CW01512019

Syllabus of Courses of Lectures on the History of Europe During the 17th, 18th and 19th Centuries

CORNELL UNIVERSITY.

SYLLABUS

OF A

COURSE OF THIRTY LECTURES

ON THE

HISTORY OF EUROPE DURING THE SEVENTEENTH CENTURY

BY

H. MORSE STEPHENS.

ITHACA:
ANDRUS & CHURCH.

TABLE OF CONTENTS

— . . . .

MODERN EUROPEAN HISTORY.

LECTURE I.

EUROPE IN 1600.

The first half of the 17th century marked by the same characteristics as the last half of the 16th, but the first traces of the modern European system, established by the Treaties of Westphalia and the Pyrenees, to be seen in the policy pursued by Henry IV of France and Cardinal Richelieu

The period covered by the 16th and first half of the 17th century a period of transition, from the ferment created by the Reformation, the discovery of the New World and of the direct sea route to Asia, the invention of printing, etc , to the settled system which lasted from the Treaties of Westphalia to the French Revolution.

The characteristic features of this transition period are the Wars of Religion

Causes of the Wars of Religion . the earnestness imparted by the Reformation supplemented by the work of the Counter-Reformation · so that war and persecution came to be considered a religious duty   religious intolerance among earnest men matched by the unscrupulous conduct of politicians

During the Wars of Religion the sense of National Unity began to be felt, binding peoples by their countries rather than their faiths . in this way the Wars of Religion helped to throw off the burden of feudalism.

Different effects of the Wars of Religion in different countries, e g , (1) in the Netherlands, (2) in France, (3) in Germany

Tendency toward strong government and standing armies to avert the horrors of religious and civil wars   France being the first country to obey this tendency becomes the most important nation in Europe during the first half of the 17th century

Where the national spirit developed, countries became strong in spite of religious internal differences, *e g.*, France, England, the United Provinces

Relative position of the powers of Europe to each other in 1600.

The condition of Germany . unsatisfactory settlement made of the religious question by the Peace of Augsburg : the pretensions and actual strength of the Holy Roman Empire , the electors, and princes of the Empire · certainty of further religious war in Germany.

The Papacy : its increased spiritual strength from the Counter-Reformation and the rise of the Jesuits

In the year 1600, though religious war impends in Germany owing to German conditions, it is practically at its close elsewhere, for Henry IV has just issued the Edict of Nantes, Philip II of Spain is just dead, and Elizabeth of England is at the very end of her reign

---

LECTURE II.

THE POLICY OF HENRY IV OF FRANCE

The character and early career of Henry IV

His part in the Religious Wars in France.

He claims the throne on the death of Henry III (1589), and struggles as Huguenot leader against the Catholics.

He adopts the Catholic religion (1593), and becomes a national king

He issues the Edict of Nantes (13 April, 1598), and thus pacifies the Huguenots: terms of the Edict.

His war with Philip II of Spain, concluded by the Treaty of Vervins (2 May, 1598)

The internal policy of Henry IV, as worked out by the Duc de Sully.

> *i* His absolutism in government, justified by the turbulence and want of patriotism of the nobles, as shown in the League: execution of Biron (31 July, 1602).
>
> *ii.* His administrative reforms.
>
> *iii.* His judicial reforms. makes seats in the Parlements hereditary
>
> *iv.* His financial reforms
>
> *v* His advancement of the material prosperity of his people :
>> *a* by encouraging agriculture.
>> *b* by undertaking public works.
>> *c.* by establishing manufactures.
>> *d* by reviving commerce
>
> *vi* His interest in trans-Atlantic exploration and emigration : foundation of Annapolis (1604), of Quebec (1608).

The foreign policy of Henry IV . the " Great Design " : the question of its authenticity

Assassination of Henry IV at Paris by François Ravaillac (14 May, 1610)

Effect of the sudden death of the King on France and on Europe.

Authorities : The most recent SMALL BOOK on the life of Henry IV is a biography by *P F Willert* in the " Heroes of the Nations " series The accounts of his reign in the small histories of modern Europe by *Victor Duruy* and by *A Ammann and G Coutanceau* are good, and in the large histories of France by *Martin*, *Michelet* and by *Dareste*, brilliant but not quite up to date The best SECONDARY AUTHORITIES are *Poirson*, Histoire du règne de Henri IV, 4 vols., *Perrens, Les mariages espagnols sous le règne de Henri IV et la régence de Marie de Medicis and *L'Église et l'État en France sous le règne de Henri IV et la régence de Marie de Medicis , *Philippson*, Heinrich IV und Philipp III , *M Ritter*, Geschichte der Deutschen Union ; *Anquez*, Henri IV et l'Allemagne , *Rott*, Henri IV, les Suisses et la Haute Italie, *Puyol*, Edm Richer · étude sur la renovation du gallicanisme au commencement du XVII ième Siècle, 2 vols , +*Henrard*, Henri IV et la princesse de Condé , and *Féret*, Henri IV et l'Église catholique , see also the essays on " La France sous Henri IV " in *Hanotaux*, Etudes Historiques sur le XVIᵉ et le XVIIᵉ siècle, and on " Ravaillac et ses complices " in *Loiseleur*, Questions historiques du XVIIᵉ siècle, as well as Vol 1, chap 6 of Les Finances françaises, by the *Baron de Nervo* Short excerpts from the PRIMARY AUTHORITIES are to be found in three volumes in the series edited by *B Zeller*, Henri IV et Sully, Henri IV et Biron, and La Fin de Henri IV. The chief PRIMARY AUTHORITIES are the various collections of the letters of Henry IV, including the Lettres Missives ed by *Berger de Xivrey*, 8 vols , and the Correspondance avec Maurice le Savant, ed by *de Rommel*, *Benoit*, Histoire de l'édit de Nantes, 5 vols , the first three volumes of *Th Ritter*, Briefe und Acten zur Geschichte des Dreissigjahrigen Krieges, the Mémoires of *Villeroy*, *Agrippa d'Aubigné* and *De Thou*, the Mémoires-journaux of *L'Estoile*, the Chronologie novenaire of *Palma Cayet*, the Négociations of *Jeannin*, the Journal of *Bassompierre*, and above all, the Économies royales, or Mémoires, of *Sully*, with the recent criticisms by *Pfister* in the Revue Historique, vols. 54, 55, 56

[Books marked with a * are *not* in the University Library]

LECTURE III

THE THIRTY YEARS' WAR TO THE DEATH OF GUSTAVUS ADOLPHUS

The approach of renewed religious war in Germany changes in German conditions since the Peace of Augsburg (1555) : political effect of the Reformation · secularization of ecclesiastical estates.

The spread of Calvinism · the Ecclesiastical Reservation . the Counter-Reformation.

Forewarnings of the war (1) the case of the Elector of Cologne (1584) , (2) the case of the city of Aachen (Aix-la Chapelle), (1589) : (3) the case of the town of Donau-werth (1607).

Formation of the Protestant Union (1608), and of the Catholic League (1609).

The Emperor and his political position in Germany : the three lay electors, Brandenburg, Saxony, and the Elector Palatine : the three ecclesiastical electors · Mayence, Cologne and Trèves : the Duke of Bavaria

The Emperor as head of the House of Hapsburg · his position in Bohemia, Austria and Hungary . the Emperors Rudolf II, and Matthias

The succession to Juliers-Cleves (1609), and interference of Henry IV of France, and the Dutch.

The outbreak of the Thirty Years' War : the " throwing from the windows " at Prague (23 May, 1618) . accession of the Emperor Ferdinand II and election of the Elector Palatine as King of Bohemia (1619) : the battle of the White Mountain (8 Nov , 1620), and occupation of the Palatinate by Spain Maximilian of Bavaria made Elector (1623) . triumph of the Catholic League

Intervention of Christian IV, King of Denmark (1625), to the aid of the Protestants Wallenstein at the head of the Emperor's army : the siege of Stralsund . Christian IV makes peace at Lubeck (22 May, 1626).

Height of the Catholic success the Emperor Ferdinand issues the Edict of Restitution (6 March, 1629) . Diet of Ratisbon (1630)

Gustavus Adolphus, King of Sweden, comes to the rescue of Protestantism ; he conquers Pomerania (1630) the sack of Magdeburg by Tilly (May, 1631) Brandenburg and Saxony join Gustavus Adolphus : the battle of Breitenfeld or Leipzig (17 Sept , 1631) Gustavus conquers Bavaria and takes Munich . Gustavus face to face with Wallenstein :

Gustavus Adolphus killed at the battle of Lutzen (16 Nov., 1632)

The character of Gustavus Adolphus his military genius : the Swedish nation and army : his political schemes the startling changes caused by his intervention in the Thirty Years' War, and his death

Assassination of Wallenstein (25 Feb , 1634) : his character and political aims.

End of the earnest period of the Thirty Years' War.

Authorities : Of SMALL BOOKS in English, *S R Gardiner*, The Thirty Years' War, and *C R. L Fletcher*, Life of Gustavus Adolphus ("Heroes of the Nations") may be recommended In French, *Charveriat*, Histoire de la guerre de Trente ans, 2 vols, is readable, and in German *Winter*, Geschichte des dreissigjahrigen Krieges The best SECONDARY HISTORY, based on original documents, is *Anton Gindely*, Geschichte des dreissigjahrigen Krieges, 5 vols , of which a popular and compressed edition has been translated into English by *A Ten Brook* ; but *Schiller*, Geschichte des dreissigjahrigen Krieges is still read as a German classic among more special books should be noted *Gindely*, Rudolf II und seine Zeit, 2 vols , *Stieve*, Der Ursprung des dreissig-jahrigen Krieges, 2 vols , *Hurter*, *Geschichte Kaiser Ferdinands II, 4 vols , and *Friedensbestrebungen Kaiser Ferdinands II, *Opel*, Der Niedersachsich - Danische Krieg , *Gindely*, Wald-stein wahrend seines ersten Generalats, 2 vols , *Droysen*, Gustav Adolf , *Gforer*, Gustav Adolph, Konig von Schweden und seine Zeit, 3 vols , *Harte*, History of Gustavus Adolphus, 2 vols. ; *Vincent Chapman*, History of Gustavus Adolphus and of the Thirty Years' War, 2 vols , *Buhring*, Venedig, Gustav Adolf und Rohan , *K. A. Muller*, Kurfurst Johann Georg der Erste , *Ranke*, Geschichte Wallensteins , *Forster*, Wallenstein als Feldherr und Landesfurst , *Von Janko*, Wal-lenstein , *Hildebrand*, Wallenstein und seine Verbindungen mit den Schweden , *Hallwich*, *Wallenstein's Ende and Gestalten aus Wallenstein's Lager, and *Villermont*, Tilly ou la Guerre de Trente Ans Among PRIMARY AUTHORITIES consult *Abelin*, Theatrum Europæum, 2 vols , and Arma Suecica, 4 vols , *J L Gottfried*, Fortgesetze historische Chronick , *Lotichius*, Rerum Germanica-rum sub Matthia, Ferdinandis II et III imperatoribus gestarum libri 55 , *Khevenhiller*, Annales Ferdinandei, 12 vols , *Brachelius*, Historia sui temporis , *Riccius*, De bellis Germanicis libri x , Ko-nung Gustaf II Adolfs Skrifter, ed. by *Styffe, Irmer*, Die Verhand-lungen Schwedens und seiner Verbündeten mit Wallenstein und dem Kaiser, 3 vols , *Forster's* and other collections of *Wallenstein's* Letters ; *M Ritter*, Briefe und Acten zur Geschichte des Dreissigjahrigen Krieges in den Zeiten des Vorwaltenden Einflusses der Wittelsbacher, 5 vols , and *S R Gardiner*, Letters and other Documents illustrating the relations between England and Germany at the Commencement of the Thirty Years' War (Camden Society, 1865)

[Books marked with a * are *not* in the University Library]

LECTURE IV.

THE POLICY OF RICHELIEU

The government of France from the death of Henry IV (1610) to the ministry of Richelieu (1624) a period of court intrigues, of weakness of the central authority, and of vacillating foreign policy

The Regency of Marie de Medicis in the name of her son, Louis XIII (1610–1617) her favourites : the one event of importance the Spanish marriages, Louis XIII marrying Anne, daughter of Philip III of Spain, and the heir to the Spanish throne marrying Elizabeth, sister of Louis XIII (1612) . murder of Concini, Maréchal d'Ancre (24 April, 1617).

The States-General held in 1614. what it was, what it might have done and how it failed

The government of the favourite, the Duc de Luynes (1617–1621) : the escape of Marie de Medicis from Blois (1619) : the struggle between mother and son : attack commenced on the political power of the Huguenots capture of St. Jean d'Angély (1621) : Treaty of Montpellier (1623).

Richelieu (born 5 Sept , 1585 , Bishop of Luçon, 16 April, 1607 , Cardinal, 5 Sept., 1622), becomes chief minister of France (19 April, 1624) : his early career : his character . his political aims

Richelieu's policy .

i To make the crown of France all-powerful by over-
coming the nobility : the conspiracy of Gaston,
Duke of Orleans, the King's brother (1626) . the
edict against duelling and execution of Montmo-
rency-Boutteville (1627) . the " Day of Dupes"
(11 Nov., 1630) and imprisonment and exile of
· Marie de Medicis the exiles, including Gaston
of Orleans, seek the help of Lorraine and Spain
execution of Montmorency (30 Oct , 1632) . the
plots of the queen, Anne of Austria . her relations with the Duke of Buckingham birth of
the Dauphin (5 Sept , 1638) : the conspiracy of
Cinq Mars . his execution (12 Sept., 1642)

ii. To unite the force of France by destroying the political power of the Huguenots the rights possessed by the Huguenots under the Edict of
Nantes : their unpatriotic spirit a remnant of the
ideas of the 16th century · the civil war of 1625–
26 , the siege of La Rochelle (1627–28) . help
sent to the Huguenots by England . the capture
of La Rochelle (28 Oct , 1628) the Peace of
Alais (28 June, 1629), granting the Huguenots
religious liberty, but destroying their political
independence

iii To overthrow the power of the House of Hapsburg
Richelieu's adoption of part of the " Grand Design . " his endeavours to assist the Protestant
powers, and to cut the communication between
Germany and Spain marriage of Charles I of
England with Henrietta Maria (1 May, 1625) the
first war in Italy (1624–26) : the Valtelline restored to the Grisons : the second war in Italy
(1628–30) against Spain, the Empire and Savoy ·
Richelieu in the field : Richelieu takes Pignerol
(March, 1630), and by Treaty of Cherasco re-
establishes the Duke of Mantua (6 April, 1631) .
Richelieu supports the Protestant Netherlands

Richelieu and the German Protestants he sends
Père Joseph to the Diet of Ratisbon (1630) he
induces Gustavus Adolphus to enter Germany
his relations with Sweden : France intervenes in
the Thirty Years' War (1635)

Death of Richelieu (4 Dec , 1642), followed by that of
Louis XIII (14 May, 1643) . the relations between them effect of Richelieu's policy on the French monarchy and the
position of France in Europe

Authorities The most accessible SMALL BOOK in English is *J H
Bridges*, France under Richelieu and Colbert Among SECONDARY
WORKS, founded on documents, consult *J B Perkins*, France under
Richelieu and Mazarin, **Perrens* works cited under Lecture II, *B
Zeller*, La minorité de Louis XIII, **Le Connétable de Luynes, *Riche-
lieu et les ministres de Louis XIII, **Puyol* Louis XIII et le Béarn,
Bazin, Histoire de France sous Louis XIII, 4 vols , *Picol* Histoire des
États Généraux vols 4. 5, *Georges d'Avenel* Richelieu et la Monarchie
absolue, 4 vols , *Topin*, Louis XIII et Richelieu, *Houssaye*, Le Cardinal
de Bérulle et le Cardinal de Richelieu, **Georges d'Avenel*, La Jeunesse
de Richelieu (Revue des Questions historiques, 1869), **La Garde*
Le Duc de Rohan et les Protestants sous Louis XIII, the *Vicomte
de Meaux*, La Réforme et la Politique Française en Europe, 2
vols , *G Fagniez*, articles on Père Joseph in the Revue Historique,
vols 26, 27, 28, 35, and in the Revue des Questions historiques, 1889,
1890, and above all the first volume (all yet published) containing the
latest account of Richelieu's youth, *Gabriel Hanotaux*, Histoire du
Cardinal de Richelieu The great PRIMARY AUTHORITY is the collection of Lettres, instructions diplomatiques et papiers d'État of Richelieu, edited by *Georges d'Avenel*, (Collection des Documents inédits.
8 vols) . with his Maximes d'État in the same collection, and his Mémoires , see also the Mémoires of *Rohan, Omer Talon Montglat,
Brienne, Mathieu Molé, Madame de Motteville, D'Estrées* and
Fontenay-Mareuil, the Correspondance of *Cardinal de Sourdis*, and
the *Mercure François*

LECTURE V.

THE THIRTY YEARS' WAR . FROM 1632 TO 1648

Change in the character of the war after the death of Gustavus Adolphus : the religious pretexts recede : national and personal ambitions make Germany their field : the mercenary troops become more numerous

Wallenstein's army brought directly under the Emperor Bernard of Saxe-Weimar comes to the front . the Swedish armies and the policy of Chancellor Oxenstiern

The battle of Nördlingen (5 and 6 Sept., 1634) its important results : victorious position of the Emperor and the Catholics the Elector of Saxony makes peace with the Emperor at Prague (30 May, 1635) : the plans of Oxenstiern : if the Swedes could have been pacified and the French had not intervened, the Thirty Years' War might have ended

The intervention of Richelieu he occupies Lorraine : he receives Alsace from the German Protestant princes for active aid (Nov , 1634) · he purchases Bernard of Saxe-Weimar and his army (Oct , 1635) . he signs an alliance with Oxenstiern (April, 1635) : he signs a treaty with the Dutch, made apprehensive by the death of Isabella of the neighborhood of the Spaniards, for the division of the Catholic Netherlands (8 Feb , 1635) : he negotiates with the Swiss, and the Dukes of Savoy, Mantua and Parma . effect of Richelieu's intervention the prolongation of the war

France invaded by the Spaniards on the north-west and by the Imperialists (1636) the Swedish general Baner forced back to the Baltic : closer alliance made between Richelieu and Oxenstiern · Baner defeats the Saxons and Imperialists at Wittstock (4 Oct , 1636).

Ferdinand III elected Emperor (22 Dec , 1636) death of Ferdinand II (15 Feb 1637)

The last years of Richelieu's foreign policy the successes

of Bernard of Saxe-Weimar on the Rhine · his ambitions
capture of Breisach (17 Dec , 1638) death of Bernard (18
July, 1639) the Spaniards invade France (1640) . battle of
Chemnitz (14 April, 1639) and death of Baner (20 May,
1641) Richelieu tries to divert Spain from German affairs by
causing a revolution in Catalonia (1640) and encouraging
the insurrection of Portugal (1640).

The first negotiations for a general peace (1640–41) accession of Frederick William as Elector of Brandenburg
(1640) : he secures his neutrality (1642).

The progress of the war after the death of Richelieu rise
into prominence of Condé, Turenne and Torstenson Spain
unable to assist the Emperor with further subsidies Torstenson destroys the Imperial and Saxon army at Breitenfeld (2
Nov , 1642) : outbreak of war between Denmark and Sweden
(1643) Treaty of Bromsebro (1645) Condé defeats the
Spaniards at Rocroi (19 May, 1643) . Turenne reorganizes
Bernard's army : the battles of Freiburg (16 Aug., 1644)
and Jankau (6 March, 1645) · the Elector of Saxony makes
a truce with the Swedes (31 Aug , 1645) the battles of
Marienthal (5 May, 1645) and Nordlingen 3 Aug , 1645)
the invasion of Bavaria the Elector Maximilian makes a
truce (15 March, 1647) : battle of Zusmarshausen (17 May,
1648) : Condé wins the battle of Lens (10 Aug , 1648) the
Swedes seize the Castle of Prague (26 July, 1648) : the Emperor determines on peace

The treaties of Westphalia (24 Oct., 1648), close the Thirty Years' War . the Emperor makes peace with France and
Sweden : but Spain remains at war with France

Authorities : *S R Gardiner*, The Thirty Years' War still
remains the best SMALL BOOK in English ; *Gindely* should be supplemented among SECONDARY AUTHORITIES by *Barthold*, Geschichte des
grossen Deutschen Krieges vom Tode Gustav Adolfs ab, mit besondere
Rucksicht auf Frankreich, 2 vols , *Droysen*, Bernhard von Weimar,
2 vols. , *Sugenheim*, Frankreich's Einfluss auf und Beziehungen zu
Deutschland, vol 1 ; *Koch, Geschichte des Deutschen Reichs unter
der Regierung Ferdinands III, 2 vols ; *Dudik Schweden in Bohmen
und Mahren ; *Biedermann*, Deutschlands trubste Zeit oder Der

Dreissigjahrige Krieg in seine Folgen fur den deutsche Culturleben, the *Duc d'Aumâle*, Histoire des princes de la maison de Condé, vols 5, 6 The PRIMARY AUTHORITIES as for Lecture 3, with the additions of *Georges d'Avenel*, Richelieu's letters cited for Lecture IV, *Szilágyi*, Actes et Documents pour servir à l'histoire de l'alliance de Rakoczy avec les Français et les Suédois, *Bougeant*, Histoire des Guerres et des Négociations qui précédèrent le Traite de Westphalie, 3 vols, and *Axel Orenstierna's* Skriften och Brefvexling, 6 vols, and omitting *Gardiner*, Letters, *Styffe*, *Irmer* and *Wallenstein*

[Books marked with a * are *not* in the University Library]

LECTURE VI

THE TREATIES OF WESTPHALIA

The history of the Treaties of Westphalia . a congress for peace resolved upon in 1641 suggested by the Elector of Mayence in 1639 approved by the Imperial Diet at Ratisbon (1640–41) suggested that two congresses, in one of which the Emperor should deal with the Swedes, Dutch and Protestant princes, and in the other with France, should be held to arrange terms of peace, at Lubeck and Cologne at the wish of the Swedes Osnabruck and Munster chosen instead . by a resolution of the Imperial Diet, with the assent of the Emperor, the German princes and free cities allowed to be represented at the congresses

Meeting of the congresses (1644) . the chief ambassadors Cardinal Chigi, Papal Nuncio, and Contarini, Venetian ambassador, Mediators, Trautmannsdorf, Nassau and Volmar for the Emperor, Longueville, D'Avaux and Abel Servien for France, John Oxenstiern and Salvius for Sweden, Saavedra and Zapata for Spain delays about precedence . the envoys of France and Sweden present their demands (June 1645) . effect of the military operations on the negotiations . the part played by the Elector of Bavaria the Treaties of Westphalia signed at Munster (24 Oct., 1648)

Chief points of the Treaties of Westphalia .

A With regard to non-German powers *i* France received the Three Bishoprics (Metz, Toul and Verdun) occupied in 1552, Alsace, except Strasbourg and reserving the rights of the Empire, Breisach and the right to garrison Philippsburg, and Pignerol : the Duke of Lorraine not to be aided by the Emperor and left to make a separate treaty with France *ii* Sweden received Western Pomerania with the island of Rügen, Stettin, Wismar, the archbishopric of Bremen and the bishopric of Verden, with representation in the Diet of the Empire . *iii* The independence of the Swiss cantons was officially recognized *iv* The Protestant Netherlands, which had been recognized as independent by Philip IV of Spain (30 Jan , 1648) were declared independent of the Empire, and received certain districts in Brabant and Luxembourg

B With regard to German powers *i* Brandenburg received, in compensation for part of Pomerania, the archbishopric of Magdeburg, and the bishoprics of Halberstadt, Cammin and Minden [The succession to Cleves-Juliers was settled in 1666 by Brandenburg · receiving Cleves, the Mark and Ravensberg, and Neuburg receiving Juliers and Berg] *ii* Saxony retained Lusatia and part of Magdeburg : *iii* Mecklenburg received, in compensation for Wismar, the bishoprics of Schwerin and Ratzeburg *iv*. Hesse-Cassel received the abbey of Hirschfeld *v* Bavaria received the Upper Palatinate and retained the electorate conferred in 1623 *vi* Charles Louis, eldest son of the expelled Elector Palatine, received the Lower (Rhine) Palatinate, and a new electorate was created for him

C With regard to the religious question *i* The terms of the Peace of Augsburg were confirmed, fixing the date for ecclesiastical property at 1 Jan., 1624 *ii* The Ecclesiastical Reservation was acknowledged by the Protestants : *iii* The Calvinist was recognized as fully as the Lutheran religion.

D With regard to the Empire · (effect of the book "Hippolithus a Lapide") . *i*. Territorial supremacy, including the right of making alliances, granted to the States

of the Empire *ii* Prerogatives of the Imperial Diet proclaimed *iii* Concurring jurisdiction of the Imperial Chamber and Aulic Council acknowledged.

E General amnesty declared, and the Peace of Westphalia made a fundamental law of the Empire

Effect of the Treaties of Westphalia on Germany : the
practical disintegration of the Holy Roman Empire

Effect of the Treaties of Westphalia on Europe commencement of a new era, in which political succeeded religious distinctions opening of 150 years in which the diplomacy of kings became the chief factor in history.

Authorities : All SECONDARY HISTORIES of the Thirty Years'
War devote their concluding chapters to the Treaties of Westphalia,
but see also *Kerviler*, Abel Servien, *Contarini*, Relazione del con-
gresso di Munster, *Odhner* Die Politik Schwedens im Westphalischen
Friedenscongress , *J S Putter*, Geist des Westphalischen Friedes and his
Historical Development of the Political Constitution of the Germanic
Empire, vol ii The PRIMARY AUTHORITY is *J G von Meiern*, Acta
Pacis Westphalicae oder Westphalische Friedenshandlungen und
Geschichte, 6 vols , but *Bougeant*, cited under Lecture V, and his
Histoire du Traité de Westphalie, 2 vols , are useful as being founded
on *D'Avaux* Mémoires

[Books marked with a * are *not* in the University Library]

LECTURE VII.

THE FRONDE AND THE TREATY OF THE PYRENEES

Richelieu on his deathbed nominated Mazarin his successor six months later the child Louis XIV succeeded to the
throne the Parlement of Paris declared Anne of Austria,
the queen-mother, Regent she gave both power and affec-
tion to Mazarin : character and previous career of Mazarin.

Mazarin followed accurately Richelieu's foreign policy :
during his administration Condé and Turenne won their first
victories and the Treaties of Westphalia were signed

What France gained by the Treaty of Westphalia : a footing on the Rhine by the annexation of Alsace, which also enabled her to surround the independent duchy of Lorraine and the Spanish province of Franche Comté.

Spain refused to make peace with France owing to the outbreak of civil war known as the " Fronde."

The nature of the Fronde " playing at civil war " : its fruitlessness and intrigues . its real want of importance

The Fronde, *first phase* (1648-49) · part played by the Parlement of Paris and the Parisians *second phase* (1650-51)· arrest of Condé Turenne invades France with a Spanish army the battle of Rethel (15 Dec , 1650) : the Cardinal de Retz Mazarin goes into exile (Feb , 1651) *third phase* (1651-52) . Condé raises an insurrection in the south : Mazarin returns (Dec., 1651) Turenne joins the royal party : battle of the Faubourg Saint-Antoine (2 July, 1652) : Mazarin again goes into exile (Aug , 1652) *fourth phase*, the king and the queen-mother re-enter Paris (21 Oct , 1652) : Condé joins the Spaniards De Retz imprisoned : Gaston of Orleans exiled to Blois : final return of Mazarin (Feb. 1653,). end of the Fronde

Mazarin pursues the war with Spain with vigor : Turenne commanding the French and Condé the Spanish army . Mazarin makes an alliance with Cromwell · the battle of the Dunes (14 June, 1658), capture of Dunkirk and overthrow of the Spaniards formation of the League of the Rhine (14 Aug , 1658) : the new Emperor, Leopold I (elected 1657) bound by the terms of his capitulation not to send help to Spain

Negotiations for peace with Spain Mazarin's hands freed by the death of Cromwell (1658).

The Treaty of the Pyrenees signed by Mazarin and Don Luis de Haro in the Isle of Pheasants (7 Nov , 1659)

Its terms . (1) France received Artois and Roussillon, conquered by Richelieu

(2) Spain abandoned all claims to Alsace

(3) Charles IV, Duke of Lorraine, was to be restored, but all his fortresses were to be dismantled.

(4) The Prince de Condé was to be forgiven and reinstated

(5) France abandoned the King of Portugal

(6) Louis XIV was to marry Maria Theresa, elder daughter of Philip IV, King of Spain, who was to abandon all claims to the succession in Spain on payment of a dowry of 500,000 crowns

Importance of the Treaty of the Pyrenees as the supplement to the Treaties of Westphalia

Marriage of Louis XIV to the Infanta (1660)

Death of Mazarin (9 March, 1661) : success of his foreign policy · his internal policy · neglect of the finances : destruction of feudal castles in France

Life and work of Saint Vincent de Paul

Authorities : The best SECONDARY HISTORIES, founded on documents, for the administration of Mazarin are *Chéruel*, Histoire de la France pendant la Minorité de Louis XIV, 4 vols , and *Histoire de la France sous le Ministère de Mazarin, 3 vols , *J B Perkins*, France under Richelieu and Mazarin , *Comte de Cosnac*, Mazarin et Colbert , *Bazin*, Histoire de France sous le Ministère du Cardinal Mazarin , *Gaillardin*, Histoire du règne de Louis XIV, vols 1, 2 ; *Comte de Sainte-Aulaire*, Histoire de la Fronde, 2 vols , *Duc d'Aumâle*, Histoire des Princes de Condé, vols 5. 6 , *Victor Cousin*, La Jeunesse de Mazarin, Madame de Longueville, 2 vols , Madame de Sablé, Madame de Chevreuse and Madame de Hautefort , *Chantelauze*, Le Cardinal de Retz et l'affaire de chapeau, and Le Cardinal de Retz et ses missions diplomatiques à Rome , *Valfrey*, Hugues de Lionne , *Barante*, Vie de Mathieu Molé , *Moreau*, Choix de Mazarinades, 2 vols , *Feillet*, La Misère au temps de la Fronde , *Loth*, Saint Vincent de Paul et sa mission sociale ; *Bourelly* Cromwell et Mazarin, and *Tessier*, Le Chevalier de Jant et les relations de la France et du Portugal au temps de Mazarin   The chief PRIMARY AUTHORITY is the collection ed by *Chéruel*, of the Lettres du Cardinal Mazarin pendant son Ministère, 6 vols , (Collection des Documents inédits) , for the period of the Fronde there are many interesting personal memoirs to be used with caution, among which may be noted the Mémoires of *Madame de Motteville, Omer Talon, Gourville, Mademoiselle de Montpensier, Montglat, Brienne, Guy Joly, Mathieu Molé*, and, above all, those of *Cardinal de Retz*

[Books marked with a * are *not* in the University Library]

LECTURE VIII

— ———· —

EUROPE IN THE MIDDLE OF THE 17TH CENTURY

I. FRANCE

Importance of the study of the history of France in the
17th century rests on the fact that, during the Age of Louis
XIV, its institutions were copied all over Europe, while its
foreign policy was the keynote of political history ; it was
France which led the way to strong central government at
home, supported by standing armies, and the adoption of
foreign alliances independent of religious considerations

Government of France as moulded by Richelieu and
Mazarin for the use of Louis XIV *i* The Monarchy :
growth of its powers . its strength . the Court : *ii*
The Nobility · blows dealt by Richelieu . tendency to become
a caste distinction between grande and petite noblesse sur-
vival of privilege . *iii.* The Church in France · its struggle
with the Huguenots contrast between Gallican and Ultramontane ideas · *iv* The States-General . and its failure to
resemble the English Parliament of the 17th century *v*
The Central Administration its strengthening the great aim
of the French monarchy . creation of the "Intendants" .
vi. Local Administration . distinction between pays d'élection
and pays d'États · the provincial Estates the provincial
spirit the cities and towns privileges of the municipalities :
the "Bourgeoisie" *vii.* The Judicial Administration . the
Parlement of Paris the provincial Parlements the "Noblesse de la Robe" · the strength of the Bar ; the pays du
droit coutumier and the pays du droit écrit *viii.* The Financial Administration . the Farmers-general . the taille, the
gabelle, the aides, the douanes *ix* Manufactures and Commerce : Lyons, Marseilles, Bordeaux, Dieppe and Le Hâvre
the guilds the ouvriers ; *x* Agriculture : the seigneur, the

farmer and the peasant grande culture and petite culture : " copyhold " tenure and its relics of feudalism · "noble land " · .*xi* The condition of the poor · hospitals charity : .*xii*. Material condition : roads and canals : public works : .*xiii* Intellectual condition education : colleges and village school . the Académie Française provincial academies · the press : .*xiv* The army and navy their organization · their power concentrated in the hands of the monarchy.

Position of France in Europe in the middle of the 17th century *i* Geographical conditions . additions made by Richelieu and Mazarin · search for a defensible frontier . boundaries of language and race disregarded · existence of non-French territories in France : Lorraine, Franche Comté, and Avignon *ii* Growth of political tradition the Foreign Office . the diplomatists

Extra-European expansion of France. *i* New France : Canada and Acadia efforts at colonization : *ii* The French Antilles ; San Domingo their importance to France . *iii*. The French East India Company of Richelieu (1640) : Madagascar

Strength and weakness of France in the 17th century.

Authorities : The chapters on the condition of France in the SECONDARY HISTORIES, noted under Lectures 2, 4 and 7, and especially in *Hanotaux*, Histoire du Cardinal de Richelieu, vol 1, *Georges d'Avenel*, Richelieu et la Monarchie absolue, and *Chéruel*, Histoire de la France pendant la minorité de Louis XIV, and *Histoire de la France sous le ministère du Mazarin See also *Chéruel*, Histoire de l'administration monarchique en France, 2 vols , **Dareste*, Histoire de l'administration et des progrès du pouvoir royal en France , *Picot*, Histoire des États-Généraux, 5 vols , *Caillet*, L'Administration en France sous le ministère de Richelieu , **Luçay*, Les origines du pouvoir ministériel en France Les Secrétaires d'État depuis leur institution jusqu'à la mort de Louis XV , *+Hanotau r*, Origine de l'institution des intendants de province , **Thomas*, Une province sous Louis XIV situation politique et administrative de la Bourgogne de 1661 à 1715 , **Monin*, Essai sur l'histoire administrative du Languedoc pendant l'intendance de Basville (1685-1719) **Arbois de Jubainville*, L'administration des intendants d'après les archives de l'Aube, *Baron de Nervo*, Les Finances Françaises, 2 vols , *Clamageran*, Histoire de l'impôt en France, 3 vols , *Fagniez*, L'Industrie en France sous Henri IV, and Le Commerce de la France sous Henri IV (Revue Historique, vols 16, 23) , *Levasseur*, Histoire des classes ou-vrières en France, 2 vols , *Daresle*, Histoire des classes agricoles en France , *Susane*, *Histoire de l'ancienne infanterie française, 8 vols , and *Histoire de la cavalerie française, 3 vols , *Guérin*, Histoire mari-time de la France, 4 vols , *Gilles de la Tourelle*, Théophraste Renau-dot, and *Parkman*, Pioneers of France in the New World

LECTURE IX

EUROPE IN THE MIDDLE OF THE 17TH CENTURY

2 THE EMPIRE, THE HOUSE OF AUSTRIA, AND THE GERMAN PRINCES

The Holy Roman Empire, in its inception the lay authority ruling western Europe in conjunction with the Pope, became towards the close of the Middle Ages the ruling power in Germany, and by the Treaties of Westphalia lost even that function

The form, precedence and tradition of the Empire only was left to hold Germany together, and the different states and categories of states of the Empire must be regarded as independent political units, very loosely federated

The constitution of the Empire, as it was retained after the Treaties of Westphalia . (1) the Elective Emperor · (2) the Imperial Diet comprising (i) the College of Electors, (ii) the College of Princes, (iii) the College of Free Cities · (3) the Imperial Chamber · (4) the Aulic Council · (5) the Circles

Distinction between immediate and mediate members of the Holy Roman Empire

The Diet of Ratisbon (1663) declared perpetual, and en-voys plenipotentiary take the place of Princes and Electors in person

The House of Austria still remains the most powerful sovereignty in Germany from its hereditary dominions, not from the constant election of its head as Emperor . but it looks for expansion to the East, not to the West and gradually ceases to act chiefly for German interests

The dominions of the House of Austria · (1) Austria proper, Styria, Carinthia, etc.. [the Tyrol ceded by Ferdinand II to his brother (1623) returned to the Austrian dominions (1665)] their administration : the powers of the provincial Diets and extent of local self-government · (2) Bohemia · a home of Protestantism · its sufferings during the Thirty Years' War deprivation of its local autonomy and attempts at Germanizing the Czechs · (3) Hungary and Croatia its constant war with the Turks · division of the kingdom of St Stephen at commencement of the 17th century (i) Transylvania, 2082 square miles, (ii) the Turks, 1859, (iii) Austria, administered by the Palatine of Hungary and the Ban of Croatia, 1222 · (i) Transylvania : the reign and policy of Gabriel Bethlen (1613–29) George Rakoczy I (1629–48) George Rakoczy II (1648–60) . intervention in the Thirty Years' War : encouragement of Protestantism struggle with the Turks . (ii) Turkish Hungary . its condition under Turkish rule : (iii) Austrian Hungary the power of the Diet.

Administration of the hereditary dominions . the councils at Vienna the army and foreign politics the influence of the Jesuits

The ecclesiastical electorates : Mayence, Cologne and Trèves

The lay electorates (1) Saxony its condition at the Treaties of Westphalia its wealth and compactness · the Elector the recognized chief of the German Protestants : policy of John George I . the ambitions of Saxony turn eastward . (2) Brandenburg . John Sigismund, Elector, becomes Duke of Prussia (1616) as a feudatory of Poland the claims on Pomerania and Juliers-Cleves the policy of George William during the Thirty Years' War accession of the Great Elector (1640) compensation for Pomerania and settlement of

Juliers-Cleves case (1666) gives Brandenburg a German interest Brandenburg's advantages from the Northern War (1656–60) (3) Bavaria · the Elector Maximilian and the Counter-Reformation his part in the Thirty Years' War (4) The Elector Palatine importance of his position on the Rhine with regard to France.

The lay princes of the Empire their varying power introduction of primogeniture in 16th and 17th centuries its effects their love of independence

The ecclesiastical princes of the Empire the Catholic and Protestant bishoprics their chapters fill the place of provincial Estates or Diets and make their government oligarchical.

The free cities of the Empire : their decline during the Thirty Years' War · decay of the Hanseatic League only Hamburg, Bremen and Lubeck renew the League (1630) · trade passes to the Dutch and the English

The knights of the Empire · their dependence on the Emperor

General character of the administration in Germany the provincial Diets · tendency to imitate France

Depopulation and misery caused by the Thirty Years' War . poverty of Germany

Intellectual condition : the foundation of universities and academies

Authorities · Among books in English may be noted *Léger*, Autriche-Hongrie, translated by Mrs Birkbeck Hill , *Coxe*, History of the House of Austria, 4 vols, and *Vehse*, Memoirs of the Court, Aristocracy and Diplomacy of Austria, 2 vols , for Austria , *Tuttle*, History of Prussia, vol. 1, and *Carlyle*, History of Frederick the Great, vol 1 for Prussia, and *J S Putter*, Historische Entwickelung der heutigen Staatsverfassung des deutschen Reichs, translated by Dornford, vol 2 All histories, whether of the Empire or of separate states, give a general review of the condition of Germany at the time of the Treaties of Westphalia but special reference may be made to *Erdmannsdorffer*, Deutsche Geschichte, 1648–1740, vol 1, *Biedermann*, Deutschlands trubste Zeit oder Der Dreissigjahrige Krieg in seine Folgen fur den deutsche Culturleben and *Hauser*, Deutschland nach dem dreissigjahrige Kriege

LECTURE X

EUROPE IN THE MIDDLE OF THE 17TH CENTURY

3 THE NETHERLANDS

The situation of the Netherlands at the beginning of the century the Protestant Netherlands, the Seven United Provinces of Holland, Zealand, Gelderland, Friesland, Utrecht, Groningen and Overyssel, had practically secured their independence and the Catholic Netherlands, now Belgium, were governed by the Infanta Isabella, to whom they had been granted as a dowry by Philip II

The two parties in the Protestant Netherlands the supporters of the Stadtholder, Maurice of Nassau, and the republicans led by John van Olden Barneveldt the strength of the former among the country gentlemen, noblemen and peasants, of the latter among the burghers of the cities, and especially of Amsterdam

The war of independence with Spain closed by a twelve years' truce, negotiated by Henry IV of France (1609)

The political struggle combined with a religious difference the Arminians or Remonstrants against the Gomarists or Calvinists · the Synod of Dort condemns the Arminians (1618) execution of Barneveldt (19 May, 1619)

The end of the truce (1621) · part played by the Dutch in the Thirty Years' War · owing to the prudence of Maurice and Frederick Henry, the Stadtholders, they only occupy Cleves and resist Spanish invasion at intervals

The Catholic Netherlands under Isabella remain contented with their local government and in comparative tranquility, but when France joins in the Thirty Years' War, Artois is lost, and after Mazarin's treaty with Cromwell, the English and French conquer nearly up to Brussels : by the Treaty of the Pyrenees, the Catholic Netherlands are deprived of Artois (1659)

Meanwhile by the Treaty of Westphalia (30 Jan , 1648)

with Spain, William II, elected Stadtholder 1647, promises
to support the Spanish rights to the Catholic Netherlands in
return for the closing of the Scheldt to commerce by this
means the United Provinces secure a buffer against France,
and Amsterdam secures her commercial supremacy at the
expense of Antwerp

The Stadtholder resolves on a coup d'état attempt to
seize Amsterdam (30 July, 1650) death of William II
(Nov., 1650) the stadtholderate declared vacant government divided between the States-General and the Provincial
Estates · election of John de Witt as Grand Pensionary
(1653)

War between England and the United Provinces (1652–54)
owing to the Navigation Act passed by the English Parliament and aimed at the Dutch carrying trade

The prosperity of the Dutch in the first half of the 17th
century . their naval and commercial monopoly : its causes .
its political, social and material effects

The Dutch in Asia : the first voyage of Houtman (1596) :
they seize the spice and pepper trade . foundation of Batavia
(1619) : rivalry with the English massacre of Amboyna
(1623) . expulsion of the Portuguese . their settlements at
the Cape of Good Hope and in India, China and Japan.

The Dutch in South America : their establishment in Brazil (1624–37) : the government and great views of Maurice of
Nassau (1637–44)· their expulsion by the Portuguese (1655).

The Dutch in North America . foundation of New Amsterdam . the New Netherlands and the emigration thither.

Contrast between the Protestant and Catholic Netherlands

Authorities : *Motley*, History of the United Netherlands, Vols 3
and 4, and Life and Death of John of Barneveldt, 2 vols , *Wenzelbur-
ger*, Geschichte der Niederlande, vol 2 , and *Kervyn de Lettenhove*,
La Flandre pendant les trois derniers siècles, 3 vols , for reference
Grotius, Annales et Historiæ de rebus Belgicis, *Meteranus Novus,
Meinsma, Geschiedenis van de Nederlandsche Oost-Indische Bezittin-
gen, 2 vols and *De Jonge*, De Opkomst van het Nederlandsch Gezag
in Oost-Indie, 8 vols

LECTURE XI.

EUROPE IN THE MIDDLE OF THE 17TH CENTURY

4 SWEDEN AND DENMARK

The position acquired by Sweden by the Treaties of West-phalia she becomes the chief territorial power on the Baltic, as possessor of Finland, Carelia, Ingria, Esthonia, and Western Pomerania with an outlet on the North Sea as possessor of Bremen and Verden , she controls the mouths of the Elbe, the Weser and the Oder, but her own southern provinces are occupied by Denmark Sweden is recognized as the chief military power in Europe

The Chancellor, Axel Oxenstiern his policy : his organi-zation of the Swedish monarchy on an oligarchical basis · the material condition of Sweden its sturdy Lutheranism

The reign of Queen Christina, only child of Gustavus Adolphus she takes the direction of affairs (1644) on the outbreak of war with Denmark : the Treaty of Bromsebro (13 Aug , 1645) her influence in favour of peace in the ne-gotiations at Osnabruck her internal government . she ab-dicates in favour of her cousin, Charles X (6 June, 1654) her later life : her fondness for literature and science · she becomes a Catholic (1655), and dies at Rome (19 April, 1689).

The reign of Charles X : as a soldier he desires to utilize the Swedish army : he invades Poland (1656) : previous relations between Poland and Sweden . the conduct of the Great Elector · Charles X attacks Denmark (1657) and by the Treaty of Roskild (7 March, 1658) obtains the Danish provinces of Sweden, including Halland, Scania and the island of Börnholm · he proposes to divide Denmark and attacks Copenhagen (1659) : the Dutch and other powers interfere : death of Charles X (23 Feb , 1660)

Accession of Charles XI : regency of the queen-mother, Hedwiga the war closed owing to the mediation of the powers by the Treaty of Oliva with Poland, by which Poland ceded Lithuanian Livonia to Sweden and John Casimir resigned his claims to the Swedish throne (3 May, 1660), by the Treaty of Copenhágen with Denmark, confirming that of Roskild (7 June, 1660) and by that of Kardis with Russia (1661) confirming the cession to Sweden of Ingria and Carelia

Position of Denmark at the Treaties of Westphalia · she rules over Norway and the southern provinces of Sweden, and thus controls the commerce of the Baltic : her relations. with the Empire owing to her connection with Schleswig and Holstein

The rivalry between Denmark and Sweden the key note of Danish foreign policy . the government of Christian IV (1588–1648) · the aristocratic constitution of Denmark · Christian's court his fondness for Norway and foundation of Christiania his misfortunes during the Thirty Years' War . foundation of the Danish East India Company (1615) and occupation of Tranquebar in India

The reign of Frederick III : the government of Ulfeldt and the nobles . Ulfeldt joins Charles X of Sweden and induces him to attack Denmark : Denmark's losses at Roskild

The revolution of 1660 overthrow of the power of the nobles the monarchy of Denmark made hereditary and absolute a States-General promised but never called : resumption of lands granted to noblemen : improvement in administration.

The Germanizing of Denmark . the situation of Norway : its poverty, and hatred for Sweden

The supremacy of the Baltic definitely moved from Denmark to Sweden.

Authorities: As a SMALL BOOK in English, see *Otté*, Scandinavian History, and in French, *Geffroy*, Les États Scandinaves Among SECONDARY AUTHORITIES consult the large general history by *Fryxell*, (not translated), *Carlson*, Geschichte Schwedens, vols 5, 6, translated and continued from *Geijer*; *Cronholm*, Sveriges Historie under Gustaf II Adolphs Regering, 6 vols , (not translated), *Grauert, Chris-

tina, Königin von Schweden, und ihr Hof, 2 vols., *Archenholtz*
Mémoires pour servir à l'histoire de la reine Christine, 4 vols., *Allen*
Geschichte des Königreich Dänemark, and *Spittler* Geschichte der
Dänschen Revolution im Jahre 1660, being vol 5 of his Sämmtliche
Werke.

[Books marked with a * are *not* in the University Library.]

LECTURE XII.

EUROPE IN THE MIDDLE OF THE 17TH CENTURY

5 RUSSIA AND POLAND

The contrast between the Slavs of the Greek Church in
Russia, and the Slavs of the Roman Church in Poland, the
former being essentially Asiatic, and the latter essentially
European

The backwardness of Russia and its Asiatic character due
to historical circumstances, but chiefly to the conquest by the
Mongol hordes, and its derivation of Christianity from Constantinople.

The epic character of the great struggle with the Mongols,
and its effect in forming the Russian people

The reign of Ivan the Terrible (1533–84) marks the
emergence of Moscow as the centre from which the Russian
Empire was to grow : he takes the title of Tsar (1547) his
wars with the Tartars on the south and east, and with the
Poles and Lithuanians and Livonians on the west and north-
west . his endeavors to reach the Baltic : his relations with
the powers of western Europe, and especially with Elizabeth
of England : opening up of trade between Russia and England by way of the White Sea and Archangel ; the Muscovy
Company invasion of Siberia · the government of Ivan
the Terrible . his autocracy : his struggles with the nobility .
his " States-General " his personality

Russian history in the 17th century until the time of Peter the Great, a commentary on the aims and ideals of Ivan the Terrible.

The reign of Feodor Ivanovitch (1584–98) : institution of serfdom and creation of the patriarchate . the reign of Boris Godúnov (1598–1605) : the " false " Dimitri civil war and anarchy : the Poles of Moscow (1612) election of Michael Románov as Tsar (1613).

The reign of Michael Románov (1613–45) restoration of peace and tranquility · moral and material condition of Russia

The insurrection of the inhabitants of Little Russia and the Cossacks against Poland under Bogdan Khmelnitzski (1648) . he appeals to the Tsar · war with Poland : by truce of Androussovo (1667) Russia obtains the left bank of the Dnieper as its frontier with Kiev and Smolensk on the right bank.

The condition of Poland in the 16th century the turbulence of the nobles . the pacta conventa . the right of confederation ; the liberum veto (1652) the influence of France the work of the Jesuits · the Counter-Reformation

The most notable events the Union of Lublin (1569) uniting Poland and Lithuania the death of the last of the Jagellons, hereditary Grand Dukes of Lithuania (1572) and election to the throne of Poland thrown open · the secularization of Prussia by Albert of Hohenzollern, Grand Master of the Teutonic Knights, as a fief of Poland (1525) followed by the suppression of the Knights of the Sword (1561) on yielding Riga to Sweden, Livonia to Poland, and making Kettler, the last Grand Master, Duke of Courland, as a feudatory of Poland

The reign of Sigismund III Vasa (1587–1632) · his Catholicism : failure to obtain the throne of Sweden . the reign of Ladislas VII Vasa (1632–48) : Poland during the Thirty Years' War · election of John Casimir Vasa : his wars with Sweden and Russia : by the Treaty of Wehlau (1657) the Elector of Brandenburg is recognized as Duke of Prussia, free from the suzerainty of Poland : the insurrection of Bogdan Khmelnitzski : the Truce of Androussovo

In the middle of the 17th century Russia is growing politically stronger from her concentrated autocracy and Poland
politically weaker from her anarchic constitution

Authorities : *Morfill*, Story of Russia and Story of Poland , *Rambaud*, Histoire de la Russie, translated by L B Lang, 2 vols. , *Salvandy*, Histoire de Pologne avant et sous le Roi Jean Sobieski, 3 vols

---

LECTURE XIII

EUROPE IN THE MIDDLE OF THE 17TH CENTURY

6   THE OTTOMAN TURKS

The extent of Islam at the commencement of the 17th
century : origin of the Turks

The Ottoman Turks reach the height of their power in the
16th century Sulaiman (Solyman) the Magnificent (1520–
66) . the European possessions of the Turks   their northern
capital at Buda · their control of the Levant   their power in
Northern Africa and over the Mediterranean : Barbarossa
and Dragut . blow dealt to them by the loss of the passage
of the Asiatic trade through Egypt · Venice induces the
Turks to oppose the Portuguese in Asia : organization of the
Turkish power : the Sultan as Caliph . the Ulemas : the
Janissaries

Resistance of the Knights of St John   the defence of
Malta (1565)

Attitude of Europe towards the Turks : spasmodic attempts of the Popes to stir up Christendom against them · the
battle of Lepanto (7 Oct., 1571) : the alliance with France
the "capitulations" . the Levant Company and the Dutch
traders.

Poland and Hungary the bulwarks of Christendom against
the Turks . their suzerainty over the Danubian provinces and

Transylvania : the religious attitude of the Turks · the Greek Church and the Turks . their welcome of renegades

Fortunately for Christian Europe during the critical period of the Wars of Religion and the Thirty Years' War, the Turks remained quiet the Sultans degenerated in character . and between the death of Sulaiman the Magnificent (1566) and the accession of Muhammad Kiuprili to power (1656) their only conquests were Cyprus, taken (1571) and Tunis retaken (1574) causes of this sudden degeneracy

The Janissaries become Sultan-makers · they are permitted to marry and the tax of Christian children ceases

Internal dissensions mark the reign of Muhammad III (1595–1603) Ahmad I (1603–17) makes truce of Comorn with the Emperor (11 Nov., 1606) : treaties with England and the United Provinces, and war with Persia . the imbecility of Mustapha I (1617–18, 1622–23) the reign of Othman II (1618–22) and his murder Murad IV (1623–40) his capture of Bagdad (25 Dec , 1638) · his cruelty Ibrahim I (1640–48) recapture of Azov (1642) · attack on Crete (Candia) (1645) order to murder all Christians : assassinated by the Janissaries accession of Muhammad IV (1648) troubles during his minority

Appointment of Muhammad Kiuprili, a renegade Albanian, to be Grand Vizier with full powers (1656) his great reforms . he restores the force of the Ottoman Turks · his internal policy the execution of the Greek patriarch his foreign policy his victories over Venice, Russia, Transylvania and the Empire his death (1662)

Ahmad Kiuprili, Grand Vizier (1662–76) . he attacks Transylvania the Emperor Leopold resolves to resist the Turks and calls for the help of Christendom · the Diet of the Empire agrees and Louis XIV sends 6000 Frenchmen Montecuculi defeats the Turks at the battle of Saint Gothard (1 Aug , 1664) and saves Vienna the truce of Vasvar (10 Aug., 1664) : the siege of Candia Morosini surrenders to Ahmad Kiuprili (27 Sept., 1669) the Cossacks call in the help of the Turks against Poland (1672) Ahmad Kiuprili

takes Kammietz and conquers Podolia by the Treaty of
Budziak or Buczac (18 Oct , 1672) Poland cedes Podolia and
the Ukraine to the Turks and promises to pay tribute the
treaty disavowed by the Polish Diet (1673) John Sobieski
defeats the Turks at Choczim (10 Nov., 1673) and Lemberg
(24 Aug., 1675) by the Treaty of Zurawna (27 Oct , 1676)
the Turks retain Kammietz and Podolia but give up the
Ukraine and the tribute death of Ahmad Kiuprili (30 Oct ,
1676)

The greatness of the Kiuprilis the sudden resurrection of
the Ottoman power its significance

Authorities · *Creasy*, History of the Ottoman Turks, and *Stanley
Lane-Poole*, The Story of Turkey and The Story of the Barbary Corsairs are readable books , *Ranke*, Fursten und Volker von Sud-Europa ,
Die Osmanen und die spanische Monarchie im 16ten und 17ten Jahrhundert (vols 35, 36 of his Sammtliche Werke), is more scientific ,
their works are mainly based on *Von Hammer*, Geschichte des Osmanischen Reichs, 4 vols , translated into French as L'Histoire de
l'Empire Ottoman, 18 vols , and on *Zinkeisen*, Geschichte des osmanischen Reichs in Europe, 7 vols.

LECTURE XIV

-

EUROPE IN THE MIDDLE OF THE 17th CENTURY

7 ITALY

Italy at the commencement of the 17th century the idea
of Italian unity preached by Dante and Machiavelli had been
extinguished by the vitality of local life and local rivalries
the Italians preferred local to national patriotism · therefore
Italy was largely ruled by foreign powers

The divisions of Italy and their relations to each other

The chief Italian states I. The States of the Church

alteration in the character of the Popes they become more
Italian and temporal in their aspirations their attitude towards European affairs : their influence in Italy their nepotism their administration of their States Clement VIII—
Aldobrandini,—his anti-Spanish policy · annexed Ferrara
(1598) · died 1605 Leo XI—Medici,—1605 Paul V—Bor-
ghese,—1605-21 his quarrel with Venice Gregory XV—
Ludovisi,—1621-23 : Urban VIII—Barberini, —1623-44 his
anti-Spanish policy and friendship for Richelieu . his administration fortification of Rome : annexation of Urbino (1631).
war with Parma (1641-44) Innocent X—Pamfili,—1644-55
destruction of Castro : his negotiations with Mazarin . condemnation of Jansenism favouritism Alexander VII—
Chigi,—1655-67 rise in power of the " congregations "
the plague at Rome (1656) his quarrel with Louis XIV .
Avignon occupied by the French (1663-65) submission of
the Pope : the Roman nobility : the beautification of Rome.

II Kingdom of the Two Sicilies . i Sicily its feudal nobility · the rising against Spain (1647) and its suppression.
ii. Naples the government of the Spaniards · Ossuna tries
to revolt (1620) . the tax on fruit imposed by Arcos : the
rising of Masaniello (1647) . action of the Duc de Guise :
suppression of the insurrection (April, 1648)

III Grand Duchy of Tuscany the later Medici · the tran-
quil reign of Ferdinand II (1620-70) : his encouragement of
science and art

IV Duchy of Parma government of the Farnesi . the
war with the Pope (1641-44, 46-48)

V Duchy of Modena : government of the Este their
friendship for France

VI Duchy of Mantua : the war for the Mantuan succession (1627) on the death of Vincent Gonzaga II . Richelieu
supports Charles Gonzaga, Duc de Nevers · sack of Mantua
by the Imperialists (18 July, 1630) by the Treaty of Cherasco (1631) Charles is acknowledged but Savoy gets part of
Montferrat

VII Duchy of Guastalla Duke Ferdinand Gonzaga I

claims Mantua (1627). influence of Spain and the Emperor

VIII. Duchy of Milan the Spanish government its exactions

IX Republic of Venice the decline of its commerce its political importance in the Levant and in Italy. the government of the Republic its internal policy. its foreign policy the quarrel with Pope Paul V. Fra Paolo Sarpi struggle with the Turks : the war in Crete (1645–69)

X Republic of Genoa its weakness. its troubles with Corsica wealth of its bankers. the city bombarded by the French (1664)

XI Republic of Lucca its commercial prosperity

XII Duchy of Savoy : the importance of its position holding the keys of Italy Charles Emmanuel II (1580–1630) a faithful ally of Philip II, whose daughter he had married he ceded Bresse to Henry IV (1601) in exchange for Saluzzo Henry IV's dream of a kingdom of the Alps : the Mantuan succession (1627) Savoy gets part of Montferrat (1631) : the French alliance of Victor Amadeus I (1630–37) married to a daughter of Henry IV cession of Pignerol · reign of Charles Emmanuel II (1638–75) his policy schemes on Genoa the House of Savoy looks at Italy " as an artichoke to be eaten up leaf by leaf "

Authorities : Among SMALL BOOKS IN ENGLISH, or translated into English, may be noted *Trollope* Paul the Pope and Paul the Friar, *H F Brown*, History of Venice, *Malleson*, Studies in Genoese History, and, for Masaniello and Naples during this period, *Von Reumont*, The Carafas of Maddaloni Naples under Spanish Dominion Among SECONDARY HISTORIES consult *Botta*, Storia dell' Italia, vols 5–8, *Ranke*, Die romischen Papste im 16ten und 17ten Jahrhundert, 3 vols , translated by Austin, vol 3, *Brosch*, Geschichte des Kirchenstaates, 2 vols , *De Mouy*, L'Ambassade du Duc de Créqui (1662–65), 2 vols , *Giannone* Istoria civile del Reyno di Napoli, *Baldacchini*, Storia Napolitana dell' anno 1647, *Hervey de Saint Denis*, Insurrection de Naples en 1647, translated from *Rivas*, 2 vols , *Loiseleur*, Mazarin et le Duc de Guise in his Questions historique du XVIIe siècle, *Von Reumont*, Geschichte Toscanas unter die Medici, 2 vols , *Cantú*, *Milano e il suo territorio* and *Ragionamenti sulla Storia Lombardo nel secolo XVII*, *Giovini*, Biografia da fra Paolo, *Darn*, Histoire de Venise, vols x–xiv, *Costa-Beauregard*, Mémoires historiques sur la Maison royale de Savoie, 3 vols., *Belgiojoso*, Histoire de la Maison de Savoie, 4 vols , *Carutti*, Storia della diplomazia della corte di Savoia, 2 vols , and *Claretta*, Storia del regno di Carlo Emanuele II, 2 vols The PRI-MARY AUTHORITIES are to be found in *Muratori* and the *Archivio Storico Italiano*, while for the attempt of Guise on Naples may be noted *Modène* Mémoires and *Loiseleur and Baguenault de Puchesse* L'expédition du Duc de Guise à Naples, and for the quarrel between the Pope and Venice, *Sarpi*, Opere.

LECTURE XV.

EUROPE IN THE MIDDLE OF THE 17TH CENTURY.

8   SPAIN AND PORTUGAL

The extent of the dominions of Spain at the commence-ment of the 17th century Naples, Sicily, the Milanese. Rous-sillon, Franche Comté, the Catholic Netherlands, Central and South America, the Philippine Islands.

The policy of Philip II and its effect on the strength of Spain at home and abroad

The weakness of Spain at home · bad internal administra-tion sterilizing effect of South American gold . colonial administration.

The weakness of Spain abroad : the war with England and the Protestant Netherlands . the attitude of France and the Empire.

Yet the seeming power of Spain overshadowed Protestant Christendom : policy of Henry IV of France, James I of En-gland, Richelieu, Mazarin, and Cromwell toward Spain

Reign of Philip III (1598–1621) : the administration of the Duke of Lerma (1598–1618) his internal policy the expulsion of the Moriscoes (1609) his foreign policy . peace with England (1604) · truce with the Protestant Netherlands (1609) · the French alliance and marriages (1612) : Lerma becomes a cardinal and is dismissed (1618) : succeeded by his son, the Duke of Ucedo

Reign of Philip IV (1621–65) . administration of the Count-Duke Olivares (1621–43) : Spain in the Thirty Years' War Spinola occupies the Palatinate (1621) · renewal of war with the Dutch (1621) . Spain struggles with France for supremacy in Northern Italy and is three times worsted (1) in the affair of the Valtelline (1625), (2) in the Mantuan succession (1627–30), (3) in the Valtelline (1635)   Richelieu determines to overthrow the power of Spain . the revolt of Catalonia and of Portugal (1640) : dismissal of Olivares.

Administration of Don Luis de Haro (1643–65)   the Spaniards invade France and are defeated at Rocroi (1643) : and again at Lens (1648) · Spain recognizes the independence of the Protestant Netherlands at Munster (1648) : Spain tries to take advantage of the Fronde in France : Cromwell assists Mazarin . defeat of Spain : conclusion of the Treaty of the Pyrenees (7 Nov., 1659) : Spain loses Roussillon and Artois : Louis XIV marries Marie Therèse of Spain . the question of the Spanish Succession : death of Philip IV (17 Sept , 1665)

Condition of Portugal during the " Sixty Years' Captivity " to Spain (1580–1640)   ruin of her commerce : loss of her monopoly of the Asiatic trade : the Dutch seize the Spice Islands and establish themselves in Brazil : discontent felt in Portugal   preparations for revolt : negotiations with Richelieu

The Revolution of 1640 : the Duke of Braganza hailed as John IV · independence of Portugal recognized by France and Holland   help sent · the Asiatic possessions and Brazil rise against Spain · commencement of the war of independence   difficulties of John IV : his death (1656).

Reign of Affonso VI (1656–67) : government of the queen-mother (1656-62): Schomberg organizes the Portuguese army: by the Treaty of the Pyrenees (1659), Mazarin promises to abandon his support of Portugal · but he brings about the marriage of Charles II of England with Catherine of Braganza (1662) · importance of the English alliance administration of Castel Melhor (1662–67) . continuation of the war of independence . victories of Schomberg : court revolution (1667) · Dom Pedro declared Regent and Affonso VI sent to the Azores   treaty of peace with Spain signed at Lisbon (13 Feb., 1668) and independence of Portugal recognized

Significance of the Portuguese revolution   condition of Portugal and its importance as an ally of England

Authorities : As SMALL BOOKS may be noted *Dunham*, History of Spain and Portugal, vols 3, 4, which is old-fashioned but fairly correct for Spain, and *Morse Stephens*, Story of Portugal   As SECONDARY AUTHORITIES consult, for Spain, the volumes on this period in *Lafuente*, and other consecutive histories of Spain, *Weiss, L'Espagne depuis le règne de Philippe II jusqu'à l'avènement des Bourbons, 2 vols , *Melo, Guerra de la Cataluña, translated by Léonce de Lavergne, *Watson, History of the Reign of Philip III, and *Dunlop, Memoirs of Spain during the reigns of Philip IV and Charles II, 2 vols both old-fashioned but containing much that is valuable ; for Portugal, *Rebello da Silva, Historia de Portugal durante os seculos XVI et XVII, 5 vols , *Latino Coelho, Historia de Portugal desde os fins do seculo XVII até 1814, *Vertot*, Révolutions de Portugal, and *Tessier, Le Chevalier de Jaut, Relations de la France avec le Portugal au temps de Mazarin   Among PRIMARY AUTHORITIES for Spanish history during the century may be noted in addition to general collections, *Morel-Fatio*, L'Espagne au XVIe et XVIIe siècle   Documents historiques et littéraires, **Denans de Courchetet*, Histoire des negociations et du traité de paix de Pyrénees, and *Mignet*, Négociations relative à la succession d'Espagne sous Louis XIV, vol 1 ; for Portugal, **Borges de Castro and Judice Biker*, Collecção dos actos publicos celebrados entre a Coroa de Portugal e as mais potencias desde 1640, and *Carte, History of the Revolutions of Portugal with the Letters of Sir R. Southwell to the Duke of Ormond

[Books marked with a * are *not* in the University Library.]

LECTURE XVI.

FRANCE UNDER LOUIS XIV AND COLBERT: TO THE REVOCATION OF THE EDICT OF NANTES, 1685

Louis XIV assumes the actual government of France on the death of Mazarin (1661) · his personality : his political aims   how far he continued the work of Richelieu and Mazarin, how far he was an originator

His first ministers   the chancellors Séguier (–1672), d'Aligre (1672–77), and Le Tellier (1677–85)   Hugues de Lionne (–1671), Pomponne (1671–79), and Colbert-Croissy (1679–96) foreign affairs . Le Tellier (–1666) and Louvois (1666–91) war · Fouquet (–1661) and Colbert (1661–83) finances · Colbert (1668–76) and Colbert-Seignelay (1676–90) marine

The work of Colbert . he arranges the finances of France he builds up manufactures by a protective policy . he encourages commerce and occupies San Domingo   he creates the French navy · his personal probity · his hatred of war · his love of public works ; Riquet makes the great canal of Languedoc.

Louvois and his work   he organizes the army . his military reforms · formation of uniformed regiments, etc. : the great French generals, Turenne and Condé, Luxembourg and Vauban

The internal policy of Louis XIV . he attracts the nobility to court and keeps them out of politics   he builds up the administrative system · the intendants of the provinces · the official new nobility . the police system · the suppression of local liberties and municipal government . the King and his ministers the pivot of the highly centralized government

The position of the Parlements   especially the Parlement of Paris   growing importance of the noblesse de la robe

The splendour of Louis XIV : he establishes himself at Versailles : importance given by him to the Court . influence of society and social observances   effect of the removal from Paris   his absolutism in society as well as in politics

Louis XIV and the Catholic Church · his quarrel with Pope Alexander VII (1664–66) his quarrel with Pope Innocent XI, the claims of the Gallican Church . the assembly of 1682 · the attitude of Louis XIV to the Papacy the Jansenists and their doctrines · the position of the Huguenots : the new policy adopted by the King · the dragonnades · revocation of the Edict of Nantes (22 Oct., 1685).

Condition of the French provinces under Louis XIV · continuance of provincial life among the petite noblesse and the bourgeois . prosperity of the cities, and, under Colbert, of industry and commerce

Louis XIV and literature the classic age : French tragedy and comedy. created by Corneille, Racine and Molière · the great French preachers, Bossuet, Mascaron, Fléchier and Bourdaloue , the prose writers, Pascal and La Bruyère Boileau and the canons of poetry · history and Mezeray the work and position of the Académie Française

Louis XIV and art the painters, Poussin, Le Sueur and Le Brun the architects, Mansart and Perrault : the gardener, Le Nôtre foundation of the Academies of Sciences and of Inscriptions and of the School of Rome

Private life of Louis XIV ; his principal mistresses, Mdlle de La Vallière, Madame de Montespan and Mdlle. de Fontanges death of the Queen (1683) · he marries privately Madame de Maintenon (1684)

The year of the Revocation of the Edict of Nantes (1685) marks a change in the character and policy of Louis XIV he is henceforth guided by Madame de Maintenon and his confessors Père La Chaise, and Père Le Tellier . Colbert is dead and the Spanish Succession becomes his one aim

Impression which the days of the glory of Louis XIV made on Europe the imitators of his ideas and of his splendour.

Authorities *Voltaire*, Siècle de Louis XIV is still the best LITTLE BOOK on the period Among SECONDARY AUTHORITIES may be noted *Gaillardin*, Histoire du règne de Louis XIV, Vols. 3, 4 , *Lair*, *Louise de La Vallière et la jeunesse de Louis XIV, and *Nicolas Fouquet, 2

vols , *Chéruel*, *De l'administration de Louis XIV (1661-72) and *Mémoires sur le surintendant Fouquet, 2 vols , *Clément*, *Histoire de Colbert et de son administration, 2 vols , *Le Gouvernement de Louis XIV, ou la cour, l'administration, les finances et le commerce de 1683-89, *La Police sous Louis XIV, and *Madame de Montespan , *Neymarck*, Colbert et son temps, 2 vols ; *Rousset*, Histoire de Louvois, 4 vols , *Kerviler*, Le chancelier Pierre Séguier ; *Gazier*, Les dernières années du Cardinal de Retz, *Loyson*, L'Assemblée du clergé de France de 1682 , *Michaud*, Louis XIV et Innocent XI, 4 vols , *Bausset*, Histoire de Bossuet, 4 vols , and Histoire de Fénelon, 4 vols ; *Puaux et Sabatier*, Étude sur la révocation de l'Edit de Nantes, and *Martin*, La Monarchie au XVIIème siècle ; essai sur le système et l'influence personnelle de Louis XIV The PRIMARY AUTHORITIES for the administration of Louis XIV are *Clément*, Lettres, instructions et mémoires de Colbert, 7 vols , *Boislisle*, Correspondance des controleurs-généraux des finances avec les intendants des provinces, 2 vols, and *Depping*, Correspondance administrative sous le règne de Louis XIV, while among the vast number of memoirs, etc , may be noted the Journal of *Lefèvre d'Ormesson*, the Mémoires of *Madame de Motteville, Mademoiselle de Montpensier, La Fare, Gourville* and *Foucault*, *Cosnac*, Souvenirs du règne de Louis XIV, 8 vols , and above all the Letters of *Madame de Sevigné*

[Books marked with a * are *not* in the University Library]

LECTURE XVII

THE FOREIGN POLICY OF LOUIS XIV: TO THE TREATIES OF NYMWEGEN, 1678

Position of the powers of Europe towards each other, when Louis XIV assumed the government of France (1661) : effect of the restoration of Charles II in England, (1660) ideas of religious unity give way to the conception of national unity concentrated in the person of the Monarch exceptions, the Protestant Netherlands, ruled by a burgher aristocracy, and England . extinction of feudal relics in England and development of commercialism the contest for the commerce of the world between England and the Dutch

Advantages possessed by France in the new era of diplomatists and standing armies Louis XIV understands and
dominates the new era : his foreign office and diplomatists .
his army, its organization and its generals his navy

Louis XIV resolves to use these advantages to enlarge the
borders of France, and, for internal and external reasons, de-
cides on a war policy.

Louis XIV and diplomatic privileges : the case of D'Es-
trades at London (1662), and of Créqui at Rome (1664)

Louis XIV and England . marriage of Henrietta of England, sister of Charles II, to the Duke of Orleans, brother
of Louis XIV (1661) purchase of Dunkirk (Nov , 1662).

Louis XIV and Spain : his hopes of the succession . his
claims for diplomatic precedence granted

Louis XIV and Germany . he sends help to the Emperor
against the Turks (1664) his influence with the League of
the Rhine and the west German princes

Louis XIV and the Turks he defeats the Barbary Corsairs (1665), and sends help to the Venetians in Candia.

Louis XIV and the Dutch . his relations with John de
Witt effect of Colbert's policy on the Dutch.

The naval war between England and the Dutch (1664–67) .
causes of the war in commercial rivalry : the republican party
and the House of Orange . capture of New Amsterdam battle of Lowestoft (3 June, 1664) : the bishop of Munster attacks the Dutch Louis XIV declares war against England :
battle of the Downs (1–4 June, 1666) · Louis XIV makes
peace with England (March, 1667) the Dutch in the Med-
way . Treaty of Breda (31 July, 1667) England abandons
the trade of the Spice Islands, but keeps the New Netherlands in North America

The War of Devolution (1667–68) · pretext for the war,
(see Appendix V) . isolation of Spain Louis XIV takes the
border fortresses of the Catholic Netherlands, and occupies
Franche Comté · the Triple Alliance by the treaty of Aix-
la-Chapelle (2 May, 1668), France keeps French Flanders
but restores Franche Comté to Spain

The Triple Alliance between England, Sweden, and the Dutch (23 Jan., 1668) · its importance the principle of the Balance of Power, which is one of the keynotes of European policy for more than a century, invoked to check the ambition of Louis XIV

The position in the Protestant Netherlands : the policy of John de Witt Perpetual Edict against the House of Orange character of William III

Louis XIV breaks up the Triple Alliance by the Treaty of Dover with England (1 June, 1670), and by detaching Sweden (April, 1672) : secret treaty with the Emperor for dividing the Spanish Succession (Nov , 1671).

Louis XIV attacks the Dutch (1672) : their sole ally the Great Elector, Frederick William of Brandenburg · passage of the Rhine (12 June, 1672) · the Dutch cut their dykes (18 June) · murder of John de Witt (20 Aug) : William III elected Stadtholder the Great Elector forced to make peace

The naval war England joins France the battle of Solebay (7 June, 1672) the Dutch successful in 1673 peace between England and the Dutch (19 Feb., 1674).

The continental war coalition formed against Louis XIV by the Emperor and the Great Elector (Oct , 1672) joined next by Spain and the Duke of Lorraine (Aug , 1673), Denmark and the Elector Palatine (Jan and March, 1674), the Empire (May, 1674), and the Great Elector (July, 1674) the Electors of Trèves and Cologne forced to abandon France (1673) : Sweden remains her only ally

Campaign of 1673 capture of Maestricht (29 June, 1673) ◦ Turenne's strategy : campaign of 1674 Louis XIV occupies Franche Comté Condé wins the battle of Senef (11 Aug., 1674) : Turenne crosses the Rhine and ravages the Palatinate campaign of 1675 Turenne reoccupies Alsace, and is killed (26 July) naval victories of Du Quesne in the Mediterranean death of De Ruyter (1676) . subsequent campaigns : capture of the border fortresses

Treaties of Nymwegen (Niméguen) signed (10 Aug ,

1678, 5 Feb , 1679) · France obtained from Spain Franche
Comté, Valenciennes and other towns in French Flanders,
and recognition of rights in Alsace the Dutch ceded nothing :
the treaty supplemented by that of Saint Germain-en-Laye
(7 Sept., 1679), by which Brandenburg and Denmark restored all conquests to Sweden

Authorities Among SECONDARY WORKS dealing with the diplomatic and military history of the period, founded on documents, may
be noted, *Filon*, La France et l'Autriche au XVIIe Siècle , *Lefèvre-*
Pontalis, Jean de Witt, 2 vols , translated into English ; *Baillon*, Hen-
riette Anne d'Angleterre duchesse d'Orléans , *Forneron*, Louise de
Kéroualle, duchesse de Portsmouth , *Rousset*, Histoire de Louvois, 4
vols , *Peter*, Der Krieg des Grossen Kurfursten gegen Frankreich ,
Depping, Geschichte des Krieges der Munsterer und Kolner gegen
Holland , *Von Ennen*, Frankreich und der Niederrhein, 2 vols , *Pié-*
pape, Histoire de la réunion de la Franche-Comté à la France, 2 vols.,
Roy, Turenne ; *Michel*, Vauban , *Jal*, Abraham Du Quesne et la marine de son temps, 2 vols , and *Paulhat*, Louis XIV et la compagnie
des Indes. The chief PRIMARY AUTHORITIES are *Mignet*, Négociations relatives à la succession d'Espagne, 4 vols , *Griffet*, Recueil de
lettres pour servir à l'histoire militaire de Louis XIV, 8 vols , and the
Mémoires of *Turenne*, and the *Maréchal de Gramont*

[Books marked with a * are *not* in the University Library]

LECTURE XVIII

PRUSSIA UNDER THE GREAT ELECTOR

The scattered nature and diverse character of the dominions ruled by Frederick William, Elector of Brandenburg and
Duke of Prussia, known as the Great Elector, in 1648 : his
centre in Brandenburg, not yet entirely evacuated by the
Swedish troops . Eastern Pomerania still full of Swedes ·
Prussia only held in feudal subjection to Poland and Cleves
garrisoned by the Dutch

Contrast between the policy pursued in Brandenburg and in the rest of Germany during the latter half of the 17th century · the importance of the reign of the Great Elector . he prepares the way for the future greatness of the House of Hohenzollern

The Great Elector's national policy · his desire to hold Prussia free from Polish suzerainty the motive for his actions in the Northern War of 1656–60 (see Lecture XI) · that relief granted by the Treaty of Wehlau (1657) confirmed by the Treaty of Oliva (1660) his desire to get the Dutch garrison out of Cleves the motive for aiding the Dutch in 1672 . his desire to conquer Western Pomerania the motive for joining the coalition against Louis XIV

To carry out his schemes the Great Elector, like Louis XIV, creates and organizes a standing army, and looks solely to national interests.

In 1666 he finally divides the Juliers-Cleves dominions, and takes Cleves, Ravensberg and Mark · in the same year he occupies Magdeburg, which falls to him by the Treaties of Westphalia on the death of Augustus of Saxony in 1680

Part taken by the Great Elector in the wars against Louis XIV in 1672 he aids the Dutch, but makes peace in 1673 : in 1674 he joins the coalition against France, and is attacked by Sweden he defeats the Swedes at Fehrbellin (18 June, 1675), takes Stettin (1677), and Stralsund (1678) : but at the Treaty of Saint-Germain-en-Laye (17 Sept , 1679) has to restore all Western Pomerania except a small district

The Great Elector and the Emperor : his German policy : he joins the League of the Rhine . strives for the leadership of the Protestant princes with Saxony his friendship with Denmark . his attitude towards Poland his claim to Jagernsdorf in Silesia, confiscated by Ferdinand II in 1623, and to Liegnitz on death of the last duke (1675) compromised in 1686 by the Emperor Leopold's ceding to him Schwebus in Silesia.

The internal policy of the Great Elector . his struggle for absolutism and centralized administration with the nobility, united in their provincial Estates, and with the municipal rights of the cities · local jealousy of his different provinces. (1) In Brandenburg the Estates were enfeebled and could not meet without being convoked : no Estates of the province, only provincial Estates in the Old, and New, Mark. (2) In Cleves the nobility Lutheran and opposed to the Calvinist Elector · their alliance with the Dutch · the administration in the hands of the Estates the resistance of the nobility overthrown by the use of troops in 1651 and 1654 . the administration taken into the hands of the Elector (3) In Prussia the nobility with full feudal power taxing and ruling their dominions their friendship with and imitation of the Polish nobility . independent attitude of the Estates, supported by the city of Konigsberg · the Great Elector's struggle for the recognition of his sovereignty (1660–63) the execution of Kalkstein (1670)

The keynote of the struggle the definition of the position of the Elector and the Estates the main battle over taxation in Brandenburg (1653), in Cleves (1661), in Prussia (1663) the right of self-taxation of the Estates is acknowledged but in Cleves from 1670, in Brandenburg from 1678, in Prussia and in Magdeburg from 1682 the direct taxes are recognized as permanent, and future taxes are imposed without asking the Estates excise introduced by Grumbkow (1677)

In return for the subordination of the nobles, the Great Elector recognizes serfdom on their properties, and re-establishes it in Prussia

To carry out his ambitious hopes for his House, the Great Elector saw that Brandenburg must be a military power his efforts to create a standing army at his accession it consisted of 1200 men, at his death of 30,000

Material progress encouraged by the Great Elector : agriculture improved ; marshes drained ; canal made from the Elbe to the Oder , Berlin becomes a city , welcome of more than 20,000 Huguenots after the Revocation of the Edict of Nantes

Death of the Great Elector (28 April, 1688) comparison between his aims and methods and those of Louis XIV.

Authorities In English see *Carlyle*, History of Frederick the Great, vols 1, 2 and *Tuttle*, History of Prussia, vol 1. Among SEC-ONDARY HISTORIES consult *Berner*, Geschichte des preussischen Staats, *Stenzel*, Geschichte des preussischen Staats, vols 1, 2, *Droysen*, Geschichte des preussischen Politik, vol 3, *Ranke*, Zwolf Bucher preussischer Geschichte, *Treitschke*, Deutsche Geschichte, vol 1, *Philippson*, Geschichte des preussischer Staatswesens, vol 1, *Bornhak*, Geschichte des preussischen Verwaltungsrechts, vol 1, *Isaacsohn*, Geschichte des preussischen Beamtenthums, vol 2, *Cavaignac*, Les Origines de la Prusse contemporaine, vol 1, and *Peter*, work cited under Lecture XVII The PRIMARY AUTHORITY is the collection, edited by *Erdmannsdorfer* and others, of the Urkunden und Actenstucke zur Geschichte des Kurfursten Friedrich Wilhelm von Brandenburg

[Books marked with a * are *not* in the University Library]

LECTURE XIX.

THE FOREIGN POLICY OF LOUIS XIV TO THE TREATIES OF RYSWICK, 1697

The rivalry of William III, Prince of Orange, and Louis XIV · the character of William III . his adherence to the doctrine of the Balance of Power · the question of the Spanish Succession

The position of Louis XIV after the Treaties of Nymwegen his friendship with Charles II and James II of England the "chambers of reunion," and Alsace and Franche Comté : he seizes Strasbourg and purchases Casale (Sept., 1681): secret alliance between the Emperor, William III, Spain and Sweden (1681) to preserve the arrangements made at Nymwegen in 1678 : prevented from acting by the invasion of the Turks and the siege of Vienna (1683) the Imperial Diet makes a truce of twenty years with Louis XIV, and consents to the reunions (Aug , 1684) · the question of the Palatine Succession (1685) · pretensions of Louis XIV formation of the League of Augsburg (9 July, 1686) between the allies of 1681, joined by Victor Amadeus II, Duke of Savoy, the Elector of Bavaria, and others

Louis XIV and the Mediterranean . Du Quesne bombards Tripoli, and Algiers, and Genoa (1684) : Seignelay improves the French navy

Louis XIV and Pope Innocent XI . the ambassador's right of asylum occupation of Avignon (1687)

Louis XIV and the administration : Colbert succeeded by Le Peletier (1683–89), and Pontchartrain (1689–99) Louvois by Barbézieux (1691–1701) . Colbert-Croissy assisted by Colbert-Torcy (1689), and succeeded by him (1696).

Effect of the Revocation of the Edict of Nantes (1685) in Europe, especially in England and Germany

Outbreak of war (1688) : its causes (1) the Palatine Succession . (2) the electorate of Cologne, France supporting Cardinal von Furstenberg and the Emperor, Joseph Clement of Bavaria Louis XIV devastates the Palatinate, occupies Bonn, Cologne, Mayence and Trèves, and takes Philippsburg (1689).

The position changed by the Revolution of 1688 in England, by which William III became King of England effect of this change on the position of Louis XIV . he sends an army and a fleet to support James II in Ireland

Campaign of 1690 De Tourville defeats the English and the Dutch off Beachy Head (10 July), but James II is defeated at the battle of the Boyne (11 July), and leaves Ireland Luxembourg defeats the Prince of Waldeck at Fleurus (1 July, 1690), and Catinat the Duke of Savoy at Staffarda (17 Aug , 1690)

The campaign of 1691 Louis XIV prepares to invade England he takes Mons (9 April) Catinat takes Nice (2 April) Noailles takes Urgel death of Louvois

The campaign of 1692 Russell defeats De Tourville at the battle of La Hogue (29 May) . end of the French supremacy in the Channel · regular naval war abandoned for privateering Duguay-Trouin and Jean Bart : the invasion of England abandoned · Louis XIV takes Namur (5 June) Luxembourg defeats William III at Steenkirk (3 Aug.) the Duke of Savoy invades Dauphiné

The campaign of 1693 Luxembourg defeats William III at Landen or Neerwinden (29 July), and takes Charleroi (11 Oct) Catinat defeats the Duke of Savoy and Prince Eugène at Marsaglia (4 Oct) · Noailles takes Rosas

Exhaustion of France feebleness of the ministers depreciation of the currency.

Defensive campaign of 1694 death of Luxembourg (4 Jan , 1695) William III recaptures Namur (1695) Louis XIV makes peace with Victor Amadeus II of Savoy, who recovers Pignerol and Casale, and whose daughter marries the grandson of Louis he declares himself the ally of France

Negotiations for peace opened at Ryswick (May, 1697) peace decided by Vendôme's capture of Barcelona (10 Aug)

The treaties of Ryswick signed 20 Sept and 30 Oct., 1697, by which (1) Louis XIV recognized William III as King of England, but refused to expel James II (ii) the Dutch allowed to garrison the frontier towns of Belgium as " barrier fortresses " (iii) Louis XIV restored to the Empire Philippsburg, Breisach and Freiburg, and all places adjudged to him since the treaties of Nymwegen, except Strasbourg, Longwy, Sarrelouis and Landau · (iv) Leopold, Duke of Lorraine, restored to his father's dominions, with all fortresses dismantled

Position of the powers of Europe at the Treaties of Ryswick awaiting the settlement of the Spanish Succession

Authorities Of the SECONDARY HISTORIES cited for Lectures XVI and XVII, *Voltaire*, **Gaillardin*, **Clément*, Le Gouvernement de Louis XIV de 1683-89, *Rousset*, **Michaud*, *Bausset*, **Martin*, **Fiton*, **Von Ennen*, **Roy*, **Michel* and **Jal* are still valuable, and of the PRIMARY AUTHORITIES, *Boislisle*, *Depping*, *Foucault*, **Cosnac*, *La Fare*, *Madame de Sevigné*, and **Griffet* To the SECONDARY AUTHORITIES should be added for this period, *Macaulay*, History of England vols 1-4 , **Sirtema de Grovesteins*, Guillaume III et Louis XIV, 8 vols , **Reynald*, Louis XIV et Guillaume III, 2 vols , **Noailles*, Histoire de Madame de Maintenon et des principaux événements du règne de Louis XIV, 4 vols , *Geffroy*, Madame de Maintenon , **Legrelle*, Louis XIV et Strasbourg ; **Gérin*, Le pape Alexandre VIII et Louis XIV , *Schulte*, Markgraf Ludwig von Baden und der Reichs-

krieg gegen Frankreich, 2 vols , *Carutti*, Storia del regno di Vittorio
Amedio II, and *D'Haussonville*, Histoire de la réunion de la Lor-
raine à la France, 4 vols   To the PRIMARY AUTHORITIES add *Louis
XIV* Œuvres, 6 vols , and Mémoires pour l'instruction du Dauphin,
ed *Dreyss*, 2 vols , *Spanheim*, Relation sur la cour de France en 1690 ,
Madame de Maintenon Correspondance générale and Œuvres ed by
Lavallée, 12 vols , the various collections of the Letters of the *Duchesse
d'Orléans*, known as the Princess Palatine , *Catinat*, Mémoires et
Correspondance, 3 vols., the Mémoires of *Mdlle de Lafayette*, *Madame de Caylus*, the *Abbé Choisy*, and *Torcy*, and the Journal of *Dangeau*, vols 1-6

[Books marked with an * are *not* in the University Library]

LECTURE XX.

THE SIEGE OF VIENNA BY THE TURKS, 1683 POLAND UNDER JOHN SOBIESKI

The Emperor Leopold I and Hungary . his efforts (1) to
extirpate Calvinism, (2) to destroy local independence, in the
portion of Hungary left to him . the situation after the
Treaty of Vasvar (1664) : the conspiracy of 1670   the Palatine office abolished and a policy of religious persecution
and Germanization adopted . the insurrection of Tokoli
(1675-79) encouraged by Louis XIV to embarrass the Emperor   effect of Western on Eastern European politics . the
Treaty of Nymwegen (1678) followed by the Diet of Œdens-
berg (1681) by which the Palatine was restored, arbitrary
taxes abolished, all offices granted to Magyars, and liberty
of worship promised to the Protestants

The Emperor Leopold and Transylvania   attitude of that
province to the Turks (see Lecture XIII).

The Turks recognize Tokoli as Prince of Hungary, and
under the command of Kara Mustapha Kiuprili march on
Vienna (1683)   the siege of Vienna (March–Sept , 1683) .

its significance in history help sent to the Emperor by other states heroic defence of Vienna appeal for the help of John Sobieski, King of Poland : attempt of Louis XIV to isolate the Emperor

John Sobieski, King of Poland, elected 21 May, 1674 the disastrous reign of John Casimir Vasa (1648-69) . the feeble reign of Michael Koributh Vichnevetski (1669-74) Sobieski's difficulties in Poland since the Treaty of Zurawna (27 Oct , 1676) . his treaties with Russia and the Dutch his fame as a general his desire for a crusade against the Turks his friendship with Pope Innocent XI his differences with Louis XIV . he resolves to come to the help of the Emperor

John Sobieski with Charles V, Duke of Lorraine, defeats the Turks in their camp (12 Sept , 1683) and raises the siege of Vienna : pursuit of the Turks . capture of Gran . execution of Kara Mustapha Kiuprili

War with the Turks · *first phase* (1684-89) : excitement caused in Christendom by the siege of Vienna the " Holy League " . the Venetians under Morosini conquer the Morea (1684-87) · the Poles in Moldavia (1686) · the Duke of Lorraine takes Buda (3 Sept , 1686) · he and Louis of Baden defeat the Turks at Mohacs (12 Aug , 1687) . the Janissaries depose Muhammad IV and place Sulaiman II on the throne (Nov , 1687) the Prince of Transylvania declares himself a vassal of Hungary . capture of Belgrade (Sept , 1688) : Louis of Baden invades Servia . the Russians attack the Turks Mustapha Kiuprili appointed Grand Vizier (1689).

The Emperor Leopold's action on the conquest of Hungary . he punishes the friends of Tokoli · executions at Eperies the crown of Hungary made hereditary, instead of elective, in the House of Hapsburg · abolition of the coronation oath : persecution of the Protestants

War with the Turks *second phase* (1689-91) the Emperor has to detach the Duke of Lorraine to fight Louis XIV on the Rhine Louis of Baden commands against the Turks Mustapha Kiuprili appoints Tokoli Prince of Transylvania

and recaptures Belgrade (1690) accession of Ahmad II
Louis of Baden defeats the Turks at Szalankemen (19 Aug ,
1691) Mustapha Kiuprili killed : Transylvania conquered ·
the Hapsburgs recognized as Princes of Transylvania (Dec.,
1691) . John Sobieski's last campaign he extends the frontier of Poland to the Pruth (1691)) . Louis of Baden sent to
the Rhine

War with the Turks · *third phase* (1691–98) . unimportant
operations (1691–95) : accession of Mustapha II (1695) . he
takes command of the Turkish army he invades Hungary
and takes many fortresses confusion caused by the death of
John Sobieski : Peter the Great takes Azov (28 July, 1696)
Prince Eugène destroys the Turkish army at Zenta (11 Sept ,
1697) : the Turks sue for peace

Reasons which induced the Emperor Leopold to make
peace with the Turks . the imminence of the falling in of the
Spanish Succession intervention of the English and Dutch.

Treaty of Carlowitz (26 Jan , 1699) ; (i) the Emperor obtained Hungary, except the Banat of Temesvar, the whole
of Transylvania, Croatia and Slavonia to the Save (ii)
Venice obtained Dalmatia and the Morea (iii) Poland recovered Podolia with Kammietz . (iv) Russia got Azov.

Since the siege of Vienna the Turks have receded in Europe the Treaty of Carlowitz marks the first stage of their
decline

The condition of Poland under John Sobieski rivalry between the Poles and Lithuanians . the factious nobility : Sobieski's schemes for reform rejected he finds himself without
subsidies or support attitude of foreign powers · Sobieski
wishes to abdicate . approach of civil war . Sobieski's ad-
vancement of civilization in Poland . death of John Sobieski
(17 June, 1696) election of the Elector Augustus of Saxony
to be King of Poland (1 June, 1697)

Authorities: Among SMALL BOOKS *Léger*, Autriche Hongrie ;
Creasy, Ottoman Turks and *Morfill*, Story of Poland, as before, with
*Malden, History and Consequences of the Defeat of the Turks before
Vienna in 1683 As SECONDARY AUTHORITIES see *Coxe*, History of

the House of Austria, 4 vols ; *Teutsch*, Geschichte der Siebenburger Sachsen ; *Klopp*, Das Jahr 1683 und der folgende grosse Turkenkrieg bis zum Frieden von Carlowitz, 2 vols , *Thürheim*, Feldmarschall Ernst Rudiger, Graf Stahremberg ; *Roder von Diersburg*, Des Markgrafen Ludwig Wilhelm von Baden Feldzüge wider die Turken, 2 vols ; *Arneth*, Prinz Eugen von Savoyen 3 vols. ; *Von Hammer*, Histoire de l'Empire Ottoman vols. 12, 13, *Coyer*, Histoire de Jean Sobieski, 3 vols , and *Salvandy*, Histoire de Pologne avant et sous Jean Sobieski, 3 vols , are old-fashioned and do not give sources, but interesting There is much that is useful in *Farges*, Recueil des instructions données aux ambassadeurs et ministres de France en Pologne

[Books marked with a * are *not* in the University Library]

LECTURE XXI.

RUSSIA UNDER PETER THE GREAT

Condition of Russia under the first Románovs, internal and foreign policy of the Tsars (see Lecture XII).

The reign of Alexis Románov (1645–75) : autocracy legalized the government of the boyars, disorganization of the administration popular risings. Stenka Razin (1666–71) : Nikon's reform of the Russian liturgy : the code of Alexis : his wars with Poland and Sweden · he accepts the suzerainty of the Cossacks of Little Russia, and the Ukraine, and of the Zaporogues. by truce of Androussovo with Poland (1667), he receives Smolensk and Kiev

The reign of Feodor Alexievitch (1675–82).

Accession of Peter the Great, youngest son of Alexis, born 9 June, 1672, the rising of the Streltsi at Moscow Ivan V proclaimed joint Tsar with Peter : Princess Sophia made Regent

The government of Sophia and Vasili Galitzin (1682–89) : they confirm the peace of Kardis with Sweden and the treaty of Androussovo. Galitzin's expedition against the Crimean

Tartars (1687–89) overthrow of Sophia (1689) Peter the Great assumes the government.

The boyhood of Peter the Great : his education his character his passion for boat-building · his foreign friends Lefort his amusements and occupations · his longing for a navy · condition of Russian commerce ·. Archangel : the Baltic · the government of the boyars . by death of Ivan V Peter becomes sole Tsar (8 Feb., 1696)

Peter the Great's first war · the capture of Azov (28 July, 1696) by treaty with the Turks, Azov granted to Russia (1700).

Peter the Great's visit to Western Europe (1697–98) ; its political results : its effect on Peter's character.

Destruction of the Streltsi (1698) first steps taken for the formation of a regular army and navy . forcible introduction of Western usages

First appearance of Russia in European politics · negotiations between Augustus I, Elector of Saxony and King of Poland, Frederick, Elector of Brandenburg, Frederick IV, King of Denmark, and Peter the Great for an attack on Sweden . motives of the attack · Brandenburg also suggests the partition of Poland : Peter's desire for a port on the Baltic

Peter the Great invades Ingria the Russians defeated by Charles XII at the battle of Narva (13 Nov , 1700) Charles XII moves against Poland

The Russians take Noteburg (22 Oct., 1702), and Peter the Great founds St Petersburg : occupation of Ingria and Carelia capture of Narva (20 Aug., 1704).

The Empress Catherine · private marriage (1707) . public marriage (1712) · her influence over Peter · Menshikov

Closeness of the alliance between Peter and Augustus I · the devastation of Livonia · the Swedes defeated at Kalisch (29 Nov., 1706) · Augustus makes peace with Charles XII at Altranstadt (1706) Peter left without allies : the war in Lithuania : fortification of Moscow.

Charles XII invades the Ukraine (1708) : treachery of Mazeppa, Hetman of the Cossacks , the battle of Liesna (9 Oct ,

1708) the winter of 1708–9 destruction of the Swedish army at Poltáva (11 July, 1709) escape of Charles XII. importance of the victory . Russia takes rank with European nations the result of a trained and disciplined army immediate effects of the victory . Augustus, aided by Peter, resolves to recover the Polish throne and to conquer Livonia · the Russians made safe in Ingria and Carelia, with an outlet to the Baltic the Emperor offers his sister to the Tsarevitch Alexis, who marries Princess Charlotte of Brunswick-Wolfenbüttel (25 Oct 1711) league of Russia, Denmark and Prussia formed against Sweden by treaty of Marienwerder (1 Nov., 1709) Elbing promised to Prussia

Early suggestions of a partition of Poland by Prussia and Saxony to Peter the Great

Internal reforms · the new administration the Privy Council takes the place of the Council of Boyars . the new departments . formation of the eight governments the taxes and financial system · commerce and monopolies encouragement of foreigners ecclesiastical reforms reformation of the monasteries . the Senate . unpopularity of these changes . local insurrections and discontent.

Continuance of the war with Sweden : capture of Viborg (21 June, 1710), of Riga (July) and of Revel (September) . occupation of Livonia and Esthonia marriage of Peter's niece Anne to the Duke of Courland . occupation of Courland.

The Turks declare war against Peter the Great (1 Dec., 1710) Peter the Great invades Moldavia . he is surrounded by the Turks on the Pruth and by treaty of 11 July, 1711, agrees to surrender Azov, which was given up to the Turks in 1712

The campaigns in Pomerania (1711–13) sequestration of Stettin.

Peter the Great's position at the time of the Treaties of Utrecht

The greatness of the work Peter had done for Russia.

Authorities: Of SMALL BOOKS the most readable is still, despite some mistakes and misconceptions, *Voltaire*, Histoire de l'empire de Russie sous Pierre le Grand, which should be checked by the chapters on his reign in *Morfill*, Story of Russia, and *Rambaud*, Histoire de la Russie, translated by L B Lang, 2 vols The best SECONDARY AUTHORITIES are *Schuyler*, Peter the Great, 2 vols , *Bruckner*, Peter der Grosse, and *Herrmann*, Russland unter Peter der Grosse The University Library, owing to the gift by Mr Eugene Schuyler of his invaluable collection, is rich in books on this subject most of these volumes are in Russian but among those of historical and biographical interest in other languages may be noted *Obolenski and Possell*, Tagebuch des Generalen Patrick Gordon, 3 vols , and *Possett*, Der General und Admiral Franz Lefort, sein Leben und seine Zeit, 2 vols

———————————

LECTURE XXII

--

CHARLES XII OF SWEDEN.

The reign of Charles XI of Sweden (1660–97) during his minority and the government of his mother, Hedwiga, peace was made with Poland, Denmark and Russia [see Lecture XI] and Sweden joined the Triple Alliance [see Lecture XVII] the political position of Sweden the government of the nobles · they grant to themselves the crown lands

Charles XI assumes the government (1672) . his alliance with France he invades Brandenburg : he is attacked by Denmark and the Dutch : his navy is defeated by Cornelis van Tromp (11 June, 1675) and his army by the Great Elector at Fehrbellin (18 June, 1675) : he defeats the Danes at Lund (11 Dec., 1675) but loses all Pomerania and his fleet is destroyed by Admiral Juel (11 June, 1678) : by the Treaty of Saint-Germain-en-Laye (17 Sept , 1679) he recovers all his lost territory by the influence of Louis XIV his alliance with the Dutch (1681) · he sends them 6000 men (1688–98).

The Revolution of 1682 absolute power placed in the hands of the king by the Estates : he attacks the nobility by resuming all lands granted to them since 1609 . his excellent administration economy and large savings encouragement of Swedish commerce

Christian V, King of Denmark (1670-99) · the administration of Griffenfeld (1670-76) . result of the war with Sweden · his troubles with Holstein-Gottorp the Convention of Altona (1691) his attempts to imitate Louis XIV his creation of a privileged nobility · excellence of his navy and commerce · his administration . he invades Schleswig (1698) and is succeeded by Frederick IV in the following year.

Charles XII of Sweden (1697-1718) his education and character he is declared of age (1699) · danger threatened to Sweden by the alliance against her of Denmark, Brandenburg, Saxony and Russia.

The first campaign of Charles XII · he comes to the help of the Duke of Holstein-Gottorp (1700) he attacks Copenhagen Frederick IV makes the Treaty of Travandahl (18 Aug , 1700), granting practical sovereignty to the Duke in Schleswig

The second campaign of Charles XII · he defeats the Russians at Narva (30 Nov , 1700) and the Saxons at Klissow.

Charles XII despises Russia and resolves to drive Augustus I out of Poland · the Polish Diet declares the throne of Poland vacant election of Stanislas Leczinski as King of Poland (12 July, 1704) · Charles XII invades Saxony . by the Treaty of Altranstadt (24 Sept , 1706) Augustus recognizes Stanislas as king . commanding position of Charles XII in European politics expectation of his intervention in the War of the Spanish Succession : visit of Marlborough to him

Charles XII invades the Ukraine (1708) : his army destroyed or captured by Peter the Great at Poltáva (11 July, 1709) . he escapes to Bender : his efforts to induce the Turks to attack Russia · he is arrested by the Turks and imprisoned at Adrianople (1713)

The Northern War during the residence of Charles XII at

Bender : Augustus I tears up the Treaty of Altranstädt and with Peter the Great reconquers Poland : Stanislas Leczinski escapes to Sweden (1710) and goes to Bender (1713) . the Russians conquer Esthonia and all the shores of the Gulf of Finland · Frederick IV of Denmark invades Sweden, but is defeated by Stenbock at Helsingborg (10 March, 1710) Stenbock defeats the Danes at Gadebusch (20 Dec., 1712) and burns Altona : he is joined by the Duke of Holstein-Gottorp : Stenbock forced to surrender at Tönning (May, 1713) the Danes conquer Bremen and Verden campaign of the Russians, Prussians, Saxons and Danes in Pomerania : the whole province occupied, except Stralsund

Position of the northern powers at the Treaties of Utrecht . exhausted condition of Sweden : triumphant attitude of Russia, Prussia and Denmark . Sweden ceases to be a great power . the position given her by the Treaties of Westphalia too great for her to hold · sources of her strength and weakness

The character and career of Charles XII

Authorities : The best SMALL BOOK is still *Voltaire*, Charles XII, but the summary of facts in *Otté*, Scandinavian History, and *Geffroy*, Les États scandinaves, is useful For more detailed information see *Lundblad*, Geschichte Karls des Zwölften, 2 vols , *Beskow*, Karl der Tolfte and *Sarauw*, Die Feldzüge Karls XII, while *Schuyler*, Peter the Great, *Morfill*, Story of Poland, and *Tuttle*, History of Prussia, can be studied for the Russian, Polish and Prussian sides of the Northern War The general histories of Sweden by *Fryxell* and by *Geijer*, translated into German and continued by *Carlson*, devote much space to the reigns of Charles XI and Charles XII.

LECTURE XXIII.

THE WAR OF THE SPANISH SUCCESSION, 1701–14

Causes of the War of the Spanish Succession : the reign of Charles II of Spain (1665–1700) : his feeble health : intrigues for the succession to the Spanish dominions importance of the question to European nations · the doctrine of the Balance of Power.

The Secret Partition Treaty between Louis XIV and the Emperor Leopold (19 Jan , 1668) Louis to have the Netherlands, Franche Comté, Navarre, Naples, Sicily and Catalonia. Leopold to have Spain, the Indies and the Milanese these terms made impossible by the Treaties of Ryswick.

The claimants to the Spanish Succession and their claims Philip, Duke of Anjou, grandson of Louis XIV, the Archduke Charles, younger son of the Emperor Leopold, and the Electoral Prince of Bavaria (See Appendix V)

The First Partition Treaty between William III and Louis XIV (11 Oct , 1698) · the Electoral Prince to have Spain, the Indies and the Netherlands, Charles to have the Milanese, Philip to have Naples, Sicily, the Tuscan ports and Guiposcoa arrangement accepted by Spain death of the Electoral Prince of Bavaria (6 Feb , 1699)

The Second Partition Treaty between William III and Louis XIV (15 May, 1700) . Charles to have Spain, the Indies, the Netherlands and Sardinia, Philip to have the same as before with the addition of the Milanese, which was to be exchanged for Lorraine.

Intrigues at Madrid · Charles II makes a will in favour of Philip (7 Oct , 1700) and dies (1 Nov , 1700).

Louis XIV accepts the will and acknowledges his grandson as ruler of all the Spanish dominions (16 Nov , 1700) : William III and the Dutch reluctantly recognize Philip V of Spain : diplomatic precautions of Louis XIV his first mistake, expulsion of the Dutch from the barrier fortresses : formation of the Grand Alliance (7 Sept , 1701) between the Emperor, William III, the Dutch and the King of Prussia . second mistake of Louis XIV : he recognizes the Pretender as King of England (17 Sept , 1701) on the death of James II death of William III (19 March, 1702) and accession of Queen Anne . the Grand Alliance against Louis XIV strengthened by the assistance of the Empire (30 Sept , 1702) . its leading spirits the Duke of Marlborough, Prince Eugène and the Grand Pensionary Heinsius · the allies of France were the Dukes of Modena, Mantua, Guastalla and Savoy, and the Electors of Bavaria and Cologne.

War of the Spanish Succession. campaign of 1701 Eugène turns the position of Catinat in Lombardy and defeats Villeroi at Chiari (1 Sept)

Campaign of 1702 Eugène surprises Villeroi at Cremona (1 Feb). the Dukes of Modena and 'Guastalla abandon France Vendôme defeats Eugène at Luzzara (15 Aug) Louis of Baden invades Alsace and seizes Landau Bavaria declares war and seizes Ulm (8 Sept.) Villars defeats Louis of Baden at Friedlingen (14 Oct.) . Marlborough takes Liége and other fortresses on the Meuse

Campaign of 1703 French plan of marching on Vienna Francis Rakoczy raises an insurrection in Hungary . critical position of the Emperor . Villars enters Bavaria : Vendôme enters the Tyrol Vendôme has to retire owing to the conduct of Victor Amadeus of Savoy, who joins the allies (8 Nov.) importance of this event : the Duke receives from the Emperor Alessandria, Valenza, the Val Sesia and the Lomelline : failure of the invasion of the Tyrol . Villars defeats the Austrians at Hochstadt (21 Sept) : Tallard recaptures Landau (17 Nov.) . Marlborough takes Bonn (May) and occupies the electorate of Cologne · insurrection of the Protestants in the Cevennes.

Campaign of 1704 : Vendôme conquers Piedmont successes of Rakoczy Marlborough joins Eugène in Bavaria and crushes Tallard at Blenheim (13 Aug.) . Louis of Baden takes Landau and Marlborough Trèves importance of the battle of Blenheim Sir George Rooke seizes Gibraltar (4 Aug) : Portugal recognizes the Archduke Charles as King of Spain.

Campaign of 1705 . Joseph I succeeds Leopold as Emperor (May) he pursues a conciliatory policy towards Hungary · Villars puts down the revolt in the Cevennes, takes Wissembourg and invades Baden Vendôme besieges Turin and defeats Eugène at Cassano (16 Aug) : Marlborough in the Netherlands Galway invades Spain from Portugal · Peterborough takes Barcelona (13 Sept) and Catalonia declares for the Archduke Charles.

Campaign of 1706 · Galway occupies Madrid (2 July) but the Spaniards rise for Philip V and drive him out (Aug.) : Peterborough takes Valencia and relieves Barcelona · Eugène relieves Turin, defeats Orleans and drives the French out of Italy (7 Sept) Villars retakes Lauterbourg and Haguenau : Marlborough crushes Villeroi at Ramillies (23 May) and occupies the Catholic Netherlands

Campaign of 1707 : Berwick defeats Galway at Almanza (15 April) : all Spain, except Catalonia, supports Philip V · Naples acknowledges the Archduke Charles · the Emperor confiscates the duchy of Mantua he grants Montferrat and Casale to the Duke of Savoy, but adds Mantua to the Milanese Eugène and the Duke of Savoy invade France and besiege Toulon : Villars storms Stolhofen (23 May), invades Germany and invites Charles XII of Sweden to join him · Marlborough undertakes no military operations, but keeps Charles XII from intervening

Campaign of 1708 · Rakoczy, utterly defeated, escapes to Poland Stanhope takes Port Mahon in Minorca the Austrians, under Daun, occupy Naples and Sardinia : Pope Clement XI prepares to resist Vendôme conquers the Catholic Netherlands, but is defeated by Marlborough and Eugène at Oudenarde (11 July) the allies invade France . capture of Lille (22 Oct.)

Louis XIV negotiates for peace the demands of the allies Louis appeals to France and continues the war

Campaign of 1709 . the Pope by the approach of Austrian troops is forced to recognize the Archduke Charles as King of Spain (15 Jan) Marlborough and Eugène take Tournay (2 Sept.) the battle of Malplaquet (11 Sept.).

Negotiations of Gertruydenburg.

Campaign of 1710 Stahremberg and Stanhope defeat Philip V at Almenara (27 July) and Saragossa (20 Aug) the Archduke Charles occupies Madrid (21 Sept) · Vendôme makes Stanhope prisoner at Brihuega (9 Dec) and defeats Stahremberg at Villa Viciosa (10 Dec) Marlborough and Eugène take Douai (25 June), Bethune (29 Aug) and Aire (8 Nov)

General weariness of the war — change of ministry in England — the Archduke Charles succeeds his brother, Joseph I (17 April, 1711) — he is elected Emperor as Charles VI — effect of this change

Campaign of 1711 : Marlborough takes Bouchain (12 Sept). Torcy and Bolingbroke, the French and English ministers, secretly arrange preliminaries of peace — Ormond succeeds Marlborough in command of the army — Duguay-Trouin takes Rio de Janeiro (23 Sept)

The congress of plenipotentiaries to decide on terms of peace meets at Utrecht (Jan., 1712).

Campaign of 1712 — the English make a truce (17 July) — Villars defeats Eugène at Denain (24 July) and retakes Marchiennes, Douai and Bouchain

The Emperor refuses to accept the Treaties of Utrecht, signed 11 April, 1713, and continues the war

Villars takes Spires, Worms, Landau and Fribourg

The Emperor makes peace with France at Rastadt (4 March, 1714) and the Empire at Baden (7 Sept., 1714)

Contrast between the War of the Spanish Succession and the Thirty Years' War

Authorities : For a short account of the War of the Spanish Succession see *Stanhope*, History of England during the Reign of Queen Anne, 2 vols — Among general SECONDARY AUTHORITIES see *Wyon*, History of Great Britain during the Reign of Queen Anne, 2 vols., *Coxe*, Memoirs of the Kings of Spain of the House of Bourbon, vols 1, 2, *Reynald*, Louis XIV et Guillaume III, Vol 2, and *Guerre de la succession d'Espagne, *Moret*, Quinze Ans du règne de Louis XIV, 3 vols , *Noailles*, Histoire de Madame de Maintenon, 4 vols , *Von Noorden*, Europaische Geschichte im Achtzehnten Jahrhundert, vols 1-3, *Krohn*, Die letzten Lebensjahre Ludwigs XIV, *Ennen*, Der Spanische Erbfolgekrieg und der Churfurst Joseph Clemens von Coln, and *Landau*, Kaiser Karl VI als Konig von Spanien. Among diplomatic SECONDARY AUTHORITIES see *Courcy*, La coalition en 1701 contre la France, 2 vols , *Legrelle*, La Diplomatie Française et la succession d'Espagne, 4 vols , and *Gædeke*, Die Politik Œsterreichs in der spanischen Erbfolgefrage — Among military SECONDARY AUTHORITIES see *Coxe*, Memoirs of the Duke of Marlborough, 6 vols , *Alison*, Military Life of the Duke of Marlborough, *Stanhope*, History of the War of the Succession in Spain, *Parnell*, The War of the Succession

in Spain, *l'ogué*, Villars, *Arneth*, Prinz Eugen von Savoyen, 3 vols ,
and *Leben des Feldmarschalls Graf Guido Starhemberg, and *Roder-
von Diersburg*, Kriegs und Staatschriften des Markgrafen Ludwig
Wilhelm von Baden uber den spanischen Erbfolgekrieg   The chief
PRIMARY AUTHORITY is *Pelet*, Mémoires militaires relatifs à la succession d'Espagne, 11 vols (Collection des Documents inédits), but see
also *Grimblot*, Letters of William III and Louis XIV, 1697-1700,
**Hippeau*, Avènement des Bourbons au trône d'Espagne correspond-
ance inédite du Marquis d'Harcourt, 2 vols , *Baudrillart*, Philippe V
d'Espagne et la Cour de France, 2 vols , *Murray*, Letters and Despatches of Marlborough, 5 vols , *Rambuteau*, Lettres du Maréchal
de Tessé, *Lamberty*, Mémoires pour servir à l'histoire du XVIIIième
siècle, 14 vols , *Louville*, Mémoires secrets sur l'établissement de la
maison de Bourbon en Espagne, 2 vols , and the Mémoires of *Berwick, Villars, Duguay-Trouin, Forbin*, and *Torcy*, with the Journal
inédit, 1709-1711, of *Torcy*, edited by *Masson*

[Books marked with i * are *not* in the University Library]

LECTURE XXIV

THE TREATIES OF UTRECHT

The first negotiations made by Louis XIV after Ramillies
(1706) . he tries to detach the Dutch from the Grand Alliance · refusal of the Grand Pensionary, Heinsius, to treat
separately (19 Nov.)

. Second negotiations at the Hague with the allies after
Oudenarde and the loss of Lille (May–June, 1709) · hard
terms offered to Louis XIV (28 May) he refuses to accept
them (2 June)

Conference at Gertruydenburg after Malplaquet (March–
July, 1710) Louis XIV willing to accept the terms offered
at the Hague : the conference broken up (25 July)

Effect on the situation of the accession of the Tories to
power in England (1711) and of the recall of Marlborough

Death of the Dauphin (14 April, 1711)

Congress for peace opened at Utrecht (12 Jan , 1712) the chief plenipotentiaries, Torcy for France, Bolingbroke for England, Heinsius for the Protestant Netherlands progress of the negotiations treaties of peace signed between France, England, the Netherlands, Prussia, Savoy, etc , at Utrecht (11 April, 1713) ; the Emperor Charles VI continues at war with France

Treaties signed between France and the Emperor at Rastadt (4 March, 1714), confirmed by the Empire at Baden (7 Sept , 1714) and between Spain and Portugal at Madrid (6 Feb , 1715) but the Emperor makes no peace with Spain and refuses to acknowledge Philip V

The whole series may be considered together as the Treaties of Utrecht.

Chief provisions A The Spanish succession ı Philip V recognized as King of Spain and the Indies, on condition that the crowns of Spain and France should never be united causes of this decision. ıı. Charles VI received the Milanese, Naples, Sardinia and the Catholic Netherlands ııı. Victor Amadeus II received Sicily ıv England received Gibraltar and Minorca.

B Louis XIV of France maintained his borders as settled by the Treaties of Ryswick, but surrendered recent conquests in Germany . he ceded Acadia (Nova Scotia) to England, recognized the Protestant Succession, and promised to expel the Stuart Pretender and to dismantle Dunkirk

C England received Gibraltar and Minorca from Spain and Acadia from France her sovereignty in Newfoundland (subject to certain fishing rights) and Hudson's Bay recognized . the Protestant succession in the line of Hanover acknowledged and by an Assiento she obtained certain rights of commerce with Spanish South America

D. The Emperor Charles VI received the Catholic Netherlands, subject to an arrangement with the Dutch, Naples, Sardinia and the Milanese, together with Mantua, whose last Gonzaga duke had died in 1708

E The creation of the Electorate of Hanover (1692) recognized by the powers

F   The Elector of Bavaria and the Elector Archbishop of
Cologne, Prince Joseph Clement of Bavaria, restored to their
dominions.

G   The title of the King of Prussia recognized, and he received Upper Gelderland as heir of the Prince of Orange

H   The Dutch have the closing of the Scheldt to commerce and their right to garrison the eight "barrier fortresses" in the Catholic Netherlands—Charleroi, Furnes,
Ghent, Menin, Mons, Namur, Tournay and Ypres—confirmed

I   Victor Amadeus II had the cessions of Alessandria,
Valenza, the Val Sesia and the Lomelline, granted in 1703,
and of Casale and Montferrat, granted in 1707 from the
duchy of Mantua, confirmed, and received Sicily, with the
title of King of Sicily

J   The Catalans abandoned

Importance of the Treaties of Utrecht   comparison with
the Treaties of Westphalia   its most notable points . France
left upon the Rhine and in close alliance with Spain,
England shows further development in the direction of commerce and colonies, the dominions of the House of Hapsburg
become nominally larger but really more unwieldy and less
German, Prussia takes a step in advance among the nations
in becoming a kingdom, and the House of Savoy also becomes
a kingdom with the most powerful interests in Italy

The doctrine of the Balance of Power in the Treaties of
Utrecht . neglect of the Principle of Nationality

Authorities   Most of the general and diplomatic SECONDARY AU-
THORITIES cited under Lecture XXIII devote much space to the
Treaties of Utrecht   Good special volumes have been written by
Giraud, Le traité d'Utrecht and *Weber*, Der Friede von Utrecht,
and a PRIMARY AUTHORITY of importance is *Torcy* Mémoires

[Books marked with a * are *not* in the University Library]

LECTURE XXV

GERMANY IN 1715

Comparison between the condition of Germany after the Treaties of Utrecht and the Treaties of Westphalia

The Holy Roman Empire . constant election of the chief of the House of Austria to be Emperor owing to the votes he commanded as the leading Catholic power decreasing influence of the Emperors in German affairs the perpetual capitulation changes in the constitution of the Empire *i* Recognition of Prussia as a kingdom . the Emperor Leopold agrees to give the Elector Frederick of Brandenburg the title of King of Prussia, as Prussia is a state independent of the Empire, in return for assistance in the War of the Spanish Succession the other powers of Europe recognize the title by the Treaties of Utrecht as a member of the Empire he remains Elector of Brandenburg *ii* College of Electors the Emperor Leopold makes the Duke of Hanover an Elector (1692), at the same time restoring the full electoral powers to the kingdom of Bohemia opposition of the other Electors and of the Princes of the Empire league formed against the new electorate (1700) the Emperor promises to make no further electorates without the consent of the Empire (1706) electorate of Hanover accepted by the Diet (1710) *iii* College of Princes the Emperor's right to create new princes limited (1654) settlement of the " collegiate " votes creation of new princes made still more difficult and dependent on the consent of the Electoral College, the Princely College, and his Bench (1711) growth of the custom of primogeniture and its effect on the votes which accumulate . exception of Saxony · *iv* College of Free Cities its decay owing to the falling off in the prosperity of the cities . only the three Hansa cities remained powerful : conquest of Munster by Bishop Galen (1661), of Erfurt by the Elector of Mayence (1664), of Magdeburg by the Elector of Brandenburg (1666), of Brunswick by the Duke of Brunswick (1671) and seizure of Strasburg by Louis XIV (1681) general tendency of the Free Cities to decline in importance · *v.* The Imperial Diet its policy after it becomes perpetual and occupied only by envoys disputes about precedence its cumbrous procedure inefficiency of its military action *vi* The Imperial Chamber its seat moved from Spires, after the burning of that city by the French in the devastation of the Palatinate in 1689, to Wetzlar in 1691 : quarrels among the assessors the Chamber dissolves (1700) its reorganization · *vii* The Aulic Council its claim to deal with cases concerning States · *viii* The religious question : the application of the doctrine "*cujus regio, ejus religio*" failure of the modifications arranged by the Treaties of Westphalia . the persecution of the Protestants in the Palatinate *ix* The question of Coinage . agreement made between Saxony, Brandenburg and Brunswick at Zinna (1667) and at Leipzig (1690) *x* The Gregorian Calendar adopted by the Protestant States by a Decree of the Diet (1700)

The House of Austria additional dominions gained by the Treaties of Utrecht, no additional strength the more valuable gains of the Treaty of Carlowitz in Hungary and Transylvania tend to turn its policy still more towards the East : internal administration the rebellion of Francis Rakoczy (1703) the short reign of Joseph I (1705-1711) his concessions to the Hungarians and consequent overthrow of Rakoczy his concessions to the Protestants of Silesia at the request of Charles XII of Sweden . his penal code and the promises of his reign · the Emperor Charles VI and his views on internal government

The House of Prussia the aims of Frederick III, Elector of Brandenburg (1688-1713) to become a king and to increase his dominions his character his policy *i.* His foreign policy : he pursues the ideas of the Great Elector he joins the League of Augsburg (1688) and sends 15,000 men to serve under William III against France (1691-99) : he sends 6000 men to assist the Emperor against the Turks (1691-99) .

he sends 26,000 men to serve through the War of the Spanish Succession (1702–13) his conduct in the Northern War
(see Lecture XXII) his propositions to Peter the Great for
a partition of Poland . *ii* His arrangements for the title of
king he promises aid in the War of Spanish Succession, to
excuse the Emperor's debts to him, to vote for an Austrian
prince for Emperor, and only to use his title as Elector in
the 'Imperial Diet he crowns himself at Konigsberg as
Frederick I, King of Prussia (18 Jan , 1701) importance of
this step for the future of his House · the title recognized by
the Treaties of Utrecht *iii* His territorial policy he restores Schwebus to Austria (see Lecture XVIII) without
abandoning his claims on Silesia (1694) he buys Nord-
hausen of the Elector of Saxony (1697) he takes possession
of Elbing in Polish Prussia (1703) he seizes Mœurs and
Lingen as heir of William III (1702) and takes possession
of Gelders, which is granted to Prussia by the Treaties of
Utrecht instead of Orange · he is elected Prince of Neufchâtel
(1707) and purchases the county of Tecklenburg *iv*. His
internal policy he follows the lines of the Great Elector and
prepares the way for Frederick William I

Accession of Frederick William I (25 Feb , 1713) . by
Treaties of Utrecht his royal title is recognized and his possession of Neufchâtel and Gelders he inherits the county
of Limburg . he occupies Stettin and Wismar in sequestration
during the war against Sweden.

Other states of Germany . *i* Electoral Saxony division
made on the death of John George I (1656) its prosperity
sacrificed to the Polish policy of Augustus I (see Lecture
XXII) when elected King of Poland (1697) he became a
Catholic, but was yet allowed to remain the Director of the
Protestant party in the Diet, his change of faith being personal and not political by a convention (1700) religious
matters were left to the Duke of Saxe-Weissenfels *ii*.
Ducal Saxony : the rule of Duke Ernest the Pious of Saxe-
Gotha : great division made (1680) but no more votes al-
lowed to the House *iii*. Bavaria . Ferdinand Maria, Elect-

or (1651–79), he refuses to be a candidate for the Empire (1657) quarrels with the Elector Palatine about the Vicariate of the Empire Maximilian Emmanuel, Elector (1679–1726) candidature of his son, the Electoral Prince, for the throne of Spain he joins Louis XIV in the War of the Spanish Succession his campaigns in the Tyrol he is put to the ban of the Empire, and from the battle of Blenheim in 1704 to 1714 Bavaria is administered by the Emperors he acts as Governor-General of the Spanish Netherlands under Charles II from 1692 to 1701, and again under Philip V from 1702 until he is driven out after the battle of Ramillies (1706) restored to his dominions by the treaty of Rastadt : condition of Bavaria under Austrian rule. iv The Palatinate · the last Protestant Electors of the House of Simmern, Charles Louis I (1648–80) and Charles Louis II (1680–85) Charles Louis I joins the league against Louis XIV (1672) devastation of the Palatinate by Turenne (1675) the question of the succession (1685) . the claims of Louis XIV . Philip William of Neuburg succeeds : fresh devastation of the Palatinate by Duras (1689) : destruction of Heidelberg, Mannheim, Spires, etc accession of John William (1691) his ardent Catholicism · persecution of the Protestants : extensive emigration : Philip William pays 300,000 scudi (a scudo at this time almost equalled a dollar) to Louis XIV to compensate for his claims his internal government he moves his capital from Heidelberg to Mannheim (1720) v Hanover character and career of Ernest Augustus, 4th son of the Duke of Brunswick-Luneburg, and first Elector of Hanover his reputation as a statesman and a soldier he makes peace between England and the Dutch (1667) he becomes William III's chief German ally, and his intermediary with Brandenburg and the Emperor . he takes the title of Duke of Hanover (1679) he helps to form the League of Augsburg (1688), and is made Elector of Hanover (1692) his share in the Treaty of Ryswick · he establishes primogeniture in his family his death (1697) . the Elector George I · his increased importance in German affairs after being recognized

as heir to the crown of England (1701) he unites the
Duchy of Zell (1705) his policy his territorial importance
between Brandenburg and the United Provinces : his attitude
to France and the Emperor · admitted to the Diet as an
Elector (1710) . acknowledged as heir to England by the
Treaties of Utrecht (1713) . death of the Electress Sophia
(8 June, 1714) . he succeeds Queen Anne in England (1
Aug , 1714) *vi* The ecclesiastical electors and princes of
the Empire . methods of their government restrained by
the capitulations made with them at their election by the
chapters . the power of the chapters large sums paid to the
popes

The petty princes of Germany : their imitation of Louis
XIV in their absolutism, in refusing to summon or consult
their Estates or Diets, in their extravagance, and in their
court ceremonials.

Authorities : For the condition of Germany in 1715 in addition to
works like those of *Léger*, cited under Lecture IX dealing with general history, see *Biedermann* Deutschland im achtzehnten Jahrhundert
Vol 1, Deutschlands politische, materielle und sociale Zustande , for
the Empire see *Putter*, Historical Development of the Constitution of
the Germanic Empire, translated by *Dornford*, vol. 11 for Austria
*Krones, Handbuch der Geschichte Œsterreichs, 5 vols , **Coxe*,
History of the House of Austria, 4 vols , and **Bidermann* Geschichte
der Œsterreichischen Gesammt-Staats-Idee , for Prussia, in addition
to the general works cited under Lecture XVIII, *Ledebur*, Konig
Friedrich I von Preussen, *Waddington*, L'Acquisition de la Couronne
royale de Prusse par les Hohenzollern, *Varnhagen von Ense*, Leben der
Konigin Sophie Charlotte, 3 vols , **Bourgeois*, Neufchâtel et la poli-
tique prussienne de 1709 à 1713, and **Lavisse*, Études sur l'histoire de
Prusse , for Electoral Saxony *Bottiger*, Geschichte des Kurstaates und
Konigreichs Sachsen, 3 vols ; for Ducal Saxony *Gelbke*, Herzog Ernst
der Erste genannt der Fromme aud **Beck*, Ernst der Fromme , for
Bavaria *Schreiber*, Geschichte Bayerns, 2 vols. , and for Hanover
Kocher, Memoiren der Kurfurstin Sophie von Hannover, *Leibnitz*,
Correspondance avec l'electrice Sophie, vols 7–9 of his Werke, and
Spittler, Geschichte des Furstenthums Hannover in vols. 6 and 7 of
his Sammtliche Werke.

[Books marked with a * are *not* in the University Library]

LECTURE XXVI

Decreasing naval importance of the Mediterranean countries. the commerce of the Levant passes to the Dutch and
the English after the loss of Candia, Venice becomes an
Adriatic instead of a Mediterranean power injury inflicted
by the Barbary corsairs efforts of Louis XIV to become
master of the Mediterranean: the Dutch and English fleets
in that sea significance of the capture of Gibraltar by the
English (1704) the English become the preponderating
naval power in the Mediterranean by the cession of Gibraltar
and Minorca (1713).

The Turkish power after the Treaty of Carlowitz (1699)
(see Lecture XX) · the reign of Mustapha II (1695–1703)
his military disasters compensated by his naval successes over
the Venetians while surrendering. the Adriatic to Venice
and Hungary, except the Banat, to the Emperor, the Turks
retained the islands of the Archipelago Hussain Kiuprili,
Grand Vizier (1697–1702) he endeavors to reorganize the
Turkish army and navy he reduces Bussora, pacifies North
Africa, and regulates Turkish authority in Arabia · the
Turks begin to be influenced by European ideas and to trans-
late European books : revolt of the Janissaries and overthrow
of Mustapha II (1703). early years of the reign of Ahmad
III (1703–30) · he announces his accession to the Christian
powers Charles XII of Sweden induces the Sultan to attack
Russia (see Lecture XXI) the Treaty of the Pruth (11
July, 1711) the government of the Danubian Provinces,
Wallachia and Moldavia

Italy during the half century before the Treaties of Utrecht
(See Lecture XIV)

I. The Popes abandon the territorial aggrandisement of the
States of the Church. their attitude towards the Catholic
powers, and particularly towards Austria, France and Spain

loss of their political influence   Clement IX—Rospighosi—
1667-70   his friendly relations with France   Clement X—
Altieri—1670-76   he makes Quebec a bishopric (1676)
Innocent XI—Odescalchi—1676-89   his endeavors to reform
abuses   his abandonment of nepotism   his quarrels with
Louis XIV (see Lectures XVI, XIX)   Alexander VIII—
Ottoboni—1689-91   he makes peace with Louis XIV   Innocent XII—Pignatelli—1691-1700 .   his economy and up-
rightness   his attitude towards France   Clement XI—Albani
—1700-21   his attitude on the Spanish Succession   he is
forced to recognize the Archduke Charles .   he issues the bull
"Unigenitus" (1713) :   action of the Papacy during this
period towards the Jansenists, the Jesuits and the Quietists
(See Lecture XXVII)

II   Kingdom of Naples   its welcome to the Archduke
Charles (1707) ·   he promises to observe its local rights
separated from Sicily by the Treaties of Utrecht (1713) and
given to the House of Austria.

III. Kingdom of Sicily   given to Victor Amadeus II,
Duke of Savoy, by the Treaties of Utrecht   he is crowned
at Palermo (24 Dec., 1713) .   the character of Victor Amadeus II   growth of the House of Savoy by his policy ·   he ac-
quires Alessandria, etc , (1703),   Montferrat and Casale
(1707) and the restoration of Savoy and Nice (1713) ·   he
marries his two daughters to two grandsons of Louis XIV,
to the Duke of Burgundy, father of Louis XV. and to Philip
V of Spain ·   his internal policy :   his encouragement of public works :   his code of laws ·   his quarrel with Pope Clement
XI   he taxes ecclesiastical property

IV   Northern Duchies :   the reign of Cosmo III, the last
Grand Duke of Tuscany of the line of Medici (1670-1723)
he pays large sums to remain neutral during the War of the
Spanish Succession ·   bad management of his duchy and
misery of his people .   Francesco, Duke of Parma, remains
neutral during the War of the Spanish Succession.   but
Rainaldo, Duke of Modena, takes part in it and obtains the
Duchy of Mirandola from the Emperor   the Duchy of Man-

tua is divided by adding Mantua to Milan and giving Mont-
ferrat to Savoy in 1707 by the Emperor, because Charles IV
Gonzaga supported Louis XIV in the War of the Spanish
Succession, but a small district is given to the Duke of Guas-
talla Milan and Mantua granted to the Emperor by the
Treaties of Utrecht (1713).

V. Venice her success under Morosini in the war against
the Turks · by the Treaty of Carlowitz the Republic obtains
the Morea, the Ionian Islands and Dalmatia, and becomes
the preponderant power on the coasts of the Adriatic close
alliance formed between the Emperor and the Venetians

Spain the reign of Charles II (1665–1700) the regency
of the queen-mother, Donna Marianna (1665–75). the government of Père Nithard (1665–69) : he is forced to retire
by Don John · the king declared of age (1675) the government of Don John (1675–79) · Spain loses French Flanders and Franche Comté by the Treaty of Nymwegen
(1678). the influence of the first wife of Charles II, Marie
Louise of Orleans (1679–89) : her quarrels with her mother-
in-law influence of his second wife, Marianna of Neuburg,
exercised in favor of Austria Spain is invaded by the
French (1694–97), but loses nothing by the Treaty of Rys-
wyck (1697) intrigues for the Spanish Succession, and the
partition treaties part played by Charles II the influence
of Porto Carrero outweighs that of the queen, and the king
leaves his dominions to Philip, Duke of Anjou · steady decline of Spanish power and prosperity

The reign of Philip V his reception in Spain he falls
under the influence of his wife Marie Gabrielle of Savoy,
who is controlled by the Princess Orsini or Des Ursins the
War of the Spanish Succession in Spain Philip V twice
driven from Madrid the Spaniards rally around him : he
devotes himself to his new country by the Treaties of
Utrecht Spain loses her continental possessions as well as
Gibraltar and Minorca . death of the queen (14 Feb., 1714) .
influence and character of Madame des Ursins.

Portugal the reign of Pedro II (1685–1706) the signa-

ture of the Methuen Treaty (27 Dec., 1703) with England
its results part taken by Portugal in the War of the Spanish Succession accession of John V (1706).

Authorities For the Turks see the books cited for Lecture XIII ,
for Italy, the books cited for Lecture XIV with *Michaud*, Louis XIV
et Innocent XI, 4 vols , for Spain, *Dunham*, *Weiss*, *Dunlop* and
Mignet, cited under Lecture XV, *Reynald*, *Landau*, *Legrelle*, *Hippeau*, *Baudrillart*, *Stanhope*, *Parnell*, *Rambuteau*, *Louville* and *Berwick*, with *Coxe*, Memoirs of the Kings of Spain of the House of Bourbon, vols 1, 2, *Alexander Stanhope*, Spain under Charles II, 1690-99,
Combes, La Princesse des Ursins, the Correspondance avec Madame
de Maintenon, and the Lettres inédites of the *Princesse des Ursins*, and
the Mémoires of *Saint-Simon*

[Books marked with a * are *not* in the University Library.]

_____

LECTURE XXVII.

THE PAPACY IN THE 17TH CENTURY. THE JESUITS AND THE JANSENISTS.

The spiritual power of the Papacy in the 17th century, as
opposed to its political and territorial power.

Gradual decline in the spiritual power to be observed in
the first half of the 17th century, the Age of the Thirty
Years' War, when political considerations were becoming
paramount over religious considerations more rapid decline
during the latter half of the century, when Catholic monarchs, like Louis XIV openly quarrelled with the Pope, and
tried to check his spiritual authority

The effect of the Counter-Reformation on the position of
the Papacy its chief agents the Jesuits . with the decline of
the Jesuits from their original energy the Counter-Reformation dies away

The main lines of the work of the Jesuits *i* Education :
success of their method of teaching : their colleges and universities they control higher education in Catholic countries .

ii The Confessional they become the confessors of kings
and statesmen · Père La Chaise and Père Le Tellier : *iii.*
Missions. A Among the Protestants · their work in England, Sweden and Poland. B Among the heathen · in
Asia, in India and China · in America, in Canada and Paraguay

The decline in Jesuit energy after the death of General
Acquaviva (1615) · the generalship of Muzio Vitelleschi
(1615–45) "professed" members begin to accept offices of
power education ceases to be generally free devotion to
the prosperity of the Society takes the place of devotion to
the Papacy limitation of the general's power (1661) the
Society becomes interested in commerce its commercial
centre at Lisbon the Society supports absolutism against the
Papacy . it supports Louis XIV against Innocent XI it
opposes the Jansenist influence · Père La Chaise and Archbishop Harlay of Paris Innocent XI and Alexander VIII
endeavor to check the power of the Society and even forbid
its admitting novices Clement XI condemns its practices in
foreign missions in Asia (1715)

The Jesuit theology the adoption of "free will" doctrines · the Dominicans quarrel with them for differing from
St Thomas Aquinas growth of causistry its application to
politics and the result to private life the *Lettres Provinciales*
of Pascal and its effect it kills scholastic morality : the theological distinction between the Jesuits and the Jansenists
Père Le Tellier and Archbishop Noailles of Paris after the
issue of the bull *Unigenitus* the Jesuits rally to the Papacy
and become Ultramontane

The Jansenists their doctrines a reaction against the theology of the Jesuits . their nickname of Catholic Puritans .
the *Augustinus* of Cornelius Jansen, Bishop of Ypres, published after his death in 1640 : its theological views the
doctrines of grace, sin and forgiveness . its rapid success,
even among priests and bishops, but still more among the
educated laity, of France and the Catholic Netherlands Duvergier, Abbé de Saint-Cyran his application of Jansenist
views to life his influence on Angélique Arnauld Port Roy-

al his imprisonment by Richelieu (1638–42) the Jansenists implicated in the Fronde their quarrel with the Jesuits :
Port Royal becomes the home of moral and intellectual France :
the influence exerted by Arnauld, Nicole, Lemaître de Sacy,
Pascal and Racine the publication of the Port Royal educa-
tional works · influence possessed by the Jansenists in France.

First struggle with the Papacy (1642–69). Urban VIII
condemns generally the *Augustinus* (1642) : the " five propositions " declared heretical by the bull *In Occasione*, issued
by Innocent X (31 May, 1653). Arnauld denies that the
" five propositions " are contained in the book by Jansen :
Alexander VII declared that they were : the Jansenist writers deny the infallibility of the Pope in dealing with matters
of fact Louis XIV imprisons De Sacy and persecutes the
Jansenists, including the nuns of Port Royal . Clement IX
makes the " Peace of Clement IX " (1668) when the Jansenists agreed to condemn the " five propositions " without
acknowledging whether they were contained in Jansen's
book or not

In spite of the King's dislike of them the Jansenists become more powerful in France, especially in bourgeois and
legal circles.

Second struggle with the Papacy (1702–15) the *Réflexions
morales* of Quesnel and the *Cas de conscience* Archbishop
Noailles exhibits moderate Jansenist opinions he distin-
guishes between human and divine faith in the Pope's infallibility on questions of fact . opposition of Père Le Tellier,
the King's confessor, and the Jesuits : they appeal to Rome :
Clement XI tries to settle the question by the bull *Vineam
Domini* (15 July, 1705) · the nuns of Port Royal refuse to
accept the bull : the community suppressed (11 July, 1709)
and Port Royal ordered to be destroyed (22 Jan , 1710) .
persecution of the Jansenists · use of *lettres de cachet* 101
propositions from Quesnel's book condemned by the bull
Unigenitus (8 Sept , 1713) · the Parlement of Paris, led by
D'Aguesseau declines to register the bull as law without
modifications . Noailles and fifteen bishops refuse to accept

it : a council summoned to depose them . when they were saved by the death of Louis XIV.

The Quietists : Molinos and his doctrines condemned by Pope Innocent XII (1687) · Madame Guyon her mysticism . her relations with Fénelon : controversy between Bossuet and Fénelon · Innocent XII condemns Fénelon's *Explications des Maximes des Saints* (1699) . Louis XIV and his attitude towards the Quietists

Marie Alacoque (1647–90) and the worship of the Sacred Heart : the Abbé de Rancé and the monastery of La Trappe.

Authorities : For an account in English of the Jansenist movement see *Beard*, Port Royal, 2 vols Among SECONDARY AUTHORITIES consult *Crétineau-Joly*, Histoire religieuse, politique et littéraire de la compagnie de Jésus, 6 vols , *Sainte-Beuve*, Port Royal, 7 vols., *Reuchlin*, Geschichte von Port Royal, 2 vols , *Soyres* The Provincial Letters of Pascal, *Victor Cousin*, Jacqueline Pascal, *Lafitau*, Histoire de la Constitution Unigenitus, *Bigelow*, Molinos the Quietist,*Guerrier*, Madame Guyon, sa vie, sa doctrine et son influence, *Matter*, Le Mysticisme en France au temps de Fénelon, *Bausset*, Histoire de Bossuet, 4 vols , and Histoire de Fénelon, 4 vols., *Réaume*, Histoire de Bossuet, 3 vols , *Phélipeaux* Relation de l'origine, du progrès et de la condamnation du Quiétisme, with the works of *Arnauld, Pascal, Bossuet* and *Fénelon*

[Books marked with an * are *not* in the University Library]

LECTURE XXVIII

THE LAST YEARS OF THE REIGN OF LOUIS XIV.
FRANCE IN 1715

The government of France during the last thirty years of the reign of Louis XIV influenced by Madame de Maintenon : but carried on by the King in spite of his decreasing powers and increasing belief in himself he devotes himself more and more to foreign politics and the question of Spanish Succession, leaving internal administration to his ministers who inherit the offices of Colbert and Louvois without their ability

The change in the King's character between the Treaty of

Nymwegen and the outbreak of war with the League of Augsburg Louis XIV becomes moral and religious the gaiety of the Court disappears it becomes more ceremonious falling off in the tone of Parisian society the poisoning affairs Madame de Brinvilliers the king is governed by Madame de Maintenon and his confessors the great result of this change of character, the Revocation of the Edict of Nantes (1685)

Character and position of Françoise d'Aubigné, Madame de Maintenon her previous career. her rivalry with Madame de Montespan. she brings the king and queen together. after the death of the queen (1683) she is secretly married to Louis XIV: nature of her influence at court her ardent zeal for the Catholic religion, and prudery her difficult position. her foundation of Saint Cyr

Character and influence of Père La Chaise, confessor of Louis XIV (1675–1709) and of his successor, Père Le Tellier (1709–15) they control the ecclesiastical policy of the king in favour of the Jesuits they demand the persecution of the Huguenots and the Jansenists .

The ministers of the last years of Louis XIV their inability to control or oppose the King they act as head clerks and fear responsibility the typical minister Michel de Chamillart the last ministers Boucherat (1685–99), Louis Phélypeaux, Comte de Pontchartrain (1699–1714) and Daniel Voysin (1714–15), Chancellors, Torcy (1696–1715), foreign affairs; Le Peletier (1684–89), Louis, Comte de Pontchartrain (1689–99), Chamillart (1699–1708) and Desmarets (1708–15), finances, Barbézieux (1691–1701), Chamillart (1701–1709) and Daniel Voysin (1709–14), war, Louis, Comte de Pontchartrain (1690–93), and Jerôme, Comte de Pontchartrain (1693–1715), marine .

The French nation approves the successful war of 1688–97 against the League of Augsburg, but welcomes the Treaties of Ryswick: general delight at the acceptance of the Spanish Succession for the Duke of Anjou · "the Pyrenees have ceased to exist" confidence felt by the people in the success of Louis XIV.

Surprise felt at the defeats of Blenheim and Ramillies general discontent at the mismanagement of Chamillart his financial methods the creation and sale of sinecure offices Chamillart made the scapegoat and succeeded by Desmarets, the nephew of Colbert (1708) improvement of credit Desmarets raises loans : the armies thus raised defeated · despair of the French people at the defeat of Oudenarde.

The terrible winter of 1708–1709 . general misery of the people . the loss of Lille leaves the way open to Paris : the appeal of Louis XIV to his people on the advice of Torcy · France rallies round the king voluntary gifts to the royal treasury melting down of the royal plate ladies contribute their jewelry . result of the wave of enthusiasm to make Louis XIV persist in his resistance effect of the defeat of Malplaquet the rising of Spain and the accession of the Tory ministry in England enable Louis XIV to get much better terms at Utrecht and Rastadt than had ever been expected by him · his position at the close of the war France retains the towns she had gained at Ryswick (1697) in Europe, and only loses Açadia (Nova Scotia) in North America.

Religious persecution increased in France during the War of the Spanish Succession the suppression of the Camisards in the Cevennes (1703–1705) . Le Tellier increases the King's ardour against the Jansenists . destruction of Port Royal (1710) Louis XIV's indignation at the opposition made by the Parlement of Paris, led by D'Aguesseau, to registering the bull *Unigenitus* his intention of deposing the bishops, who favoured Jansenism influence of Le Tellier

Last year of Louis XIV's foreign policy · his intrigues with the English Tories to secure the accession of the Catholic "Old Pretender" in England he prepares a fleet for the support of the Pretender

Bad effect of the financial maladministration decline of agricultural, industrial and commercial prosperity Vauban's *Dîme Royale*

Gloom of the Court during the last years of the life of Louis XIV . contrast with its gay opening years death of the Dauphin, only son of Louis XIV (14 April, 1711) · his

education by Bossuet his three sons (1) Louis, Duke of
Burgundy, educated by Fénelon, died 18 Feb , 1712, leaving
an only child, who succeeded as Louis XV , (2) Philip, Duke
of Anjou became King of Spain as Philip V in 1700 , (3)
Charles, Duke of Berry, died 4 May, 1714 . the illegitimate
children of Louis XIV his fondness for them their position.

Death of Louis XIV (1 Sept , 1715) effect of his reign
on France and Europe his personal character   ,

Louis XIV and Asia · the French East India Company
foundation of Pondicherry (1674) embassy to Siam (1685)

Louis XIV and America . the development of Canada the
work of the Jesuits the government of Frontenac . occupation of Louisiana

Authorities Of the SECONDARY AUTHORITIES cited under Lecture
XVI *Voltaire, Bausset, *Martin*, and *Michel*, of those cited under
Lecture XIX *Noailles and *Geffroy*, of those cited under Lecture
XXIII *Moret* and *Krohn* are still useful, and may be supplemented
for the light thrown on the character of Madame de Maintenon by
Lavallée, Histoire de la maison royale de Saint Cyr, and by *Proyart*,
Vie du Dauphin, père de Louis XV, 2 vols, by *Lanier*, Étude his-
torique sur les relations de la France et du royaume de Siam de 1662 à
1703, and by *Parkman*, Count Frontenac and New France under Louis
XIV, The Jesuits in America in the 17th century, and Lasalle and the
Discovery of the Great West. Among PRIMARY AUTHORITIES on administration and finance *Depping*, *Boislisle* and *Foucault*, cited under
Lecture XVI, should be supplemented by *Esnault*, Michel Chamillart;
correspondance et papiers inédits, by *Desmarets*, Mémoire sur l'administration des finances depuis le 20 février 1708 jusqu'au 1 septembre 1715 and by *Vauban*, Le Dîme royale , while for the court of Louis
XIV and his personality during the latter years of his reign to the
Correspondance of *Madame de Maintenon*, the Letters of the *Duchesse
d'Orléans*, and the Mémoires of *Madame de Caylus, Choisy* and *Torcy*,
cited under Lecture XIX, must be added the Letters of the *Duchesse
de Bourgogne*, the Journal of *Dangeau*, vols 7-15, and above all the
Mémoires of the *Duc de Saint-Simon*, edited by Chéruel, 21 vols · the
famous work of Saint-Simon, however, must be read with caution and
on this subject reference may be made to *Chéruel* Saint-Simon con-
sidéré comme historien de Louis XIV, and to *Baschet*, Le Duc de
Saint-Simon, son cabinet et ses manuscrits

[Books marked with a * are *not* in the University Library.]

·

LECTURE XXIX

LITERATURE AND PHILOSOPHY IN THE 17TH CENTURY

Importance of the 17th century literature the literary languages of Europe created development from the study of the classics, which characterized the Renaissance, into the use of the vernaculars effect of this literary movement on the growth of nationalities the study of the classics as models continued literature ceases to concern itself mainly with religion and deals with more sides of human interest

Spain produces the first man of letters of genius of the 17th century : the life, character and works of Cervantes (1547–1616) *Don Quixote* and its effects · the Spanish drama Lope de Vega (1562–1635) and Calderon (1600–87)

The Elizabethan period of English literature . Shakespeare (1564–1614) and his contemporaries and successors : the English drama the growth of English prose Bacon (1561–1626)

Development of French literature under Richelieu and Mazarin the Académie Française founded 1635 · Malherbe (1555–1628), La Rochefoucauld (1613–80) the application of literature to politics : the Mazarinades journalism : the rise of the French drama : Pierre Corneille (1606–84).

The Age of Louis XIV the classic or "golden" age of French literature what literature owed to Louis XIV, patronage but not inspiration : the greatest writers of the time were born and had begun to write before Louis XIV impressed his personality on France · tragedy · Racine (1639–99) : comedy Molière (1622–73) poetry influence of classicism correctness takes the place of inspiration Boileau (1636–1711), the critic, and his influence . development of French prose Pascal (1623–62) the influence of Port Royal : La Fontaine (1621–95) and his *Fables* La Bruyère (1644–96) and his *Characters* : fiction Mdlle de Scudéry (1607–1701) : Fénelon (1651–1715) *Telemaque* theology and history .

Bossuet (1627–1704) . the great French preachers, Bossuet, Bourdaloue (1632–1704) and Fléchier (1632–1710) · memoir-writers Madame de Motteville (1621–89), Cardinal de Retz (1614–79) and Saint-Simon (1675–1755) . letter-writers · Madame de Sevigné (1626–96)

Growth of taste for literature in France · the Hôtel de Rambouillet and the "précieuses" · their successors

Tendency of later writers of the Age of Louis XIV to fulsome adulation of the king

English literature of the Puritan period · Milton (1608–74)

Influence of the Age of Louis XIV on the literature of other countries in Germany, French becomes the language of the courts and educated people · consequent sterility of German literature : in Italy much poetry on classical lines is produced · Tassoni (1565–1655), Guidi (1650–1712), and Filicaja (1642–1707) in Spain imitation of French style also produces sterility in England the literature of the reign of Charles II shows French influence : Dryden (1631–1701) . Congreve (1670–1729).

Relation of literature to philosophy in the 17th century

Revolution effected in philosophical method by Bacon (1561–1626) . Descartes destroys the scholastic methods (1596–1650) the speculations of Spinoza (1632–77) the theories of Leibnitz (1646–1716) : the Monads

In political philosophy France produced no great thinkers : but Hobbes (1588–1680) and Locke (1632–1704) start the lines of thought which were to lead to great results in the 18th century.

Finally Grotius (1583–1646) and Puffendorf (1632–94) create and develop international law

Variety of the literary and philosophical movements of the 17th century their diverse characteristics

LECTURE XXX.

ART AND SCIENCE IN THE 17TH CENTURY

The revolution in thought and method effected by Bacon and Descartes creates a new era in science experiments take the place of theories and the 17th century is marked by many important scientific discoveries on the other hand art tends to lose its virility and, despite two painters of genius, the art of the 17th century is governed by classical conventions: and is thus on an inferior level to its condition during the Renaissance.

The Spanish school of painting. Velasquez (1599–1660): Murillo (1617–82). the greatness of Velasquez

The Flemish school of painting. Rubens (1577–1640): Van Dyck (1599–1641). Teniers the elder (1582–1649): Teniers the younger (1610–85)

The Dutch school of painting. the isolated greatness of Rembrandt van Ryn (1608–69). characteristics of the Dutch school. Gerard Douw (1613–80) · Jan Steen (1626–79) · Paul Potter (1625–54) Ruysdael (1630–81). Cuyp (1606–62) Wouverman (1620–68): Van der Velde (1633–1707).

The Italian school of painting, its decline from the great days of Italian art into sentimentalism · Guido Reni (1574–1642) · Sassoferrato (1605–85): Salvator Rosa (1615–73).

The French school of painting its conventionality Poussin (1593–1672). Le Brun (1619–90). Claude Lorraine (1600–82).

The English school of painting · devoted to portraits influence of Van Dyck: Lely (1618–80) Kneller (1648–1723).

Architecture dominated by classic ideals and styles · their inappropriateness: the forms patronized by Louis XIV are adopted in other European countries.

The other arts absence of great sculptors. improvement in engraving · classical style of decoration

Commencement of classical gardening · the gardens of
Vaux and Versailles Le Nôtre

Music in the 17th century the development of the opera
in Italy its popularity · melody cultivated as well as harmony the Roman school Carissimi (1582–1672) his
church music . he introduces the orchestra into the churches
his cantatas and songs · Scarlatti (1659–1725) · founder of
the Neapolitan school · his songs and operas : Lully (1633–
87) develops the music written for masques : he becomes
the chief musician to Louis XIV his operas, ballets and
musical comedies his services to theatrical music in France :
association with Molière and Quinault : music in England
Purcell (1658–95) . his genius.

Bacon and Descartes, by overthrowing old methods of
thinking and arguing, prepare the way for experimental science scientific experiments become fashionable science not
yet divided and differentiated attempts at universality of
scientific knowledge Leibnitz (1646–1716)

The great mathematicians Napier, the inventor of loga-
rithms (1550–1617) Descartes (1596–1650) and the application of numerical exponents to geometry . Pascal (1623–62)
and conic sections Newton (1642–1727) and the infinitesi-
mal calculus and mathematical optics . the *Principia* : Ber-
nouilli (1654–1705) and the application of the calculus

The great biologists : Harvey and the demonstration of
the circulation of the blood (1578–1657) . Sydenham (1624–
89) · Boerhaave (1668–1738).

The great astronomers : Galileo (1546–1642) and the
demonstration that the earth moves round the sun · Kepler
(1571–1631) and the laws of planetary motion . Cassini
(1625–1712) and the measurement of the earth · Huyghens
(1629–95) and the discovery of the satellites of Saturn
Newton (1642–1727) and the lunar theory · Gregory (1633–
75) and the invention of the reflecting telescope Halley
(1656–1742) and eclipses

The great physicists . Galileo (1546–1642) the inventor of
the thermometer and the pendulum Torricelli (1608–47)

the inventor of the barometer · Descartes and the law of re-
fraction   his theory of " whorls "   Boyle (1626–91) and the
air pump   Huyghens and the pendulum clock   Newton
(1642–1727) and the theory of gravitation

These names and discoveries only indicate the progress
and first gains of experimental science   the 17th century was
in this respect also the commencement of modern history

Effect on the material conditions of life of the discoveries
of men of science   contrast between the intellectual and
material conditions of life at the beginning and the end of
the 17th century.

APPENDICES.

Appendix I.

	Emperors, Holy Roman Empire	Kings of France	Kings of Great Britain	Kings of Spain	Electors of Brandenburg, after Kings of Prussia.	Tsars of Russia.
1600	Rudolf II (since 1576)	Henry IV (since 1589)	Elizabeth (since 1558)	Philip III (since 1598)	Joachim Frederick, Elector of Brandenburg since (1598).	Boris Godúnov (since 1598)
1603			James I			
1606						Vasíl Shuiiski (The false Dimitri)
1608					John Sigismund, (also Duke of Prussia, (1616)	
1610		Louis XIII				Interregnum
1612	Matthias (King of Hungary, 1609)					
1613						Michael Románov
1619	Ferdinand II				George William.	
1621				Philip IV		
1625			Charles I			
1636	Ferdinand III					
1640					Frederick William, the Great Elector.	
1643		Louis XIV				
1645						Alexis
1649			Commonwealth Oliver Cromwell, Protector. Richard Cromwell, Protector Charles II.			
1653						
1658	Leopold I					
1660						
1665				Charles II		

Year	England	Spain	Empire	Prussia	Russia
1676					Feodor II
1682					{Ivan V {Peter I
1685	James II				
1688	William III and Mary II			Frederick I, (King of Prussia, 1701)	
1689					
1694	William III, alone				
1696					Peter I, alone
1700		Philip V			
1702	Anne				
1705			Joseph I.		
1711			Charles VI		
1713				Fred'k William I	
1714	George I				

Appendix II.

	Kings of Sweden.	Kings of Denmark.	Kings (elected) of Poland.	Sultans of the Turks	Kings of Portugal.	(Governors) Catholic Netherlands (Now Belgium).
1600	Sigismund, King of Poland (since 1592)	Christian IV (since 1588)	Sigismund III (since 1587)	Muhammad III (since 1595)	(United to Spain)	Archduke Albert, Infanta Isabella, (since 1599)
1603				Ahmad I		
1604	Charles IX					
1611	Gustavus Adolphus					
1617				Mustapha I		
1618				Othman II		
1621						Infanta Isabella, alone
1622				Mustapha I (again)		
1623				Murad IV		
1632	Christina		Ladislas VII.			
1633						Cardinal-Infant Ferdinand.
1640				Ibrahim	John IV	
1641						Dom Francisco de Mello
1644						Marquis of Castel Rodrigo
1647						Archduke Leopold
1648		Frederick III.	John Casimir.	Muhammad IV		
1649						
1654	Charles X.					
1656					Affonso VI	
1659						Archduke John.
1660	Charles XI					Marq. of Fromista.

1664						Marquis of Castel Rodrigo
1668					(Pedro, Regent)	Duke of Feria
1669			Michael Koributh Vichnevetski.			
1670		Christian V.				Count of Monterey
1674			John Sobieski.			Duke of Villahermosa.
1675						
1678						Alexander Farnese of Parma.
1683				Sulaiman II	Pedro II	Marquis of Castanaga
1687				Ahmad II		
1691						Maximilian Emmanuel, Elector of Bavaria.
1692				Mustapha II		
1695			Augustus I, Elector of Saxony			
1697	Charles XII					
1699		Frederick IV				
1701						
1702						
1703				Ahmad III		Marquis of Bednar Elector of Bavaria, *again*
1704			Stanislas Leczinski			
1706					John V	
1709			Augustus I (*again*)			(*Council of State*).
1710						
1714						(Conseil de la Conférence) Count of Konigseck

Appendix III.

	The Popes	Dukes of Savoy	Kings of The Two Sicilies	Grand Dukes of Tuscany	Dukes of Parma	Dukes of Modena.
1600	Clement VIII (Aldobrandini) (since 1592)	Charles Emmanuel I (since 1580)	Philip III, King of Spain (since 1598).	Ferdinand I, de Medici (since 1587).	Ranuccio I, Farnese (since 1592)	Cesare d'Este (since 1597).
1605	Leo XI (Medici)					
1605	Paul V (Borghese).					
1609						
1621	Gregory XV (Ludovisi).		Philip IV, King of Spain			
1622				Cosmo II, de'Medici	Odoardo Farnese.	
1623	Urban VIII (Barberini)			Ferdinand II, de'Medici.		
1628						Alfonso III, d'Este
1629		Victor Amadeus I.				Francesco I, d'Este
1630		Francis Hyacinth				
1637		Charles Emmanuel II				
1638						
1644	Innocent X (Pamfili)				Ranuccio II, Farnese	
1646						
1655	Alexander VII (Chigi)					
1658						Alfonso IV, d'Este
1662						Francesco II, d'Este
1665	Clement IX (Rospigliosi)		Charles II, King of Spain.			
1667						
1670	Clement X (Altieri)			Cosmo III, de'Medici		
1675		Victor Amadeus II				

Francesco Farnese | Rainaldo d'Este

Philip V, King of
  Spain
Archduke Charles,
  of Austria

Naples   *Sicily*
Emperor   Victor Amadeus II,
Charles VI   Duke of Savoy

Appendix IV.

	Electors Palatine.	Electors of Saxony	Dukes, aft Electors, of Bavaria	Dukes, aft Electors, of Hanover	Elector-Archbishops of Mayence	Elector-Archbishops of Cologne	Elector-Archbishops of Trèves	Princes of Orange-Nassau
1600	Frederick IV (since 1583)	Christian II (since 1591)	Maximilian (since 1596)		Wolfgang von Dalberg (since 1582)	Ernest of Bavaria (since 1583)	Lothar von Metternich (since 1599)	Philip William (since 1584)
1601					John Adam von Bicken			
1604					John Schweickhard von Kronenberg			
1610	Frederick V (King of Bohemia, 1619) (expl'd 1620 died 1632)							
1611		John George I						
1612						Ferdinand of Bavaria		
1618			*Electors* Maximilian					Maurice (Stadtholder, since 1587).
1623							Philip von Sotern	
1625								Fred'k Henry (Stadtholder)
1626					George Frederick von Greiffenklau			
1629					Anselm Casimir von Wambold			
1647	Charles Louis I				John Philip von Schönborn			William II (Stadtholder)
1648								

1650					Maximilian Henry of Bavaria	William III (Stadtholder, 1672, King of Great Britain, 1689)
1651	John George II		Ferdinand			
1652						Charles Caspar von der Leyen
1656						
1673					Lothar Frederick von Metternich Damian Hard von der Leyen	
1675						
1676					Charles Henry von Metternich.	John Hugo von Orsbeck
1679	Charles Louis II Philip William		Maximilian Emmanuel.	Ernest Augustus	Anselm Francis von Ingelheim	
1680	John George III					
1685						
1688					Joseph Clement of Bavaria.	
1690	John William					
1691	John George IV					
1692				Electors Ernest Augustus.		
1694	Augustus I, (King of Poland, 1697).					
1698				George, (King of Great Britain, 1714)	Lothar Francis von Schonborn	
1702						William IV (never Stadtholder)
1711						Charles Joseph of Lorraine

Appendix V

[Table representing the relationship of the claimants to the Spanish Succession.]

PHILIP III, KING OF SPAIN (1598-1621) = MARGARET, OF AUSTRIA

```
Anne = LOUIS XIII,        Elizabeth of France, (1)= PHILIP IV =(2) his niece,        Maria = FERDINAND III
       King of            daughter of               (1621-65)   Marianna of                   Emperor (1637-58)
       France             Henry IV                              Austria
       (1610-42)
                                                   CHARLES II                          Marianna = PHILIP IV
                                                   (1665-1700)                                     of Spain
LOUIS XIV.                                         =(1) Marie Louise
(1642-1715) = Marie Thérèse                            of Orleans                      Charles,
                                                   =(2) Marie of                       Archduke
                                                       Neuburg                         aft Emperor
                                                         s p                           CHARLES VI

                            Louis = Maria of Bavaria
                            the                        Margaret
                            Dauphin                    Theresa (1)= LEOPOLD = Eleanor
                            d 1711                                   Emperor     of
                                                                    (1658-      Neuburg
                                                                     1705)
Louis = Marie    Philip, Duke of Anjou
Duke of   of     aft                      Maximilian = Maria        JOSEPH I,
Burgundy Savoy   PHILIP V, of Spain       Emmanuel,    Auto-        Emperor
d 1711                                    Elector of   nina         (1705-11)
                                          Bavaria
Louis XV
                                          Joseph Ferdinand
                                          d 1699
```

CORNELL UNIVERSITY.

S Y L L A B U S

OF A

URSE OF THIRTY LECTURES

ON THE

HISTORY OF EUROPE DURING THE
EIGHTEENTH CENTURY

BY

H. MORSE STEPHENS.

ITHACA :
ANDRUS & CHURCH.

TABLE OF CONTENTS

Page

MODERN EUROPEAN HISTORY.

LECTURE I.

THE REGENCY OF ORLEANS, AND THE SCHEMES OF ALBERONI.

Condition of Europe and of France at the time of the death of Louis XIV

The Parlement of Paris revokes the will of Louis XIV, and the Duke of Orleans becomes Regent of France with full powers ; revocation of the precedence granted to the natural children of Louis XIV

The character of the Regent , his attitude towards politics ; Dubois made minister , the character of Dubois.

The foreign policy of the Regent ; the schemes of Alberoni cause the Regent and Dubois to enter into a close alliance with England (1716)

The condition of Spain in 1715 ; Philip V marries Elizabeth Farnese, of Parma , her character, and ambition ; dismissal of Madame des Ursins ; Alberoni by his influence over the queen becomes the director of Spanish policy ; character and ideas of Cardinal Alberoni ; his administration ; Philip V hopes to enforce his claim to the throne of France in case of the death of Louis XV ; the queen aims at obtaining Parma and Tuscany for her children.

The attitude of England ; the accession of George I places the Whigs firmly in power ; Stanhope, a friend of the Emperor, becomes the director of English foreign policy ; the principal objects of English policy the maintenance of the the treaties of Utrecht, and the exclusion of the Stuarts from the English throne ; failure of the Jacobite rising of 1715 in the north of England.

The alliance formed between England and France is joined by the United Provinces, and becomes the Triple Alliance ; the execution of the treaties of Utrecht guaranteed by the allies (Jan , 1717).

Causes of the outbreak of war between Spain and the Emperor Charles VI , the Spaniards conquer Sardinia (Aug. 1717) and attack Sicily (July, 1718).

The Emperor joins the Triple Alliance, which thus becomes the Quadruple Alliance.

The Spanish War , Byng destroys the Spanish fleet off Cape Passaro (11 Aug , 1718) ; a French army under Berwick invades Spain (April, 1719)

The plots of Alberoni , he endeavors to induce Sweden and Russia to support the Jacobites , he prepares a fleet for the Old Pretender ; he conspires with the natural children of Louis XIV for the overthrow of the regency of Orleans , discovery of the conspiracy of Cellamare

All the plots of Alberoni foiled ; he is exiled from Spain (5 Dec., 1719).

Peace signed between Spain and the Quadruple Alliance (Feb., 1720) , the Emperor Charles VI, obtains Sicily , Victor Amadeus II of Savoy receives Sardinia in compensation for the loss of Sicily ; the succession to Parma and Tuscany guaranteed to the children of Philip V by his second marriage , Saint-Simon's embassy to Spain

The internal history of France during the regency of Orleans ; cessation of the persecution of the Jansenists , exile of Père Le Tellier , Law and his financial schemes , the mania for speculation in France , the Mississippi Company , ruinous results of Law's administration , dismissal of Law (1720) , Dubois made a cardinal (1721)

Louis XV declared of age (Feb , 1723), death of Dubois, (10 Aug , 1723) and of the Regent Orleans (7 Dec., 1723)

Authorities : The most recent books in English on this period, are *Perkins*, France under the Regency, and *Armstrong*, Elizabeth Farnese , or the Termagant of Spain. Among SECONDARY AUTHORITIES may be noted, *Coxe*, Memoirs of the Kings of Spain of the House of

Bourbon, Vol II, *DeCourcy*, L'Espagne après la paix d'Utrecht, *Combes*, La Princesse des Ursins, *Seithac*, L'Abbé Dubois, *Wiesener*, Le Régent, l'abbé Dubois et les Anglais, *Châteauneuf*, Histoire du régent Philippe d'Orleans, *Thiers*, Histoire de Law, translated by F Fiske as The Mississippi Bubble, *Horn*, Jean Law, *Séché*, Les derniers jansé istes, Vol 1, *J Rousset*, Vie d'Alberoni, *Lemontey*, Histoire de la Régence, et de la minorité de Louis XV, and *O Weber*, Die Quadrupel-Allianz vom Jahre 1718 For the part played by England see, *Stanhope*, History of England Vol 1, and *Lecky*, History of England in the Eighteenth Century, Vol 1 The PRIMARY AUTHORITIES for the history of Spain include, Lettres inédites and the Correspondance of the Princesse des Ursins, Apologia dell' operazione del Card Alberoni durante il suo ministerio; and *Alberoni*, Lettres intimes à Rocca, *Baudrillart*, Philippe V d'Espagne et la Cour de France, *St Simon* Lettres et dépêches sur l'ambassade d'Espagne [ed Drumont]. For the history of the regency in France, see the Mémoires of *Saint Simon, Madame de Staal-Delaunay, Duclos*, and *Mathieu Marais*, the Souvenirs of *Madame de Crequy*, the Journal of *Dangeau* Vols xvi-xviii, and *Buvat* Journal de la Régence Many documents of importance are contained in *Lamberty*, Mémoires pour servir à l'histoire du XVIII ième siècle Vols viii-xii

·

LECTURE II

THE END OF THE NORTHERN WAR.

The military situation in Northern Europe at the time when Charles XII of Sweden suddenly arrived in Stralsund from Adrianople (22 Nov, 1715); entire conquest of Pomerania by the Danes, Saxons, Russians and Prussians (1716)

Charles XII appoints Gorz his chief minister; the schemes of Gorz; his relations with Alberoni; Gorz endeavors to make peace between Sweden and Russia; Peter the Great not unwilling so long as the Baltic provinces which he had conquered were guaranteed to him

Charles XII invades Norway (1716); George I of England, who had purchased Bremen and Verden, determines to support Denmark , second invasion of Norway by the Swedes (1718) ; Charles XII killed at Frederikshall (30 Nov , 1718)

Revolution in Sweden ; Ulrica Eleanor, younger sister of Charles XII, declared Queen , the monarchy of Sweden made elective ; all power granted to an oligarchy of nobles , execution of Gorz

The Swedish Government resolves to make peace ; George I is confirmed in the possession of Bremen and Verden (20 Nov., 1719) ; treaty signed with Augustus I of Poland , by treaty with Prussia (21 Jan , 1720), Frederick William I of Prussia obtains the district of Pomerania between the Oder and the Peene, including Stettin, with the islands of Usedom and Wollin ; by treaty with Denmark, Sweden recovers the rest of Western Pomerania and the island of Rugen, but confirms the cession of Schleswig to Denmark ; by the treaty of Nystadt with Russia (10 Sept , 1721), Sweden surrenders the provinces bordering on the Gulf of Finland to Russia, but recovers the rest of Finland.

These treaties, which conclude the Northern War, reduce Sweden to the rank of a second-rate power, and mark the advance of Russia and Prussia towards the supremacy of the Baltic.

Condition of Poland during the reign of Augustus I of Saxony (1710–34)

Condition of Denmark under Frederick IV (1699–1730)

The last years of the reign of Peter the Great ; execution of the Russian heir-apparent, Alexis ; the development of the European policy of Peter , difficulties met with in establishing a Western system of administration ; Peter the Great's Asiatic policy ; his war with Persia , he lays down the lines of future Russian development.

Death of Peter the Great (8 Feb , 1725) ; his character and greatness

Reign of Empress Catherine I (1725–1727), and of Peter II (1727–1730) , exile of Menshikov, (1727).

Anne, Duchess of Courland, younger niece of Peter the Great, made Empress (1730).

Authorities : The best SMALL BOOKS upon the period are, *Morfill*, Story of Russia, and Story of Poland, *Voltaire*, Histoire de l'empire de Russie sous Pierre le Grand, and Charles XII, *Otté*, Scandinavian History, *Geffroy*, Les États Scandinaves. The best SECONDARY BOOKS are, for Russia, *Schuyler*, Peter the Great, *Rambaud*, Histoire de la Russie, translated by L B Lang; *Bruckner*, Peter der Grosse, and *Hermann*, Russland unter Peter der Grosse ; for Sweden, the general histories by *Fryxell*, and by *Geijer*, translated into German and continued by *Carlson*, *Lundblad*, Geschichte Karls des Zwolften ; *Beskow*, Karl der Tolfte, and *Sarauw*, Die Feldzuge Karls XII ; and for Denmark, *Allen*, Histoire de Danemark

---

LECTURE III.

POLICY OF THE EMPEROR CHARLES VI

Charles VI refuses to recognize Philip V as king of Spain until after the successful war waged by the Quadruple Alliance ; improvement made in the Austrian position in Italy by the exchange made of Sardinia for Sicily.

The Emperor and the Turks, improvement in the position of the Turks since the treaty of Carlowitz (1699) ; they recover Azov from the Russians by the Treaty of the Pruth (1711) ; under the influence of the Grand Vizier, Ali Cumurgi, the Sultan, Ahmad III, declares war upon the republic of Venice (1714), the Vizier conquers the Morea (1715), and besieges Corfu, heroic defence of Corfu (1716), the Venetians appeal to the Emperor for help, Charles VI declares war against the Turks

The campaigns of Prince Eugène ; he defeats the Turks at Peterwardein (5 Aug, 1716), and takes Temesvar : he besieges Belgrade, and wins his greatest victory over the Turks there, (16 Aug, 1717) ; surrender of Belgrade to the Austrians

Peace made between the Emperor and the Turks at Passarowitz, (July, 1718) ; by this treaty Austria received the Banat of Temesvar, completing its possession of Hungary, and the city of Belgrade , the Venetians abandoned the Morea to the Turks, but were confirmed in their possession of Corfu, and received certain districts in Albania and Dalmatia , importance of the treaty of Passarowitz ; it marks the further declension of the Turkish power in Europe

The position of Charles VI towards Spain ; the Congress of Cambray (1724).

The Emperor and the Pragmatic Sanction , the terms of this decree which was propounded by Charles VI in 1713 ' (1) the dominions of the House of Hapsburg declared indivisible , (2) male heirs to succeed by primogeniture ; (3) in default of male heirs the succession to devolve upon the female heirs, first of Charles VI, then of Joseph I, and finally of Leopold I.

Owing to the Emperor's having only daughters, he endeavors to obtain an oath of adhesion to the Pragmatic Sanction from the different states forming the Austrian dominions, and a guarantee from the powers of Europe.

The different provinces of the House of Hapsburg assent to the Pragmatic Sanction by 1724

The desire for a universal guarantee of the Pragmatic Sanction, the key note of the foreign policy of Charles VI.

The question of the Ostend Company, founded by the Emperor in order to obtain a share of the Asiatic trade , the English and the Dutch oppose the new Company , the Emperor Charles is thus alienated from his former allies, and a negotiation is entered into with Spain

The policy of Spain after the dismissal of Alberoni ; the abdication of Philip V (1724), and his subsequent return to the throne , the schemes of Ripperda ; an alliance formed between Charles VI and Philip V at Vienna (30 April, 1725) ; Charles VI renounced his claims to Spain, promised to secure the succession to Parma and Tuscany to Don Carlos, son of Philip V and Elizabeth Farnese, and agreed to aid Spain to recover Gibraltar and Minorca , Philip V guaranteed the Pragmatic Sanction, renounced all claims to Naples, Sicily, the Milanese, and the Catholic Netherlands, and threw open all Spanish ports to the Ostend Company

Formation of the League of Hanover (Sept., 1725) in opposition to the Austro-Spanish Alliance , France and England joined by the Dutch, Denmark and Sweden

Catherine I of Russia guarantees the Pragmatic Sanction and joins the Austro-Spanish Alliance (1726), and her example is followed by King Frederick William I of Prussia.

Dismissal of Ripperda (May 17, 1726) , the Spaniards attack Gibraltar

Change of power in France ; the Duc de Bourbon chief minister (1723–26) , marriage of Louis XV to Marie Leczinska, daughter of Stanislas, ex-King of Poland ; Cardinal Fleury appointed chief minister (June, 1726).

A general European war averted by the peace-policy of the English and French ministers, Walpole and Fleury

Authorities : Among SMALL BOOKS in English upon the reign of Charles VI may be noted *Léger*, Autriche-Hongrie, translated by Mrs Birkbeck Hill, and for the war with the Turks, *Creasy*, History of the Ottoman Turks   The chief SECONDARY AUTHORITIES on Austrian history of this time are, *Krones*, Handbuch der Geschichte Oesterreichs, *Arneth*, Karl VI (in Allgemeine Deutsche Biographie, vol xv), *Hofler*, Fragmente zur Geschichte Kaiser Karls VI, (Sitzungsberichte der Kaiserlichen Akademie der Wissenschaften, vol lx , Vienna, 1868), *Beer*, Zur Geschichte der Politik Karls VI, (Historische Zeitschrift, 1862), *Arneth*, Prinz Eugen vols ii, iii   *A Wolf*, Geschichte der pragmatischen Sanction, *Forster* Die Hofe und Kabinette Europas im 18te Jahrhundert, *Vehse*, Memoirs of the Court of Austria, translated by Demmler, and *Bidermann* Geschichte der Oesterreichischen Gesammtstaatsidee   The SECONDARY authorities for Turkish history are *Hammer*, Histoire de l'empire ottoman and *Zinkeisen*, Geschichte des Osmanischen Reichs in Europa. For the policy of Spain see *Coxe* and *Armstrong*, cited under Lecture I, with *Ripperda*. Memoirs and *Montgon* Mémoires , and for England *Stanhope* and *Lecky*, cited under Lecture I, with *Coxe*, Memoirs of Sir Robert Walpole. As PRIMARY AUTHORITIES for the Turkish war reference should be made to *Arneth*, Relationen der Botschaften Venedigs uber Oesterreich im 18te Jahrhundert (in the Fontes rerum Austriacarum, vol. xxii), and the Feldzuge des Prinzen Eugens, and for diplomatic history Lettres et Mémoires entre les ministres des cours de la Grande-Bretagne, de France, et d'Espagne [1727]

LECTURE IV.

THE WAR OF THE POLISH SUCCESSION

Charles VI abandons Spain, and makes peace with the allies of the League of Hanover (May, 1727), suspending the Ostend Company, and referring other disputed questions to a Congress of the Powers

Spain abandons the siege of Gibraltar, and makes peace with England, (March, 1728) ; meeting of the Congress of Soissons ; by the Treaty of Seville, (Nov., 1729) Spain makes an offensive and defensive alliance with England, France, and the Dutch, who guarantee the succession of Don Carlos to Parma and Tuscany

The Treaty of Seville is accepted by the Emperor after the death of the last Farnese Duke of Parma (Jan , 1731) , England guarantees the Pragmatic Sanction ; Charles VI dissolves the Ostend Company ; Don Carlos takes possession of Parma

The Emperor Charles VI submits the Pragmatic Sanction to the Diet of the Empire (Jan , 1732) , it is accepted by the ecclesiastical Electors, and the Electors of Brandenburg and Hanover, but rejected by the Elector Palatine, and the Electors of Saxony and Bavaria

The peace-policy of Cardinal Fleury ; his endeavors to improve the finances of France , renewal of the attack on the Jansenists

The peace-policy of Sir Robert Walpole who had become prime minister of England in 1721 , his foreign policy governed by commercial considerations , the death of George I (1727) only increases Walpole's power

In spite of the peaceful tendencies of Walpole and Fleury, the death of Augustus I, King of Poland and Elector of Saxony, causes a general war

The two chief candidates for the Polish throne Augustus II, Elector of Saxony, son of the late king, and Stanislas Leczinski, who had been king from 1704 to 1709, and was father-in-law of Louis XV of France.

Stanislas was elected king, and was supported by a small body of French troops; on the other hand, the Emperor Charles VI, recognized Augustus of Saxony in return for a guarantee of the Pragmatic Sanction, and the Empress Anne of Russia sent troops to his assistance

The Russians under Munnich take Dantzig, the last refuge of Stanislas, who escapes to France and Augustus II is elected king of Poland (Feb , 1734) , Biren made Duke of Courland (1737).

Fleury resolves to attack the Emperor on the pretext that Charles VI had shown himself hostile to Stanislas, and forms the League of Turin with Spain and Sardinia for the expulsion of the Austrians from Italy (Oct , 1733); his main intention in entering upon war to acquire Lorraine for France, an intention quickened by the betrothal of Francis, Duke of Lorraine, to Maria Theresa, heiress of Charles VI.

The campaign of 1733 ; the French, under Berwick, conquer Lorraine and under Villars take Milan ; Walpole refuses to assist the Emperor , campaign of 1734 , the French take Phillipsburg where Berwick is killed, and Don Carlos conquers Naples , campaign of 1735 ; Don Carlos conquers Sicily , but little is effected in Northern Italy and on the Rhine ; first appearance of Russian troops in western Europe, an army being sent by the Empress Anne to the help of Charles VI

Preliminaries of peace signed between France and Austria (3 Oct , 1735) (1) Stanislas Leczinski renounced the throne of Poland to Augustus of Saxony, and received the Duchy of Lorraine with the title of King ; (2) Francis, Duke of Lorraine, the future son-in-law of the Emperor, guaranteed Tuscany on the death of the last of the Medici , (3) Don Carlos recognized as King of the two Sicilies, and surrendered the Duchy of Parma to the Emperor , (4) Charles Emmanuel III, King of Sardinia, received Novara and Tortona ; (5) France to receive Lorraine on the death of Stanislas.

These preliminaries of peace were eventually ratified in

the Treaty of Vienna (1738), when France also guaranteed the Pragmatic Sanction.

Charles VI endeavors to obtain revenge for his losses in the war of the Polish Succession by attacking the Turks (1737); he is aided by the Empress Anne, the Turks generally successful, by the Treaty of Belgrade (1 Sept, 1739) Austria restored to the Turks, Belgrade, Orsova, and all the territories acquired by the Treaty of Passarowitz, except Temesvar

Death of the Emperor Charles VI (26 Oct, 1740)

Authorities For the military history of the war of the Polish Succession see, *Pajol*, Les Guerres sous Louis XV Vols 1, 11, for the policy of Austria see *Kiones Arneth Beer, A Wolf, Forsler, Vehse,* and *Bideiman,* cited under Lecture III, *Hofler,* Der Congress von Soissons (Fontes rerum Austriacarum, xxxi, xxxviii), for the policy of France see *Lacretelle* Histoire du XVIII 1ème siècle, *Jobez,* La France sous Louis XV, *Tocqueville,* Histoire philosophique du règne de Louis XV, *Bonhomme,* Louis XV et sa famille, and *D'Haussonville* Histoire de la réunion de la Lorraine à la France Among PRIMARY authorities on French history should be noted the Mémoires of *Duclos, Barbier, D'Argenson, Mathieu Marais* and *Luynes*

LECTURE V

FREDERICK WILLIAM I OF PRUSSIA, AND THE EMPRESS ANNE OF RUSSIA

The character of Frederick William I, King of Prussia

The foreign policy of Frederick William I; in spite of his love for military organization, he avoided war as much as possible; his only important territorial conquest was the district of Pomerania between the Oder and the Peene, which gave him the port of Stettin on the Baltic, after the conclusion of the Northern War, Frederick William I supported the doctrine of the balance of power in Europe, the key note of his German policy was his desire to inherit the duchies of Juliers and Berg, which it was arranged should fall to Brandenburg on the extinction of the House of Neuburg, now ruling in the Palatinate, on the promise of the Emperor to secure Juliers and Berg to him, Frederick William I guaranteed the Pragmatic Sanction, deserted the League of Hanover, and signed the treaty of Wusterhausen (12 Oct., 1726); Frederick William I's attitude to Austria, and to the Empire; he disapproves of the election of Augustus II to the throne of Poland, nevertheless supports Charles VI in the War of the Polish Succession, position of the Juliers-Berg question at the time of the death of Frederick William I

The internal policy of Frederick William I; his creation of the administrative system, he deprives the nobility of all share in civil administration, which is entrusted to a middle-class bureaucracy; his centralized system and paternal government, his improvement of the finances, and economic administration; his attitude towards religion; he welcomes the Lutheran exiles from Salzburg.

The military policy of Frederick William I, he introduces strict discipline, and a new system of drill; his passion for tall soldiers; the excellence of his army; he fills the ranks of all grades of officers from the nobles alone. he recruits the army partly by compulsory service, partly by voluntary enlistment, he increases the army from 38,000 to 84,000 men

Frederick William I and his family; his quarrels with the Crown Prince, afterwards Frederick the Great

Death of Frederick William I (31 May, 1740)

Accession of Frederick II; his character and early training; his life at Rheinsberg

Russia under the Empress Anne; circumstances under which Anne obtained the throne. she overthrows the party of Russian nobility which had placed her in power, and restores autocracy; she is influenced by her lover, Biren, who becomes Duke of Courland (1737), she carries out the policy of Peter the Great in home administration, and maintains western ideas in the administration of Russia ; she employs German generals and ministers , discontent of the Old Russian party at the policy of Anne.

The foreign policy of the Empress Anne , she maintains the alliance with the Emperor Charles VI, entered into by Catherine I, and guarantees the Pragmatic Sanction ; she carries out the ideas of Peter the Great with regard to the Poles and the Turks ; in the war of the Polish Succession she places Augustus II of Saxony upon the throne of Poland ; in the war with the Turks (1736-1739) a Russian army under Munnich and Lascy conquers the Crimea and takes Azov , by the treaty of peace with the Turks, (18 Sept , 1739) Russia abandons the Crimea and obtains Azov but promises to maintain no fleet on the Black Sea

Death of the Empress Anne (29 October, 1740)

Accession of Ivan VI, great nephew of Anne, under the regency of Biren , by a *coup d'état* (Nov 1740) Biren is overthrown and the mother of the infant king, Anne of Mecklenburg, is made regent ; Elizabeth, younger daughter of Peter the Great, supported by the Old Russian party, overthrows this government and is proclaimed Empress (5 Dec , 1741),—(See Appendix v)

Authorities Of books in English on this period of Prussian history see, *Tuttle*, History of Prussia, and *Carlyle*, History of Frederick the Great Among general SECONDARY HISTORIES consult *Berner*, Geschichte des preussischen Staats, *Stenzel*, Geschichte des preussischen Staats, *Droysen*, Geschichte der preussischen Politik, vol iv *Ranke* Zwolf Bucher preussischer Geschichte, *Philippson*, Geschichte des preussischen Staatswesens, *Bornhak*, Geschichte des preussischen Verwaltungsrechts, *Isaacsohn*, Geschichte des preussischen Beamtenthums *Stadelmann*, Preussens Konige in ihrer Thatigkeit fur die Landeskultur, vol 1, and *Cavaignac*, Les Origines de la Prusse contemporaine , more special studies of the reign are contained in *Forster*, Friedrich Wilhelm I, Konig von Preussen, the Memoirs of the *Margravine of Baireuth*, and the numerous articles of *Schmoller* in different periodicals, of which a complete list is given in *Historische Zeitschrift*, vol lvii For the early history of Frederick the Great, see *Lavisse*, La jeunesse du grand Frédéric, and Le grand Frédéric avant l'avènement, and *Hamilton*, Rheinsberg For the Empress Anne reference may be made to *Morfill's* Story of Russia, and *Rambaud*, Histoire de la Russie.

LECTURE VI.

THE WAR OF THE AUSTRIAN SUCCESSION.

Important changes caused in the Europe in 1740 by the deaths of Frederick William I of Prussia (31 May), of the Emperor Charles VI (20 October), and of the Empress Anne of Russia (29 October)

The two questions with regard to the succession of Charles VI ; (1) the succession to the Hapsburg dominions, (2) the succession to the Empire.

The claimants to the Hapsburg succession : (1) the Elector of Bavaria, (2) the Elector of Saxony and King of Poland, (3) the King of Spain, (see Appendix vi) ; nevertheless Maria Theresa, elder daughter of Charles VI, whose peaceful accession had been guaranteed by the powers of Europe under the Pragmatic Sanction, ascended the throne, and declared her husband, Francis of Lorraine, who, since 1737, had been Grand Duke of Tuscany, to be joint ruler with her of the Austrian dominions.

Of the guarantors of the Pragmatic Sanction only England and the United Provinces supported Maria Theresa ; Saxony, Spain, and Bavaria were openly hostile , Sardinia and France favored the opposition ; Russia was in the throes of revolution , and Prussia took the opportunity to attack Austria

The First Silesian War ; Frederick II, afterwards known as Frederick the Great, lays claim to Silesia , the nature of his claims ; the Prussians invade Silesia ; Frederick wins the battle of Mollwitz (10 April, 1741),

England's attitude towards Maria Theresa , the declared opposition of France and Spain to her succession causes the English Cabinet to support her claims ; war had been declared between England and Spain in October, 1739 ; causes of this war ; its influence in defining England's attitude towards Austria , retirement of Sir Robert Walpole (January,

1742) ; position attained by England during Walpole's peace administration , the aims of his policy

The attitude of France towards Maria Theresa ; Fleury, like Walpole, was essentially a peace minister, but a war party existed in France as in England , the French war party desired to attack Austria, owing to the close relations between France and Spain , the schemes of Belleisle , a league formed for the overthrow of Austria , France is joined by Spain, Bavaria, the Rhenish Electors, Saxony, Sardinia, and (5 June, 1741) by Frederick the Great of Prussia

The attitude of Russia towards Maria Theresa , the Regent, Anne of Mecklenburg, proposes to assist her and to maintain the Pragmatic Sanction ; France induces Sweden to declare war against Russia (4 Aug., 1741)

Maria Theresa appeals to the Magyar nobility '' *Moriamur pro rege nostro, Maria Theresa* ''

The question of the election of an emperor to succeed Charles VI ; Maria Theresa puts forward her husband, Francis of Lorraine , the French support the Elector of Bavaria ; he receives the adhesion of Frederick the Great, and of Augustus II of Saxony, and Poland ; he is unanimously chosen (24 January) and crowned as the Emperor Charles VII (21 Feb , 1742)

War of the Austrian Succession ; campaign of 1741 , the French and Bavarians invade Bohemia ; Frederick the Great makes the Convention of Klein Schnellendorf with Maria Theresa (9 October) , the French take Prague (25 November) , the Russians under Lascy defeat the Swedes at Williamstrand (3 Sept) ; Elizabeth, daughter of Peter the Great, seizes the throne of Russia (5 December) ; death of Ulrica Eleanor, Queen of Sweden (5 Dec) ; Frederick the Great refuses to observe the terms of the Convention , dissensions between France and Prussia ; the election of the Emperor Charles VII ; the effect of Maria Theresa's appeal to the Magyars.

Campaign of 1742 , the Austrians under Khevenhiller conquer Bavaria , Frederick the Great defeats the Austrians at Chotusitz (17 May), the policy of Carteret ; through the mediation of England, Maria Theresa makes peace with Frederick the Great (28 July, 1742), and, by the Treaty of Berlin, cedes Silesia to Prussia , the Elector Augustus II makes peace with Maria Theresa at Dresden (7 September) , critical position of the French army in Prague , escape of part of the French army (16 December), and surrender of remainder (25 December) , the campaign in Italy , the policy of Charles Emmanuel III, King of Sardinia , he eventually joins the Austrians and takes Modena ; campaign in Finland ; the Swedish army surrenders to the Russians at Helsingfors (4 Sept)

Campaign of 1743 death of Fleury (29 January) ; attitude towards politics of Louis XV ; the failure of the war causes the ruin of Belleisle , the ministry of D'Argenson , the English cabinet induces the United Provinces to support Maria Theresa ; an English army invades Southern Germany , George II defeats the French under Noailles at Dettingen (26 June) ; Treaty of Worms (13 September), between Maria Theresa, England, and Sardinia, by which the Austrians cede Pavia, Piacenza, and other districts to Charles Emmanuel III, in return for effective assistance in Italy ; this alliance is met by the Treaty of Fontainebleau between France and Spain (25 October), closely uniting the two Bourbon kingdoms , by the Treaty of Abo (23 June), peace is made between Sweden and Russia , southern Finland to the Kiumen ceded to Russia ; Adolphus Frederick of Holstein, Bishop of Lubeck, recognized as heir to the Swedish throne ; Christian VI of Denmark makes an alliance with George II of England (December).

Campaign of 1744 · the French prosecute the war more vigorously , influence of Madame de Châteauroux , France declares war against England and Austria ; Marshal Saxe invades the Catholic Netherlands, Charles of Lorraine invades Alsace ; illness of Louis XV , Frederick the Great marries his sister Ulrica to Adolphus of Holstein, heir to the Swedish throne and thus offends the Empress Elizabeth of

Russia, Frederick the Great resolves again to attack Austria; he forms the Union of Frankfort with the Emperor Charles VII and the Elector Palatine; he declares himself forced as an Elector to defend the Emperor; the Second Silesian war; Frederick invades Bohemia and takes Prague, Charles of Lorraine, recalled from Alsace, evacuates Bavaria; the Prussians retire from Bohemia, death of the Emperor Charles VII (20 January, 1745), dismissal of Carteret, who is succeeded in the control of English foreign policy by Pelham (Nov, 1745)

Campaign of 1745 Maria Theresa signs the Treaty of Fussen with the new Elector of Bavaria, Maximilian Joseph (22 April), by which Bavaria renounced all claims to the Austrian Succession, guaranteed the Pragmatic Sanction, and promised to vote for the election as Emperor, of Francis of Lorraine, Marshal Saxe defeats the English at Fontenoy (11 May) and takes the fortresses of the Catholic Netherlands, the Jacobite rising distracts the attention of the English government; Augustus II of Saxony and Poland declares himself on the side of Maria Theresa (18 May), and invades Silesia with the Austrians; Frederick the Great defeats the invaders at Hohenfriedberg (4 June), and at Soor (30 Sept); Francis of Lorraine elected Emperor by seven votes to two (13 Sept.); Frederick the Great defeats the Saxons at Kesseldorf (12 December), takes Dresden, and conquers Saxony, the Spaniards take Milan (16 December); by the Treaties of Dresden (25 December) Maria Theresa confirms the cession of Silesia and all privileges granted to Frederick by the Emperor Charles VII, and Augustus pays 1,000,000 thalers in gold, while Frederick recognizes the Emperor Francis and evacuates Saxony

Campaign of 1746: the Austrians recover Milan (19 March), and defeat the French and Spaniards at Piacenza (15 June), death of Philip V of Spain (9 July); the Spaniards and French withdraw from Italy, the Austrians take Milan, in the Netherlands Marshal Saxe takes Brussels and Antwerp and defeats the English and Austrians at Raucoux

(11 October), the Austrians and Sardinians invade Provence

Campaign of 1747 . the Conference of Breda ; Marshal Saxe invades Holland ; revolution in Holland ; William IV of Orange-Nassau declared Stadtholder and the Stadtholderate made hereditary in his family : Marshal Saxe defeats the English and Austrians under Cumberland at Lauffeld (2 July) ; the battle of the Col d'Assiette (19 July).

Campaign of 1748 , the Empress Elizabeth of Russia disgusted at the language used by Frederick the Great about herself, sends help to Maria Theresa ; England and France determine upon peace.

Preliminaries of peace signed at Aix-la-Chapelle (30 April), and accepted by all the powers by the end of the year

Authorities. The most recent and most thorough SECONDARY BOOKS on the diplomatic history of this period are the *Duc de Broglie*, Frédéric II et Marie Thérèse, 1740-42, Frédéric II et Louis XV, 1742–44 Marie Thérèse impératrice, 1744-46, Maurice de Saxe et D'Argenson, 1746-48, and Etudes diplomatiques , fin de la guerre de la succession d'Autriche For the Austrian side see *Arneth*, Geschichte Maria Theresias, vols 1-3, *A Wolf*, Œsterreich unter Maria Theresia and Aus dem Hofleben Maria Theresia nach den Memoiren des Fürsten J. Khevenhiller, and *G. Wolf*, Aus der Zeit der Kaiserin Maria Theresia , for the Emperor Charles VII, *Heigel*, Der osterreichische Erbfolgestreit und der Kaiserwahl Karl's VII , for Prussia, *Carlyle*, History of Frederick the Great, *Tuttle*, History of Prussia, *Koser* Konig Friedrich der Grosse, *Preuss* Friedrich der Grosse, Preussische Staatschriften aus der Regierungszeit Friedrichs II, vols 1, 2, ed *Koser*, and *Von Rauwer*, Konig Friedrich II und seine Zeit, with *Frederick the Great*, Histoire de mon temps , for Holland, *Beer*, Uber Holland und der Œsterreichische Erbfolgekrieg (in the Sitzungsberichte des kaiserlichen Akademie fur Wissenschaft, vol lxvii), for England, *Ballantyne*, Lord Carteret , and for France, Correspondance de Louis XV et du Maréchal de Noailles, ed *Rousset*, the Mémoires of *D'Argenson*, ed *Rathery*, *Duclos*, and the *Duc de Luynes*, *Taillandier*, Maurice de Saxe, *Vitzthum*, Maurice comte de Saxe et Marie Joseph de Saxe, dauphine de France and *Zevort*, Le Marquis d'Argenson For the military history of the war in western Europe consult, *Pajot*, Les guerres sous Louis XV, vols. 2, 3, *De Vault*,

Guerre 'de la succession d'Autriche, ed *Avers, Crousse,* La guerre
de la succession d'Autriche dans les provinces Belgiques, and *Morris,*
Opérations Militaires dans les Alpes pendant la guerre de succession
d'Autriche, and of the first Silesian war, *Grunhagen,* Geschichte des
ersten Schlesisches Krieges and Die Kriege Friedrichs des Grossen,
ed by the German general staff, vols 1–3

LECTURE VII.

THE TREATY OF AIX-LA CHAPELLE AND THE AUSTRO FRENCH ALLIANCE

The first negotiations for peace ; Conference of Breda
(1746–1747) ; the Conference broken up by the refusal of
Maria Theresa to negotiate with France , the overthrow of
D'Argenson

Negotiations resumed at Aix-la-Chapelle , the chief
plenipotentiaries were, for England; Lord Sandwich, for
France, Saint-Severin, for Spain, Soto-Mayor, and for Austria, Kaunitz , Maria Theresa refuses to surrender a
principality in Italy for Don Philip ; the Conference broken
up.

After the defeat of Lauffeld, England resolves that peace
shall be made, and on 30 April, 1748, England, France, and
the Dutch sign preliminaries of peace at Aix-la-Chapelle ,
Austria is forced to assent and by the end of 1748, the Treaty
of Aix-la-Chapelle is accepted by all the powers

Conditions of the Treaty of Aix-la-Chapelle : (1) Francis
I acknowledged as Emperor, the Pragmatic Sanction again
confirmed, the Catholic Netherlands recovered, Silesia, part
of Lombardy, Parma, and Piacenza lost : (2) France evacuates the Catholic Netherlands, which had been conquered by
Marshal Saxe, acknowledges the Protestant Succession in
England, and undertakes to expel the Pretender ; (3) England receives again the commercial advantages given by

Spain by the Treaties of Utrecht, and the *status quo ante bellum* is restored in Asia and America , by this clause England recovers Madras, and France, Cape Breton ; (4) Spain acknowledges the Emperor Francis I and Don Philip receives a principality in Italy ; (5) the Dutch are confirmed in the right to garrison the barrier fortresses , (6) Don Philip of Spain, second son of Philip V and Elizabeth Farnese, and younger brother of Don Carlos, King of the Two Sicilies, receives Parma, Piacenza, and Guastalla, which are to revert to Austria on the failure of male heirs ; (7) Charles Emmanuel III recovers Savoy and Nice, and is confirmed in the possession of the districts of Lombardy, ceded to him by the Treaty of Worms ; (8) Frederick the Great of Prussia, confirmed in the possession of Silesia

The two states which profited most by the Treaty of Aix-la-Chapelle were Prussia and Sardinia ; France and Spain gained nothing ; Austria lost less than might have been expected ; England was saved from extinction in India

After the close of the War of the Austrian Succession, Maria Theresa, dissatisfied with the sacrifice of Silesia, which England had imposed upon her, seeks to alter the policy of Austria , her one desire the recovery of Silesia.

Kaunitz becomes the director of Austrian foreign policy (1749) ; character and policy of Kaunitz , he suggests an alliance between France and Austria, and is sent to Versailles to accomplish this end

Louis XV and his foreign policy , contrast between his avowed policy and secret diplomacy ; the influence of Madame de Pompadour , her dislike of Frederick the Great makes her ready to negotiate with Maria Theresa.

The relations between Austria and Spain ; the character of Ferdinand VI , he enters into close alliance with Maria Theresa (1752) ; the relations between England and Austria ; Maria Theresa attempts to revive commerce in the Catholic Netherlands, and thus offends the maritime powers of England and the United Provinces.

The relations between Austria and Russia ; the Empress

Elizabeth, owing to her dislike to Frederick the Great, allies herself with Maria Theresa

The two issues which threatened to bring on a general war, (1) the desire of Maria Theresa to recover Silesia, (2) the rivalry between England and France in Asia and America ; the expectation of a general war, in which England and Prussia should be pitted against Austria and France

Events which led to the outbreak of the Seven Years' War

The rivalry between France and England in India , the French and English support opposing native princes , the schemes of Dupleix ; first successes of Clive ; the defence of Arcot (1751) ; the recall of Dupleix

The rivalry between France and England in America ; the defeat of Braddock (9 July, 1755).

Maria Theresa refuses to assist England against France ; Frederick the Great and George II by the Convention of Westminster (16 January, 1756), make an alliance and guarantee each other's territories

Outbreak of war between England and France ; the Duc de Richelieu takes Minorca (2 June, 1756) ; war formally declared.

Louis XV disgusted at the alliance between Prussia and England resolves to accept the propositions of Kaunitz ; Madame de Pompadour presses the change, and a secret treaty of alliance is signed between Austria and France (1 May, 1756).

Maria Theresa on this basis combines a general league against Frederick the Great, which is joined by the Empress Elizabeth of Russia, and most of the other continental states

Frederick the Great, hearing of these negotiations, invades Saxony (26 Aug , 1756), and thus commences the Seven Years' War.

The Emperor Francis declares that Frederick had exposed himself to penalties by thus attacking the Empire, and the Diet declares war against Prussia (January, 1757) the Empress Elizabeth makes an offensive alliance with Austria against Prussia (2 Feb , 1757), and prepares an army ; Ber-

nis, who had made the secret treaty with Austria on the part
of France for Madame de Pompadour, becomes the director
of French foreign policy, and concludes the second treaty of
Versailles with Austria (1 May, 1757).

Importance of the diplomatic revolution effected by Kaunitz, the classic policy of France from the time of Richelieu had been based on enmity against the House of Hapsburg; causes of this change of front, unpopularity of the
Austro-French alliance in France, its effects upon Europe

Authorities: The best SECONDARY WORK on the Treaty of Aix-la-
Chapelle is the *Duc de Broglie*. La paix d'Aix-la-Chapelle for the
diplomatic revolution, see for the Austrian point of view, *Von Arneth*,
Geschichte Maria Theresias, Vol iii, and for the French side, *Bernis*,
Mémoires et lettres, ed *Masson*, for the struggle between the French
and English in India, see *Malleson*, History of the French in India,
for the situation in Prussia, *Carlyle*, History of Frederick the Great
should be used with care, and more reliance can be placed on *Tuttle*,
History of Prussia, Vol iii, on *Taysen*, Zur Beurtheilung des siebenjahrigen Krieges, and on the studies by *Ranke*, in his Sämmtliche
Werke, Vol xxx, for Saxony, see *Vitzthum*, Die Geheimnisse des
Sächsischen Kabinets Ende 1745 bis Ende 1756; and for Russia, *Vandal*, Louis XV et Elisabeth de Russie For Austria, the works of *Von
Arneth*, *A Wolf* and *G Wolf*, cited under Lecture VI, may still be
used with *Beer*, Aufzeichnungen des Grafen William Bentinck, for
Prussia, the works cited under Lecture VI with *Valory*, Mémoires,
and for France, with *Barbier*, *D'Argenson*, *De Luynes*, *Duclos*, *Crequy*,
and *Rousset*, Correspondance de Louis XV et du Maréchal de Noailles,
should be consulted, *Campardon*, Madame de Pompadour et la cour
de Louis XV, *Goncourt*, Madame de Pompadour, *Broglie*, Le Secret
du Roi, *Rousset*, Le Comte de Gisors, and *Boutaric*, Correspondance
secrète inédite de Louis XV

LECTURE VIII

THE SEVEN YEARS' WAR

The position of the powers of Europe at the outbreak of
the Seven Years' War, difference of the aims of England
and Prussia; the chief desire of Maria Theresa and the Em-

press Elizabeth was to humble Frederick the Great, and to reduce Prussia to a second rate power , the desire of France was not so much to defeat Prussia as to check the colonial expansion of England

The United Provinces, owing to the death of the Stadtholder, William IV, and the minority of his son, pursue a peace policy and declare neutrality

England desires to fight at sea and in America and India, but is drawn into the continental war by the connection with Hanover ; Pitt perceives the solidarity of the struggle upon the Continent with the maritime and colonial war, and advocates vigorous support of Frederick the Great ; Prussia has to bear the assault of Austria, Russia, and France ; excellence of the Prussian army ; Frederick the Great as a statesman and a general

The Seven Years' War   the campaign of 1756 · Frederick the Great invades Saxony (26 August), and occupies Dresden , the Saxon army surrounded at Pirna , the Austrians come to their assistance ; the battle of Lobositz (1 October) ; surrender of the whole Saxon army at Pirna (16 October) , anger of Louis XV at the attack on Saxony

The campaign of 1757 ; scheme of an invasion of Prussia by the Austrians, French, Imperialists, Russians and Swedes ; Frederick takes the offensive and invades Bohemia ; he defeates the Austrians at Prague (6 May) ; Marshal Daun advances to the relief of Prague and defeats Frederick at Kolin (18 June) ; the Prussians retire from Bohemia , the French under D'Estrées defeat the Duke of Cumberland at Hastenbeck (26 July) ; Cumberland makes the Convention of Klosterseven (10 September) , the Russians defeat the Prussians at Gross Jagersdorf (30 August), and conquer the Duchy of Prussia ; the Imperialists with a French army under Soubise utterly defeated by Frederick the Great at Rossbach (5 November) ; the Russians retire and the Swedes are driven out of Pomerania ; Frederick defeats the Austrians at Leuthen (5 December), and recovers the whole of Silesia , Pitt is appointed Secretary of State, and repudiates the Convention of Klosterseven, grants a subsidy to Frederick, and places an English and Hanoverian army under the command of Ferdinand of Brunswick ; failure of an English expedition against Rochefort.

Campaign of 1758 ; renewal of the alliance between England and Prussia, and between Austria, France and Russia ; Choiseul becomes chief minister of France and supports more strongly the Austro-French alliance, Frederick takes Schweidnitz (16 April), and invades Bohemia ; he has to retreat to meet a Russian invasion ; battle of Zorndorf (25 August), Frederick defeated by the Austrians under Marshal Daun at Hochkirch (5 October), the Austrians retire into Bohemia ; Ferdinand of Brunswick drives the French out of Hanover and Westphalia, crosses the Rhine, and defeats them at Crefeld (26 June), the English take Louisburg and Cape Breton (June), but Abercromby is repulsed from Ticonderoga, capture of Fort Duquesne, unsuccessful English attacks on the French coast

Campaign of 1759 : Frederick utterly defeated at Kunersdorf by the Russians and Austrians (10 August) ; Saxony occupied by the Austrians and Imperialists ; surrender of a Prussian army at Maxen (21 November) ; desperate position of Frederick the Great, Ferdinand of Brunswick defeats the French at Minden (1 August) ; English victories at sea, Boscawen defeats one French fleet at Lagos (17 August), and Hawke another off Quiberon (21 November), Lally fails to take Madras ; Wolfe defeats Montcalm, and takes Quebec (18 September).

Campaign of 1760 Loudon defeats the Prussians at Landshut (23 June) ; he is in turn defeated by Frederick at Liegnitz (15 August), the Russians and Austrians occupy Berlin, Frederick recovers his capital and defeats Daun at Torgau (2 November) ; Ferdinand of Brunswick keeps the French out of Hanover and Westphalia, Eyre Coote defeats the French at Wandewash (22 January), and overthrows the power of France in India ; Amherst takes Montreal (8 September), and completes the occupation of Canada, death of George II of England (25 October).

Campaign of 1761 exhaustion of the nations of Europe engaged in the war ; Loudon takes Schweidnitz ; Frederick fights no pitched battle , Ferdinand of Brunswick prevents Broglie from advancing ; the Russians fail to take Stettin ; the English capture the islands of Dominica and Belleisle ; Choiseul signs the Pacte de Famille between France and Spain ; resignation of Pitt

Campaign of 1762 . Spain declares war against England (January) , the English take Martinique, Havana, and Manilla , Lord Bute becomes Prime Minister of England (May) , he refuses to continue paying subsidies to Frederick , death of Empress Elizabeth of Russia (5 January) , her successor, Peter III, makes a offensive and defensive alliance with Frederick (5 May) ; revolution at St Petersburg (9 July) , Peter III deposed , Catherine II becomes Empress , she declares neutrality , Frederick takes Schweidnitz (October) ; the Prussians invade South Germany , the Diet of the Empire declares neutrality ; negotiations for peace ; a truce signed between Austria and Prussia.

The Seven Years' War concluded by the Treaties of Hubertsburg and Paris.

By the Treaty of Hubertsburg (15 February, 1763), the *status quo ante bellum* restored between Austria and Prussia , Silesia again guaranteed to Prussia ; Frederick promises to vote for Joseph as King of the Romans, and to evacuate Saxony.

By the Treaty of Paris (10 February, 1763), France surrenders Canada, Nova Scotia, Cape Breton, certain West India Islands, and Minorca to England ; Spain cedes Florida to England ; the English restore Belleisle, Guadeloupe, and Martinique to France, and Havana to Spain.

General results of the Seven Years' War ; policy of Frederick the Great and its results , the policy of Pitt and its results.

Authorities : An excellent short book in English is *Longman,* Frederick the Great and the Seven Years' War , the volumes devoted by *Carlyle,* in his History of Frederick the Great to this period, are the

most valuable in his book   For the military history of the war, see
Frederick the Great, Histoire de la guerre de Sept Ans in his Works,
Lloyd, History of the late War in Germany, *Jomini*, Grand Military
Operations, *Tielcke*, Beytrage zur Kriegskunst und Geschichte des
Krieges von 1756 bis 1763, *Archenholtz* Geschichte des siebenjahr-
igen Krieges in Teutschland; *Schoning*, Der siebenjahrige Krieg,
Schafer, Geschichte des siebenjahrigen Krieges, *Westphalen*, Ge-
schichte der Feldzuge des Herzogs Ferdinands von Braunschweig-
Luneburg, *Renouard*, Geschichte des Krieges in Hannover, Hessen
und Westphalen, and *Pajol*, Les guerres sous Louis XV, Vols iv, v
For the diplomatic history of the war see *Filon*, L'ambassade de
Choiseul à Vienne en 1757-58; *Bisset* Memoirs and Papers of Sir A
Mitchell, *Bonhomme*, Madame de Pompadour général d'armée, and
Beaulieu-Marconnay, Der Hubertsburger Friede   For the policy of
Pitt, see *Stanhope*, History of England from the peace of Utrecht,
Vols v-vii   For the struggle in India, *Malleson*, History of the
French in India; and in America *Parkman*, Montcalm and Wolfe

LECTURE IX.

THE SUPPRESSION OF THE JESUITS.

The condition of the southern countries of Europe in the
middle of the 18th century ; their internal development under reforming kings or great ministers , influence exerted by
the philosophic doctrines of the time towards toleration and
general reform , altered attitude towards the Pope and the
Church

The Popes of the 18th century   Clement XI—Albani—
1700-1721 , his disputes with the king of Sicily ; Innocent
XIII—Conti—1721-24 , Benedict XIII—Orsini—1724-30 ,
he confirms the condemnation of the Jansenists, and maintains the bull " Unigenitus " as an article of faith ; his personal piety and amiability ; rapacity and misgovernment of
Cardinal Coscia ; Clement XII—Corsini—1730-40 ; punishment of Coscia ; Benedict XIV—Lambertini—1740-58 ; his

skill as a statesman , his philosophical tendencies and moderation ; he corresponds with Voltaire , his buildings at Rome ; he dies before the opposition to the Jesuits reaches its height , Clement XIII—Rezzonico—1758–69 ; he refuses to consent to the suppression of the Society of Jesus

The general discontent in Roman Catholic countries caused by the commercial operations of the Jesuits , the Society ceases to be self-sacrificing and devoted to the Papacy ; faults and virtues of the Jesuits in the 18th century

The first attack on the Jesuits was directed by Pombal, who had become chief minister of Portugal under King Joseph ; causes of Pombal's hatred of the Jesuits , they oppose his measures of reform , they monopolize what remained of Portuguese commerce with India, and they fought against the cession of Paraguay to Portugal , Pombal forbids the Jesuits to come to court without leave (1757) ; the Tavora plot (1758) , Pombal deports the Jesuits to Italy (1759), and confiscates all their property in Portugal , Pope Clement XIII defends the Jesuits , execution of Malagrida (1761)

The example of Pombal followed in other countries · (1) in France : discredit caused by the failure of Jesuit traders . Choiseul determines to limit their prerogatives , he is supported by the Parlements, who remembered the persecution of the Jansenists , the Parlement of Paris condemns the constitutions of the Society (1761) ; abolition of the Society in France by a royal edict (1764) , (2) in Spain ; Charles III banishes the Jesuits from his kingdom (1767) , (3) in Italy , the Jesuits are expelled from Naples and Parma

Pope Clement XIII defends the Society of Jesus , he attacks the weakest of their opponents, excommunicates the Duke of Parma, and declares the duchy confiscated (1768) , the Catholic powers support Parma , the French occupy Avignon, and the Neapolitans Benevento ; Spain, the Two Sicilies, France and Portugal demand the suppression of the Society of Jesus (Jan , 1769) , death of Pope Clement XIII (3 Feb., 1769)

Election of Pope Clement XIV—Ganganelli—(19 May,

1769 ; his character and previous career , he is pressed by
Cardinal Bernis on the part of France to suppress the Jesuits ;
difficulties of his position , he makes friends with Parma
and Portugal and secures the evacuation of Avignon and
Benevento ; eventually, he issues a brief suppressing the
Jesuits, on 27 July, 1773.

Effect upon Europe of the overthrow of the Jesuits ; their
suppression typical of the changed attitude of the Catholic
powers towards the Pope and of the people towards the Catholic religion

Attempts made to replace the Jesuits as a teaching organization ; the Oratorians ; Catherine II protects and encourages the Jesuits in the part of Poland, which fell to her
at the first partition ; the Society continues to exist in
Russia and Prussia.

Death of Clement XIV (22 Sept., 1774) , election of Pius
VI—Braschi

Internal administration of the States of the Church under
the Popes of the 18th century ; condition of the Legations ,
Rome becomes the chief place of resort for wealthy travelers ;
effect upon Protestant countries of the increased tolerance of
the Papacy

Improved personal character of the Popes in the 18th century ; decrease of personal and family ambition ; disappearance of nepotism

Significance of the suppression of the Jesuits as a typical
act of the 18th century.

Authorities · For the suppression of the Jesuits see *Crétineau-Joly*,
Histoire religieuse, politique et littéraire de la compagnie de Jésus,
Vols. v, vi ; *Sénac de Meilhan*, Histoire abregée de l'expulsion des
Jésuites , *Saint-Priest*, Histoire de la chute des Jésuites, and *Masson*,
Le cardinal de Bernis depuis son ministere.

LECTURE X.

THE FIRST PARTITION OF POLAND

The internal history of Russia from the death of Peter the Great, formation of two opposing parties of which one desires to continue the progress in western civilization commenced by Peter, and the other desires to recur to old Russian customs and system of government ; the church, nobles, and the mass of the population favor throughout the century a reaction against Peter's innovations ; it was due to the personal character of successive rulers that Russia was further developed on western lines.

Both the Empress Anne (1730), and the Empress Elizabeth (1741), were raised to the throne of Russia because they were believed to be in harmony with old Russian ideas, but both empresses, when firmly established, carried on the system of Peter the Great in internal government and placed the administration in the hands of foreigners, mostly of Germans

Although the Russians disliked the western system, and the employment of foreigners introduced by Peter the Great, they enthusiastically believed in his foreign policy, and in the ideas he had formed for the expansion of Russia, the foreign policy of the government was popular or unpopular in so far as it adhered to, or parted from the lines laid down by Peter the Great

The foreign policy of the Empress Elizabeth, her alliance with Maria Theresa, her hatred for Frederick the Great of Prussia

The Empress Elizabeth is succeeded by her great nephew, Peter III (19 Jan., 1762), unpopularity of Peter as a foreigner and adherent of foreign ideas ; Peter III is overthrown by his wife Catherine (9 July 1762) ; the Empress Catherine II desires to emphasize her belief in the policy of Peter the Great, to satisfy the Old Russian party, she resolves to pursue an aggressive policy in Poland, causes of the popularity of this policy in Russia , Catherine expels Charles of Saxony from Courland, and restores Biren.

Attitude of Frederick the Great towards Poland ; he desires to unite the rest of Prussia to his dominions , this had been a keynote of Hohenzollern policy since the proposal of Frederick I to Peter the Great to dismember Poland , further, Frederick was afraid that Saxony and Poland might be permanently united, and thus counterbalance the power of Prussia

The attitude of Maria Theresa towards Poland ; her determination that Russia and Prussia should not divide Poland without giving her a portion ; she is urged in this direction by her son Joseph II, who had become Emperor in 1765.

Condition of Poland itself ; its poverty and bad government under the Saxon kings ; the Roman Catholic majority persecute the Protestants and the Greek Church ; non-catholics are excluded from all office, and from sitting in the Diet (1736).

The two parties in Poland ; the Pro-Saxon and the Anti-Saxon parties , Louis XV supports the Pro-Saxon party owing to the marriage of the Dauphin to a Saxon princess.

Death of Augustus II, king of Poland (5 Oct , 1763) ; his death followed by that of his eldest son (Dec., 1763) , the new Elector of Saxony, Frederick Augustus, was too young to obtain the throne of Poland ; the Pro-Saxon party is thus left without a candidate.

Election of Stanislas Poniatowski as king of Poland (7 Sept , 1764), by the influence of Russia and Prussia.

The reign of Stanislas Poniatowski , he endeavors to revoke the decree of 1736, and to admit non-Catholics to office (1766) ; the Confederation of Radom ; the reforms of 1768 , Catherine declares her intention of maintaining the Polish constitution

The Poles resent the interference of Russia ; formation of the Confederation of Bar (28 Feb , 1769) ; Choiseul desires to support the Confederation of Bar, and incites the Turks to attack Russia ; the Russians suppress the Confederation of

Bar , the Turks declare war against Russia (6 Oct , 1768).

The Russo-Turkish war , the Russians conquer Moldavia (1769), and Wallachia (1770) , a Russian fleet under Orlov incites the Greeks to rebel.

Frederick the Great proposes the partition of Poland , he comes to an agreement with the Emperor Joseph II , the proposition is made to the Empress Catherine

The negotiations for the partition of Poland (1770–72) , a final agreement made by the Treaty of St Petersburg (Aug , 1772) ; the Polish Diet consents to the partition treaty (Sept , 1773)

By the first partition of Poland (1) Frederick received West Prussia, with the exception of Dantzig and Thorn, thus connecting his eastern dominions , (2) Maria Theresa received the county of Zips, and Red Russia ; (3) Russia received Polish Livonia and part of Lithuania ; while (4) Stanislas Poniatowski remained king of the diminished central district.

The respective advantages gained by the three powers in the first partition of Poland

Conclusion of the Russo-Turkish war , campaign of 1773 ; death of the Sultan, Mustapha III (Dec , 1773) , campaign of 1774 , victories of the Russians , treaty of Kutschuk Kainardji (21 July, 1774), the Russians restore Moldavia and Wallachia, but retain Azov and Kinburn , the Tartars of the Crimea declared independent of Turkey , Russian ships allowed free passage through the Dardanelles and on the Danube , Russia acknowledged as the protector of the Danubian principalities , the Austrians sieze the Bukovina, which is ceded by the Turks (7 May 1775).

Effect of the partition of Poland and of the treaty of Kutschuk Kainardji upon the position of the Empress Catherine II

Authorities: The best SMALL BOOK on this subject is *Sorel*, La Question d'Orient au XVIIIième Siècle Among larger works s̈ *Beer*, Die erste Theilung Polens and Friedrich II und Van Swieten , *De Smitt*, Frédéric II, Catherine et le partage de la Pologne , *Michael*, Englands Stellung zur ersten Theilung Polens , *Von der Bruggen*,

Polens Avflosur g, *Schlozer* Friedrich der grosse und Katharina die Zweite, *Janssen*, Zur Genesis der ersten Theilung Polens, *Gross-Hoffinger*, Die Theilung Polens, *Roepell*, Pole um die Mitte des xviii Jahrhunderts; *Barral*, Études sur l'histoire diplomatique de l'Europe, and *Broglie*, Le secret du Roi The celebrated work of *Rulhiere*, Histoire de l'anarchie de Pologne et du démembrement de cette ré publique, was left unfinished, and only goes to 1770; it was continued in much inferior style by *Ferrand*, Les trois démembrements de la Pologne

---

LECTURE XI.

FRANCE UNDER LOUIS XV

The internal government of France during the 18th century; the administrative machinery created in the 17th century retained without modification, the central government, the work of the intendants.

The Court of Louis XV and its influence on internal politics after the death of Fleury, its influence in foreign politics; the power of the king's mistresses; the attempt of Damiens to murder the king (5 Jan 1757); Madame de Chateauroux (1740-44), Madame de Pompadour (1745-64); the ministers of the first period, Machault, D'Argenson, Belleisle; the ministers of the second period; Bernis, Choiseul.

The private foreign policy of the king; he opposes the diplomacy of his ministers, the Comte de Broglie.

The foreign policy of Choiseul; its chief features, the Pacte de Famille (1761) and the marriage of Marie Antoinette to the heir of France (1770); popularity of the Spanish and unpopularity of the Austrian alliance in France, Favier, annexation of Lorraine on death of Stanislas Leczinski (1766), purchase of Corsica from the Genoese (1767) and its conquest (1768); the dismissal of Choiseul (1770).

The weak points in the internal administration, confusion

and mismanagement in the finances , condition of the provinces ; steady improvement in trade and manufactures , decline in the prosperity of agriculture , state of the corn trade ; the Pacte de Famine.

The part played by the Parlements and especially by the Parlement of Paris down to the time of the dismissal of Choiseul , the reforms of 13 Dec , 1756 ; the strength and weakness of the Parlements ; their attempt to interfere in internal politics ; their Jansenist proclivities cause them to support Choiseul against the Jesuits

The last mistress of Louis XV ; the career and character of Madame du Barry, and her influence ; she secures the dismissal of Choiseul ; during her power (1770-74) France is governed by D'Aiguillon, Terrai, and Maupeou , the work of these ministers , D'Aiguillon, and foreign policy , the financial policy of Terrai , he declares partial bankruptcy , Maupeou and the Parlements ; he exiles the former judges and creates the Parlements Maupeou (1771).

Degradation of the Court of France in the last days of Louis XV ; his conduct destroys the prestige of the French monarchy

Condition of France during the reign of Louis XV ; its advance in material wealth ; general improvement in education ; the work of the Oratorians.

Rise of the French school of Political Economists known as the Physiocrats ; their works drew attention to the importance of the agricultural interest , Quesnay , attempts made to improve agriculture ; effect of the Physiocratic theories on commerce , Gournay , political economy becomes fashionable , the works of the Marquis de Mirabeau

Intellectual condition of France under Louis XV ; effect of the works of the Philosophes , Voltaire and his influence , Diderot and the publication of the *Encyclopédie Méthodique* ; Jean Jacques Rousseau , his influence on political and social ideas, and upon education ; the *Contrat Social*, the *Profession du Foi d'un Vicaire Savoyard*, the *Nouvelle Héloise* and *Émile*.

Position of affairs at the death of Louis XV (10 May,
1774) ; weakness of the administrative machine ; prosperity
and intelligence of the middle classes ; political insignificance
of the nobility ; condition of the Church ; evil effect of
privilege, general expectation of a new order of things in-
spired by the intellectual movement

Authorities Among SECONDARY HISTORIES may be noted *Lacretelle*, Histoire de France , *Jobez*, La France sous Louis XV, and *Tocqueville*, Histoire philosophique du règne de Louis XV. The memoirs
dealing with the period are described in *Aubertin*, L'esprit public au
XVIIIième siècle , among them may be particularly noticed those of
the *Duc de Luynes, Président Hénault, D'Argenson*, ed , *Rathery,
Barbier, Madame du Haussel, Pierre Narbonne* and *Bachaumont*
(those of the *Duc de Richelieu* are a compilation by *Soulavie*) and the
Souvenirs of *Madame de Crequy* and *Tilly*   On the finances *Stourm*,
Les Finances de l'ancien régime et de la Révolution may be consulted , on the latter years of Louis XV, *Vatel*, Histoire de Madame Du
Barry, and *Flammermont*, Le chancelier Maupeou et les Parlements,
and on the king's personality, *Bonhomme*, Louis XV et sa famille,
contain the latest information

LECTURE XII.

FRANCE UNDER LOUIS XVI.

The character of Louis XVI ; his attitude towards measures of internal reform ; his attitude towards foreign politics ;
his interest in naval affairs ; attempted reorganization of the
French army . the Comte de Guibert.

The foreign policy of Vergennes (1774-87) ; his ability
and the greatness of his views ; his adherence to the Spanish
and the Austrian alliance ; influence of Marie Antoinette in
foreign affairs , Vergennes and the smaller states of Europe ;
Vergennes and Italy ; Vergennes and the Turks; embassy
of Choiseul-Gouffier , Vergennes and Russia , the embassy

of Ségur , Vergennes' attitude towards Joseph II and Frederick the Great ; the part taken by France against England during the War of American Independence , Vergennes induces Spain to declare war against England , gains made by France by the Treaty of Versailles (1783) ; intervention of France in the Dutch Revolution of 1786 ; death of Vergennes (13 Feb 1787) , ability shown by Vergennes in concealing the real weakness of France ; Vergennes succeeded as minister for foreign affairs by Montmorin

Internal administration during the reign of Louis XVI ; influence of the Court ; extravagance of Marie Antoinette , her unpopularity at Court and among the people.

The ministry of Maurepas (1774–81) , he calls Turgot to office ; recall of the Parlements (12 Nov , 1774)

The reforms of Turgot (1774–76) ; his former career and economic ideas ; he attempts to reform the financial administration , opposition to his schemes , his proposals he establishes internal free trade in corn and attacks all restrictions on freedom of labor and freedom of trade ; his desire to overthrow the relics of feudalism, and to improve agriculture , dismissal of Turgot (12 May, 1776).

The financial administration of Necker (1774–81) ; he endeavors to draw up a balance sheet for France ; his financial methods and proposed reforms ; excitement caused by the publication of the Compte Rendu ; dismissal of Necker (19 May, 1781)

Attempt at improving local administration ; formation of Provincial Assemblies.

The financial administrations of Joly de Fleury and D'Ormesson (1781–83).

The financial administration of Calonne (1783–87) , his system of loans , his propositions of increased taxation , increase of the deficit , convocation of the Assembly of Notables (1787) ; first mention of summoning a States-General , dismissal of Calonne (1 May, 1787)

Administration of Loménie de Brienne , his struggle with the Parlements ; his measures of reform , excitement in

France at the exile of the Parlements . the Assembly at Vizille (21 July, 1788) ; promise of a speedy convocation of the States-General , dismissal of Loménie de Brienne (26 Aug., 1788)

Second administration of Necker ; he makes preparations for the elections to the States-General ; second meeting of the Notables (Nov. 1778)

Attitude of the King, Queen and the Court during these years , growing unpopularity of the Queen ; the affair of the Diamond Necklace.

Increasing demand for reform in France ; general desire to remodel the administrative system and submit it to some degree of popular control , the financial condition precipitates a political crisis ; the King and his ministers look upon the States General as a financial expedient , the people as the commencement of political and administrative reform.

Position of France at home and abroad on the eve of the French Revolution.

Authorities Among SECONDARY WORKS see *Jobez*, La France sous Louis XVI , *Droz*, Histoire du règne de Louis XVI , *Tratchevsky*, La France et l'Allemagne sous Louis XVI, and *Tocqueville*, Coup d'œil sur le règne de Louis XVI Works dealing with the condition of France during this period are cited in the Syllabus of Lectures on the French Revolution, but special reference may be made to the Correspondance secrète entre Marie Thérèse et Mercy-Argenteau, ed *Arneth* and *Geffroy*, to *Foncin*, Essai sur le ministère de Turgot, to *Lavergne*, Les Assemblées provinciales sous Louis XVI and to *Loménie*, Beaumarchais et son temps.

LECTURE XIII.

THE WAR OF AMERICAN INDEPENDENCE.

Interest taken in Europe in the struggle of the American colonists for independence , unpopularity of England on the Continent , France and Spain desire to revenge themselves for the humiliations of the Seven Years' War and the Peace of Paris , Austria is bound to France by the treaty of 1757 , Frederick the Great of Prussia had been disgusted by the way in which he had been deserted by England after the fall of Pitt ; Catherine of Russia was jealous of the commercial pretensions of England ; the republican party in Holland in its opposition to the House of Orange and to England desires to help the American colonists

Enthusiasm in France for the cause of American liberty ; Lafayette and other volunteers join Washington , Vergennes takes advantage of this enthusiasm against England , treaty of alliance formed between France and the United States, (6 Feb 1778) ; Turgot and Necker opposed to war for financial reasons , neglect of the effect which assistance to a republican movement might have in France itself , commencement of war between England and France (1778)

Spain declares war against England (1779) ; causes for this action ; influence of the Pacte de Famille

The position in the United Provinces ; war declared by England against the Dutch (Dec , 1780)

Attitude of the Empress Catherine ; formation of the Armed Neutrality or Neutral League of the North , Frederick the Great joins the League.

Complete isolation of England during the war of American Independence ; her internal troubles , weakness of the government , danger threatened in Ireland ; causes of England's fall from the great position she had occupied during the ministry of Pitt , England's only resources her naval efficiency and wealth , her naval supremacy threatened by the increased excellence of the French and Spanish navies.

England's efforts to extend the war against France to Europe in connection with the question of the Bavarian Succession frustrated by the policy of Vergennes and the Treaty of Teschen (13 May, 1779).

Owing to the absence of a base of operations on the Continent, the war was essentially naval

Campaign of 1778 ; the battle off Ushant between Keppel

and d'Orvilliers (27 July) ; D'Estaing brings help to the American colonists , Bouillé takes Dominica and other English West India islands , the English take Pondicherry.

Campaign of 1779 , Spain declares war and a French and Spanish army and fleet lay siege to Gibraltar , Eliott's defence of Gibraltar , D'Estaing takes Saint Vincent and Grenada , he is defeated in an attack on Savannah (9 Oct.), D'Orvilliers with a French and Spanish fleet commands the Channel, but fails to effect a landing in England ; Nassau-Siegen's expedition against Jersey , the French capture the English possessions on the west coast of Africa , the English take Mahé in India.

Campaign of 1780 , Rochambeau arrives in America with a French army , naval battles in the West Indies between De Guichen and Rodney (17 April, 15, 19 May) , Haidar Ali over-runs the presidency of Madras and asks for French help ; Rodney relieves Gibraltar, and defeats the Spaniards off Saint Vincent

Campaign of 1781 , Bouillé takes Tobago (2 June) , De Grasse by sea and Rochambeau on land cooperate in forcing the surrender of Cornwallis at Yorktown (19 Oct.) , Rodney takes Saint Eustatia ; battle between the English and Dutch off the Doggerbank (Aug.) ; defeat of Haidar Ali at Porto Novo (7 July).

Campaign of 1782 ; the Spaniards take Minorca , Bouillé takes Saint Kitts and Saint Eustatia , Rodney wins a great victory over De Grasse (13 Apr) , Howe relieves Gibraltar (Oct.) ; series of battles between De Suffren and Hughes off the coast of India , Bussy takes command of a French force in India , death of Haidar Ali (7 Dec)

General weariness of war , retirement of Lord North , the English ministry resolves to recognize the independence of the American colonies, preliminaries of peace signed with the United States (30 Nov 1782) , with France and Spain (20 Jan 1783) , signature of the Treaty of Versailles (3 Sept 1783), accepted later by the Dutch

Terms of the Treaty of Versailles ; England recognizes

the independence of the United States, restores Minorca and Florida to Spain, and cedes Tobago and Saint Lucia to France , the *status quo ante bellum* is restored in India, except that England obtains Negapatam from the Dutch

Results of the war of American Independence ; weakening of England by her colonial losses and by the belief that her naval supremacy had gone forever , increase in the confusion of the finances of France ; spread of a current of opinion favorable to self government and opposed to monarchy

Attitude of England and France toward each other on the eve of the French Revolution , conclusion of the commercial treaty between those powers (1786) , foreign policy of the younger Pitt, who had become prime minister of England in 1784, during the first years of his administration

French foreign policy dominated by the Austrian alliance , her inability to interfere in eastern Europe , the alliance strengthens Austria more than France ; relations between Louis XVI and Joseph II ; France intervenes in the troubles of the Emperor with the Dutch, and by the Treaty of Fontainebleau (Nov , 1785) secures the surrender to Austria of the barrier fortresses in the Netherlands

Authorities *Mahan*, Influence of sea power in history ; *Doniol*, Histoire de la participation de la France à la libération des États-Unis d'Amérique , *Balch*, Les Français en Amérique pendant la guerre de l'indépendance des États-Unis, and *Chevalier*, Histoire de la Marine française pendant la guerre de l'indépendance américaine.

LECTURE XIV.

PRUSSIA UNDER FREDERICK THE GREAT

Ruined condition of the dominions of Frederick the Great after the close of the Seven Years' War

The internal administration of Frederick , his measures for restoring prosperity , paternal government , Frederick's attitude towards agriculture and commerce , his East India

Company Frederick regards the material prosperity of his people as the chief end of the administration

Frederick's conception of monarchy ; his understanding of the "Aufgeklarte Despotismus" ; he held that his absolutism could be justified only by earnest work for the good of his people.

The administrative machinery created by Frederick the Great , following his father's example, he confides the administration to a bureaucracy composed of men of the middle class and dependent entirely upon himself ; comparison between the French and the Prussian bureaucracies the former hindered, while the latter promoted general prosperity at the close of the 18th century, because Prussia was more backward in civilization than France.

Frederick the Great's attitude towards his nobility , he employs nobles in the army rather than in civil service, and forms them into a military caste.

Frederick the Great and serfdom , he maintains the authority of the nobles upon their estates as part of the compensation for excluding them from political power and as an inducement to them to continue their services in the army ; but he endeavors to abolish, or reduce the harshness of serfdom on the royal domains

Frederick the Great and the Prussian army ; he perceives that the very existence of Prussia depends upon the efficiency of the army , he therefore devotes his attention to the maintenance of a standing army of 200,000 men, a force disproportionate to the size and population of his dominions ; the excellence and the weakness of the Prussian army during the latter years of Frederick's reign ; his camps of exercise ; perfection of drill and discipline maintained in the Prussian army , Frederick's system imitated in other countries

Admiration felt in Germany for the administrative and military system of Frederick the Great , he is thus enabled to draw upon the whole of Germany for able servants, and the Prussian idea of government penetrates beyond the borders of Prussia.

Contrast between the absolutism of Louis XIV of France and of Frederick the Great of Prussia , Louis XIV says, " I am the State,"—Frederick the Great says, " I am the first servant of the State "

Frederick the Great considered as a typical enlightened despot of the 18th century , (1) he undertakes great public works, as the making of canals and roads. the draining of marshes and the improvement of Berlin ; (2) he endeavors to simplify and codify the system of laws in the Codex Fredericiana . (3) he discourages all idea of local or municipal self-government , (4) he insists upon absolute toleration of religious worship while ready to pose as the protector of Protestantism

Frederick the Great differs from the other enlightened despots in his neglect of national higher education and in his refusal to adopt sound economic ideas in collecting his revenue , no general advance in intellectual development or in material prosperity is therefore to be perceived during his reign.

The foreign policy of Frederick the Great may be considered as national and as German , after the close of the Seven Years' War he abandons all hope of a close alliance with England and enters into intimate relations with Catherine II of Russia , with her help he carries out the first partition of Poland, and thus unites Prussia with Brandenburg , close alliance with Russia the keynote of Frederick the Great's national policy , Frederick the Great joins the Armed Neutrality started by the Empress Catherine against England (1780).

Frederick the Great's German policy ; his relations with Maria Theresa and the Emperor Joseph II , the War of the Bavarian Succession or " Potato War" , on the death of Maximilian Joseph, Elector of Bavaria (30 Dec 1777), the succession passed to the Elector Palatine, Charles Theodore, who is induced to cede Eastern Bavaria to Austria in return for a guarantee of the rest , Frederick the Great intervened, basing his interference on the rights of the princes of the

Empire ; a Prussian army invades Bohemia (1779), but no
battle takes place , France, engaged in the War of American
Independence against England, declines to interfere to help
Austria, and eventually, under the mediation of France and
Russia, the Bavarian question is settled by the Treaty of
Teschen (13 May, 1779)

By the Treaty of Teschen, Charles, Duke of Zweibrucken
or Deux-Ponts, was recognized as heir to both the Electorates
of the childless Charles Theodore, Austria received the district between Passau and Landshut, while Frederick the
Great was guaranteed the succession to Anspach and Baireuth

The schemes of Joseph II upon Bavaria induce Frederick
the Great at the close of his reign once more to stand forth
as defender of the rights of the Empire , Joseph II proposed to cede the Catholic Netherlands to Charles Theodore
in exchange for Bavaria ; to thwart this scheme Frederick
the Great in 1785 formed the Furstenbund or League of
Princes for the maintenance of the constitution of the Empire
as established by the treaties of Westphalia ; Joseph II forced
to abandon his scheme   -

Death of Frederick the Great (17 Aug , 1786).

Extension of the Hohenzollern dominions during his
reign , annexation of Silesia (1742), succession to East
Friesland under grant of Joseph I (1744) and acquirement of
royal Prussia at the first partition of Poland (1773).

Increase of the power of Prussia during his reign ; Prussia ceases to be a merely German state and becomes an
European Power

Prussia becomes, since the battle of Rossbach, the state
to which believers in the unity of Germany looked for inspiration and guidance

Character of Frederick the Great ; he is the typical monarch of the 18th as Louis XIV is of the 17th century

Authorities : For the internal development of Prussia during the
reign of Frederick the Great, see the general works by *Berner, Stenzel,
Droysen, Ranke, Philippson, Bornhak, Isaacsohn, Stadelmann,* and
Cavaignac, cited under Lecture V, with the special works on Freder-

icy by *Koser* and others, cited under Lectures VI, VII, VIII and X, and *Oncken*, Die Zeitalter Friedrichs des Grossen, *Lavisse*, Études sur l'histoire de Prusse, *Reimann*, Abhandlungen zur Geschichte Friedrichs des Grossen The PRIMARY AUTHORITIES are still Frederick's own Works, h s Politische Korrespondenz, ed *Koser*, etc, and the State Papers published by the Prussian government For his latter years see *Reimann*, Geschichte des Bairischen Erbfolgekrieges, *Taysen*, Die Militarische Thatigkeit Friedrichs des Grossen wahrend seines letzten Lebensjahres, *Ranke*, Die Deutschen Machte und der Furstenbund (in his Werke, Vols xxxi, xxxii), *G Wolf*, Œsterreich und Preussen, 1780-90, and *C W von Dohm*, Denkwurdigkeiten and Über der Deutschen Furstenbund For his personality, see in addition to *Carlyle*, History of Frederick the Great, *Lavisse*, La jeunesse du grand Frédéric and Le grand Frédéric avant l'avànement, *De Catt*, Memoiren, ed *Koser*, and *Denoiresterres*, Voltaire et Frédéric II For a contemporary account of the actual condition of Prussia and the working of the government, see *Mirabeau* (and *Mauvillon*), De la Monarchie prussienne sous Frédéric le Grand

---

LECTURE XV.

RUSSIA UNDER CATHERINE THE GREAT

Catherine's reforms in the internal administration of the Russian Empire, she follows the ideas of Peter the Great in forming a bureaucratic system entirely dependent upon the will of the ruler and consisting chiefly of foreigners, but she preserves the attachment of the people by pursuing purely Russian aims of territorial expansion

Catherine summons an assembly from all parts and all classes of the Empire to draw up a code of laws, but Russia was not sufficiently advanced in civilization for such a benefit; nevertheless, something is done to systematize the administration of justice.

Catherine's great public works; she builds canals, and improves agriculture and means of communication, she encourages commerce and manufactures

Catherine and the intellectual development of Russia ; she founds the Academy of Sciences in St Petersburg and encourages foreigners to visit and describe her country , like Frederick the Great she keeps in touch with the intellectual movement of Western Europe , her friendship with Diderot and correspondence with Grimm

Attitude of Catherine towards serfdom , she endeavors to regulate but not to abolish it ; her patronage of the middle classes

Catherine's method of government , she keeps the direction of affairs in her own hands , her diligence and insight , her attitude towards her ministers and her lovers

Catherine and her court ; she makes use of her discarded lovers in the management of affairs , the importance of the Orlovs and of Potemkin , her wisdom in selecting her lovers from among the Russians and not from foreigners

Catherine's zeal in carrying out the plans of Peter the Great and in fulfilling the ambitions of the Russian people in foreign politics keeps the Russians, and even the members of the Old Russian Party, faithful to her in spite of her being a German and of her introduction of Western ideas , her adherence to Russian ideals necessary for the maintenance of her power

The foreign policy of Catherine the Great after the first partition of Poland and the Treaty of Kutschuk Kainardji (1774) , Catherine remains on good terms with Frederick the Great, and expects the assistance of Prussia in the further partition of Poland, but she looks to Austria for assistance in the final overthrow of the Turks

Catherine's attitude towards England and France , the Armed Neutrality (1780) , the embassy of Ségur

Catherine and Joseph II ; the interview of Mohilev (1780) ; Catherine, believing the Turkish question more pressing than the Polish question, enters into a close alliance with Austria , Joseph II agrees in the hope of separating Russia from Prussia , gradual alienation of Catherine from Prussia , effect of the death of Frederick the Great (1756)

The policy of Potemkin , after being the favorite of Catherine from 1774 to 1776, he becomes her chief executive agent , he desires to overthrow the Turks and conquer Constantinople ; the Turks by the intervention of Vergennes permit the Russians free navigation in the Black Sea (1779)

Potemkin conquers the rising of Cossacks and Tartars under Pugatchev and, in 1783, conquers the Crimea which had been declared an independent state by the treaty of Kutschuk Kainardji , Catherine's famous journey to the Crimea (1787) ; Catherine proposes a Quadruple Alliance of Russia, Austria, France and Spain

The Turks declare war against Russia (Aug , 1787) , Joseph II comes to the help of Russia (1788) ; campaign of 1787) . Suvórov repulses the Turkish attack on the Crimea . campaign of 1788 ; the Austrians under Loudon take Dubitza, and under Coburg with the help of the Russians take Choczim , the Russians under Potemkin storm Ochákov (6 Dec) , Pitt prepares an English fleet , Gustávus III of Sweden declares war against Russia and invades Finland , campaign of 1789 , death of the Sultan Abdul Hamid, and accession of Selim III (7 Apr) , the Turks defeated by the Austrians and Russians at Foksany (31 July) and on the Rymnik ; the Austrians under Loudon take Belgrade (9 Oct) and under Coburg take Bucharest ; the Russians under Potemkin defeat the Turks at Tobac and take Bender , campaign of 1790 ; Coburg takes Orsova and an armistice as made between the Austrians and Turks at Giurgevo (19 Sept.) ; the Russian fleet is defeated by the Swedes at Svenska Sound (9 July), and the Treaty of Verela is signed between Sweden and Russia (14 Aug) , the Russians take Ismail (20 Dec.) ; campaign of 1791 ,·the Austrians make peace with the Turks at Sistova (4 Aug) , Catherine continues the war alone , the Russians under Repnin defeat the Turks at Matchin (9 July) , negotiations for peace

By the Treaty of Jassy (9 Jan., 1792) peace is made between Russia and the Turks by which Russia retains Ochákov and the coast line between the mouths of the Bug and the Dinestar

Political history of the war with the Turks , the attitude of Frederick William II of Prussia ; causes of the Swedish war , the attitude of England under Pitt , change in the position of affairs caused by the death of Joseph II and the accession of Leopold II (1790) , Catherine makes peace with the Turks in order to have her hands free to deal with Poland , death of Potemkin (16 Oct , 1791)

Importance of Catherine's foreign policy in maintaining her position in Russia , she brings Russia forward more prominently as a European power ; changing phases of the Eastern question.

Catherine's claim to be considered one of the typical enlightened despots of the 18th century , her difficulties and advantages.

Authorities : For short accounts of the reign of Catherine see *Morfill*, Story of Russia, and *Rambaud*, Histoire de la Russie, translated by *Lang* and for a lively account of her personality and life, *Waliszewski*, Le roman d'une impératrice, and Autour d'un trône   Among SECONDARY WORKS should be noticed, in addition to those cited under Lecture X, *Bruckner*, Katharina die Zweite , *Bilbassof*, Geschichte Katharina II, and *Herrmann*, Geschichte des russischen Staates   Of PRIMARY AUTHORITIES, *Ségur*, Mémoires , *Arneth*, Joseph II und Katharina von Russland   ihr Briefwechsel, Catharine's Correspondance avec Grimm, and the papers contained in the Russian ''Sbornik,'' are most accessible , *Beer*, Die orientalische Politik Œsterreichs seit 1774, analyzes the policy of Austria during the latter part of Catherine's reign, and the Turkish side can be read in *Von Hammer*, Histoire de l'empire ottoman, and *Zinkeisen*, Geschichte des osmanischen Reichs

LECTURE XVI.

THE EMPEROR JOSEPH II.

The administration of the Austrian dominions under Maria Theresa , her maintenance and even encouragement of local liberties and local self-government so long as they did not interfere with the ascendancy of the Catholic church , for this reason the Catholic Netherlands and the Milanese were given greater independence than Bohemia, where Czech ideas were identified with Protestantism, contentment of the scattered provinces of the House of Hapsburg under the rule of Maria Theresa, personal admiration and enthusiasm felt for her character

The conservatism of Maria Theresa in administration ; her husband, the Emperor Francis, puts order into the finances, Kaunitz manages foreign affairs ; attempt made to codify the laws, encouragement of foreign commerce, resurrection of the Ostend Company with Trieste for its headquarters

Foreign policy of Maria Theresa, her hatred of Frederick the Great, the Austro-French alliance ; its results for Austria, her share in the partition of Poland, her Italian policy, she makes use of her family to support Austrian influence abroad, thus her second son Leopold becomes Grand Duke of Tuscany, the third Ferdinand Governor-General of Lombardy and by marriage heir to the Duchy of Modena, the fourth Maximilian Elector-Archbishop of Cologne, while of her daughters Maria Carolina marries Ferdinand IV, King of the Two Sicilies, Maria Amelia, Ferdinand Duke of Parma, and Marie Antoinette, Louis XVI of France, and Maria Christina, Duchess of Saxe-Teschen, governs the Austrian Netherlands

On the death of the Emperor Francis I (18 Aug, 1765), the eldest son, Joseph II, is elected Emperor, while his second son, the Archduke Leopold, succeeds as Grand Duke of Tuscany

Character and training of Joseph II : for fifteen years he holds the position of Emperor without being ruler of the Austrian dominions, difficulties of this position, he endeavors to make the power of the Emperor more of a reality (see Lecture XIX) ; his interference in foreign affairs, his admiration for Frederick the Great followed by a still greater admiration for the Empress Catherine ; his share in the first partition of Poland and in the War of the Bavarian Succession, Maria Theresa checks his wish to effect internal reforms

Death of Maria Theresa (29 Nov., 1780) and accession of Joseph II to the Austrian dominions

The Emperor Joseph II in many ways the most typical of the enlightened despots, his personality, his ardent desire to improve the condition of his people, the three vices which led to the failure of his schemes for reform, (1) his desire to do everything *for* the people and not *by* the people : (2) his wish to weld the Austrian dominions into a homogeneous realm like France, or an administrative entity like Prussia and Russia, (3) the rapidity with which he forced his reforms on the people without any preparation.

Joseph II's national reforms . he desires to unify the administration of his dominions ; he makes German the official language in the home dominions of the House of Hapsburg ; he endeavors to destroy all local franchises and to establish the same system throughout his dominions, his efforts for administrative and judicial unity and regularity.

Joseph II's religious reforms · he issues an edict of tolerance permitting freedom of thought and worship, the visit of Pope Pius VI to Vienna (1782) ; Joseph II suppresses numerous convents and certain religious orders, and endeavors to reform the administration of the Church, he frees the Jews from their disabilities and permits them even to enter the army ; he endeavors to make education secular, and to take it out of the hands of the church.

Joseph II's attack upon infringements of personal liberty he abolishes serfdom in Hungary (22 Aug , 1785), and inaugurates a system for removing feudal burdens and forced labor, he abolishes all guilds and corporations interfering with freedom of labor

Joseph II's efforts to improve the intellectual condition of his people he establishes a system of primary education, and frees the press from the censorship

Joseph II's encouragement of public works, and improvement of means of communication.

Joseph II's encouragement of trade and commerce ; his endeavors to obtain from the Dutch the freedom of the River Scheldt

The result of Joseph II's reforms was to rouse discontent and even rebellion throughout his dominions; the Hungarian magnates were disgusted at his freeing the serfs, and the Magyars at his attempts at Germanization; the Czechs in Bohemia were apprehensive that his reforms would crush them further, the Tyrolese were in a ferment at his measures against the Church, and the Belgians were forced into open rebellion, both by his interference with their local government, and by his measures against the Catholic Church

In spite of the seething discontent in his own dominions, Joseph II pursued an active German and foreign policy

The German policy of Joseph II, he endeavors to make the Empire a reality; fears of the German princes at this action, his attempt to create a German church practically independent of the Papacy, the suspicion created that his German policy was to promote only the power of Austria heightened by his proposal to exchange the Austrian Netherlands for Bavaria, this scheme thwarted by the formation of the Furstenbund by Frederick the Great (1785)

Joseph II's Dutch policy he endeavors, while the Protestant Netherlands are torn by the struggle between the Stadtholder and the Republican party, to induce the Dutch to give up the Barrier fortresses and to free the Scheldt to commerce, by the treaty of Fontainebleau (Nov, 1785) the Barrier fortresses are given up by the mediation of France, but the closing of the Scheldt is maintained, effect of Joseph II's Dutch policy on England, it leads to the hearty support of the House of Orange and indirectly to the formation of the Triple Alliance between England, Prussia, and the United Provinces (1788)

Joseph II's Russian policy; his admiration for the Empress Catherine leads him to engage, while his dominions were in almost open insurrection, in war with the Turks.

Position of the Eastern Question during the reign of Joseph II, attitude of the Triple Alliance towards the schemes of Joseph and Catherine

Importance of the reign of Joseph II, contrast between his activity and endeavor to promote internal reforms with

the attitude taken in France by his brother-in-law, Louis
XVI

Authorities: On the policy and government of Maria Theresa during the latter years of her reign, see *Arneth*, Geschichte Maria Theresias, *A Wolf*, Œsterreich unter Maria Theresia, and the invaluable
collections of letters contained in *Arneth*, Maria Theresia und Joseph
II . Ihr Correspondenz sammt Briefen Josephs an seinen Bruder Leopold, and Briefe der Kaiserin Maria Theresia an ihre Kinder und
Freunde, and in *Arneth* and *Geffroy*, Correspondance secrète entre
Marie Thérèse et le Comte de Mercy-Argenteau avec les lettres de Marie Thérèse et Marie Antoinette   For the reign of Joseph II see *Huber*,
Geschichte Josephs II , *Gross-Hoffinger*, Leben und Regierungsge-
schichte Josephs II , *Paganel*, Histoire de Joseph II ' *Von Hock* and
Bidermann, Der Œsterreichische Staatsrath , *G Wolf*, Œsterreich
und Preussen, 1780–1790, Das Unterrichtswesen in Œsterreich unter
Josef II. and Josefina , *Ziegler*, Die politische Reformbewegung in
Siebenburgen in der Zeit Josephs II und Leopold II , *Frank*, Das Tole-
ranz-Patent Kaiser Joseph II , *Schlitter*, Die Reise des Papstes Pius VI
nach Wien (Fontes rerum Austriacarum, Vol cccxxii) , *Beer*, Die
orientalische Politik Œsterreichs seit 1774 , *Lindner*, Die Aufhebung
der Kloster in Deutsch-Tirol, 1782 87 : Ein Beitrag zur Geschichte
Kaiser Josefs II, and *Brunner*, Josef II Charakteristik seines Lebens
und seines Kirchenreform   For this reign there are also several invaluable collections of letters   *Arneth*, Joseph II und Leopold von Tos-
cana · Ihr Briefwechsel von 1781–90, Joseph II und Katharina von
Russland Ihr Briefwechsel , and Marie Antoinette, Joseph II und Leopold II Ihr Briefwechsel , *Arneth* and *Flammermont*, Corréspond-
ance secrète du Comte de Mercy-Argenteau avec l'empereur Joseph
II et le prince de Kaunitz , *Beer*, Joseph II, Leopold II und Kaunitz ,
Ihr Briefwechsel, and *Brunner*, Correspondance intime de l'empereur
Joseph II avec le comte de Cobenzl et le prince de Kaunitz.

LECTURE XVII.

THE NORTHERN COUNTRIES OF EUROPE IN 1789

The situation in Prussia at the death of Frederick the
Great (1786) , the character of his nephew and successor,
Frederick William II ; the internal policy of the new king ;
he maintains the administrative system of his uncle, but in

the place of personal supervision leaves the direction to ministers of mediocre capacity , both the army and the civil service suffer from the change of monarchs , the Prussian court ; influence of favorites, male and female ; Frederick William II's attitude towards religion ; he departs from the toleration which his uncle had established , influence of the Mystics, Rosicrucians, etc. , he revives the censorship of the press ; his extravagance , he spends the treasures accumulated by his uncle , difficulty experienced in raising an adequate revenue.

The foreign policy of Frederick William II , the management of foreign affairs left to Hertzberg, who had been minister under Frederick the Great after the death of Frederick, Catherine II of Russia strengthened her alliance with Austria and proposed to settle the Eastern question by a joint campaign against the Turks , Prussia, deprived of the Russian alliance, desires to renew its former friendship with England , the opportunity afforded by the Dutch Revolution of 1787 ; Pitt and the English Cabinet, in their apprehension of the success of the French party in the Protestant Netherlands and in their uneasiness at the conduct of Joseph II, request Frederick William II, as brother-in-law of the Stadtholder to intervene : the Prussians occupy Amsterdam (1787) ; signature of the Triple Alliance between England, Prussia and the United Provinces (15 April, 1788) , Hertzberg supported by the Triple Alliance prepares to intervene in the settlement of the Eastern question

Condition of the Protestant Netherlands during the 18th century , their commercial prosperity, but decline of their naval and military power , the two parties,—the Republican burghers and the supporters of the House of Orange , the French invasion of 1745 causes William IV of Orange to be declared hereditary Stadtholder (see Lecture VI) ; William IV, and, after his death (1750), the Grand Pensionary Fagel, pursue a policy of close alliance with England , this causes the Republicans to look for help to France ; neutrality of the Dutch during the Seven Years' War , William V undertakes the Stadtholderate in 1766 ; the Republican party especially in Holland desire to help the insurgents in America ; their conduct causes England to declare war (1780) , by the Treaty of Versailles the Dutch cede Negapatam their chief factory in India to England

The Dutch Revolution of 1787 ; William V, the Stadtholder, is accused of favoring the English during the war , riots in the cities ; William V driven from the Hague ; the Dutch Republicans appeal for help to France ; Vergennes, and after him Montmorin, is afraid to send regular troops for fear of renewing the war with England, but permits the raising of a body of French volunteers, the Legion of Maillebois , Pitt resolves to restore the power of the Stadtholder , Harris, . afterwards Lord Malmesbury, induces Frederick William II to restore William V ; the Prussians under the Duke of Brunswick occupy Amsterdam (Sept , 1787) ; the Republican party overthrown ; France dares not oppose Prussia and England , Van der Spiegel made Grand Pensionary , Lord Malmesbury concludes the Triple Alliance between England, Prussia and the United Provinces (15 April, 1788)

History of Denmark during the 18th century ; general characteristics ; the growth of commercial prosperity and of literary and scientific development under the autocracy of enlightened kings and ministers , struggle between Germanizing and nationalizing tendencies ; steady improvement in internal administration ; foreign policy based on a close alliance with England, its territorial policy for the absorption of Holstein

Reign of Christian VI (1730–46) , his Puritanism ; his encouragement of commerce and of the navy ; the Danish East India Company ; chance of uniting Denmark with Sweden lost in 1743 by the election of Adolphus Frederick of Holstein, to be heir to the throne of Sweden instead of the Crown Prince of Denmark.

Reign of Frederick V (1746-66) ; ministry of Bernstorf (1751-70) , danger threatened to Danish independence by the accession of Peter Frederick of Holstein to the throne of Russia as Peter III in 1762 ; the Tsar threatens to destroy Denmark ; Catherine, on usurping the throne of Russia, makes peace with Denmark and eventually allows Holstein to be exchanged for the bishopric of Lubeck and the duchy of Oldenburg, which are granted to the House of Holstein-Gottorp.

Reign of Christian VII (1766–1808), Struensee made chief minister (1770), his character ; his philosophical ideas and use of his power ; he represents the German, philosophical and sweeping reform party, he suppresses the censorship, abolishes the Council of State, reorganizes the army, establishes religious toleration, simplifies the collection of the revenue, encourages education and reforms the law and the judicial administration ; Struensee is accused of being too intimate with the queen, Caroline Matilda, sister of George III of England, a conspiracy is formed against him ; he is arrested (17 Jan , 1772) and executed (28 April, 1782).

Andrew Bernstorf becomes chief minister ; in foreign affairs he clings to the English alliance ; in internal affairs he carries out gradual reforms , insanity of the king , the Queen Dowager forces Bernstorf to resign (1780) and calls Guldberg to office ; Denmark joins the Armed Neutrality , the Crown Prince Frederick seizes the government (1784) and recalls Bernstorf to office ; the reforms of Bernstorf ; he prohibits the negro slave trade and (20 June, 1788) finally abolishes serfdom in Denmark ; the Jews allowed the rights of citizens , by an arrangement with Russia, Denmark attacks Sweden in 1788, but peace is made the same year by the intervention of the Triple Alliance

Sweden in the 18th century , her losses by the treaties, which concluded the Northern War and especially by the Treaty of Nystadt (1721) reduce her to a second rate power , the election of Ulrica Eleanor, younger sister of Charles XII, to the throne of Sweden (1719) instead of the rightful heir, the Duke of Holstein-Gottorp, transfers all power to the Senate, composed of the nobles , powerlessness of the Swedish monarchy ; concentration of executive, legislative and judicial authority in the hands of the nobles ; poverty, rapacity and want of patriotism ; rivalry of two parties—the " Hats " relying on France, bribed by France, looking for the reconquest of Finland and Stettin, and desirous of keeping in touch with Western Europe, and the " Caps " bribed by Russia, and hoping by Russian help to conquer Denmark and Pomerania.

Reign of Ulrica Eleanor (1719-41) and of her husband Frederick of Hesse-Cassel, Frederick I of Sweden (1720-51) , rule of the " Caps " (1721-35) , the " Hats " obtain the mastery (1738) and declare war against Russia at the request of France (4 Aug , 1741) ; the Swedes defeated at Wilmanstrand (3 Sept , 1741) and Helsingfors (1742) ; the " Caps " recover power , by the Treaty of Abo with Russia (23 Jan., 1743) a small cession of territory is made to Russia, and Adolphus Frederick of Holstein, Bishop of Lubeck, is elected heir to the Swedish throne at the request of the Empress Elizabeth in the place of his cousin the rightful heir, Charles Peter of Holstein-Gottorp, who had been chosen as the successor to the Russian throne ; defeat of the plan of the " Hats " to choose the Crown Prince of Denmark and thus unite the Scandinavian countries , personality of Frederick I ; his code of civil law (1736) ; his patronage of Linnæus and foundation of the Academy of Stockholm

Reign of Adolphus Frederick (1751-71) , he is married to a sister of Frederick the Great , he steadily supports the " Caps " who remain in power throughout his reign ; execution of Horn and Brahe, leaders of the " Hats " , at the demand of the Empress Elizabeth of Russia, the Swedes take part in the Seven Years' War and attack Prussia , their part in the war ; after the death of Elizabeth, Adolphus Frederick makes peace with Frederick the Great at Hamburg (20 May, 1762) ; at the instigation of his son, Gustavus, the king makes a vain attempt to overthrow the power of the Nobles and the Senate by an appeal to the Estates of Sweden (1769).

Reign of Gustavus III (1771-92) ; his character and edu-

cation , his travels , his attachment to France , his adoption
of the theory of enlightened despotism , his philosophical
ideas , he resolves to overthrow the oligarchy , he is supported by Vergennes, the French ambassador to Sweden ; by
a *coup d'état* (19 Aug , 1772) he destroys the power of the
Senate and assumes all executive authority leaving the right
of taxation to the Estates , his internal policy , sweeping reforms , he abolishes torture, encourages commerce, improves
the administration and suppresses the censorship of the
press , his difficulties with the Estates ; his autocratic action ,
the foreign policy of Gustavus III , he joins the " armed
neutrality " of 1780 , to win national support he attacks
Russia (1788) , misbehaviour of the Swedish army in Finland , the malcontents led by the king's brother, Charles,
Duke of Sudermania , Sweden attacked by Denmark (1788) ,
coup d'état of 1789 , Gustavus declares a new fundamental
law of Sweden that " the King shall administer the affairs
of State as he thinks best " , victory won by the Swedish
navy at Svenska Sound (9 July, 1790) , Treaty of Verela
signed with Russia (14 Aug , 1790) establishing the *status
quo ante bellum* , in what ways Gustavus III was a typical
enlightened despot of the 18th century

Authorities ; For Prussian history during the early years of Frederick William II see *Philippson*, Geschichte des preussischen Staatswesens vom Tode Friedrichs des Grossen bis zu der Freiheitskriege ,
Ségur, Décade historique, and *Mirabeau*, Histoire secrète de la cour
de Berlin For the Dutch Revolution see *Ségur*, Decade Historique,
Vol III ; *De Witt*, Une invasion prussienne en Hollande en 1787 ;
Bohtlingk, Die hollandische Revolution 1787 und der deutsche Furstenbund, and *Malmesbury*, Diaries and Correspondence For Danish
history see *Allen*, Histoire de Danemark , *Vedel*, Correspondance
ministérielle du comte J H G Bernstorff , the Correspondance entre
Bernstorff et Choiseul , *Host* Graf Struensee und sein Ministerium ,
Wraxall, Life and Times of Caroline Matilda, Queen of Denmark, and
Willich Struensee For the reign of Gustavus III, see *Bain*, Gustavus III and his Contemporaries , *Geffroy*, Gustave III et la cour de
France, *Possell*, Geschichte Gustavs III, and *Sheridan*, History of the
Revolution in Sweden, with for general Swedish history in the 18th
century, the histories of *Fryxell* and of *Geijer*, translated and con-
tinued by *Carlson*.

LECTURE XVIII.

THE SOUTHERN COUNTRIES OF EUROPE IN 1789.

Decreasing commercial importance of the Mediterranean during the 18th century, and consequent decreasing political importance of the countries surrounding it ; the civilization of Europe centers in the northwest of the continent, in England, France and the United Provinces , causes of this change

The condition of the Mediterranean in the 18th century ; ravages of the Barbary Corsairs ; the trade of the Levant absorbed by the English ; effect of their occupation of Gibralter and Minorca , Venice monopolizes the trade of the Adriatic ; position and government of Malta.

. Portugal in the 18th century ; its commercial and political dependence on England after the Methuen Treaty (1703) ; its attempts to get free from the English alliance, and to enter into close relations with Spain ; Spain's desire to annex Portugal ; internal government ; the monarchy depends upon Brazil for its revenue , misgovernment of Brazil , disappearance of Portugeese power in Asia.

The reign of John V (1706-50) ; he endeavors to imitate Louis XIV , the reign of Joseph (1750-77) , the earthquake at Lisbon (1 Nov., 1755) , the administration of Pombal, one of the enlightened ministers of the 18th century ; his internal policy and reforms ; his belief in autocracy ; comparison between Pombal and Richelieu , Pombal takes the lead in the suppression of the Society of Jesus (see Lect. IX) , he abolishes slavery in Portugal (25 May, 1773) but maintains negro slavery in Brazil ; he reforms the administration and the judicial system , he encourages trade and manufactures ; he promotes higher education and reorganizes the University of Coimbra ; Pombal's foreign policy , he desires to throw off the yoke of England , the Spaniards invade Portugal under the terms of the Pacte de Famille , they are defeated with the assistance of England , peace signed between Spain and Portugal (10 Feb., 1763) , reign of Maria I (1777–86), and Pedro III (1777–86) , dismissal of Pombal ; maintenance of his system ; insanity of Maria I, and assumption of the government by Prince John (1788).

Spain in the 18th century , poverty and exhaustion, material and intellectual, of the country , character of the government of the Bourbon kings of Spain , causes of the decline of the power of Spain , the royal revenue derived from the Spanish colonies in America , their misgovernment , attempts made to maintain a strong navy ; abandonment of commerce.

The latter years of the reign of Philip V (1700–46) , the reign of Ferdinand VI (1746–59) ; the influence of Farinelli ; administrations of La Ensenada (1746–56) and of Wall (1756–61) ; the reign of Charles III, formerly king of the Two Sicilies (1759–88) , Charles III one of the typical enlightened despots ; his efforts to improve the condition of Spain , his difficulties ; greatness of his ministers , Aranda and the expulsion of the Jesuits (see Lect IX) ; his internal administration , creation of a navy and encouragement of public works , Campamanes establishes a national system of education ; Jovellanos reforms the judicial system and introduces the ideas of the political economists , Cabarrus founds the Bank of St Charles, establishes a national system of credit and tries to revive commerce , reform of the currency , encouragement of public works and improvement of agriculture ; endeavor of Olavides to restore prosperity in Southern Spain , his overthrow by the Inquisition (1776).

The foreign policy of Charles III , its keynotes—the recovery of Gibraltar and the conquest of Portugal ; Spain attempts to achieve these ends by the signature of the Pacte de Famille with France (10 Aug , 1761) ; Spain declares war against England (1762), and invades Portugal ; defeat of the Spaniards and loss of Havana and Manilla ; by the Treaty of Paris (1763) Spain cedes Florida to England and recovers Havana and Manilla , France cedes Louisiana to Spain in compensation for the loss of Florida , Aranda, min-

ister for foreign affairs (1765-73) and Florida Blanca (1774-
90) ; Spain joins France against England in the War of
American Independence ; part played by the Spanish navy
during the war , by the Treaty of Versailles (1783) Spain
recovers Minorca and Florida ; expeditions made by Spain
against the Barbary corsans

Death of Charles III (12 Dec , 1788) , importance of his
reign , accession of Charles IV

Italy in the 18th century ; Austrian influence practically
supreme (see Lect XVI and Appendix VI) ; Sardinia the
only really national state in Italy

I The Papacy , Pope Pius VI—Braschi, 1775-99 ; his
administration ; his endeavor to drain the Pontine marshes ;
he founds the Clementine Museum , his difficulties with the
Emperor Joseph II, the Grand Duke Leopold and Tanucci ,
his visit to Vienna (1782).

II The Two Sicilies ; the government of Don Carlos,
afterwards Charles III of Spain (1735-59) , the administration of Tanucci, one of the most enlightened ministers of his
time , he abolishes feudalism in Naples , his attempt to reform the laws ; his encouragement of art and education , his
action against the power of the Church ; on the accession of
Charles to the throne of Spain he gives the Two Sicilies to
his third son Ferdinand IV (1759-1825) , during the minority of the young king, Tanucci remains in power , he continues his reforms , he cooperates in the suppression of the
Jesuits and occupies Benevento and Ponte-Corvo (1769), (see
Lect IX) , his struggle with the Papacy and suppression of
useless bishoprics ; after his marriage with Marie Caroline,
daughter of Maria Theresa (1768), the king falls under her
influence and dismisses Tanucci (1776) , the government of
Acton and supremacy of the queen

III Tuscany , the administration of the Grand Duke Leopold, second son of Maria Theresa (1765-90) , his reforms ,
he draws up a code of laws , he reduces the number of bishoprics and monasteries , he improves the material condition of
Tuscany ; his administrative reforms , his judicial reforms ,

he adopts the economic ideas of the Physiocrats and abolishes all restrictions on industry and commerce , his patronage of higher education , he founds the prosperity of Leghorn , he disbands his army , the Grand Duke Leopold the most enlightened of the benevolent despots

IV. Parma , the reign of Don Philip (1749-65) the administration of Du Tillot, Marquis of Felino , his reforms , his patronage of higher education , his action against the monasteries ; his encouragement of manufactures , the reign of Don Ferdinand (1765-1802) ; Du Tillot's scheme of marrying him to the heiress of Modena foiled , he marries Marie Amélie, daughter of Maria Theresa , Du Tillot's struggle with the Papacy and suppression of the Jesuits (see Lect IX) , he suppresses the Inquisition and founds the University of Parma , dismissal of Du Tillot by the influence of the duchess (1771) ; greatness of Du Tillot; ''a great minister of a little state ''

V Modena ; reign of Francesco III (1737-80) ; he supports France in the War of Austrian Succession, but after the peace of Aix-la-Chapelle (1748) becomes Governor-General of Lombardy for Maria Theresa , reign of Hercules III (1780-1803) , his avarice and unpopularity ; his heiress, Maria Beatrice, marries the Archduke Ferdinand, third son of Maria Theresa (1771)

VI Lombardy ; the Milanese and Mantua governed as possessions of Austria by the Duke of Modena, (1748-80) and by the Archduke Ferdinand (1780-96) , enlightened administration of Count Firmian (1759-82) , his reforms and encouragement of higher education

VII Kingdom of Sardinia ; the reign of Charles Emmanuel III (1730-73) ; he pursues the traditional policy of the House of Savoy , his gains in the war of the Polish Succession (see Lect. IV) and in the war of the Austrian Succession (see Lect. VII) , the reign of Victor Amadeus III (1770-96) , his close alliance with France , influenced by the enlightened spirit of the century , his buildings at Nice ; improvement of his army.

VIII. The Republic of Venice; its mastery of the Adriatic and government of the Ionian Islands; conservatism; inferiority of its administration.

IX The Republic of Genoa; its decline and prosperity during the 18th century; insurrection of Corsica (1729), Corsica declares its independence (1733;) election of Theodore, Baron Von Neuhof, as king of Corsica (1736), the Genoese request the assistance of France, the Genoese under Maillebois conquer the Corsicans (1739), the French evacuate Corsica (1743); the second insurrection of the Corsicans, headed by Paoli, also suppressed by French troops (1753–56); third insurrection under Paoli (1759); the Republic of Genoa cedes Corsica to France (1768); conquest of the island by the French

The Turks during the 18th century; steady decline of their power, the relations of the Sublime Porte with France, the wars of the Turks with Austria and Russia (see Lects. III, V, X, and XV); the Treaties of Passarowitz (1718), Belgrade (1739), Kutschuk Kainardji (1774), Sistova (1790), and Jassy (1792), causes of the decay of the Turkish power, the dismemberment of the Turkish dominions becomes one of the two problems of the Eastern question.

Authorities: For Portugal see *Morse Stephens*, Story of Portugal, *Latino Coelho*, Historia de Portugal desde os Fins do XVII Seculo até 1814, *Smith*, Memoirs of the Marquis of Pombal, and *Moore*, Alberoni, Ripperda, and Pombal For Spain see *Coxe*, Memoirs of the Kings of Spain of the House of Bourbon, and the chapters on the century in *Lafuente*, Storia general de España, *Rosseeuw Saint-Hilaire*, Histoire d'Espagne, and *Baumgarten*, Geschichte Spaniens, and the chapters on Spain in *Schlosser*, History of the Eighteenth Century For Italy see *Franchetti*, Storia d'Italia dapo il 1789, *Botta*, Histoire d'Italie depuis 1789 à 1814, *Cantú*, Histoire des Italiens, *Brosch*, Geschichte des Kirchenstaats, *Colletta*, Storia del Reame di Napoli dal 1734 sino al 1825, *Helfert*, Konigin Carolina, and Maria-Carolina Anklagen und Vertheidigung, *Potter*, Vie et mémoires de Scipion Ricci, evêque de Pistoria, *Bianchi*, Storia della Monarchia Piedmontese, *Belgiojoso*, Histoire de la Maison de Savoie, *Costa-Beauregard*, Mémoires historique sur la Maison royale de Savoie, *Daru*, Histoire de Venise, Vols xv–xvii, *Arrighi*, Histoire de Pascal Paoli, *Paoli*,

Lettres, and *Boswell*, Account of Corsica and Memoirs of Paoli For the Turks see *Creasy*, History of the Ottoman Turks , *Von Hammer*, Histoire de l'Empire Ottoman , *Zinkeisen*, Geschichte des Osmanischen Reichs, with *Vandal*, Une Ambassade française en Orient sous Louis XV , la mission du Marquis de Villeneuve, 1728-40 , *Pingaud*, Choiseul Gouffier , *Bonneville de Marsangy*, Le Chevalier de Vergennes, son ambassade à Constantinople, and *Baron de Toll*, Memoirs

---

LECTURE XIX

GERMANY IN 1789

The condition of Germany in 1789 , working out of the principles established by the Treaties of Westphalia , the establishment of the independence of the states of the Empire had destroyed the sense of German nationality , looseness of the bonds which held the Empire together.

History of the Holy Roman Empire in the 18th century conditions produced during the War of the Austrian Succession ; the weakness of the Emperor Charles VII proved how entirely the imperial power depended on the strength of the prince elected ; innovation at the election of 1745, when the envoy of Maria Theresa, as Queen of Bohemia, was permitted to vote , war of execution declared against Frederick the Great (1756), under which an army of imperial troops assisted the French at Rossbach, but when it was proposed to place Frederick under the ban of the Empire in 1758, the Protestant princes threatened to secede ; election of Joseph II as King of the Romans (1764) , he becomes Emperor (1765).

Impotence of the Diet of the Empire which, since 1668, had remained in perpetual session, and consisted only of envoys , in 1788 only fourteen princes of the Empire and eight free cities maintained representatives at Ratisbon , the Imperial Diet had thus ceased to be an operative federal bond of union.

The judicial authority of the Empire ; scandalous inefficiency of the Imperial Tribunal at Wetzlar , Joseph II commences a visitation of the Tribunal (1767–76), but effects no
valid reform ; greater vigor of the Aulic Council, especially
during the reign of Joseph II ; while the Imperial Tribunal
neglects appeals laid before it, the Aulic Council deals more
promptly with cases against princes for misuse of power

Utter inadequacy of the executive power of the Empire ,
mis-management and inefficiency of the Circles ; inability of
the Empire, as such, to carry on war proved in the campaign
of Rossbach , disputes as to raising, commanding, and paying imperial troops ; a Jew contracts for the raising of the
quota of soldiers demanded for the Bishop of Paderborn

Efforts of Joseph II to make the imperial power a reality ,
besides trying to reform the Imperial Tribunal and punishing bad rulers, he tries to take a more active part in the Imperial Diet ; jealousy aroused by this action among the
princes of the Empire , the project of exchanging the Austrian Netherlands for Bavaria increases the apprehension of
the ambitious of Austria ; Frederick the Great seizes the opportunity to form the Fürstenbund, or League of Princes
(23 July, 1785) , importance of this movement ; it accentu-
ates the rivalry between Prussia and Austria for the leadership of Germany ; Joseph's idea of uniting Germany under
the Emperor effectually thwarted.

Joseph II stands forth as the champion of the German
church ; the interference of the Rota at Rome with the me-
tropolitan court at Mayence in the case of an appeal from
Spires, causes a clause to be inserted in the capitulation of
1765, declaring it necessary to check all encroachments on
the liberties of the church in Germany , the action of Joseph
causes the Pope to withdraw his claims ; effect of Joseph
II's action minimized by his persistence in interfering with
the rights of German ecclesiastical princes of the Empire in
Austria

Imitation of the splendour and despotism of Louis XIV
almost universal among German princes during the first half

of the 18th century , followed in the second half by a general adherence to the ideas of enlightened despotism

The leading enlightened despot was Charles Frederick, Margrave of Baden-Baden, and Baden-Durlach , his writings on political economy, and attempt to put economic ideas into practice : he abolishes serfdom (23 July, 1783) and establishes a scheme of primary education , among other princes similarly enlightened may be noted Charles Theodore, Elector Palatine and Elector of Bavaria, who suppressed many convents, and with the help of Count Rumford, promoted reforms, but who persecuted the Protestants ; Frederick Augustus, Elector of Saxony , Clement Wenceslas of Saxony, Elector Archbishop of Trèves, and the Archduke Maximilian, Elector Archbishop of Cologne, who were both tolerant rulers, and Furstenberg, who administered the bishopric of Munster for many years ; against these enlightened princes may be set the Landgrave of Hesse-Cassel, who sold his subjects to England for the American war, the Duke of Wurtemberg, and the Duke of Zweibrucken or Deux-Ponts

Although government in the larger states of Germany was administered on enlightened principles towards the close of the 18th century, the government of the smaller principalities was generally oppressive

In spite of its anarchical political condition, Germany during the 18th century began to recover from the effects of the Thirty Years' War , material improvement ; still greater intellectual development , increase in the number and efficiency of German universities ; growth of German literature , its tendency ; the Court of Weimar

Distant prospect in the 18th century of German unity , Frederick the Great becomes a national hero , distrust of the schemes of Joseph II , admiration felt for the Prussian system of government , Germany hampered in its development by the existence of the Holy Roman Empire and the ideas of the treaties of Westphalia

Authorities : Many of the books cited under Lectures XIV and XVI describe the attitude of Frederick the Great and Joseph II towards

the Empire A bright and concise account of the political and social
condition of Germany on the eve of the French Revolution is given in
Rambaud, Les Français sur le Rhin For a defence of the conditions
of the Empire during the 18th century see *Putter*, Historical Development of the Political Constitution of the Germanic Empire, translated
by Dornford Among the general works on Germany may be noted
Biedermann, Deutschlands politische, materielle, und sociale Zustande
im 18te Jahrhundert , *Hausser*, Deutsche Geschichte vom Tode Friedrichs des Grossen bis zur Grundung des deutschen Bundes , *Heigel*,
Deutsche Geschichte vom Tode Friedrichs des Grossen bis zur Auflo
sung des alten Reichs , *Perthes* Politische Zustande und Personen in
Deutschland zur Zeit der französischen Herrschaft, and *Geismar*, Die
politische Literatur der Deu schen in 18te Jahrhundert , among books
on individual German states see *Hausser*, Uber die Regierung Karl
Friedrichs von Baden , *Kleinschmidt*, Karl Friedrich von Baden , *Erdmannsdorfer*, Politische Korrespondenz Karl Frederichs von Baden ,
Knies, Karl Friedrichs von Baden brieflicher Verkehr mit Mirabeau
und Dupont , *Hausser*, Geschichte des rheinischen Pfalz , *Strippel-
mann*, Beitrage zur Geschichte Hessen-Cassels , *Roth von Schrecken-
stein*, Graf von Normann Ehrenfels, Konigliche Wurttemburgischer
Staatsminister, 1756-1817 , *Schreiber*, Geschichte Baierns, and *Count
Rumford*, Memoirs

LECTURE XX

THE ENLIGHTENED DESPOTS

The most characteristic feature in government of the 18th
century was the existence and the work of the Enlightened
Despots , though differing in the degrees of their enlighten-
ment these rulers showed a common tendency to use their
authority for the good of their people.

The three most important enlightened despots, not because
they were most enlightened, but because of their political
power, were the Emperor Joseph II, the Empress Catherine
II, and Frederick the Great ; their example had much to do
in changing the conception of the duties of monarchy in

Europe ; but they did not originate the movement, and were its most illustrious rather than its most thoroughgoing representatives.

Some of the enlightened despots like the three rulers above mentioned carried on the work of government themselves , others like Joseph of Portugal, Charles III of Spain and Christian VII of Denmark showed their sympathy with the spirit of the times by supporting enlightened ministers, like Pombal, Tanucci, Aranda and Bernstorf

The origin of the conception of enlightened despotism is to be found in the works of the political philosophers, political economists and jurists of the century

The enlightened despots and their ministers were very sensitive to the criticism of the men of letters of their time, and European public opinion had much to do with initiating and encouraging schemes of internal reform , the chief leaders of the intellectual movement in Europe during the century were Frenchmen, and it was to French writers who were practically unable to influence their own country that foreign monarchs looked for advice and applause.

In the 17th century there was a general movement towards giving autocratic power or despotism to monarchs because they best realized the State with its ideals of internal peace and national independence or aggression ; in the 18th century autocratic government sought to justify its further existence on the ground that it could do more good for the people than any other system.

The following points are common to all the enlightened despots or enlightened ministers of the 18th century ; (1) their belief that autocracy logically implied extreme centralization ; (2) in their indifference to racial, national or local characteristics looking on their subjects as people to be governed according to system for their own good whether they liked it or not , (3) in their disregard of class distinctions which led them to select their servants from the most suitable persons and finally destroyed the political power of the aristocracies of the continent , (4) in their freedom from religious intolerance, most of them being sceptics, and regarding religion from an impersonal standpoint

The enlightened despots paid special attention to the following subjects, some of them distinguished themselves more in one line than another ; but their claim to be enlightened rests upon their zeal in more than one of the following particulars :

(1) Attempts to soften or abolish serfdom and other feudal abuses ; in this line Joseph II was most thorough-going of the enlightened despots, but before his time Pombal abolished slavery in Portugal (25 May, 1773) and Tanucci deprived the nobility of Naples of their feudal power, while afterwards Charles Frederick, Margrave of Baden, abolished serfdom in his dominions (23 July, 1783) and Andrew Bernstorff did the same thing in Denmark (20 June, 1788).

(2) Projects of legal and judicial reform ; promulgation of codes of law in which work Frederick the Great of Prussia, the Grand Duke Leopold of Tuscany, Gustavus III of Sweden, and Frederick Augustus Elector of Saxony were especially distinguished ; reforms in judicial administration by the abolition of torture and the introduction of more humane methods of punishment , improvement in this respect was shown in the work of all the enlightened despots owing chiefly to the influence of Voltaire and Beccaria.

(3) Efforts to promote material prosperity by the undertaking of public works, such as draining marshes, making roads and improving harbors , in these directions Catherine II in Russia, Charles III and Aranda in Spain, Pope Pius VI and Victor Amadeus III, King of Sardinia, did the most

(4) Adoption of the ideas of the political economists in collecting their revenues and encouraging manufactures and commerce , several of the enlightened despots were themselves distinguished members of the Physiocratic school, like Charles Frederick, Margrave of Baden, and the Grand Duke Leopold of Tuscany, while the Emperor Joseph II in Austria, Gustavus III in Sweden, Pombal in Portugal, and the Bernstorffs in Denmark were partisans of the new school of political economy.

(5) Encouragement of education, and especially of higher education ; all the enlightened despots established academies of literature, science and art in their capitals, and encouraged learned men , many universities were established or reorganized, notably in Italy, Germany, Denmark and Portugal , systems of national primary education were attempted by Charles Frederick, Margrave of Baden, and by Campomanes in Spain

(6) Freedom of the press established, for instance, by Struensee in Denmark (1770), Gustavus III of Sweden (1784), and by the Emperor Joseph (1783), but their example was not universally followed, though the power of the censorship was everywhere diminished

(7) Deliberate steps taken to diminish the wealth and power of the Church in Roman Catholic states , this is illustrated by the combined attack upon the Jesuits, and by the suppression of the Inquisition in Portugal, Naples, and Parma, and by the measures taken for reducing the number of bishops and monks, by the Emperor Joseph II, the Grand Duke Leopold of Tuscany, Tanucci, and the Elector Charles Theodore of Bavaria

The essential weakness of the enlightened despots was their attempt to do everything without considering whether the people were prepared for reform ; further, there could be no guarantee for the continuance of their work

Great services rendered by the enlightened despots of the 18th century to the cause of civilization and progress in Europe

Authorities: There exists no single book devoted to the history and the work of enlightened despots of the 18th century in Europe, but reference may be made to *Morse Stephens*, European History, 1789-1815, chapter 1, for a sketch of their position, and to *Sorel*, L'Europe et la Révolution française, vol. 1

LECTURE XXI.

THE FRENCH REVOLUTION.

The elections to the States-General

Meeting of the States-General (5 May, 1789) , the struggle between the Orders , the Oath of the Tennis Court (20 June) ; concentration of troops round Paris , capture of the Bastille (14 July)

Anarchy in France ; breakdown of the administrative system , restoration of order by local effort

The Constituent Assembly at Versailles ; the Declaration of the Rights of Man ; the might of 4 August , the questions of the veto and of two chambers ; approach of national bankruptcy ; Necker and Mirabeau.

The King and royal family brought to Paris (6 Oct 1789) . Lafayette *λ .ι., d.οη ⌐ ⌐ ⌐*

The work of the Constituent Assembly , the Constitution of 1791 , division of France into departments ; establishment of local self government ; abolition of the old law courts, and creation of a new judicial system ; the civil constitution of the clergy and its results , the mania for election . weakening of the central executive authority ; abolition of the relics of feudalism ; the financial situation and its results ; first issue of assignats

Political history of the Constituent Assembly ; effective authority passes from the King to the Assembly ; its refusal to openly undertake the responsibility of executive government ; decree of 7 Nov., 1789 , disorganization of the civil administration, of the army and the navy , repression of the military mutiny at Nancy (20 Aug 1790) ; the advice and the plans of Mirabeau , death of Mirabeau (4 Apr., 1791) , nature of the opposition to the Revolution , attitude of the Court , attitude of the Church ; the émigrés ; enthusiasm of the people for the Revolution ; the Federation of 14 July 1790

The foreign policy of the Constituent Assembly ; the debate on the declaration of peace and war , danger of bringing about foreign war ; Mirabeau reporter of the Diplomatic Committee ; the three questions which gave rise to foreign complications , (1) the affair of Avignon ; (2) the affair of Nootka Sound, involving the maintenance of the Pacte de Famille; (3) interference with the rights of the Princes of the Empire in Alsace

Endeavors of Mirabeau to avoid foreign war ; the Queen, Marie Antoinette, looks to her brother, the Emperor Leopold, for help ; the people believe the Court desirous of suppressing the Revolution by calling in foreign invaders

The flight to Varennes (21 June, 1791) ; its effect , definite and open breach between the King and the Revolution , the massacre of the Champ de Mars (17 July, 1791) ; the Emperor Leopold issues the Manifesto of Padua (6 July) , the Declaration of Pilnitz, signed by the Emperor Leopold and Frederick William II of Prussia, threatening France (27 Aug) ; Louis XVI accepts the Constitution of 1791 , dissolution of the Constituent Assembly (21 Sept)

The Legislative Assembly ; influence of the Girondin party ; their war policy , their decrees against the émigrés ; Louis XVI's demand of the Rhenish Electors , French armies raised and directed to the frontier , debates on the expediency of war with Austria in the Legislative Assembly and the Jacobin Club ; declared opposition to the alliance with Austria , the attitude of the Emperor Leopold , war declared by France against Austria (20 Apr , 1792) , the policy of Dumouriez , position of Louis XVI and Marie Antoinette.

Europe and the French Revolution , contemptuous views originally held by foreign rulers who believed that the Revolution would destroy the position of France among the nations ; apprehension felt as time went on in the states bordering on France at the contagion of democratic principles , admiration at first felt in England for the French Revolution , effect of Burke's writings ; attitude towards the French Revolution of the Empress Catherine, Frederick William II of Prussia, and Gustavus III of Sweden.

Effect of the outbreak of war on the development and internal history of the French Revolution

Authorities : The best small books on the Revolution are *Mignet,*
Histoire de la Révolution française, and *Carnot.* La Révolution fran-
çaise For further authorities see the Syllabus of Lectures on the
French Revolution

LECTURE XXII

THE BELGIAN REVOLUTION AND THE POLICY OF THE EMPEROR LEOPOLD

The extent of insurrectionary feeling in the Austrian dominions in 1789 , contrast between the popular movements
in the Austrian dominions and in France , causes of this
contrast ; the position in Hungary

The opposition to the policy of Joseph II reaches its
height in the Austrian Netherlands

The Belgian Revolution of 1789 ; Maria Theresa's government of the Austrian Netherlands , the administrations of
Charles of Lorraine,and of the Archduchess Marie Christine ,
Joseph's policy in the Austrian Netherlands ; he enrages the
Belgians, (1) by his political measures infringing their local
liberties and rights of local self-government · (2) by his religious policy and attempt to introduce secular education ,
stern suppression of riots in the Belgian cities ; Joseph abolishes the constitution of Hainault (31 Jan , 1789), and of Brabant (18 June, 1789) , the Belgian exiles raise an army at
Breda, and are encouraged by the Triple Alliance

The army of Belgian patriots under Van der Mersch cross
the frontier (23 Oct.) ; general insurrection , evacuation of
Brussels (12 Dec), and abandonment of the Catholic Netherlands by the Austrian troops ; meeting of a general con-

vention at Brussels under the presidency of Cardinal Frank-
enberg ; constitution promulgated for the Belgian Republic
(10 Jan , 1790) , formation of the United States of Belgium ;
influence of Van der Noot ; independence declared , death
of the Emperor Joseph (20 Feb., 1790).

The two parties in Belgium,—the Van der Nootists or Statists and the Vonckists or Democrats ; the Statists persecute
the Democrats, and drive their leaders from the country ;
jealousy felt of Van der Noot ; the Emperor Leopold offers
to restore the government of the Austrian Netherlands as it
had existed under Maria Theresa ; the offer rejected by the
Belgian leaders , the country entirely re-occupied by the Austrians without a blow (Nov.–Dec., 1790) ; comparison of the
Belgian with the French Revolution

The Revolution in Liége , the people of Liége rise in insurrection and expel the Prince-Bishop (16–18 Aug , 1789) ;
the Prussians restore the authority of the Bishop (Nov.,
1789) ; the Austrians eventually occupy Liége, at the request
of the princes of the neighboring Circle, and restore the Prince-
Bishop (13 Jan., 1791).

The Emperor Leopold ; condition of Austrian affairs at the
time of his accession (20 Feb , 1790) ; his character and previous career as Grand Duke of Tuscany ; he grants Tuscany
to his second son, the Archduke Ferdinand.

Internal policy of Leopold ; he makes concessions to the
insurgents and malcontents in the different provinces of the
House of Hapsburg , he gives up Joseph's schemes of unifi-
cation and restores local government and liberties to provinces
not in open insurrection ; he maintains Joseph's edict of religious toleration, and many other reforms, and quiets the
fear among the people of further innovation.

Leopold's foreign policy , first period ; he determines to
make peace with the Turks and to frustrate the schemes of
Prussia by breaking up the Triple Alliance , the relations between Prussia and Poland ; the treaty of 29 March, 1790, by
which the Poles agreed to cede Thorn and Dantzig to Prussia
in exchange for the retrocession of Austrian Galicia ; Leopold

breaks up the Triple Alliance ; he convinces England and the Dutch that he would hand over the Austrian Netherlands to France if they supported Prussia in its schemes against Austria ; the Prussians concentrate an army in Silesia and Leopold an army in Bohemia , the Conference of Reichenbach (June, 1790) ; by the Convention of Reichenbach (27 July), Austria engages to make peace with the Turks, the Triple Alliance guarantees the restoration of Austrian authority in the Netherlands, and Prussia promises to withdraw its support to the malcontents in Hungary and Belgium, and to support Leopold's candidature for the imperial throne , great diplomatic victory thus won by Leopold , dismissal of Hertzberg

Leopold and the Turks ; the Armistice of Giurgevo (19 Sept , 1790) , by the Treaty of Sistova (4 Aug 1791) Austria obtains from the Turks Old Orsova and part of Croatia

Leopold and the Hungarians ; the position in Hungary consequent on the measures taken by Joseph ; the Magyar nobles assume semi-independence , and send envoys to Reichenbach , Leopold marches an army to Pesth ; he refuses to grant semi-independence to Hungary ; the Hungarians submit , he is crowned king of Hungary (15 Nov , 1790) , he makes concessions to the pride of the Hungarians

Leopold and the Empire ; he is crowned Emperor (9 Oct., 1790) ; his steps to win back the leadership of the German princes which Prussia had secured by the formation of the Furstenbund in 1785 , he avails himself of the opportunity afforded by the disgust of the German princes at the measures taken by the French Constituent Assembly with regard to the rights of the princes of the Empire in Alsace

Position of Leopold in 1791 ; success of his diplomacy ; he had restored Austria to the position she had lost under Joseph II , he had won the support of the Triple Alliance ; his attitude towards France

Leopold's foreign policy , second period ; his sister Marie Antoinette appeals to him for armed help ; Leopold's dislike for war , the Manifesto of Padua (6 July, 1791) ; Leopold

desires to maintain the power of Louis XVI because the
France–Austrian alliance depended upon it ; he persuades
the king of Prussia to issue the Declaration of Pilnitz with
him (27 Aug , 1791) ; he protests, as Emperor, against the
violation of the rights of the princes of the Empire in Alsace
(3 Dec.) and defends the border princes for sheltering
French émigrés (14 Dec) , in this position he is heartily
supported by the Diet of the Empire , he signs an offensive
and defensive alliance with Frederick William II of Prussia
(2 Feb., 1792) , death of the Emperor Leopold (1 March,
1792)

Assassination of Gustavus III of Sweden (29 March,
1792) ; his brother Charles, Duke of Sudermania, becomes
regent and pursues a neutral policy for Sweden

Parties at the Court of Prussia ; Frederick William II determines to adhere to the alliance with Austria, and after the
death of Leopold becomes the leader of the alliance

Francis II, eldest son of Leopold, crowned Emperor (14
July, 1792) ; he is the last Holy Roman Emperor

Conditions under which the war with France commenced

Authorities : On Belgium in the 18th century and the Belgian Revolution, see *Juste*, Histoire de la Belgique , *Discailles*, Les Pays-Bas
sous le règne de Marie Thérèse , *Piot*, Le règne de Marie Thérèse
dans les Pays Bas autrichiens , *Borgnet*, Histoire des Belges à la fin
du XVIIIième siècle , *A Wolf*, Maria Christina, Erzherzogin von
Œsterreich, and Leopold II und Maria Christina , ihr Briefwechsel,
Magnette, Joseph II et la liberté de l'Escaut, 1781-85 , *Delplace*,
Joseph II et la révolution brabançonne , *Juste*, La révolution brabançonne, Les Vonckistes, La république belge, and Le Comte de Mercy-
Argenteau et l'abandon de la Belgique , *Verhagen*, Le Cardinal de
Franckenberg , *Lorenz*, Kaiser Joseph II und die Belgische Revolution
nach den Papieren des Grafen Murray in his Drei Bucher Geschichte
und Politik ; *Zeissberg*, Zwei Jahre Belgischer Geschichte (in the Sitzungsberichte des kaiserlichen Akademie fur Wissenschaft, 1891) , *Discailles*, Le général Van der Mersch avant la révolution brabançonne ,
Galesloot, Chronique des événements les plus remarquables arrivés à
Bruxelles (1780-1827) , *Gérard*, Rapedius de Berg , mémoires et documents pour servir à l'histoire de la révolution brabançonne , *Vreede*,
Van der Spiegel en zijne tijdgenooten, and *Staes* De Belgische repub-
lick van 1790 On the revolution in Liége see *Borgnet*, Histoire de la

révolution liégeoise de 1789, *C W von Dohm*, Die Lutticher Revolution von 1789, and *Chestret*, Papiers de Jean Remi de Chestret pour servir à l'histoire de la révolution liégeoise For the policy of Leopold see *Schels*, Geschichte Œsterreichs unter der Regierung Leopold II, *Zeissberg*, Kaiser Leopold II (in Allgemeine Deutsche Biographie), *Sorel*, L'Europe et la Révolution française, *Von Sybel*, Geschichte der Revolutionszeit, *Vivenot*, Quellen zur Geschichte der Deutschen Kaiserpolitik Œsterreichs wahrend der Franzosischen Revolutionskriege, *Huffer*, Diplomatische Verhandlungen aus der Zeit der Franzonischen Revolution, an I *Creux*, Pitt et Frédéric Guillaume II, l'Angleterre et la Prusse devant la question d'Orient en 1790 et 1791

LECTURE XXIII.

THE STRUGGLE OF THE FRENCH REPUBLIC AGAINST EUROPE

French reverses at the commencement of the war ; the invasion of the Tuileries (20 June, 1792) ; the proclamation of the Duke of Brunswick ; the plan of campaign, the Austrians invade French Flanders, and the Prussians Lorraine and Champagne, rapid advance of the invaders, excitement in Paris ; general belief in France that the Court sympathized with the invaders, capture of the Tuileries and suspension of the king (10 Aug)

Desperate efforts made for the defence of France, the work of Danton and of Vergniaud ; desertion of Lafayette (20 Aug) ; the Prussians take Verdun (2 Sept) ; the massacres in the prisons of Paris (2–6 Sept.), Dumouriez repulses the Prussians at Valmy (20 Sept) ; the Duke of Brunswick retires from France, gallant defence of Lille.

Meeting of the National Convention (20 Sept, 1792), declaration of the French Republic ; parties in the Convention, the Girondins and the Mountain

Successes of the French armies ; war declared against the

king of Sardinia ; Montesquiou occupies Savoy, and Anselme Nice (Sept., 1792) , Custine invades Germany and takes Spires (1 Oct.), Worms (4 Oct) and Mayence (21 Oct.) ; Dumouriez invades the Austrian Netherlands, defeats the Austrians at Jemappes (6 Nov.), and occupies the whole of Belgium and Liége , excitement and delight caused in France by these successes . Savoy and Nice declared annexed to the French Republic (9 Nov) and Belgium (13 Dec) ; the Revolutionary Propaganda

The position in the Convention , execution of Louis XVI (21 Jan, 1793) ; the Convention increases the number of its enemies , Dumouriez's plan for conquering the United Provinces , France declares war against England and Holland (1 Feb., 1793) , other countries join in the war against France, namely, Spain, Portugal, Tuscany, the Two Sicilies, and eventually on 22 March, the Holy Roman Empire ; only Sweden, Denmark, Switzerland, and the United States of America remain neutral.

Campaign of the Spring and Summer of 1793 ; change in the character of the war , disorganization of the French armies ; the thirteen armies of the Republic , England becomes the paymaster of the coalition , the policy of Pitt and Grenville in England ; Thugut becomes chief minister in Austria, and Haugwitz in Prussia ; the Austrians under the Prince of Coburg, defeat the French at Neerwinden (21 March), and, with the help of the English under the Duke of York, drive the French out of Belgium , desertion of Dumouriez (5 Apr.) , the English and the Austrians invade France and take Valenciennes (28 July) the Prussians take Mayence (22 July) , the Austrians and Imperialists invade Alsace , Toulon occupied by the English and Spaniards (4 Aug) , the Spaniards invade France at both ends of the Pyrenees

Effect of the disasters on the Convention ; establishment of the Revolutionary Tribunal (9 March) and of the first Committee of Public Safety (7 Apr) , struggle between the Girondins and the Mountain ; overthrow of the Girondins

(31 May-2 June) ; outbreak of civil war ; the rising in Normandy , Lyons and Marseilles declare for the Girondins , insurrection in La Vendée ; the Constitution of 1793 ; formation of the Great Committee of Public Safety (July-Sept , 1793) , it establishes the Reign of Terror

The Reign of Terror in France , suspension of the constitution of 1793 and autocracy of the Great Committee , causes of the power of the Great Committee ; its chief means for maintaining its authority ; (1) the Revolutionary Tribunal ; executions in Paris , (2) the Representatives on Mission , their repression of internal disturbances , the Great Committee restores discipline in the army and navy, and concentrates the resources of France for the foreign war ; incidents of the Reign of Terror , the worship of Reason ; the Noyades at Nantes

Campaign of the Autumn and Winter of 1793 , plans of Carnot ; Houchard raises the siege of Dunkirk and defeats the English and Hanoverians at Hondschoten (8 Sept) ; Jourdan raises the siege of Maubeuge and defeats the Austrians at Wattignies (16 Oct) , Hoche defeats the Prussians at the Geisberg (25 Sept) , Pichegru drives the Austrians and Imperialists across the Rhine , Dugommier recovers Toulon (18 Dec) , the Spaniards driven across the frontier ; capture of Lyons (9 Oct.) and defeat of the Vendeans

Opposition to the Great Committee of Public Safety and the Reign of Terror in the Convention and in Paris ; execution of the Hébertists (14 March, 1794) and of the Dantonists (5 April) , increased stringency of the Reign of Terror : the position of Robespierre , the worship of the Supreme Being (7 May)

Campaign of 1794 , victories of the French armies ; Jourdan defeats the English and Austrians at Fleurus (26 June), and with Pichegru occupies Belgium , Moreaux defeats the Prussians at Kaiserslautern and occupies Trèves , the French defeat the Sardinians and invade Spain , the English under Lord Howe defeat the French navy in the battle of 1 June ; the English occupy Corsica.

With the French victories and the repulse of the invaders
the necessity for submitting to the Reign of Terror ceases,
identification of Robespierre and his friends with the Reign
of Terror, overthrow and execution of Robespierre and his
friends on 9 Thermidor (28 July), end of the Reign of Terror, end of the power of the Great Committee of Public
Safety; its method of government retained but the personnel
changed every month.

Characteristics of the Reign of Terror in France, triumph
of the French Republic over the powers of Europe

Authorities : A brief account of the war can be found in *Morse
Stephens*, European History, chapters iii, iv For secondary and primary authorities see Syllabus of Lectures on the French Revolution

LECTURE XXIV

THE SECOND AND THIRD PARTITIONS OF POLAND

The reign of Stanislas Poniatowski

The designs of the Empress Catherine for the further partition of Poland ; the Poles look for help to Prussia which
desires to annex Thorn and Dantzig, the Treaty of Warsaw
(29 March, 1790) ; the action of the Polish envoys at the
Conference of Reichenbach (June, 1790) ; causes of the independent attitude of Poland in 1790

Internal reforms effected in Poland during the reign of
Stanislas, attempts made to create a national army, and to
abolish the feudal army, to establish a national system of
finance, and to provide a national scheme of education, the
aims of the Polish patriots, they desire to make Poland a
state instead of a loose confederation of nobles, attitude of
Russia, Prussia and Austria towards the reform party in
Poland.

Meeting of the Constituent Diet (6 Oct , 1788) , it appoints a committee to draw up a new constitution for Poland, raises the national army to 60,000 men, and decrees a large levy of taxes

The Polish Constitution of 1791 ; it is accepted by the Diet (3 May, 1791) , mainly the work of Kollontai ; it abolished the elective monarchy, the Liberum Veto, the right to confederate and the capitulations , it declared the throne of Poland hereditary in the House of Saxony after the death of Stanislas , it created a regular government conferring the legislative authority on the king, senate, and elected chamber, and the executive authority on the king aided by six ministers responsible to the legislature , the middle classes of the cities were admitted to political rights and allowed to elect deputies to the legislature , the nobility agreed to pay taxes to the extent of ten per cent of their income ; serfdom was not abolished, but the Diet declared its willingness to give all arrangements made between a lord and his serfs for the benefit of the latter the sanction of the law , comparison between the French and the Polish constitutions of 1791

Prussia and Austria at Pilnitz acknowledge the new Polish Constitution, but Catherine of Russia, fearing it would make Poland a strong state, determines to overthrow it , the Confederation of Targovitsa protests against the abolition of the Liberum Veto and the Constitution of 1791 , the Confederates request Catherine to aid them , she issues a manifesto declaring herself the guarantor of the ancient Polish Constitution (18 May, 1792) and orders a Russian army under Suvórov to invade Poland ; the Russians defeat Joseph Poniatowski at Zielencé (18 June) and Kosciuszko at Dubienka (17 July) , Kollontai and the Polish constitutional leaders go into exile ; a new Diet is called which abrogates the Constitution of 1791

Frederick William II of Prussia refuses to aid the Polish patriots and sends a Prussian army into Poland , it was owing to his interests in Poland that he took so slight a part in the war against France after the battle of Valmy .

Second treaty of partition signed by Catherine and Frederick William (4 Jan , 1793) and agreed to by Stanislas and the Polish Diet at Grodno under the pressure of Russian troops (24 Sept , 1793) , by this second partition Russia annexed Minsk, Podolia, Volhynia and Little Russia, while Prussia received Posen, Gnezen, Kalisch and the cities of Dantzig and Thorn , wrath of the Emperor Francis II at receiving no share in the second partition of Poland ; he resolves that the war with the French Republic shall not keep him from looking after Austrian interests in Poland.

The Polish insurrection of 1794 , Kosciuszko raises the standard of national independence at Cracow (23 March) , general insurrection throughout Poland , Kosciuszko defeats the Russians at Raclawice (4 Apr) and occupies Warsaw (19 Apr.) , the Prussians besiege Warsaw (July–Sept., 1794) , retirement of the Prussians ; a Russian army under Suvórov enters Poland ; Kosciuszko defeated and taken prisoner at Maciejawice (12 Oct) ; capture of Warsaw (9 Nov) ; complete overthrow of the patriots

Stanislas Poniatowski removed from Poland (7 Jan , 1795) ; he abdicates (25 Nov. 1795)

Third and final partition of Poland (3 Jan , 1795) , Prussia receives Warsaw and the neighbouring provinces ; Austria receives Cracow and the rest of Galicia , Russia rectifies its frontier as arranged in 1793 ; extinction of Poland as an independent state

Causes of the failure of Poland to maintain her independence , comparison between the Polish insurrection of 1794, and the successful national resistance of France to foreign invaders the same year

Influence of Polish affairs upon the progress of the war against France ; weakening of the Prussian and Austrian armies upon the French frontier , commencement of dissensions between Prussia and Austria.

Authorities: For a short account of the second and third partitions of Poland, see *Morfill*, Story of Poland Consult also *Ferrand*, Les trois démembrements de la Pologne , *Von der Bruggen*, Polens Auflosung , *Smitt*, Suworow und Polens Untergang , *Herrmann*, Die Œsterreichisch-Preussische Allianz von 7 Feb , 1792 und die zweite Theilung Polens , *Zeissberg*, Geschichte der Raumung Belgiens und des Polnischen Aufstandes, 1794 (in the Archiv fur Œsterreichische Geschichte, Vol lxxii) , *Vivenot*, Quellen zur' Geschichte der Deutschen Kaiserpolitik Œsterreichs während der Französischen Revolutionskriege, Vol v; *Sybel*, Geschichte der Revolutionszeit , and *Sorel*, L'Europe et la Révolution française

---

ɔ

LECTURE XXV.

THE TREATIES OF BASLE

The government of the Thermidorians in France ; they continue the system of vigorous organization and centralization initiated by the Great Committee of Public Safety, but discontinue the methods of the Reign of Terror

The internal policy of the Thermidorians ; they retain the supremacy of the Committees and the power of the Deputies on Mission ; rising cry for vengeance against the Terrorists , execution of Carrier (Nov , 1794) ; closing of the Jacobin Club, and repeal of the Law of Maximum (Dec., 1794) ; readmission to the Convention of most of the proscribed Girondins (Dec , 1794), and of the remainder (March, 1795)

Foreign policy of the Thermidorians , the continued victories of the republican armies change the attitude of France from that of a nation fighting for existence to that of a conqueror , change introduced into the character of the war ; Merlin of Douai lays down the bases on which France might honorably make peace (4 Dec , 1794) and the Convention finally abandons the idea of the Republican Propaganda.

The campaign of 1794-5 ; the French under Pichegru conquer the United Provinces ; occupation of Amsterdam ; capture of the Dutch fleet in the Texel , retreat of the Austrians , the remains of the English army under the Duke of York return to England , the Thermidorians refuse to annex the Protestant Netherlands , the Dutch Republicans, who had been exiled in 1787, return , organization of the Batavian Republic , alliance formed between the French and Batavian Republics (March, 1795) , Jourdan defeats the Austrians at Aldenhoven (2 Oct.), and occupies Aix-la-Chapelle, Bonn, Cologne, and Coblentz , two French armies invade Spain, and take Rosas and Vittoria ; defeat of the émigrés landed at Quiberon Bay from English ships (July, 1794).

Result of French victories at home and abroad

Increasing vehemence of the attacks on the Terrorist leaders , the Thermidorians are ousted from power by the returned Girondins and deputies of the Marsh ; action of the Jeunesse Dorée in Paris , insurrections of 12 Germinal (1 April, 1795), and 1 Prairial (20 May) , disarmament of the Faubourg Saint-Antoine , reaction in the provinces against the Terrorists , preparations made for drawing up a new constitution for France.

Changed attitude of Europe toward France , general readiness to make peace with France, now that she had abandoned the Revolutionary Propaganda, and had shown herself too formidable to be conquered , commencement of negotiations for peace ; treaty of peace signed with Tuscany (9 Feb., 1795) ; the French Republic thus received into the comity of nations

The negotiations at Basle ; importance of the demands made by the French Republic , the question of the natural limits of France , treaty of peace signed with Prussia (5 April, 1795) , line of demarcation established protecting the Northern States of Germany from French invasion , importance of this provision, which placed North Germany under obligations to Prussia , by a secret article Prussia recognized the river Rhine as a natural boundary of France, and promised to cede her possessions on the left bank in exchange for ecclesiastical states to be secularized in Germany

The Treaty of Basle with Prussia followed by other treaties

s gued at the same place, the most important, the treaty of peace with Spain (22 July) ; the political situation in Spain, power of Godoy, the queen's lover, who is created Prince of the Peace

Other treaties signed at Basle ; with Hesse-Cassel (29 Aug), and other German states

Importance of the Treaties of Basle in the history of Europe, Prussia's assent to the proposition that the French boundary should be the Rhine, thus diminishing the Empire, and her readiness to further break up the Empire by annexing ecclesiastical territory.

Austria's reasons for continuing the war ; the policy of Thugut, France enters into friendly negotiations for the exchange of Madame Royale, daughter of Louis XVI.

Persistence of England in continuing the war ; influence of the advice of the French émigrés ; popular feeling in England with regard to the French Republic ; Pitt and Grenville refuse to believe in the stability of the government of France

Work of the Thermidorians, sudden change in the position of France from an invaded country, seemingly on the point of dissolution, to a victorious and triumphant nation

Authorities : For authorities on the internal history of France during the rule of the Thermidorians, see Syllabus of Lectures on the French Revolution . For the Treaties of Basle and the events leading to them, see *Sorel*, Europe et la Révolution française and La Paix de Bâle (Revue Historique, Vols v-vii), *Hausser*, Deutsche Geschichte vom Tode Friedrichs des Grossen, *Sybel*, Geschichte der Revolutionszeit, *Gentz*, Ueber den Ursprung und Charakter des Kriegs gegen die Französische Revolution, *Zeissberg*, Zur Deutsche Kaiserpolitik Œsterreichs. ein Beitrag zur Geschichte des Revolutionsjahre, 1795 (Sitzungsberichte der Kaiserlichen Akademie der Wissenschaften, 1889), *Hüffer*, Diplomatische Verhandlungen aus der Zeit der Französischen Revolution, *Vivenot*, Quellen zur Geschichte der Deutschen Kaiserpolitik Œsterreichs während der Französischen Revolutionskriege, Vertrauliche Briefe des Freiherrn von Thugut, Herzog Albrecht von Sachsen-Teschen als Reichsfeldmarschall, and Thugut, Clerfait und Wurmser, *Witzleben*, Prinz Friedrich Josias von Coburg-Saalfeld, Herzog zu Sachsen, and above all, *Kaulek*, Papiers de Barthélemy, Ambassadeur de France en Suisse, 1792-97.

LECTURE XXVI.

THE FRENCH DIRECTORY AND THE FIRST VICTORIES OF BONAPARTE

The Constitution of the year III (1795), its most important feature, the entire separation of the executive and legislative authority, the former being confided to five Directors, the latter to two Chambers, the Council of Ancients, and the Council of Five Hundred.

The Convention resolves that the Directors and two-thirds of the first legislature, under the new constitution, shall be elected from among themselves discontent expressed among those who wished to suppress the Terrorists at this resolution, insurrection of 13 Vendémiaire (5 Oct, 1795) in Paris, and its suppression.

The first Directors Barras, Reubell, Revellière-Lépeaux Carnot, and Letourneur

The foreign policy of the Directory, adoption of the principles of the Thermidorians, readiness to make peace on the terms of receiving the natural boundaries of France, the only enemies of the Republic left were England, Austria and Sardinia ; the treasonable intrigues of Pichegru, the activity of the émigrés ; exchange of Madame Royale (20 Dec, 1795), attitude of Austria, England, Prussia, Spain, and the smaller states of Europe toward the French Republic, the Directory endeavors to form an alliance with Prussia and Spain

Failure of the French armies upon the Rhine in the winter campaign of 1795, owing to the treachery of Pichegru, Napoleon Bonaparte takes command of the army of Italy (27 March, 1796), his previous career

Campaign of 1796 in Italy, first stage, Bonaparte turns the Maritime Alps and separates the Sardinian from the Austrian army, he defeats the Sardinians under Colli at Montenotte (12 April), Millesimo (13 April), Dego (15 April), Ceva (16 April), and Mondovi (22 April) ; Victor Amadeus III of Sardinia signs the Armistice of Cherasco (28 April), and subsequently makes peace with the French Republic, ceding Savoy and Nice to France

Campaign of 1796 in Italy , second stage ; Bonaparte crosses the Po, and (10 May) forces the passage of the Adda at the bridge of Lodi ; the Austrians evacuate Lombardy , Bonaparte occupies Milan and besieges Mantua , the Dukes of Parma and of Modena are forced to sue for peace ; Bonaparte occupies the Legations of Ferrara and Bologna , Pope Pius VI signs the Armistice of Foligno (24 June).

Campaign of 1796 in Italy ; third stage , an Austrian army under Wurmser, invades Italy for the relief of Mantua , Bonaparte breaks up the siege and defeats the Austrians at Castiglione (5 Aug) ; Wurmser retreats, but in the following month enters Italy by the valley of the Brenta, and throws himself into Mantua , Bonaparte summons delegates from the whole of Northern Italy to meet at Milan

Campaign of 1796 in Italy ; fourth stage , the Emperor Francis II makes a great effort to recover North Italy and appeals to his people , the Austrian army under Alvinzi invades by the Brenta ; the French repulsed at Caldiero (12 Nov) ; Bonaparte wins the battle of Arcola (16 Nov.) ; retreat of the Austrians.

Campaign of 1796 in Italy , fifth stage , the Austrians make a last effort to relieve Mantua by way of Lake Garda ; Bonaparte defeats Alvinzi at Rivoli (14 Jan , 1797) , surrender of Mantua (2 Feb , 1797) ; Bonaparte advances on Rome ; Pope Pius VI signs the Treaty of Tolentino (19 Feb , 1797)

Effect of the campaign of 1796 on Italy, on Austria, and on Europe ; its effect on the position of the Directors in France,

Campaign of 1796 in Germany ; Jourdan and Moreau invade Southern Germany, but are out-manœuvred and driven back by the Archduke Charles , famous retreat of Moreau ; effect of this campaign in Germany , Frederick William II of Prussia signs a secret supplement to the Treaty of Basle (5 Aug , 1796 , Baden, Wurtemburg, and Bavaria enter into negotiation with the French Republic

Charles IV of Spain under the influence of Godoy signs an offensive and defensive treaty with the French Republic at San Ildefonso (19 Aug , 1796), and declares war against England ; the English abandon Corsica , Sir John Jervis defeats the French and Spanish fleet off Cape St Vincent (14 Feb., 1797) ; the English send an army under Stuart to defend Portugal against Spain.

The Directory and England ; Lord Malmesbury sent to Paris to discuss the bases of peace (Nov –Dec 1796) ; stormy weather foils Hoche's expedition for the invasion of Ireland.

Internal policy of the Directory , Hoche pacifies Brittany and La Vendée ; financial condition of France

Death of the Empress Catherine of Russia (17 Nov , 1796) , the Emperor Paul withdraws all assistance from the enemies of France

Campaign of 1797 , Bonaparte invades the Tyrol and approaches Vienna ; preliminaries of peace between France and Austria signed at Leoben (17 April, 1797), by which Austria agreed to recognize the Rhine as the frontier of France which involved the cession of Belgium, and to take Venice in exchange for Lombardy ; a Congress was determined on at Rastadt to arrange terms of peace between the French Republic and the Empire.

The elections of 1797 in France ; Barthélemy elected a Director in the place of Letourneur ; the majority of the legislature opposes the Directors ; negotiations for peace with England which had been commenced at Lille broken off , Hoche and Bonaparte support the Directors ; the *Coup d'état* of 18 Fructidor (4 Sept , 1797) ; Merlin of Douai and François de Neufchâteau elected Directors in the places of Carnot and Barthélemy ; death of Hoche (15 Sept)

Bonaparte's policy in Italy , he occupies Venice , he dissolves the ancient government of Genoa and forms the Ligurian Republic , he forms the Northern Italian States, except Piedmont into the Cisalpine Republic (9 July) ; he annexes the Ionian Islands ; effect of Bonaparte's Italian policy.

Signature of the treaty of Campo-Formio between Austria and France (17 Oct , 1797); the Preliminaries of Leoben followed , its open and its secret clauses ; capture of Mayence by Hatry (29 Dec , 1797).

Critical position of England in 1797 : she remains the only nation in arms against the French Republic , the mutiny at the Nore and other naval mutinies ; Duncan defeats the Dutch fleet off Camperdown (11 Oct , 1797).

Bonaparte arrives in Paris (5 Dec , 1797) , he requests permission to conduct an expedition to Egypt

Authorities : As a small book, *Morse Stephens*, European History, 1789-1815, chapter v There exists no satisfactory SECONDARY HISTORY of the Directory , *Barante*, Histoire du Directoire is out of date, but remains the only elaborate attempt to treat the period consecutively , reference may be made to *Thibaudeau*, Mémoires sur la Convention et le Directoire, and much valuable light is thrown by the Prussian despatches published in *Bailleu*, Preussen und Frankreich von 1795-1807 For Napoleon's campaign in Italy, the account given by *Thiers*, Histoire de la Révolution Française is unsurpassed for graphic power and substantial accuracy , for a shorter sketch see *Jung*, Histoire de Bonaparte, and *Lanfrey*, Histoire de Napoleon , for the re settlement of Italy, *Gaffarel*, Bonaparte et les républiques Italiennes and for military details, *Jomini*, Histoire critique et Militaire des Campagnes de la Révolution de 1792 à 1801, and *Pommereul*, Campagnes du général Bonaparte en Italie The primary authority is the Correspondance de Napoleon

---

LECTURE XXVII.

THE SECOND COALITION AGAINST THE FRENCH REPUBLIC

Bonaparte's expedition to Egypt (1798) ; he takes Malta (12 June) ; he reaches Egypt, occupies Alexandria (1 July), wins the battle of the Pyramids (21 July) and occupies Cairo (24 July) , Nelson destroys the French fleet at the Battle of the Nile (1 Aug) , Bonaparte and his army thus prevented from leaving Egypt.

Treilhard elected a Director in the place of François de Neufchâteau (May, 1798)

Foreign policy of the Directors, their efforts against England, the expedition to Egypt intended for the overthrow of England's power in Asia; the intrigues of the Directors in Ireland, they send a force to assist in the Irish insurrection of 1798 under Humbert which surrenders to Cornwallis (Aug., 1798)

Pitt endeavors to form a new coalition against the French Republic.

The position in Prussia; death of Frederick William II and accession of Frederick William III (16 Nov., 1797), character and training of the new king, he dismisses his father's favorites, undertakes reforms, endeavors to put the finances in order and appoints trustworthy ministers, in foreign politics he resolves to maintain absolute neutrality between France and England in spite of the special missions of Thomas Grenville and Sieyès, policy of Haugwitz

The position in Austria, detestation felt for the French by the Austrian people, popularity of the Emperor Francis II, riot in Vienna against the French ambassador Bernadotte (13 April, 1798), Austria entertains the proposals of Pitt for a new coalition

The position in Russia; character of the Emperor Paul; he is ready to abandon the policy of Catherine and to interfere in the affairs of Western Europe, he agrees to join the coalition and to send armies to coöperate with the Austrians and the English

The position in the smaller states of Europe, Sweden, Denmark and the Turks maintain an attitude of friendly neutrality towards France, Portugal requests the withdrawal of the English army under Stuart, it occupies Minorca, Spain remains in close alliance with France

Revolution in Switzerland; the French intervene; formation of the Helvetian Republic (April, 1798).

The French in Italy, murder of General Duphot in Rome (27 Sept., 1797); General Berthier occupies Rome (15 Feb,

1798) : Pope Pius VI leaves Rome ; he is eventually made prisoner by the French and dies at Valence (29 Aug , 1799) , formation of the Roman Republic (Feb., 1798), Ferdinand IV, king of the Two Sicilies, after the news of Nelson's victory of the Nile, drives the French from Rome , General Championnet occupies Rome (15 Dec , 1798), defeats the Neapolitan army, occupies Naples (Jan , 1799), and establishes the Parthenopean Republic , the French occupy Piedmont (Nov., 1798), and Tuscany (March, 1799)

General feeling in Europe at these aggressions of the French Directory , the Second Coalition, freed from the fear of Bonaparte, resolves to act , commencement of war , the French defeated at Stockach (25 March), and at Magnano (5 April), murder of the French plenipotentiaries at Rastadt (28 April, 1799).

Campaign of 1799 in Italy ; a Russian army under Suvórov occupies Milan (28 April), and Turin (27 May), and besieges Genoa , the Russians defeat the French under Macdonald at the Trebbia (17-19 June) ; Ferdinand IV reoccupies Naples , the Austrians occupy Northern Italy ; Suvórov defeats the French under Joubert at Novi (15 Aug), and the Austrians defeat Championnet at Genola (4 Nov) ; the siege of Genoa

Campaign of 1799 in Switzerland , Masséna defeats the Russians under Korsákov at Zurich (26 Sept.) ; Suvórov's attempt to cross the Alps , Masséna compels the Archduke Charles to retire

The campaign of 1799 in Holland , the English under Abercromby and Mitchell seize the remnant of the Dutch fleet in the Texel (27 Aug) ; an English army under the Duke of York, and a Russian army under Hermann, land in Holland ; the invaders are repulsed by General Brune , by the Convention of Alkmaar (18 Oct) the invaders agree to evacuate Holland

Bonaparte's campaign in Syria , he conquers Palestine (Feb , 1799) and lays siege to Acre , he defeats the Turks at Mt. Tabor (16 Apr.) ; he abandons the siege of Acre

(20 May) and retires into Egypt , he defeats the Turks in Egypt and re-establishes French supremacy there , he resolves to return to France without his army

Effect of the campaign of 1799 upon the allied Powers , wrath of the Emperor Paul with the English and the Austrians , he resolves to abandon the Coalition and enters into negotiations with France

Effect of the campaign of 1799 on the position in France , struggle between the Legislature and the Directory , reversal of the condition of affairs in 1797 , Sieyès succeeds Reubell as Director (May, 1799) ; *Coup d'état* of 30 Prairial (18 June, 1799) ; Gohier, Roger Ducos, and Moulin succeed Treilhard, Merlin of Douai and Revellière-Lépeaux as Directors ; the policy of Sieyès and of Talleyrand

Bonaparte escapes the English cruisers in the Mediterranean and reaches France (9 Oct.) and Paris (16 Oct) , he resolves to overthrow the government of the Directory , revolution of 18 Brumaire (9 Nov) ; Bonaparte, Sieyès and Roger Ducos declared provisional Consuls

Effect of the revolution of 18 Brumaire on France and on Europe

Authorities : For a short sketch see *Morse Stephens*, European History, 1789-1815, chapter vi Among larger works based on primary authorities and containing documents, see *Huffer*, Diplomatische Verhandlungen aus der Zeit der Franzosische Revolution and Die Kabinetsregierung in Preussen und Johann Wilhelm Lombard , *Vivenot*, Zur Geschichte des Rastadter Kongresses, *Helfert*, Der Rastadter Gesandtenmord, and *Wertheimer*, Erzherzog Karl und die zweite Koalition bis zum Frieden von Lunéville (Archiv fur Œsterreichische Geschichte, lxvii) For the military history in Europe see *Jomini*, cited under Lecture XXVI , *Bunbury*, Some Passages in the Great War with France, and *Michailowski-Danilewski und Milutin*, Geschichte des Krieges Russlands mit Frankreich im Jahre 1799 , and for Bonaparte's Campaign in Egypt the works on Napoleon cited under Lecture XXVI with *Boulay de la Meurthe*, La Campagne en Egypte en 1798-99 , *Gaffarel*, Bonaparte en Egypte, and *Berthier*, Relation des campagnes du Général Bonaparte en Egypte et en Syrie.

LECTURE XXVIII

THE TREATIES OF LUNÉVILLE AND OF AMIENS

Constitution of the year VIII, executive power assumed by Bonaparte as First Consul; Cambacérès and Le Brun appointed Second and Third Consuls.

The foreign policy of Bonaparte as First Consul; he negotiates with Russia; the Emperor Paul's admiration for Bonaparte; he orders Louis XVIII to leave Russia and proposes that Bonaparte should make himself King of France, Bonaparte negotiates with Prussia Frederick William IV expresses personal admiration for Bonaparte, but refuses to abandon his attitude of neutrality; Bonaparte negotiates with the new Pope, Pius VII—Chiaramonti; he resolves to continue the war with Austria and with England

Bonaparte's campaign of 1800 in Italy, the defence of Genoa by Masséna; surrender of Genoa (4 June); Bonaparte crosses the Alps by the Great St Bernard; battle of Montebello (9 June), Bonaparte utterly defeats the Austrians under Melas at Marengo (14 June, 1800), the French reoccupy the whole of Northern Italy without further fighting, Bonaparte re-establishes the Cisalpine and Ligurian Republics

Campaign of 1800 in Germany, struggle between Moreau and the Archduke Charles, Moreau reaches Munich; Moreau ordered to continue the campaign into the winter, he defeats the Archduke John at Hohenlinden (5 Dec); Macdonald crosses the Splugen and with Brune threatens Vienna, Moreau also approaches Vienna; the Emperor Francis II sues for peace

Signature of the Treaty of Lunéville (9 Feb, 1801); by this treaty the Emperor Francis again acknowledges the Rhine to be the frontier of France and recognizes the Cisalpine Republic, Austria again receives Venice; the Duke of Modena, whose heiress had married the Austrian Archduke Ferdinand, receives the Breisgau in exchange for his duchy

which is absorbed in the Cisalpine Republic, Tuscany is
converted into the Kingdom of Etruria and conferred upon
the son of the Duke of Parma, a relative of the King of Spain,
and the Grand Duke Ferdinand is promised a principality in
Germany, Ferdinand IV, King of the Two Sicilies, was allowed to retain his dominions and the Pope received back the
States of the Church with the exception of Bologna and Ferrara, agreement made for the re-constitution of the Holy
Roman Empire and the secularization of the German ecclesiastical principalities

Further arrangements in Italy, the Cisalpine Republic is
reorganized after the new form of government in France, and
Bonaparte is appointed its first Consul, the Ligurian Republic re-established with the provision that its Doge should be
appointed by France

The Emperor Paul of Russia, his proposals to Bonaparte
for a joint campaign against England, his mad freaks and
unpopularity in Russia, assassination of the Emperor Paul
(23 March, 1801).

Bonaparte's action against England, his desire to strike at
her commerce, re-establishment of the Armed Neutrality or
Neutral League of the North, originally established by the
Empress Catherine in 1780 between Russia, Prussia, Sweden,
and Denmark, the English bombard Copenhagen and destroy the Danish fleet (2 April, 1801).

War between Spain and Portugal, Bonaparte orders that
the Portuguese ports should be closed to English trade and
certain cessions made to Spain ; the Prince Regent of Portugal refuses, the Spaniards invade Portugal and defeat the
Portuguese armies, by the Treaty of Badajoz (6 June, 1801),
Portugal cedes Olivenza to Spain, the English occupy
Madeira and Goa

The campaign in Egypt (1800-1801), Kléber's victory
at Heliopolis (20 March, 1800), assassination of Kléber
(14 June, 1800), an English army under Abercromby lands
in Egypt (19 March, 1801), battle of Alexandria (21
March), surrender of Alexandria and Cairo, the French
agree to evacuate Egypt (2 Sept, 1801)

Desire for peace in both England and France ; Pitt resigns
office and is succeeded by Addington (March, 1801), nego-
tiations for peace, signature of the Treaty of Amiens (25
March, 1802), by the terms of this treaty England restores
Martinique and Guadeloupe to France, but retains Trinidad,
conquered from Spain, and Ceylon, conquered from the
Dutch, England promised to restore Malta to the Knights of
St John, if their independence was guaranteed by the Great
Powers

By the Treaties of Lunéville and Amiens, Europe was for
the first time entirely at peace, since France declared war
against Austria in 1792, position of the powers of Europe
towards each other ; France had come out of the struggle
not only with undiminished power but with a general recognition of the Rhine as her frontier, commanding position of
Bonaparte as first Consul ; attitude towards France of England, Austria, Prussia, Russia and Spain

Authorities : For the campaign of Marengo see *Thiers*, Histoire
du Consulat et de l'Empire, for the Treaty of Lunéville, *Krones*, Geschichte Œsterreichs im Zeitalter des Französischen Kriege und der
Restauration, *Beer*, Zehn Jahre Œsterreichschen Politik, 1801-10, and
Fournier, Gentz und Cobenzl Geschichteder Œsterreichischen Diplomatie in den Jahre 1801-05 For the Treaty of Amiens, *Pellew*, Life
of Lord Sidmouth, and *Ross*, The Correspondence of the Marquess
Cornwallis

LECTURE XXIX

LITERATURE AND PHILOSOPHY IN THE EIGHTEENTH CENTURY

Characteristics of 18th century literature, it is an age of
polished prose rather than of poetry ; dominated at first by
severe classicism, it is later affected by mock sentimentalism,
and ends with a return to simple naturalism.

Importance of 18th century literature, its influence on politics , its effect on the enlightened despots ; its share in paving the way for the ideas of the French Revolution , the epoch of patrons ; the position held by men of letters

Services rendered by 18th century literature to the discoveries of experimental science , the *Encyclopédie Méthodique*

French literature in the 18th century , decline of poetry , the drama , tragedy , Voltaire (1694–1778) , comedy ; Marivaux (1688–1763) ; Crébillon (1674–1762) ; dramatic criticism ; Diderot , importance of the French stage , epic poetry , its decline , Voltaire's *Henriade* ; other poets ; Gresset (1709–1777) ; prose writers , historians , Vertot (1655–1735), Voltaire, Rulhière (1735–1791) , fiction ; Lesage (1668–1747) , *Gil Blas* , Prevost (1697–1763) , *Manon Lescaut* , Bernardin de Saint Pierre (1737–1814) , *Paul et Virginie* , theology ; the preacher Massillon (1663–1742) ; the chief French writers turn their attention to political, philosophical, and social questions , Montesquieu (1689-1755) , *L'Esprit des lois* ; Holbach (1723–1789) ; Helvétius (1715–1771) , Raynal (1713–1796) , Jean Jacques Rousseau (1712–1778) , his political philosophy , the *Contrat Social* , his theory of education , *Émile* , his sentimentality ; the *Nouvelle Héloïse* , the Encyclopædists , Diderot (1713–1784) , D'Alembert (1717–1783) ; the typical man of letters of the 18th century, Voltaire (1694–1778 ; his character, literary merits, and influence

English literature of the 18th century , influence of classicism ; the Age of Anne, Pope (1688–1744) , Swift (1667–1745) , Addison (1672–1719), Steele (1671–1729), and the *Spectator* , Bolingbroke (1678–1751) , Defoe (1663–1731) , the middle period of the century , sentimentalism , Sterne (1713–1768) , Johnson (1709–1784) and his influence , Goldsmith (1728-1774) , poetry ; Gray (1716–1771) , return to nature , Cowper (1731–1800) , fiction , Richardson (1743–1814), Fielding (1707–1754), Smollett (1721–1771) , history , Robertson (1721–1793) ; Hume (1711–1777) ; Gibbon (1737–1794) , classical scholarship , Bentley (1662–1742) , Porson (1759–1808) ; political philosophy , Burke (1730–1797).

Italian literature in the 18th century, its decadence; influence of the academies, poets and play-wrights, Metasta-sio (1698-1782), Goldoni (1707-1793); Gozzi (1713-1786); Alfieri (1749-1803), prose writers, Beccaria (1738-1794); Filangieri (1752-1788), the study of history, Muratori (1672-1750).

Danish literature in the 18th century, Holberg (1684-1754)

Spanish literature in the 18th century; its affectation

German literature in the 18th century, its beginning and development; the importance of Lessing (1729-1781) as poet and critic, Klopstock (1724-1803); Wieland (1733-1813); Herder (1744-1803); German literature reaches its height with Schiller (1759-1805) and Goethe (1749-1832); causes of the rise of German literature; its significance, its characteristics; the German universities; the court of Weimar

Relation of literature to philosophy in the 18th century.

Attitude of philosophical writers toward religion; the Frenchschool, Voltaire, Rousseau; D'Alembert; Holbach; Helvétius, the more rigid philosophical thinkers; Condillac (1715-1780), Condorcet (1743-1794), the English Deists; Bishop Butler (1692-1752), and the *Analogy*; the speculative philosophy of Berkeley (1684-1753); Hume (1711-77), the importance of Kant (1724-1804), his influence on the subsequent history of philosophy, Fichte (1762-1814), Hegel (1770-1831)

The 18th century writers of political philosophy; influence of Locke and the English thinkers; importance of Montesquieu, Rousseau, and Voltaire, Beccaria and Filangieri, the Abbé de Saint-Pierre (1658-1743).

Political economy and its development in the 18th century, Quesnay (1694-1774); the Marquis de Mirabeau (1749-1791); Adam Smith (1723-1790) and the publication of the *Wealth of Nations*

Characteristic features of the literary and philosophical movements of the 18th century

LECTURE XXX.

ART AND SCIENCE IN THE EIGHTEENTH CENTURY

The tendency noticed in the 17th century towards the decadence of art under the influence of conventionality and sentimentalism, increases in the 18th century, while the development of experimental science leads to startling discoveries and general progress

Decline of art in the 18th century, its causes; extended study of the theory of art, Diderot (1713–1784), Reynolds 1723–1792), improvement of education in art; importance of Rome in this respect; revival of the study of ancient Greek art, Winckelmann (1717–1768), development of the arts of engraving and etching, general diffusion of knowledge of the great works of art; royal and noble patronage of art, the formation of the great galleries of Europe, Dusseldorf, Dresden, dilettantism

The Italian school of painting, the Roman school, Batoni (1708–1787), Raphael Mengs (1728–1779), though German by birth, belongs to this school; the Venetian school Canaletto the elder (1697–1768), Canaletto the younger (1724–1780), Guardi (1712–1793).

The French school of painting, its representatives in the 18th century; Boucher (1703–1770) and classicism; Watteau (1684–1721), and graceful conventionality, Greuze (1726–1805) and sentimentalism; new ideas introduced by David (1748–1825), his greatness as a draughtsman, his influence on the French school of art

The English School of painting, Hogarth (1697–1764); his merits and faults, foundation of the Royal Academy (1768), the great English portrait painters, Reynolds (1723–1792); Gainsborough (1727–1788); Romney (1734–1802)

Sculpture; the one great sculptor of the 18th century, Canova (1757–1822), his unique position

Effect of the increased study of Greek and Roman art;

the excavation of Herculaneum and Pompeii, the Clementine museum, the antiquarians; Visconti (1722–1784, the great collections of gems and of classical antiquities

Architecture, it continues dominated by 17th century ideals and pseudo-classicism; imitation of Versailles

Music in the 18th century, while the graphic arts decline in originality and vitality, music with improvement of musical instruments, the growth of the orchestra, and the better understanding of its theory and principles, becomes the most original and characteristic expression of 18th century civilization, importance of music as a civilizing agent, immense popularity of the opera. Italy becomes the home of the opera, which absorbs all minds, the opera in France, in Austria, in England; invention and growth of the oratorio in England; development of German music, harmony, the age of the great masters, culminating in Beethoven

Music in Italy, development of the opera, the mass, and the song, melody, the great singers of the 18th century, Farinelli (1705–1782), Caffarelli (1758–1826), the composers of the Neapolitan school, Leo (1694–1742); Piccini (1728–1800), Paisiello (1741–1816); the Venetian school; the teaching of singing, Porpora (1687–1767)

Music in France, Rameau (1683–1764), the opera in France, the rivalry between Gluck and Piccini, cultivation of musical taste in France in the direction of theatrical music; Grétry (1741–1813), Méhul (1763–1817)

Music in England; the opera, rivalry between Handel and Pononcini, the greatness of Handel (1684–1759), development of the oratorio, church music in England

Music in Germany; the first great German master, Johann Sebastian Bach (1685–1750); the opera in Germany, Gluck (1714–1787), Mozart (1756–1791), Mozart and his influence on the development of music, his operas and masses; his orchestral compositions, music and its headquarters at Vienna; Haydn (1732–1809); Beethoven (1770–1827), importance of music in German civilization

Popularity of experimental science in the 18th century, men of science occupied with the application and extension of

the scientific knowledge and of the discoveries made in the
17th century ; application of science to industrial development

The great mathematicians , Euler (1707–1783) , De Moivre
(1667–1754) ; D'Alembert (1717–1783) ; Lagrange (1736–
1813) ; Laplace (1749–1827) and the *Mécanique céleste* ,
Monge (1746–1818) and descriptive geometry

The great biologists ; Morgagni (1682–1771) and anatomy ,
Spallanzani (1719–1799) and his discoveries on the nature of
blood , introduction of vaccination , Jenner (1749–1823)

The great naturalists Buffon (1707–1788) , Daubenton
(1716–1800), Lacépède (1756–1825); Lamarck (1744–1829)

The great botanists Linnæus (1707–1778) and his classifi-
cation of plants ; Jussieu (1747–1836) and the natural order

The great mineralogists and geologists Werner (1750–
1817 ; Hauy (1743–1822) the founder of mineralogy , Dolo-
mieu (1750–1801)

The great astronomers Clairaut (1713–1765) ; Mauper-
tuis (1698–1756) , Bradley (1692–1762) ; Herschel (1738–
1822) and the discovery of Uranus ; Lalande 1732–1807) ,
Bailly (1736–1793) and the history of astronomy.

The great physicists influence of Newton (1642–1727) ,
Franklin (1706–1790) and electricity , Volta (1745–1827)
and the voltaic pile , Galvani (1737–1798) and galvanism ,
Réaumur (1683–1757) and the improvements in the thermometer ; Fontana (1730–1803) , influence of the discoveries
of Priestley and Lavoisier on physics.

The great chemists ; Cavendish (1731–1810) , Lavoisier
(1743–1794), and Priestley (1733–1805), and the resolution
of air and water into their component parts , Berthollet
(1748–1822) ; Scheele (1742–1786) , Fourcroy (1765–1809)

Application of scientific discoveries, Watt (1736–1819), and
the steam engine , Boulton (1728–1809) , Hargreaves, Ark-
wright (1732–1792), Crompton and Cartwright, and the development of textile industry.

Improvements in civil engineering , extension of canals ,
the Duke of Bridgewater in England , Brindley (1716–1772) ,
Smeaton ; Telford.

The practical character of the 18th century is to be seen in
its application of science to human needs.

APPENDICES.

Appendix I.

Emperors, Holy Roman Empire	Kings of France,	Kings of Great Britain	Kings of Spain.	Kings of Prussia.	Tsars of Russia.
Charles VI (since 1711)	Louis XV, Orleans, *Regent.*	George I, (since 1714) *Stanhope.* *Walpole.*	Philip V (since 1700) *Alberoni* (to 1719)	Frederick William I (since 1713)	Peter I (since 1689).
. . .	*Bourbon*	. . .	Luiz I	. . .	
. . .	*Fleury.*	George II	Philip V (again). *Ripperda* (to 1726)	. . .	Catherine I
. . .	. . .		. . .		Peter II Anne Ivan VI
Maria Theresa succeeds to Austrian dominions)	. . .	*Wilmington*	. . .	Frederick II	Elizabeth
Charles VII, Elector of Bavaria.	*D'Argenson* (to 1747).	*Pelham*		. . .	
Francis I, (husband of Maria Theresa)	. . .	*Newcastle* *Devonshire* (with *Pitt*) *Newcastle* (with *Pitt*)	Ferdinand VI *La Ensenada*	. . .	
Kaunitz	*Bernis*	. . .	*Wall* .	*Hertzberg*	
. . .	*Choiseul*				

	Austria	France	England	Spain	Prussia	Russia
1759				Charles III		
1760			George III			
1761			(*Pitt* resigns). *Bute*	*Squillace.*		Peter III.
1762						Catherine II.
1763			*G Grenville*			
1765	Joseph II		*Rockingham.*			
1766			*Grafton.* *North.*	*Aranda*		
1770		*D'Aiguillon*				
1773		Louis XVI				
1774		*Turgot* *Necker.*				
1776				*Florida Blanca*		
1780	(Death of Maria Theresa)					
1781		*Joly de Fleury* *D'Ormesson*				
1782			*Rockingham.* *Shelburne.* *Portland* *W. Pitt.*			
1783		*Calonne.*				
1786		*Loménie de Brienne* (to 1790). *Necker* (to 1790).			Frederick William II	
1787						
1788				Charles IV.		
1790	Leopold II					
1792	Francis II	Republic. *Committee of Public Safety*		*Aranda.* *Godoy*	*Haugwitz*	
1793						
1794	*Thugut.*	Directory.				
1795						
1796	*Cobenzl.*					
1797					Fred'ick William III.	Paul I.
1799		Consulate				
1801			*Addington*			Alexander I.

Appendix II.

Kings of Sweden.	Kings of Denmark.	Kings (elected) of Poland.	Sultans of the Turks.	Kings of Portugal.	Governors of the Catholic Netherlands (now Belgium) under Austria.
Charles XII (since 1697)	Frederick IV (since 1699).	Augustus I, Elector of Saxony (since 1709).	Ahmad III (since 1703).	John V (since 1706)	Count of Königseck (since 1714).
Ulrica Eleanor and Frederick I.					Prince Eugène of Savoy.
	Christian VI.	Augustus II, (Elector of Saxony).	Mahmud I.		Archduchess Maria Elizabeth.
Frederick I (alone)					Count Frederick von Harrach-Rohrau.
					Archduchess Maria Anna and Charles of Lorraine.
	Frederick V.			Joseph. Pombal.	Charles of Lorraine (alone).
	J. H. Bernstorff.				
Adolphus Frederick (of Holstein-Gottorp).		(Interregnum). Stanislas Poniatowski.	Othman III. Mustapha III.		

Gustavus III	Christian VII. Struensee A. Bernstorff.	(First Partition)	Abdul Hamid I	Pedro III and Maria I	Archduchess Maria Christina and Albert of Saxe-Teschen
	(Prince Frederick, Regent).			Maria I (alone).	
		(Second Partition.)	Selim III		Archduke Charles (Annexed by France).
Gustavus IV.		(Final Partition).		(Prince John, Regent).	

The Popes	House of Savoy, after 1720 Kings of Sardinia.	Kings of the Two Sicilies	Grand Dukes of Tuscany	Dukes of Parma	Dukes of Modena
Clement XI (Albani) (since 1700).	Victor Amadeus II Duke of Savoy (since 1675), King of Sicily (since 1713), King of Sardinia, 1720	*Naples.* Emperor Charles VI (since 1713) *Sicily* Victor Amadeus II of Savoy, I of Sicily (since 1713)	Cosimo III de'Medici (since 1670)	Francesco Farnese (since 1694).	Rainaldo d'Este (since 1694)
		. . Emperor Charles VI.			
Innocent XIII (Conti)	. . . . .		Giovanni Gastone de'Medici		
Benedict XIII (Orsini)				Antonio Farnese	
Clement XII (Corsini)	Charles Emmanuel III of Savoy, I of Sardinia		.		
	.	Don Carlos, aft Charles III of Spain *Tanucci*	.	Don Carlos, aft. King of the Two Sicilies Emperor Charles VI	
	.		Francis of Lorraine Emperor 1745-65		Francesco II d'Este

Benedict XIV (Lambertini).	.					Maria Theresa.
Clement XIII (Rezzonico)	.		Ferdinand IV		Don Philip *Du Tillot* (to 1771)	
Clement XIV (Ganganelli)	.				Leopold, aft. Em-peror	Don Ferdinand
Victor Amadeus III of Savoy, II of Sardinia.						
Pius VI (Braschi)	.	*La Sambuca.* Acton	.	Ferdinand III	.	Ercole III d'Este
Charles Emmanuel IV of Savoy, II of Sardinia.						
	.	Parthenopean Republic. Ferdinand IV.	.		.	Cisalpine Republic · Cisalpine Republic
Pius VII (Chiaramonti)	.	.	(King of Etruria) Louis of Parma.	.	Don Ferdinand . Cisalpine Republic	Ercole III d'Este. Cisalpine Republic
Victor Emmanuel I						

Appendix IV.

Electors Palatine.	Electors of Bavaria.	Electors of Saxony.	Electors of Hanover.	Elector-Archbishops of Mayence.	Elector-Archbishops of Cologne.	Elector-Archbishops of Trèves.	Princes of Orange-Nassau.
John William (since 1690).	Maximilian Emmanuel (since 1679).	Augustus II (since 1694), I of Poland (since 1697).	George I (since 1698), (King of Great Britain since 1714).	Lothar Francis von Schönborn (since 1694).	Joseph Clement of Bavaria (since 1688).	Charles Joseph of Lorraine (since 1711).	William IV (since 1711), (Stadtholder 1747).
Charles Philip.						Francis Louis of Neuburg.	
	Charles Albert (Emp. Charles VII, 1742-45).				Clement Augustus of Bavaria.		
			George II (King of Gt. Britain)	Francis Louis of Neuburg Philip Charles von Eltz.		Francis George von Schönborn	
		Augustus III. II of Poland. Brühl (to 1763).					
Charles Theodore.	Maximilian Joseph I.			John Frederick von Ostein.			
							William V (Stadtholder 1766).

				John Philp von Walderdorf	
			Maximilian Frederick von Kongseck-Rotheufels.		
		Emerich Joseph Breidbach.			
	George III (King of Gt Britain)				
				Clement Wenceslas of Saxony.	
		Frederick Chas. von Erthal.			
Frederick Christian (Feb) Frederick Augustus (Dec.)			Archduke Maximilian.		
		Charles Dalberg.			Batavian Republic.
Charles Theodore (unites the electorates).					
Maximilian Joseph II					

Appendix V.

Table representing the Succession to the Russian Throne

MARIA MILOSLAVSKI (1) = ALEXIS ROMÁNOV (1645–75) = (2) NATALIA NARISHKIN

FODOR
MIRVITCH
1675–82)

IVAN V (1682–96) = Prascovia
Solikov

Sophia,
Regent
(1682–89)

Eudoxia Lapushkin (1) = PETER THE GREAT = (2) CATHERINE I
(1682–1725)   (1725–27)

Anne = Charles Leopold, Duke of
Mecklenburg-Schwerin

ANNE (1730–40)
= Frederick
William, Duke
of Courland

Anne = Antony Ulric of
Brunswick-Wolfenbuttel

IVAN VI (23 Aug – 5 Dec, 1741)

Alexis = Charlotte
d 1718 | Sophia of
        | Brunswick-
        | Wolfenbuttel

PETER II
(1727–30)

Anne = Charles Freder-
ick, Duke of
Holstein-
Gottorp

PETER III = CATHERINE II (1762–96)
(5 Jan –9 July,
1762)

ELIZABETH
(1741–62)

Appendix VI.

Table representing the claimants to the Austrian Succession (1740) with children of Maria Theresa

MARGARET THERESA of Spain (1)=LEOPOLD I=(2) ELEANOR of Neuburg
Emperor 1658-1705

JOSEPH I=Wilhelmina Amelia of Hanover, Emperor 1705-11

CHARLES VI=Elizabeth Christina of Brunswick-Wolfenbuttel, Emperor 1711-40

Maria Elizabeth, Governor of the Austrian Netherlands

Maria Anna=John V, King of Portugal (1725-41)

...onda Sobieski (2)=Maximilian Emanuel=(1)Maria Antonina, Elector of Bavaria

Joseph Ferdinand died 1699

Maria Josepha (elder daughter)=Augustus II, King of Poland, Elector of Saxony (1734-63)

Maria Amelia (younger daughter)

MARIA THERESA=FRANCIS I of Lorraine, GrandDuke of Tuscany, Emperor 1745-65 (1740-80)

Maria Anna=Chas. of Lorraine, Governor of the Austrian Netherlands (1744-61)

Charles Albert, Elector of Bavaria (1726-45) Emperor CHARLES VII, (1742-45) (elder son)

...lement ...igustus, ...ector of ...ologne ...724-61 ...unger son)

Maximilian Joseph I Elector of Bavaria (1745-77)

...SEPH II Emperor 1765-92

LEOPOLD II Emperor 1790-92

Ferdinand=Maria Beatrice of Este, heiress of the last Duke of Modena, Governor-General of Lombardy

Maximilian Elector of Cologne (1784-1803)

Maria Christina=Duke Albert of Saxe-Teschen, Governor of the Austrian Netherlands (1781-92)

Maria Amelia=Ferdinand, Duke of Parma

Maria Caroline=Ferdinand IV, King of the two Sicilies

Marie Antoinette=Louis XVI, King of France

CORNELL UNIVERSITY.

— —   —

S Y L L A B U S

OF A

COURSE OF TWENTY=FOUR LECTURES

ON THE

HISTORY OF EUROPE DURING THE NINETEENTH CENTURY

BY

H. MORSE STEPHENS.

———   —-—

ITHACA ·
ANDRUS & CHURCH

TABLE OF CONTENTS.

MODERN EUROPEAN HISTORY.

(NINETEENTH CENTURY)

LECTURE I.

THE CONSULATE IN FRANCE AND THE RE-CONSTITUTION OF GERMANY.

The government of the Consulate ; its policy of reconciliation ; many *émigrés* permitted to return ; complete pacification of La Vendée by the Treaty of Montluçon ; suppression of brigandage ; restoration of internal peace

The financial policy of the Consulate ; the work of Gaudin ; taxes fairly levied and collected , corruption punished ; foundation of the Bank of France.

The Consulate and legal reform , commissions appointed to draw up codes

The Consulate and the Catholic Church ; Bonaparte's negotiations with the Papacy ; end of the schism which had lasted since the civil constitution was proclaimed in 1790 ; terms of the Concordat signed by Pope Pius VII and the First Consul Bonaparte (15 July, 1801) and promulgated (18 Apr , 1802)

The Consulate and education ; Bonaparte's attempt to establish a scheme of national education

The Consulate and the internal administration of France ; formation of the Prefectures ; the left bank of the Rhine organized as part of France.

The Consulate and the colonies of France ; Bonaparte desires to restore the power of France in America ; he obtains Louisiana from Spain and an extension of French Guiana from Portugal ; he re-occupies Guadeloupe and Martinique by the Treaty of Amiens , he attacks San Domingo , resistance of Toussaint L'Ouverture.

Constitutional changes made during the Consulate ; effect of the Conspiracy of the Infernal Machine (24 Sept., 1800) , Bonaparte declared, after an appeal to the Primary Assemblies, First Consul for life , he is enabled to nominate a successor.

The Constitutional authorities of the Consulate , the part played by the Counsil of State, the Senate, the Tribunate, and the Legislative Body ; the National List suppressed and replaced by Electoral Colleges.

The ministers of the Consulate ; Talleyrand, Minister of Foreign Affairs, Gaudin, of Finance, Regnier, of Justice, Chaptal, of the Interior, Berthier, of War, Decrès, of the Marine, and Fouché, of Police

The re-constitution of Germany ; the new arrangements made necessary by the cession to France of the left bank of the Rhine and by the proofs that had been given during the war of the intrinsic weakness of the political system of the Empire ; the new arrangements accepted by the Imperial · Diet (25 Feb , 1803) ; the Holy Roman Empire, as established by the Treaties of Westphalia, practically ceases to exist.

Changes made in the Colleges of the Imperial Diet ; (1) the College of Electors increased from eight electors, three ecclesiastical and five lay, to ten electors, one ecclesiastical and nine lay , the archbishops of Cologne and Treves lost their electoral dignity owing to their dominions being absorbed into France , the Archbishop of Mayence continued as an elector and received as his dominions the bishopric of Ratisbon, the principality of Aschaffenburg and the county of Wetzlar ; the nine lay electors were the five who had formerly held that dignity, Bohemia, Brandenburg, Saxony, Bavaria, and Hanover, with four new electors, the Margrave of Baden, the Duke of Wurtemberg, the Landgrave of Hesse-Cassel and the Grand Duke Ferdinand, formerly Grand Duke of Tuscany, who was made Elector of Salzburg , (2) College of Princes ; owing to the secularization of the Catholic bishoprics and monasteries this college was greatly reduced in

numbers and consisted mainly of Protestant princes; (3)
College of Free Cities, this college would have been entirely
abolished but for the intervention of France, as it was, only
six free cities were maintained out of fifty-two, namely, Augsburg, Bremen, Frankfort-on-the-Main, Hamburg, Lubeck
and Nuremberg; these changes in the Imperial Diet deprived
the Catholics, and Austria, the chief Catholic power, of their
predominance.

The secularization of the ecclesiastical states, this step,
which had been suggested by France at Basle and by Bonaparte at Leoben, was nominally undertaken to compensate
those princes of the Empire who had lost territory by the
cession of the left bank of the Rhine to France; the princes
who profited most were, however, those who were already
powerful, thus Prussia, Bavaria, Baden, Wurtemberg, and
Hanover all received important accessions of territory making
them compact and populous states, Austria received only
two small bishoprics, Brixen and Trent, but two Austrian
princes, the Grand Duke Ferdinand and the Duke of Modena
received the German states of Salzburg and the Breisgau in
compensation for the loss of their Italian principalities, the
Prince of Orange, formerly Stadtholder of the United Netherlands, received the bishopric of Fulda.

Effect of these sweeping changes destroying the Holy
Roman Empire, and building up strong German states, upon
the policy and condition of Germany.

The re-constitution of Switzerland; Bonaparte interferes
in Swiss politics; by the Act of Mediation (19 Feb., 1803),
he restores federal government but maintains the abolition of
feudalism and other reforms made by the Helvetian Republic; to the thirteen old cantons—six democratic, Appenzell,
Glarus, Schwyz, Unterwalden, Uri, and Zug, and seven
oligarchical—Basle, Berne, Freiburg, Lucerne, Schaffhausen,
Soleure, and Zurich, he added six new cantons—Vaud, Aar-
gau, Thurgau, Ticino, Saint-Gall, and the Grisons, he regulated the relations between the federal and cantonal governments, and was declared Mediator of the Confederation of
Switzerland.

Authorities: A brief account of the Consulate and of the re constitution of Germany in Switzerland is given in *Morse Stephens*, European History, 1789–1815, chap vii For the Consulate, see *Thiers*, Histoire du Consulat et de l'Empire , *Thibaudeau*, Mémoires sur le Consulat and, Le Consulat et l'Empire, and for the policy of Napoleon, the various lives and histories, particularly *Lanfrey* and *Taine* The Memoirs most valuable for the subjects treated in this lecture are those of *Chaptal, Lucien Bonaparte, Talleyrand,* and *Gaudin* , for the Concordat consult the valuable work of *D'Haussonville*, Documents inédits sur le Concordat. For the re-constitution of Germany, see *Rambaud*, Les Français sur le Rhin, *Hausser*, Deutsche Geschichte vom Tode Friedrichs des Grossen, *Oncken*, Das Zeitalter der Revolution, des Kaiserreichs und der Befreiungskriege, *Beer*, Zehn Jahre Œsterreichischer Politik, 1801–1810, and *Heigel*, Deutsche Geschichte vom Tode Friedrichs des Grossen

LECTURE II

THE POWER OF NAPOLEON AT ITS HEIGHT.

Recommencement of war between France and England, (18 May, 1803) , causes of the war , the points left unsettled by the Treaty of Amiens ; the question of Malta, which the English refused to surrender , the interference of the First Consul in Switzerland and his annexation of Piedmont (11 Sept., 1802) regarded as evidences of the desire of France further to disturb the peace of Europe , Bonaparte's wrath at the libels published upon him in England , the trial of Peltier , the embassy of Whitworth to Paris ; the English seize French ships and Bonaparte in reprisal arrests all Englishmen travelling in France and occupies Hanover.

Formation of the Grande Armée ; Bonaparte's genius for military organization ; he forms the camp of Boulogne and prepares to invade England.

Difficulties of Bonaparte's position ; the plot of Pichegru, Georges Cadoudal, and others against his life , arrest and

execution of the Duc d'Enghien (21 March, 1804) , Bonaparte offered the title of Emperor of the French by the
Senate (18 May, 1804) , the offer ratified by the French people in their primary assemblies ; coronation of Bonaparte as
the Emperor Napoleon (2 Dec , 1804) , also crowned King
of Italy at Milan (20 May, 1805).

The institutions of the Empire ; the Imperial Court , increased importance of the Senate and Council of State ,
highly centralized form of administration established under
the Empire.

In the year in which Napoleon became Emperor of the
French the Emperor Francis II declared the Austrian dominions an hereditary empire (11 Aug , 1804), and takes the
title of Emperor of Austria (7 Dec.)

Position of affairs in England at the recommencement of
war with France ; Addington, who had made the Treaty of
Amiens, succeeded as prime minister by Pitt, who advocates
a vigorous foreign policy (1804)

Pitt's endeavors to form a third continental coalition
against Napoleon , Frederick William III persists in maintaining the strict neutrality, by which Prussia had gained so
much , the Tsar Alexander I of Russia personally admired
Napoleon, but his court and people pressed him to side with
England ; the execution of d'Enghien and Napoleon's treatment of his ambassador further impelled Alexander to join
the coalition against France , the Emperor Francis gladly
entered the coalition ; Spain was the close ally of Napoleon,
while of smaller countries, Sweden, under Gustavus IV, the
Two Sicilies, and Portugal were favorable to the coalition,
and Denmark, to Napoleon.

The campaign of 1805 ; Napoleon unable to attempt the
invasion of England because the French fleet cannot command the Channel ; the scheme of Napoleon frustrated by
the conduct of Admiral Villeneuve ; Nelson in command of
the Channel ; Sir Robert Calder's action with the French
fleet (25 July), the Austrians under Mack before the declaration of war occupy Ulm (Sept) , Napoleon despairing

of invading England breaks up his camp at Boulogne and in-
vades Germany ; Mack surrenders at Ulm (20 Oct), vic-
tory of Trafalgar won by Nelson over the French and
Spanish fleets (21 Oct), Napoleon occupies Vienna , a
Russian army joins the Austrians , Napoleon defeats the
Austrians and Russians at Austerlitz (2 Dec)

The results of Austerlitz , by the Treaty of Pressburg
(26 Dec) Austria cedes Venice to the Kingdom of Italy,
Istria and Dalmatia to Napoleon, who governs them under
Marmont as the Illyrian Provinces, and the Tyrol to Bavaria , the Electors of Bavaria and Wurtemberg given the title
of King, and the Elector of Baden that of Grand Duke ,
formation of the Confederation of the Rhine , death of Pitt
(23 Jan , 1806).

The campaign of 1806 , the attitude of Prussia to Napoleon,
and of Napoleon to Prussia , influence of Queen Louisa upon
Frederick William III ; the Prussians prepare for war ; the
Prussians defeated by Napoleon at Jena and by Davout at
Auerstadt (14 Oct) ; Napoleon occupies Berlin (25 Oct) ;
the French invade Poland, occupy Warsaw (15 Dec.) and
go into winter quarters on the Russian frontier.

The campaign of 1807 ; battle of Eylau (8 Feb) ; close
alliance formed between the Tsar Alexander and Frederick
William III of Prussia by the Treaty of Bartenstein (April),
surrender of Dantzig to the French (24 May) , Napoleon
defeats the Russians at Friedland (14 June)

Interview between Napoleon and Alexander at Tilsit
(25 June, 1807), followed by the Peace of Tilsit (7 July,
1807) , by this treaty Russia ceded the Ionian Islands to
France , Napoleon promised not to restore the independence
of Poland, but created the part of Poland which Prussia had
received in the different partitions into the Grand Duchy of
Warsaw with the Elector of Saxony, to whom he gave the
title of king, as Grand Duke , Napoleon suggested to Alexander the resurrection of the Empires of the East and the
West and advised him to extend his dominions at the cost of
Sweden and Turkey

After much hesitation, Napoleon makes peace with Prussia after depriving Frederick William III of Polish Prussia and of all Prussian territory to the west of the Elbe.

After the Peace of Tilsit, Napoleon recognizes that his sole remaining enemy is England , progress of the war with England after the battle of Trafalgar , complete triumph of the English fleet and blockade of the French coasts ; the English occupy Sicily, to which island Ferdinand IV had fled before a French army in 1805, and defeat General Reynier at Maida (3 July, 1806) ; the English re-occupy the Cape of Good Hope which had been surrendered to the Dutch by the Treaty of Amiens.

Napoleon, being unable to attack England directly, resolves to ruin English commerce , he issues the Berlin Decree (21 Nov., 1806) declaring the British Islands in a state of blockade, followed by the Milan Decree, declaring any ship touching at a British port lawful prize , by the Treaty of Tilsit, Russia agrees to the continental blockade , effect of the blockade on English commerce.

The Treaty of Tilsit marks the zenith of Napoleon's power, but his splendour is most apparent during the Congress of Erfurt (Sept., 1808).

Authorities : For the history of the Empire, see *Morse Stephens, Thiers, Thibaudeau*, and *Lanfrey* cited under Lecture I , for the personality of Napoleon, *Taine* Napoléon, *Lévy* Napoléon intime, *Masson* Napoléon et les Femmes, *Bourrienne* Memoirs, *Méneval* Napoléon 1er , for the outbreak of war with England, see *Oscar Browning*, Despatches of Lord Whitworth , for the relations between Napoleon and the Tsar Alexander, see *Vandal*, Alexander 1er et Napoléon, und *Tatischeff*, Napoléon et le Tsar Alexandre d'après des Documents inédits ; for the campaigns of Austerlitz, Jena, and Friedland, see the elaborate works of *Jomini*, and *Mathieu Dumas*, with *Marbot*, Memoirs, and *Thiebault*, Souvenirs, and the numerous lives of the marshals and generals of Napoleon , for the Imperial Court, see *Madame de Rémusat*, Memoirs ; and, as the primary authority for the whole period, the Correspondence of Napoleon.

LECTURE III.

EUROPE DURING THE ASCENDENCY OF NAPOLEON

Napoleon after the Treaty of Tilsit sweeps away the last relics of the Holy Roman Empire and re-organizes Germany ; under his system the Confederation of the Rhine, of which he was entitled the Protector, became the chief power of Germany ; it consisted of thirty-two reigning princes , its population of 20,000,000 of Germans was bound to contribute 150,000 soldiers to the army of Napoleon ; and its policy was conducted by a Diet sitting at Frankfort, composed of two colleges, the College of Kings, and the College of Princes

The four kingdoms in the Confederation of the Rhine were Bavaria, Wurtemberg, Westphalia, and Saxony ; the Kings of Bavaria and Wurtemberg ally their families with that of Napoleon and receive their reward in extension of territory : the King of Saxony is made Grand Duke of Warsaw, and is included in the Confederation from the importance of his geographical position between Austria, Prussia and Russia ; the kingdom of Westphalia created by Napoleon from the dominions of Prussia to the west of the Elbe, with Hesse-Cassel, Brunswick, part of Hanover, etc , was conferred on Napoleon's youngest brother, Jerome Bonaparte.

The College of Princes consisted of the five Grand Duchies of Baden, of Hesse-Darmstadt, of Berg, created by Napoleon and conferred by him on his brother-in-law, Joachim Murat, of Frankfort, conferred on Dalberg, formerly Archbishop Elector of Mayence, and of Wurtzburg, conferred on the Grand Duke Ferdinand, formerly ruler of Tuscany, and of twenty-three princes whose principalities were of moderate extent

Effect of the new organization in Germany ; the French system of centralized administration and of military conscription everywhere introduced , serfdom, and other feudal abuses abolished , the codified law of France introduced into Westphalia and Berg , the Knights of the Empire deprived of their sovereign rights ; the petty dukes, counts, and princes, whose territories lay within those of the reigning princes were mediatized, that is to say, lost their immediate sovereignty while retaining their titles and rank as a class of privileged aristocracy

Effect of these measures , Germany becomes a confederation of more or less powerful states instead of a collection of petty feudal principalities.

Napoleon's Italian policy , he appoints his step-son, Eugène de Beauharnais, viceroy of the kingdom of Italy, which comprised the former Cisalpine Republic with the addition, after the Treaty of Pressburg, of Venice ; Napoleon kept Piedmont as part of the French dominions, and annexed the Ligurian Republic, Parma, Etruria or Tuscany, and eventually in 1810, Rome, directly to France, giving his sister Elisa the title of Grand Duchess of Tuscany and Duchess of Lucca, and his sister Pauline that of Duchess of Guastalla ; the relations of Napoleon with the Pope ; arrest of Pius VII (6 July, 1809) , the kingdom of Naples conferred upon Napoleon's brother, Joseph Bonaparte, in 1806 and on Murat in 1808 ; great reforms accomplished in Italy, but failure of Napoleon to recognize the principle of nationality

Napoleon and Holland ; changes in the character of the Batavian Republic , Louis Bonaparte made King of Holland in 1806 , dislike of the Dutch for the continental blockade ; Napoleon annexes Holland to his dominions in 1810.

Denmark during the ascendency of Napoleon ; Napoleon's scheme for seizing the Danish fleet ; the English, hearing of this scheme, bombard Copenhagen and seize the Danish fleet themselves (Sept 1807) ; friendship of Frederick VI of Denmark for Napoleon

Sweden during the ascendency of Napoleon ; Gustavus IV, the sworn enemy of Napoleon and ally of England ; after the Treaty of Tilsit the French under Brune occupy Swedish Pomerania ; the Tsar Alexander conquers Finland (1808) , insanity of Gustavus IV ; he attacks Denmark ; he is dethroned (29 March) and his uncle, the former regent, made king (10 May, 1809) ; Bernadotte, one of Napoleon's marshals, elected Prince Royal of Sweden and heir to the throne (5 Nov , 1810)

The Turks during the ascendency of Napoleon , the Sultan Selim III refused to enter Pitt's coalition against Napoleon (1805), and an English expedition under Duckworth was sent against him (1807) ; overthrow and assassination of Selim (21 July, 1807) , after an interval, Mahmud II becomes Sultan (July, 1808) ; his vigor and ability ; he is inclined to the side of France, but dislikes the establishment of the French in the Illyrian provinces , the Tsar Alexander attacks the Turks (1809) ; the Russians occupy Moldavia and Wallachia (1810), and cross the Danube (1811)

The greatest extension of Napoleon's empire attained by the annexation of the districts along the northern coasts of Germany from the borders of Holland to the mouth of the Weser, including Bremen, Hamburg, and Lubeck, (13 Dec., 1810) , this annexation caused by the difficulty of maintaining the continental blockade ; at this time the French dominions were divided into 130 departments extending from Rome to Lubeck ; the organization and administration of these departments

Napoleon's administration when at the height of his power ; excellence of his civil service , his ministers and the Council of State ; suppression of the Tribunate (1808) ; growing importance of the police department , organization of the army, and services of Clarke, Minister of War , Napoleon's legal reforms ; the codes ; his financial reforms ; his reforms in education , the formation of the University, of France (1811)

Napoleon's belief in the hereditary principle , his new nobility ; his desire for an heir ; he resolves to divorce his wife, the Empress Josephine

Failure of Napoleon to appreciate the forces working against him at the height of his power , he had failed to ruin England in spite of all his efforts ; he had roused the

national spirit, which had made France so great, against him
in Spain and in Germany ; the Grande Armée, which had
won his victories, was being destroyed, and the vacancies in
its ranks filled by foreigners and young French conscripts

Authorities See the books cited under Lecture II, with *Rambaud*,
La Domination française en Allemagne, *Beaulieu-Marçonnay*, Karl
von Dalberg und seine Zeit, *Kleinschmidt*, Geschichte des Konigreichs Westfalen, *DuCasse*, Mémoires et correspondance du Roi Jé-
rome, and *Goecke*, Das GrossherzogthumBerg unter Joachim Murat, etc

LECTURE IV.

OVERTHROW OF THE POWER OF NAPOLEON

The struggle between England and Napoleon ; the policies
represented by Castlereagh and Canning, the former desiring
to raise national insurrections against Napoleon, the latter to
form coalitions and to act directly against the French with an
English army ; duel between Castlereagh and Canning
(1809) , Lord Wellesley becomes director of English foreign
policy (1809–1812) ; the English take the remaining colonial possessions of France and Holland, Martinique and the
Mauritius (1809), Guadeloupe (1810), and Java (1811)

Napoleon resolves to attack Portugal, because the Prince-
Regent declined to join in the continental blockade , by the
Treaty of Fontainebleau with Spain (29 Oct , 1807) he ar-
ranges for the division of Portugal ; a French army under
Junot invades Portugal , the Prince-Regent escapes to Brazil ;
Junot enters Lisbon (20 Nov., 1807), occupies the whole of
Portugal and declares that the House of Braganza has ceased
to reign (1 Feb , 1808)

Napoleon's interference in the affairs in Spain ; the people
of Madrid attack Godoy, the Queen's lover, and support
Prince Ferdinand, the heir to the throne ; the royal family of

Spain appeals to Napoleon and proceeds to France ; Charles IV cedes his throne to Napoleon who proclaims his brother Joseph king of Spain (6 June, 1808) ; a French army enters Spain to support Joseph and occupies Madrid ; the Spaniards rise in insurrection ; 18,000 French soldiers surrender to the Spaniards at Baylen (20 July, 1808) , the English ministry supports the Spanish insurgents with money and arms

The Portuguese rise in insurrection against the French ; the English ministry send an army to their help under Sir Arthur Wellesley, who wins the battles of Roriça and Vimeiro (17–21 Aug , 1808) ; by the Convention of Cintra (30 Aug.) the French under Junot agree to evacuate Portugal

Napoleon in person invades Spain, and occupies Madrid (13 Dec , 1808) , Sir John Moore, with the English Army from Portugal advances to Salamanca to save Andalusia ; retreat of Sir John Moore to Corunna ; battle of Corunna (16 Jan , 1809)

The difficulties of Napoleon in the Peninsula, and the promise of support from England cause the Emperor Francis to believe the time propitious for a fresh war ; unpopularity of the French in Germany ; Napoleon's contempt for the popular feeling against him ; Stadion, who had become State-Chancellor of Austria in 1806, desired to make Austria the representative of this German national feeling , the services of Gentz , re-organization of the Austrian army by the Archduke Charles.

Campaign of 1809 ; the Archduke Charles invades Bavaria, and the Archduke John, Italy ; Napoleon enters Germany, defeats the Archduke Charles at Abensberg and Eckmuhl (20–22 Apr) and occupies Vienna (12 May) ; the battle of Aspern or Essling (21–22 May) ; Napoleon shut up in the island of Lobau ; the Tyrolese rise in insurrection under Hofer , Napoleon, joined by reinforcements, defeats the Austrians at Wagram (6 July).

By the Treaty of Vienna (14 Oct , 1809) Austria ceded Trieste, Carniola, and part of Croatia to Napoleon, who added these districts to the Illyrian provinces , Austria also ceded

Salzburg to Bavaria, and Western Galicia to the Grand
Duchy of Warsaw ; causes of the failure of Austria to arouse
German national feeling ; Stadion succeeded by Metternich ;
Napoleon marries the Archduchess Maria Louisa, daughter
of the Emperor Francis (2 Apr., 1810)

The English ministry resolves to pursue the war vigorously on land against Napoleon ; failure of the expedition to
Walcheren (Aug., 1809) ; successes in the war in the Peninsula ; gallant defence of Saragossa by the Spaniards , though
the Spanish armies were defeated, their guerilla warfare reduces the power of the French ; Arthur Wellesley, afterwards Lord Wellington, placed in command of the English
army in the Peninsula , he wins the battle of Talavera
(28 July, 1809) ; Wellington holds the lines of Torres
Vedras and repulses a French invasion of Portugal under
Masséna (1810-1811) , Wellington takes Ciudad Rodrigo
and Badajoz and defeats Marmont at Salamanca (22 July,
1812), Joseph Bonaparte evacuates Madrid , the English
forced to retreat from Burgos, and Joseph recovers Madrid
for the last time.

The growth of the national spirit in Germany ; the
Germans look to Prussia to lead them ; the Tugenbund.

The re-organization of Prussia ; the ministry of Stein ,
he abolishes serfdom and introduces other reforms , the war
ministry of Scharnhorst , he passes the youth of Prussia
through the army, and in the place of conscription adopts
universal military service ; Napoleon demands the dismissal
of Stein (1808) and of Scharnhorst (1810) , the ministry
of Hardenberg , he completes the work of Stein by making
the former serfs absolute owners of their holdings , foundation of the University of Berlin ; assistance rendered by
William von Humboldt ; Frederick William III forced to
sign an offensive and defensive alliance with Napoleon (24
Feb , 1812)

Growing disagreement between Napoleon and the Tsar
Alexander ; its causes , Napoleon resolves to invade Russia ;
Castlereagh, who came into office Jan., 1812, offers to aid

Russia ; through English mediation Russia makes peace with the Turks at Bucharest (28 May, 1812) ; Russia signs the Treaty of Abo with Sweden (24, Mch 1812) by which Bernadotte promises to aid Russia against Napoleon and to cede Finland in exchange for Norway.

Campaign of 1812 , Napoleon invades Russia (May) ; retreat of the Russians ; battle of Borodino (7 Sept) ; Napoleon occupies Moscow (14 Sept) ; the retreat from Moscow , almost complete destruction of the French army.

Campaign of 1813 , during the retreat from Moscow the Prussian contingent under Yorck abandons the French army (30 Dec , 1812) ; Prussia declares war against France (16 Mch , 1813) ; Napoleon rallies his army and wins the battles of Lutzen (2 May) and Bautzen (20 May) ; Austria signs the Convention of Reichenbach (17 June), and promises to join the allies if Napoleon refuses the terms offered to him ; Congress of Prague , Austria declares war against Napoleon (12 Aug.) ; the French under Oudinot and Macdonald defeated by Bernadotte and Blucher at Gross-Beeren and the Katzbach (23–25 Aug.) ; Napoleon defeats the Austrians at Dresden (26–27 Aug.) , surrender of Vandamme to the Russians at Kulm (30 Aug.); the Treaty of Töplitz (19 Sept., ; Bavaria and Wurtemberg desert Napoleon ; great defeat of the French at Leipzig (16–19 Oct.) , battle of Hanau (30 Oct.) ; Napoleon leaves Germany , general rising of the Germans against the French

Campaign of 1813 in the Peninsula , Wellington defeats the French at Vittoria (21 June) and invades France.

The allied armies reach the Rhine ; negotiations with Napoleon , position taken up by the Tsar Alexander, Metternich and Castlereagh

Campaign of 1814 in France, the allies invade France ; Napoleon's victories ; the Congress of Châtillon (Feb–Mch) , Frederick VI of Denmark cedes Norway to Sweden by the Treaty of Kiel (14 Jan.) ; the Dutch rise in insurrection ; Carnot's defence of Antwerp , the position in Italy ; Eugène de Beauharnais remains faithful, but Murat

negotiates with the allies ; the English occupy Genoa ; attitude of France towards Napoleon ; the country refuses to
rise to support him ; the allies sign the Treaty of Chaumont
(1 Mch.) , Napoleon's last battles , the allies occupy Paris
(31 Mch) ; abdication of Napoleon at Fontainebleau
(6 Apr)

Causes of the fall of Napoleon.

Authorities: On Napoleon's interference in Spain and Portugal
and on the history of the Peninsular War, see *Du Casse,* Mémoires et
Correspondance du Roi Joseph, *Wellington*, Despatches, *Napier*,
History of the Peninsular War, and *Gomez y Arteche*, Guerra della
Independencia , for the campaign of Wagram, see *Pelet*, Mémoires
sur la Guerre de 1809, for the reorganization of Prussia, see *Seeley*,
Life of Stein, *Pertz*, Das Leben des Ministers Freiherrn vom Stein,
Ranke, Denkwürdigkeiten des Fursten von Hardenbreg, *Stern*,
Abhandlungen und Aktenstucke zur Geschichte der Preussischen Re-
formzeit, and *Lehmann*, Scharnhorst , for Napoleon's campaign in
Russia, see *Ségur*, Histoire de Napóleon et de la Grande Armée pendant l'Année 1812 , for the campaign in Germany of 1813, and the
rising of Germany against Napoleon, see *Droysen*, Das Leben des
Grafen Yorck von Wartenburg, *Pertz*, Das Leben des Grafen Neit-
hardt von Gneisenau,'*Oncken*, Œsterreich und Preussen im Befreiungskriege, *Droysen*, Vorlesungen über die Freiheitskriege , for the defensive campaign of 1814 in France, see *Houssaye*, 1814, and for the
diplomatic proceedings of the period, *Alison*, Lives of Lord Castlereagh
and Sir Charles Stewart, the Memoirs and correspondence of *Castlereagh*, and *Vitrolles*, Mémoires

---

LECTURE V

THE CONGRESS OF VIENNA.

The abdication of Napoleon was followed by the provisional Treaty of Paris (11 April) assigning to him the
island of Elba and an income, and to the Empress Marie
Louise the duchies of Parma and Piacenza

The provisional government of France under the guidance

of Talleyrand accepted Louis XVIII as king ; on his arrival he issued the Declaration of Saint-Ouen (2 May) promising representative government, liberty of worship and of the press, responsibility of ministers, guarantee of property acquired during the Revolution, etc , which were afterwards embodied in the Charter (4 June, 1814)

By the First Treaty of Paris (30 May, 1814) France was reduced to the limits of 1792, with the addition of Avignon, and other districts within these limits, and of part of Savoy ; she received back all her colonies except the Mauritius, Saint Lucia and Tobago, which were ceded to England

It was agreed that a congress of representatives of the states of Europe should be held at Vienna to dispose of the territories on the left bank of the Rhine, taken from France and in general to settle the affairs of Europe.

The Congress of Vienna met on 1 Nov., 1814 ; it was attended by most of the sovereigns of Europe, and those who were not present sent special envoys

The most important ambassadors were Metternich for Austria, Hardenberg for Prussia, Castlereagh for England, and Razumovski and Nesselrode for Russia ; these representatives of the four victorious powers arrogated to themselves the right to arrange the decisions of the Congress.

Arrival of Talleyrand as the representative of France ; his great diplomatic campaign , he stands forth as the advocate of legitimacy, and as the defender of the smaller powers ; he adroitly makes use of the dissensions between the four great powers

The chief political questions at issue ; (1) the Tsar Alexander desired the whole of Poland and Frederick William III of Prussia the whole of Saxony, whose king had remained faithful to Napoleon , (2) the disposition of the territories on the left bank of the Rhine ; (3) the treatment of Italy, especially of Murat, who had abandoned Napoleon ; Talleyrand's attitude upon these questions

In order to oppose the claims of Russia and Prussia, Austria, England and France sign a secret treaty of alliance (3 Jan , 1815)

Eventually it is settled that Prussia shall receive Lusatia, being about two-fifth of the kingdom of Saxony, and Russia the greater part of the Grand Duchy of Warsaw, including the city of Warsaw; Prussia retained her gains in the first and second partitions of Poland, with the additions of Posen, Thorn and Dantzig, while Austria retained Eastern Galicia, and Cracow was made a free state

In order to establish strong powers upon the Rhine to curb France, Holland and Belgium are united as the Kingdom of the Netherlands and granted to the Prince of Orange, who is also made Grand Duke of Luxemburg, the districts comprising the former electorates of Tréves and Cologne, etc, were granted to Prussia, the districts further south to Bavaria, in compensation for the loss of Salzburg and the Tyrol, and the fortress of Mayence to Hesse-Darmstadt, to be garrisoned by the Germanic Confederation.

The re-arrangement of Italy, Lombardy and Venetia were given to Austria, Genoa was added to the kingdom of Sardinia in which the succession was fixed in the Carignan line, Tuscany and Modena were restored to their former rulers, both Austrian princes, Parma, Piacenza and Guastalla were given to the Empress Marie Louise for her life, with succession to the rightful heir who was for the time made Grand Duke of Lucca, the States of the Church restored to the Pope and the question of retaining Murat on the throne of Naples remained unsettled until he defied Austria and endeavored to summon Italy to arms; after the defeat of Murat at Tolentino (3 May, 1815) Naples was restored to Ferdinand IV, King of the Two Sicilies.

In the North, Sweden was confirmed in the possession of Norway, ceded to her by Denmark by the Treaty of Kiel, but Denmark lost Swedish Pomerania and received instead the Duchy of Lauenburg.

In Germany, Prussia regained her acquisitions of 1803 with Swedish Pomerania, the greater part of the kingdom of Westphalia, and Rhenish Prussia, Hanover received East Friesland and other districts, and the mediatization of the petty states of Germany was maintained.

England, in addition to the colonial gains made by the Treaty of Amiens, retained the Cape of Good Hope, the Mauritius, Malta, Heligoland, and the Ionian Islands, but restored Martinique to the French and Java to the Dutch ; Castlereagh's chief preoccupation at Vienna was, however, to secure the abolition of the negro slave trade.

Before these arrangements were finally completed, the congress was startled by the news that Napoleon had left Elba and was again master of France ; it therefore hurried through the rest of its work by reorganizing Germany and Switzerland

The Germanic Confederation took the place of the Confederation of the Rhine ; it consisted of thirty-eight states, in addition to Austria and Prussia, namely ; the four kingdoms of Bavaria, Hanover, Saxony and Wurtemberg, the eight grand duchies of Baden, Hesse-Cassel, Hesse-Darmstadt, Luxemburg, Mecklenburg-Schwerin, Mecklenburg-Strelitz, Oldenburg, and Saxe-Weimar, eleven duchies, eleven principalities, and the four free cities of Bremen, Frankfort, Hamburg and Lubeck ; the affairs of the Confederation were entrusted to a Diet presided over by Austria and consisting of an Ordinary Assembly of seventeen and a General Assembly of sixty-nine members

The Swiss Confederation was guaranteed neutrality by the powers of Europe , three new cantons, Geneva, Neufchâtel and the Valais were added ; entire independence was given to the individual cantons and the presidency of the federal diet was reserved to Zurich, Berne and Lucerne in turn.

Importance of the work of the Congress of Vienna ; it shows a reaction to 18th century ideas in trampling on the ideas of nationality and of the sovereignty of the people

The story of the Hundred Days , unpopularity and unwise conduct of Louis XVIII ; Napoleon escapes from Elba and lands in France (1 Mch , 1815) ; he reaches Paris (20 Mch) ; flight of Louis XVIII , Napoleon promises to establish representative institutions , the Additional Act

(23 Apr), he endeavors to raise France against the allies; he is defeated by the English and Prussians at Waterloo (18 June); surrender of Napoleon to Captain Maitland (15 July), he is sent to St. Helena, the allied armies occupy Paris, restoration of Louis XVIII

By the Second Treaty of Paris (20 Nov, 1815) France loses the part of Savoy granted her in 1814 and other ratifications of her frontier; she has to restore the works of art accumulated in Paris to their former owners; she is forced to pay a war contribution of 700,000,000 francs and to maintain an army of 150,000 troops of the allies in possession of her eastern fortresses for five years.

Authorities: For the history and acts of the Congress of Vienna, see *Flassan*, Histoire du Congrès de Vienne, *Kluber*, Akten der Wiener Congresses, *Angeberg*, Le Congrès de Vienne et les Traités de 1815, *De Pradt*, Le Congrès de Vienne, *Schoell*, Recueil de Pieces Officielles relatives au Congrès de Vienne, *Talleyrand*, Mémoires, *Pallain*, Correspondance inédite du Prince de Talleyrand et du Roi Louis XVIII pendant le Congrès de Vienne, *Metternich*, Memoirs, *Alison*, Lives of Lord Castlereagh and Sir Charles Stewart, *Castlereagh*, Correspondence, *Wellington*, Supplementary Despatches, *Ranke*, Hardenberg For the Hundred Days, see the books on Napoleon already cited, *Houssaye*, 1815, *Constant*, Mémoires sur les Cent Jours, *Vitrolles*, Mémoires, and *Rochechouart*, Souvenirs, and for the campaign of Waterloo, *Siborne*, History of the War in France and Belgium in 1815, *Ropes*, History of the Waterloo Campaign, *Gardner*, Waterloo, *Chesney*, Waterloo Lectures, and *Charras*, Histoire de la campagne de 1815

LECTURE VI

THE HOLY ALLIANCE

After the signature of the Second Treaty of Paris, the Tsar Alexander of Russia, influenced by Madame de Krudener, proposes the formation of a Holy Alliance declaring the obligations of monarchs to the Christian religion; it is signed by the Emperor Francis of Austria and King Frederick William III of Prussia, (26 Sept , 1815), but not by England , the objects and aims, secret and avowed, of the Holy Alliance.

Metternich recognized as the leading statesman of the Holy Alliance , his fear of democratic principles greater than his attachment to religion ; his intimacy with Castlereagh , he proposes to preserve the peace of Europe and the force of government by frequent congresses of representatives of the great powers, which should consult and act together

Metternich's Austrian policy the reverse of that of Joseph II , he believes in maintaining authority by preserving the diversity of language and law in the different provinces of the Austrian empire.

The internal policy of the Tsar Alexander I ; his attempt to establish constitutional government in Poland ; his friendship with Adam Czartoryski and other Polish patriots , his interest in the Eastern Question, and desire to overthrow the power of the Turks , he encourages the Greeks, especially through Capo d'Istria, in their desire for independence

The government of Louis XVIII in France , the system of the Charter ; representative government in two chambers ; the two parties, Royalists and Constitutionalists , suppression of the liberty of the press , repression of the partisans of the Revolution , the White Terror , the administration of the Duc de Richelieu, (1815–1818)

The Congress of Aix la Chapelle , the allies agree to evacuate France (9 Oct , 1818)

The spread of constitutional principles in Germany ; indignation of the young German party at the refusal of the Congress of Vienna to recognize the principle of nationality or the establishment of representative government ; the spirit of the universities , the Burschenschaft

Certain German rulers, notably the Kings of Bavaria and Wurtemberg and the Grand Dukes of Baden and Saxe-Weimar, grant representative constitutions to their states , Fred-

erick William III of Prussia had promised a constitution in
1815 and took steps in that direction in 1818 ; the work of
William von Humboldt , Metternich's opposition to the liberal movement in Germany

The murder of Kotzebue (23 Mch , 1819) , its effect on
Germany , Frederick William III dismisses Humboldt and
delays his promised constitution ; riots in Germany , Metternich takes advantage of these risings to oppose liberal ideas ,
the Congress of Carlsbad (Aug 1819) ; the Final Act of the
Congress of Vienna (15 May, 1820), strengthening the power
of the Diet of the Germanic Confederation against the
different states ; measures taken against German liberalism

The demand for representative government and for the
establishment in different degrees of liberal principles
stigmatized by Metternich as Jacobinism , he induces the
Holy Alliance, including the Tsar Alexander, to declare
against liberalism

The supporters of liberal principles form secret societies
all over Europe in relation with each other ; in Germany
and in Italy their cause is associated with the spirit of
nationality.

General revolution in Spain (1820) caused by the
reactionary government of Ferdinand VII , the Spanish
colonies in Central and South America fight for their independence , San Martin, Francia, Bolivar and Iturbide ; the
Spaniards demand the Constitution of 1812 , Ferdinand VII
appears to yield, but appeals for help against his people to
the Holy Alliance ; Catalonia and Navarre oppose the reforms of the Cortes

The Carbonari in Italy ; the movement for reform, both
democratic and national ; Pepe seize Naples (1820) and
forces Ferdinand IV to adopt a liberal constitution ; democratic rising in Turin

Metternich lays the question of the liberal movement in
Italy before a congress of the powers at Troppau (Oct ,
Dec., 1820) and at Laybach (Jan –Mch , 1821) ; Austria
authorized to interfere , Austrian troops suppress the liberal
movements in Naples and Piedmont.

Suicide of Castlereagh (12 Aug., 1822) ; Canning becomes English foreign minister ; his liberal ideas and dislike of Metternich ; Castlereagh's death the first blow at the solidarity of the great powers in the system of governing Europe by Congress.

Attitude of France towards the other powers,; policy of Louis XVIII ; administration of Decazes (1818–20) and of Richelieu (1820–21) , formation of an ultra-Royalist ministry under Villèle (1821)

Meeting of the Congress of Verona (Oct , 1822), summoned to deal with the revolutionary movement in Spain ; attitude taken by Canning, who declares the intention of England to recognize the independence of the South American republics and warns the allies not to interfere in Portugal ; the Congress requests France to re-establish the authority of Ferdinand VII

A French army invades Spain, occupies Madrid, and suppresses the Constitutional party in Spain ; unpopularity of this action among French liberals , plots formed against the Bourbons

Death of Louis XVIII (16 Sept , 1824) , accession of the Comte d'Artois as Charles X ; his ultra-Royalist ideas , he retains Villèle in power

Death of the Tsar Alexander I (1 Dec , 1825) , the character of his influence on European politics since the Congress of Vienna ; his death breaks up the Holy Alliance ; his successor, Nicholas I, resolves to carry out his own policy without consulting the other powers ; Metternich remains the director of the policy of Austria and Russia, but England, owing to the death of Castlereagh, and Russia, owing to the death of Alexander, no longer submit to his leadership

Authorities For the diplomatic history of this period, see *Debidour*, Histoire Diplomatique de L'Europe, *Metternich*, Memoirs, *Castlereagh*, Correspondence, *Pozzo di Borgo*, Correspondance diplomatique, and *Ranke*, Hardenberg , for special Congresses, see *De Pradt*, L'Europe après le Congrès d'Aix La Chapelle, and Le Congrès de Carlsbad, *Bignon*, Le Congrès de Troppau, and *Chateaubriand*, Le

Congrès de Verone ; for the history of the Restoration in France, see *Viel-Castel*, Histoire de la Restauration, *Rochechouart*, Souvenirs, *Hyde de Neuville*, Mémoires, *Marcellus*, Souvenirs diplomatiques, and *Villèle*, Mémoires, for Germany, see *Gervinus*, Geschichte des Neunzehnten Jahrhunderts, *Treitschke*, Deutsche Geschichte im Neunzehnten Jahrhundert, and *Pfister*, König Friedrich von Wurttemberg und seine Zeit , on Italy, see *Colletta*, Istoria di Reame di Napoli, *Pepe*, Memoirs, and *Costa de Beauregard*, La Jeunesse du Roi Charles Albert , for Spain, *Hubbard*, Histoire Contemporaine de l'Espagne, and *Martignac*, Essai historique sur la Révolution d'Espagne , and for the Tsar Alexander, *Ford*, Madame de Krudener, La Correspondance entre le Tsar Alexandre et le Prince Adam Czartoryski, and *Schnitzler*, Histoire intime de la Russie sous les Empereurs Alexandre et Nicolas

---

LECTURE VII

THE EASTERN QUESTION AND THE INDEPENDENCE OF GREECE.

The importance of the Eastern question in the history of Europe during the 19th century ; owing to the extinction of Poland, it becomes practically a Turkish question ; England and Austria devote themselves to checking the disruption of the Turkish Empire which it was the traditional policy of Russia to promote

The position of the Turks at the time of the Congress of Vienna ; loss of the old Muhammadan fanaticism and energy , the government of the Sultan Mahmud II ; quasi-independence of Egypt attained by Mehemet Ali by his destruction of the Mamelukes (1811) , discontented and independent spirit of the Christian populations under Turkish rule, of the inhabitants of the Danubian provinces of Wallachia and Moldavia, of the Slavs of Servia, and of the Greeks.

The insurrection of the Servians under Kara George (1804) , recognition of Servian independence by the Treaty of Bucharest (1812), the Turks nevertheless reconquer Servia and expel Kara George, second Servian insurrection under Milosch Obrenovitch (1815); he is for a time recognized as quasi-independent (1817)

Position of the Danubian provinces under the Treaty of Bucharest; Russia reaches the Danube.

The Greeks rise in insurrection (1821); they are encouraged, but not openly, by the Tsar Alexander I; his friendship for Capo d'Istria, failure of the first rising under Ypsilanti, gallantry of the Greek insurgents, Metternich declares against assisting them; Alexander therefore, dismisses Capo d'Istria from office; strong feeling among the educated classes in England and France in favor of the Greeks, many volunteers, including Byron, go to their assistance; large loans raised for them in England

Change caused in the attitude of Russia to the Eastern Question by the accession of Nicholas, he resolves to promote Russian interests in Turkey without consulting other powers; Nicholas agrees with Canning that the Turks shall be forced to recognize the independence of Greece (4 Apr, 1826); by the Treaty of Ackerman (7 Oct., 1826) the Turks make concessions to Russia, and the Sultan promises to appoint local boyars or nobles elected by the local divans for seven years as Hospodars or princes of the two Danubian provinces and to establish quasi-independence in Servia.

Canning becomes prime minister of England (10 April, 1827), Russia, England and France come to an agreement for securing absolute independence for Greece (6 July, 1827); the Turks encouraged by Metternich, refused to yield; death of Canning (8 Aug,), destruction of the Turkish fleet by the allies at Navarino (20 Oct, 1827); Capo d'Istria elected President of the Greek state.

Position of the Sultan Mahmud II, by the massacre of the Janissaries (15 June, 1826) he had destroyed his army; the battle of Navarino had destroyed his fleet; nevertheless, he refused to consent to the independence of Greece.

The Tsar Nicholas, in the name of the Triple Alliance,

attacked the Turks and a Russian army crossed the Pruth
(7 May, 1828) ; changes of ministry in England and France
caused England under Wellington to be less eager, and
France under Martignac to be more eager to support the
cause of the Greeks ; a French force under Maison occupies
the Morea, which is evacuated by the Egyptian troops of
Mehemet Ali ; the Russians repulsed from Shumla and Silistria , successful campaign of Paskievitch in Armenia

By an agreement between England, France and Russia,
the limits of Greece are fixed, and it is resolved that some
prince not belonging to the Royal Houses of these countries
shall be placed upon the throne of Greece (22 Mch , 1829) ,
candidature of Leopold of Saxe-Coburg-Gotha

Campaign of 1829, Diebitch reaches Adrianople , terror
of the Sultan Mahmud ; by the Treaty of Adrianople (14
Sept , 1829) the Treaty of Ackerman is renewed with the
exception that the Hospodars of the Danubian provinces are
to be appointed for life, the independence of Greece is
recognized and the Russians are permitted to occupy the
fortresses upon the Danube as a guarantee of the payment
of a large indemnity by the Turks

Conclusion of the Greek question ; Leopold refuses the
throne , murder of Capo d'Istria (9 Oct , 1831) , Otho of
Bavaria made King of the Hellenes (7 May, 1832) ; the
French evacuate the Morea.

The Tsar Nicholas I and Poland ; the government of the
Grand Duke Constantine , indignation of the Poles at the refusal of self-government ; the feeling of nationality maintained by secret societies , the Poles, who served under Napoleon, look for help to France in regaining their independence

Effect of the Revolution of Feb , 1830, in France upon
Poland ; an insurrection breaks out at Warsaw (29 Nov ,
1830) , the Russians are driven from Poland ; Chlopicki dictator of Poland (5 Dec , 1830—15 Jan., 1831) , the Poles defeat the Russians at Waver (20 Feb , 1831), and elsewhere ;
Europe refuses to help the Poles , the Austrians and Prus-

sians mass troops upon their frontiers, fearing that the insurrection will reach Austrian and Prussian Poland ; Louis
Philippe of France is not firm enough on his throne to interfere ; the Poles defeated at Ostrolenka (26 May, 1831) ;
Warsaw besieged and taken by Paskievitch (7 Sept , 1831) ;
cruel punishment of the Polish insurgents , rigorous government of the Tsar Nicholas

Policy of Nicholas towards the Turks ; by his occupation
of the Danubian fortresses he keeps them at his mercy , the
character and career of Mehemet Ali, Pasha of Egypt ; he invades Syria, with the intention of marching on Constantinople , England and France intervene to stop Mehemet Ali ;
the Sultan Mahmud calls in the help of Russia and signs an
offensive and defensive treaty with Nicholas at Unkiar
Skelessi (12 July, 1833) , the Russians evacuate the Danubian fortresses and provinses (1834)

Russia's advance into Central Asia ; conquest of the Central Asian tribes one of the national aims of the Russian people ; importance and value of the work to Europe ; the campaign of the Russians for the possession of the Caucasus
and the conquest of Circassia and Georgia ; Russian wars
with Persia ; by the Treaty of Gulistan (1813) Fateh Ali
Shah cedes Daghestan to Russia, and by the Treaty of Turk-
omanchai (1828) Russian influence becomes predominant in
Persia.

The settlement of the Eastern question presents difficult
problems to England, France and Austria, which all have an
interest in restraining Russia.

Authorities : For the history of the Eastern Question, reference
may be made to the sketch contained in *Debidour*, Histoire Diplomatique de l'Europe, to several of the other works cited under Lecture VI, to *Balleydier*, Histoire de l'Empereur Nicolas, to *Gentz*, Dé
pêches inédits aux Hospodars de Valachie, and to *Ranke*, History of
Servia , for the War of Greek Independence, the best authorities are
Finlay, History of the Greek Revolution, *Gordon*, History of the
Greek Revolution, *Soutzo*, Histoire de la Révolution Grecque, and
Tricoupis' history written in modern Greek , for the policy of Canning, see his political life by *Stapleton*, and his official correspondence

edited by *Stapleton*, for the war between Russia and Turkey, see *Chesney*, The Russo-Turkish Campaigns of 1828-29, and *Moltke*, Journal of the War between Russia and Turkey, and, for the advance of Russia into Central Asia, *Hellwald*, The Russians in Central Asia

LECTURE VIII

THE REVOLUTION OF 1830 IN FRANCE

The position of parties under the Restoration, in the Chambers appeared only ultra-Royalists, and Constitutionalists, who desire to interpret the charter of 1814 according to the principles of 1789, in the army and in military circles were many Bonapartists; and in the cities the Democratic and Republican party was very strong.

Character of the ultra-Royalist administration of Villèle (1821-28) during the latter years of Louis XVIII and the first years of Charles X, severe repression of Bonapartist plots and city riots; the Royalists endeavor to make the Constitutional party responsible for Bonapartist and Democratic excesses, the bourgeois, and educated classes of France, support the Constitutionalists; Royalism is confined to a small party of the nobility, growing importance of journalism, the work of Armand Carrel, Courier, Thiers, and Guizot.

The character, and policy of Charles X; he hopes by a vigorous foreign policy, as shown in the expedition to the Morea in 1828 and in the expedition to Algiers in 1830, to turn the minds of the people from internal politics, and by a close alliance with the absolutist powers, especially Russia, to get assistance from abroad in case of insurrection at home

The elections of 1827 give a large majority in the Chambers to the Constitutionalists, Villèle succeeded in office by Martignac (4 Jan. 1828); the new ministry satisfies neither the King nor the Chambers, and is succeeded by the ultra-Royalist ministry of Polignac (8 Aug , 1829) , the king and ministry being unable to get a majority for their measures resolve to alter the Charter in favor of increasing the royal power

Proclamation of the Ordinances submitting the press to severe censure and modifying the electoral laws (25 July, 1830).

The insurrection of July 1830 in Paris , the erection of barricades and commencement of street fighting (27, 28 July) , the failure of the troops to suppress the insurrection; Charles X, when too late, withdraws the Ordinances (29 July); he resolves to leave France with his family (31 July) , he appoints the Duke of Orleans Lieutenant-General of the kingdom, (1 Aug) and abdicates (2 Aug); he reaches England (17 Aug)

Surprise of the Constitutionalists at their sudden and complete victory , the part played by Lafayette ; the Constitutionalists resolve that although the victory had been won by the democrats of Paris it shall result in the formation of a Constitutional monarchy , the Chambers revise the Charter from the liberal point of view, and (7 Aug) elect the Duke of Orleans as King of the French under the title of Louis Philippe

Character, career and disposition of Louis Philippe , difficulties of his position at the commencement of his reign ; he represented the ideas and wishes of the bourgeois, and not of the whole people of France, which weakened him at home, while abroad, he is regarded as the creation of a new French Revolution not less dangerous to the monarchical system of Europe than the first French Revolution

The foreign policy of Louis Philippe , importance of the services rendered at this time by Talleyrand, who goes as ambassador to London ; the Monarchy of July recognized by Wellington, as prime minister of England, and cordially supported by the Reform Ministry of Lord Grey, which succeeded to power in Nov 1830 , the recognition of England was followed by that of Austria and Prussia, Metternich and Frederick William III being afraid to attack France by themselves ; the Tsar Nicholas was too much occupied with putting down the Polish insurrection to interfere in France, and did not desire to do so after Louis Philippe refused to assist the Poles

The insurrections in Belgium and elsewhere which followed the Revolution in France made the position of the king very difficult because France was held responsible for the other risings , skill shown by Louis Philippe and Talleyrand.

Internal policy of Louis Philippe , doubtfulness of his title as a legitimate or a revolutionary monarch , he re-establishes the tricolor flag ; Lafayette appointed Commandant General of the National Guards of France , the first ministry of Louis Philippe containing members of both the Constitutional and advanced Liberal parties , Laffitte, the leader of the advanced party, made chief minister (2 Nov , 1830) , changes made in the Constitution

The ministry of Casimir Perier (1831–32) , his strong government at home and his strong foreign policy , abolition of the hereditary peerage and appointment of an upper-chamber of life peers

Significance of the Revolution of 1830 in France , the bourgeois at last have an opportunity of putting into effect the principles of 1789 ; results of their experiment

Authorities : The Revolution of 1830 in France is treated at length in the first chapters of the following general histories of the reign of Louis Philippe . *Thureau-Dangin*, Histoire de la Monarchie de Juillet *Louis Blanc*, Histoire de dix Ans, *Capefigue*, L'Europe depuis l'avènement du Roi Louis Philippe, *D Houssonville*, Histoire de la politique extérieure du Gouvernement Français (1830-48), and *Hillebrand*, Geschichte Frankreichs, of special value are *Talleyrand*, Mémoires, vols. iv and v, containing his correspondence with Louis Philippe from 1830 to 1834, and reference may be made to *Guizot*, Mémoires pour servir à l'histoire de mon temps, *Lafayette*, Mémoires, *Salvandy*, Seize Mois, *Laffitte*, Mémoires, and the *Duc de Broglie*, Souvenirs.

LECTURE IX.

THE BELGIAN INSURRECTION

The mistake made by the Congress of Vienna in uniting the Protestant and Catholic Netherlands under one monarch, the hereditary antagonism of the Dutch and the Belgians, in 1815 Belgium had been for more than twenty years under French government and resented the government of the Dutch

The government of William I, King of the Netherlands; he declares Dutch the official language of the country and favors his Dutch over his Belgian subjects

The Belgians, excited by the news of the Revolution of July, 1830, in Paris, and hoping for help from the new government of France, break into insurrection (25 Aug, 1830), a Dutch attack on Brussels is repulsed (30 Aug), a provisional government formed, and a national assembly summoned

The National Assembly of Belgium meets (10 Nov.), solemnly proclaims the independence of Belgium (18 Nov), and that Belgium should be like France a constitutional monarchy and not a republic

William I appeals to the great powers for assistance, on the ground that the independence of Belgium was contrary to the decisions of the Congress of Vienna; but the Tsar Nicholas was engaged in Poland, Metternich's attention was fixed on Italy, England, under the Reform Ministry of Lord Grey, was inclined to sympathize with the Belgian insurgents and only Prussia was prepared to assist him.

The difficult position of Louis Philippe; as the king made by the Revolution of 1830 in Paris, he is looked on as responsible for the Belgian Revolution by Europe and appealed to for help by the Belgians, England was the only great power which cared much about Belgium, and it thought more of keeping Belgium separate from France than subject to Holland, Talleyrand, as French ambassador in London, agreed to act with England in settling the fate of the Belgians ; a conference of the powers summoned for this purpose in London

The Conference of London recognized the independence of Belgium (20 Dec.) and direct an armistice to be made (9 Jan , 1831) , it fixed the boundaries of the new Belgian State (20 Jan), excluding from it Luxemburg, Maestricht and the right bank of the Scheldt , discontent of the Belgians with these frontiers, which were eventually slightly modified

The Duc de Nemours, second son of Louis Philippe, elected King of the Belgians over the Duke of Leuchtenberg and the Archduke Charles ; he refuses the throne (17 Feb , 1831) , the regency of Surlet de Chokier, Leopold of Saxe-Coburg-Gotha, the English candidate, elected King of the Belgians (4 June) , he accepts the throne under certain conditions , the Conference of London, under the influence of the English foreign minister Palmerston, declares Belgium neutral under the guarantee of the Powers

William I suddenly breaks the armistice and invades Belgium (1 Aug , 1831), Leopold appeals for aid to France , vigorous action of the Casimir Perier ministry ; a French army under Gérard occupies Brussels (12 Aug , 1831); the Belgians accept the terms fixed by the Conference of London (15 Nov , 1831), the states of Europe generally recognize Leopold

William I remains obdurate ; the English and French fleets blockade Holland ; and Gérard's army is directed to take the citadel of Antwerp, the only Dutch fortress remaining in Belgium ; capture of Antwerp (23 Dec., 1832)

From that time the independence of Belgium was assured, though William I still tried to make difficulties.

The nature and character of the Belgian constitution

The effect of the Revolutions of 1830 in Paris and Belgium in Germany ; riots and risings in Rhenish Prussia where the Catholics are alarmed at the Protestant legislation of Frederick William III, and where the idea of self-government is especially strong ; insurrections and demands for self-government in other German states, notably in Hanover, Hesse-Cassel and Saxony ; expulsion of the Duke of Brunswick by his people

Resurrection of the young German movement for nationality and self-government , revival of the Tugenbund, the Burschenschaft, etc.

Metternich attributes these political risings to the growth of revolutionary ideas, and attacks constitutional government as a form of republicanism and as essentially revolutionary.

Metternich's ascendency over the mind of Frederick William III ; after 1830 he appeals to the Tsar Nicholas and hopes to revive the Holy Alliance

The Conferences of Toplitz and Munchen–Gratz (1832), the three powers guarantee each other's rights in Poland and take measures for crushing the idea of Polish nationality they also resolve against the doctrine of non-intervention and declare the right of any monarch whose position is assailed by internal rebellion to appeal for aid to other monarchs

With regard to Germany, Metternich gets a law passed in the Federal Diet that, in case of disagreement between a German ruler and his people, the Confederation could interfere to restore the power of the ruler, and it was declared that no constitution granted by himself could limit the right of a ruler to collect taxes

The effect of the Revolution of 1830 in Italy , the Carbonari force a series of insurrections ; the Empress Marie Louise is driven from Parma, and Duke Francis IV from Modena (Feb , 1831), more general insurrections in the States of the Church, the attitude of Pope Gregory XVI—Capellari ; provisional government formed for the Legations at Bologna

Metternich sends Austrian troops to restore order in Parma, Modena, and the States of the Church, the Italian insurgents look for help to France ; the attitude taken by Louis Philippe and Casimir Perier ; the French occupy Ancona (22 Feb ,

1832) which they assert their right to hold as long as the Austrians occupy the Legations ; the French evacuate Ancona when the Austrians withdraw (Dec 1838).

Significance of the movement of 1830 in Europe

Authorities : On the Belgian Revolution see *Nothomb* Essai historique et politique sur la révolution de Belgique, *Juste* La révolution de la Belgique, 1830, and Le Roi Léopold, and *Bavay* Histoire de la révolution belge de 1830, on the revolutionary movement in Germany in 1830 see *Gervinus* and *Treitschke*, cited under Lecture VI, *Bulle*, Geschichte der neuesten Zeit, *Deventer* Cinquante années de l'histoire fédérale de l'Allemagne, and *Biedermann*, 1815-1840, Funf und zwanzig Jahre Deutscher Geschichte; and in Italy *Thayer* The revolutionary movement in Italy from 1815 to 1848, *Tivaroni* Istoria della dominazione Austriaco in Italia, and *Mazzini* Works.

LECTURE X.

INSURRECTION AND CIVIL WAR IN SPAIN AND PORTUGAL.

The condition of Portugal after the Peninsular War , extent of English influence in the regency and the army ; the Portuguese expel the English (1820) and draw up a democratic constitution (1822).

John VI returns to Portugal, when Brazil declares its independence under the Emperor Pedro I (1823), on the death of John VI the Emperor Pedro issues the Charter of 1826 establishing moderate parliamentary government and then abdicates the throne of Portugal in favor of his daughter Maria da Gloria ; Canning sends an English force to Portugal to maintain order which is withdrawn in 1827.

Dom Miguel, younger brother of the Emperor Pedro, who was appointed regent in 1827, seizes the throne (1828), he declares himself an absolute monarch, and persecutes both the moderate adherents to the Charter of 1826, and the more radical supporters of the Constitution of 1822.

The reign of Dom Miguel ; both Chartists and Constitutionalists rise in rebellion (1829) and declare in favor of Maria da Gloria ; the Emperor Pedro resigns the throne of Brazil (1831) and comes to the support of his daughter's cause ; attitude of the powers of Europe to the civil wars in Portugal ; many English officers enter the Queen's service ; the siege of Oporto ; Napier destroys Miguel's fleet off Cape St Vincent (5 July, 1833); the Pedroites occupy Lisbon (24 July)

England, France and Spain recognize Maria da Gloria and form the Quadruple Alliance ; Dom Miguel surrenders to a Spanish and Portuguese army at Evora Monte (26 May, 1834), by the Convention of Evora Monte he is forever expelled from Portugal

Death of the ex-Emperor Pedro (24 Sept , 1834); troubled reign of Maria da Gloria (1834-53), constant outbreaks of civil war and frequency of military pronunciamentos in favor of the Charter of 1826 and the Constitution of 1822 ; revision of the Charter (1852)

Revival of national feeling in Portugal , rejection of Iberianist ideas

The latter years of the reign of Ferdinand VII of Spain after his restoration to absolute power by the French in 1823 , the question of the succession to the throne ; Ferdinand VII, by a Pragmatic Sanction, declares his elder daughter, Isabella, to be the heir ; opposition of Don Carlos, his brother, who claims the succession as male heir

Death of Ferdinand VII (29 Sept , 1833); Isabella, a child of three years old, recognized as Queen by the greater part of Spain, under the regency of her mother Christina, a daughter of Ferdinand IV, King of the Two Sicilies , character of Christina , the regency is recognized by England and France.

Don Carlos opposes the regency and declares himself king ; his cause is favored by the clericals and by the mountaineers of Northern Spain , outbreak of civil war , victories of the Carlists.

Rivalry of England and France in the affairs of the Peninsula , personal rivalry between Palmerston and Louis Philippe ; both countries prevented by jealousy of each other from openly assisting the Christinists, though they both as constitutional monarchies desire her success over the Carlists , legions of volunteers were however raised both in France and in England for the support of the Christinists , services of Sir De Lacy Evans

Perilous position of the Christinists , the military revolt of La Granja (13 Aug , 1836); Christina summons a Cortes, which promulgates the liberal constitution of 1837 , vigorous prosecution of the war against the Carlists ; victories of Espartero , defeat and flight of Don Carlos (1839)

Espartero forces Christina to leave Spain (1840) and rules the country as regent for three years ; his strong government and endeavor to put down brigandage and restore the prosperity of Spain.

Narvaez overthrows Espartero (1843), recalls Christina, and declares the young queen Isabella of age.

The rivalry between England and France for influence in Spain becomes more pronounced ; the policy of Louis Philippe ; the question of the Spanish marriages ; Queen Isabella married to her cousin Don Francisco d' Assisi, Duke of Cadiz, and her sister and heiress to the Duc 'de Montpensier, fifth son of Louis Philippe (1846)

Condition of Spain during the reign of Queen Isabella ; constant changes in the ministry between Narvaez, Espartero and O'Donnell ; backwardness of Spain in material and intellectual progress

Characteristics of the history of the Peninsula during the period succeeding the overthrow of Napoleon , unfitness of the Spanish and Portuguese for representative government , the meaning and effect of the pronunciamientos and civil wars

Authorities: Upon the civil wars in Portugal and the establishment of representative government there, see *Morse Stephens* The Story of Portuaul, *Smith*, Memoirs of the Duke of Saldanha, *Luz Soriano*,

Historia da Guerra civil e do Estabelecimento do Governo Parlamentar
em Portugal, *Freire de Carvalho*, Memorias para a historia do tempo
que duron a Usurpacão de Dom Miguel, *Gomes de Barros e Cunha*,
Historia da Liberdade em Portugal, and *Bollaert*, The Wars of Succession in Spain and Portugal, upon the same period in Spain, see
Hubbard, Histoire contemporaine de l'Espagne, *Los Valles* Don Carlos, *Bollaert*, and *Duncan* The English in Spain, or the War of Succession between 1834 and 1840

LECTURE XI

EUROPE DURING THE REIGN OF LOUIS PHILIPPE

The characteristics of the Monarchy of July ; its founders
model their ideas on the English parliamentary system, including the responsibility of ministers, the annual voting of
supplies, and the selection of ministers from the legislature,
but the upper House consisted of life and not of hereditary
peers, and the popular House was elected by a very restricted
franchise consisting only of large taxpayers and members of
the learned professions, allowing votes only to about three
hundred thousand persons.

The difficulties of the position of Louis Philippe ; he is
opposed on the one side by the Legitimists, who caused disturbances in the south, and on the other by the Republicans,
who rise in insurrection in the great industrial cities, and
especially in Lyons

Effect of the foreign policy of Louis Philippe and of his
refusal to help the insurgent Belgians, Poles and Italians upon
his position at home.

Death of Casimir Perier (16 May, 1832).

Repression of a Republican rising in Paris (6 June), and
arrest of the Duchess of Berry (7 Nov.), who had endeavored to raise La Vendée for the Legitimists.

Commencement of parliamentary government ; formation

of the Soult administration ; difficulties in the way of establishing regular parliamentary government in France ; absence of definite parliamentary parties , the chief parliamentary leaders, Thiers, Guizot, the Duc de Broglie, Molé, Berryer, and Odilon Barrot

Numerous industrial and democratic insurrections in France , Fieschi's attempt on the king's life (28 July, 1835), attempt of Louis Napoleon upon Strasbourg (3 Oct , 1836) ; constant ministerial changes

The foreign policy of Louis Philippe ; his intimate relations with England (1830-34) , the cause of this close alliance to be found in the distrust of him felt by the other great powers , gradual weakening of the alliance , Palmerston, the English foreign minister, endeavors to keep France from interfering in the affairs of Spain and Portugal ; Louis Philippe then weakens in his attachment for England, and negotiates with Austria, endeavoring to obtain an Austrian archduchess as wife for his eldest son ; France and England come into collision on Colonial, South American, Asiatic and African questions

The occupation and gradual conquest of Algeria by France , the resistance of Abd-el-Kader ; the campaigns of Bugeaud.

A fresh crisis arises in the Eastern Question, which nearly causes war between France and England ; the Sultan Mahmud II had not forgiven Mehemet Ali, the Pasha of Egypt, who had conquered Syria in 1832, and had only been prevented from overthrowing the Ottoman Empire by the intervention of Russia and the great powers , the Turks invade Syria, but are defeated by the Egyptians near Aleppo (20 June, 1839) ; death of Mahmud II (30 June), and accession of Abdul Medjid

The French sympathize with Mehemet Ali, but England is afraid that his success will overthrow the Turkish Empire, and therefore agrees with Russia, Prussia and Austria to intervene on behalf of the Turks ; Palmerston resolves to break the Anglo-French alliance and by the Treaty of Lon-

don (15 July, 1840) agrees with the other three great powers
to act without France , Napier and Stopford bombard Bey-
rout (12 Sept.) and Acre (2 Nov); the Egyptians retire
from Syria ; and eventually Mehemet Ali is forced to accept
an hereditary title to Egypt under certain conditions, and to
abandon all other claims , the great powers guarantee the
neutrality of the Dardanelles under Turkish sovereignty

Indignation felt in France against England ; war averted
with difficulty , ·formation of the Guizot administration
(29 Oct , 1840), which remained in office till the end of the
reign of Louis Philippe.

Growth of the Napoleonic legend in France ; attempt of
Louis Napoleon on Boulogne (5 Aug , 1840) , the remains of
the first Napoleon brought to France and interred at Paris
(15 Dec-, 1840)

Changes brought about in the political attitude and conditions of England during the reign of Louis Philippe ; the
passing of the Reform Bill (1832) transfers political power
from the aristocracy to the middle classes, and subsequent
reforms make the administration more democratic ; the accession of Victoria (1837) finally separates English from continental interests, for the Kingdom of Hanover passes to
her uncle, the Duke of Cumberland, who ascends the throne
as Ernest I , importance of this event

Marriage of Victoria to Albert of Saxe-Coburg-Gotha ,
his character, and interest in foreign politics ; the Queen's
first ministers, Melbourne and Palmerston , influence of
Wellington , Sir Robert Peel comes into power (1841) ; his
endeavors for peace

The question of Spanish marriages , Louis Philippe tricks
the English ministry, and after preventing the marriage of
Queen Isabella of Spain to the English candidate, Prince
Leopold of Saxe-Coburg-Gotha, he secures the marriage of
the young Queen to her cousin Don Francisco and of her
only sister to his own fifth son, the Duc de Montpensier
(1845).

Indignation of the English court and ministry at the

Spanish marriages, Lord John Russell comes into office with Palmerston as foreign minister (1846), resolved to isolate Louis Philippe ; the new government refuses to discourage the revolutionary movements on the point of breaking out all over Europe

Position of Austria during the reign of Louis Philippe, the death of the Emperor Francis and the accession of the Emperor Ferdinand I (1835) strengthens the position of Metternich, his close relations with the Tsar Nicholas ; occupation of Cracow (1836-41) by Austria ; annexation of Cracow by Austria (1846), Metternich's continued efforts to repress all movements for parliamentary reform or national independence in Italy and Germany, Metternich's friendship with Russia grows warmer as his influence over Prussia decreases after the accession of Frederick William IV.

Insignificent part played by Prussia during the latter years of the reign of Frederick William III in European politics ; the king's fidelity to the ideas of the Holy Alliance and to the settlement reached by the Congress of Vienna, he refuses to grant to the Prussians the constitution he had promised, under Metternich's influence he opposed liberal and parliamentary ideas all over Germany, discontent caused in Rhenish Prussia by his Protestant sympathies ; death of Frederick William III (7 June, 1840)

In spite of this opposition to liberal ideas Prussia was regarded as the one power which could unite Germany, this doctrine held especially in Northern Germany, fostered by the universities, and encouraged by Prussian statesmen and administrators ; excellence of the Prussian administrative and military system ; maintenance of the system of Scharnhorst, Prussia becomes especially the guardian of the smaller states of Germany ; she takes the first step towards hegemony by the formation of the Zollverein

The history of the Zollverein or Customs-union ; the ideas and arguments of List ; the Federal Diet of the Germanic Confederation refuses to establish a Customs-union, formation of the Zollverein (1833) : its chief members Prussia,·

Bavaria, Wurtemberg, Saxony, Hesse-Cassel, Hesse-Darmstadt, and the petty states of the Thuringian Union , joined
by Baden, Nassau, and Hesse-Homburg (1835), Frankfort
(1836), Brunswick (1841) and Luxemburg (1842) ; opposed
to it was the Steuerverein, consisting of Hanover, Oldenburg
and Schaumburg-Lippe, as well as to the two Mecklenburgs,
and the free cities of Hamburg, Bremen and Lubeck ,
commercial and political importance of the Zollverein.

Accession of Frederick William IV as King of Prussia
(1840) , his character , his hatred for France ; his liberal
ideas ; he places Eichhorn and Boyen in office, allows exiled
liberals to return, patronizes German literature and gives a
measure of liberty to the press ; he forms a States-General
out of the Provincial States with taxing and consultative
powers only (3 Feb , 1847).

Civil war in Switzerland ; the desire of the majority of
the Swiss Cantons for a stronger federal bond than that
devised by the Congress of Vienna ; changes in the constitution of individual cantons , introduction, especially since
1830, of democratic ideas ; cantonal revolutions ; formation
of the Sonderbund, by which the seven Catholic cantons of
Lucerne, Schwytz, Uri, Unterwalden, Glarus, Zug, Fribourg,
and Valais made an armed union to resist centralization and
defend the Jesuits , the majority in the Federal Diet, presided
over by Ochsenbein, decrees the dissolution of the Sonderbund (20 July, 1847) and the expulsion of the Jesuits ,
attitude of the great powers ; mutual apprehensions of
Louis Philippe and Metternich ; they deny the right of the
Swiss to alter the constitution laid down by the Congress of
Vienna ; the Sonderbund declares its intention to resist
(29 Oct ,) . the Federal Diet declares war (6 Nov ,),
General Dufour defeats the troops of the Sonderbund and
occupies their cantons, which submit (29 Nov) , declaration of the new Federal constitution, giving greater strength
to the Federal power and organizing a Swiss army, but recognizing cantonal rights in internal administration

General apprehension of democratic risings felt in 1847 ,

preparations for revolution ; the persistence of liberal and national ideas.

Authorities In addition to the works on the reign of Louis Philippe by *Thureau-Dangin, Capefigue, D'Haussonville, Hillebrand* and *Louis Blanc*, cited under Lecture VIII, see, for the later part of his reign and for other points touched on in this lecture, *Duvergier de Hauranne*, Histoire du gouvernement parlementaire en France, *Regnault*, Histoire de huit ans (1840–48), *Guizot*, Mémoires pour servir à l'histoire de mon temps, *Odilon Barrot*, Mémoires, *Mazade*, Monsieur Thiers, *Thiers*, Discours parlementaires, *Berryer*, Discours parlementaires, *Duc de Broglie*, Souvenirs, *Talleyrand*, Mémoires, *Rousset*, Conquête de l'Algérie, and *Ideville*, Le Maréchal Bugeaud   For the history of English foreign policy see *Le Strange*, Correspondence of Lord Grey and the Princess Lieven, *Dalling and Ashley*, Life of Lord Palmerston, *Torrens*, Life of Lord Melbourne, *Walpole*, Life of Lord John Russell, *Gordon*, Lord Aberdeen, *Greville*, Memoirs, *Stockmar*, Memoirs and *Martin*, Life of the Prince Consort   For the history and development of the Zollverein see *Treitschke*, Deutsche Geschichte im neunzehnten Jahrhundert, *Weber*, Der Deutsche Zollverein; Geschichte seiner Entstehung und Entwickelung, and *Festenberg-Packisch*, Geschichte des Zollvereins , for the early years of the reign of Frederick William IV of Prussia, *Ranke*, Aus dem Briefwechsel Friedrich Wilhelms IV mit Bunsen and Friedrich Wilhelm IV (in his Werke, Vols 50–52), *Wagener*, Die Politik Friedrich Wilhelms IV and *Biedermann*, Dreissig Jahre Deutsche Geschichte , and for the war with the Sonderbund, *Adams*, The Swiss Confederation, *Crétineau-Joly*, Histoire du Sonderbund, *Dandliker*, Geschichte der Schweiz, and *Vulliemin*, Histoire de la Confédération Suisse

LECTURE XII

THE REVOLUTION OF 1848 IN FRANCE

Growing unpopularity of the Monarchy of July during the administration of Guizot ; the government alienates moderate liberals by refusing to grant the smallest measure of electoral reform , while its rigidly Bourgeois and Capitalist sympathies exasperated the Democratic and Labor parties.

The growth of democratic and socialist ideas among the working classes of France ; the influence of Saint-Simon, Fourier, Prudhon, etc

The movement for parliamentary reform and democratic revolution in 1847 ; the banquets and toasts to liberty, equality and fraternity ; Odilon Barrot and Ledru-Rollin

The Revolution of February, 1848; riots in Paris (22 Feb), resignation of Guizot (23 Feb., 1848) ; appointment of Bugeaud as commandant of Paris, barricades erected in the streets ; Louis Philippe forbids Bugeaud to act, he abdicates the throne (24 Feb) and leaves France

Significance of the Revolution of February, overthrow of the Bourgeois Monarchy.

The mob of Paris bursts into the Chambers and the Hôtel de Ville ; proclamation of the Republic ; rejection of the idea of the regency to be held by the Duchess of Orleans during the minority of her son, the Comte de Paris, formation of the Provisional Government, consisting of six leading republican deputies, three journalists and a working man, e g., Dupont de l'Eure, Arago, Lamartine, Ledru-Rollin, Crémieux, and Marie, deputies. Marrast, Louis Blanc, and Floçon, journalists, and Albert, Garnier-Pagés installed as Mayor of Paris.

Importance and conduct of Lamartine as provisional minister of foreign affairs, and of Ledru-Rollin as provisional minister of the interior ; Lamartine assures Europe that the revolution in Paris was not intended to encourage revolution elsewhere, while Ledru-Rollin imitated the extreme policy of the Convention, attempted to appoint pro-consuls and established public workshops

The extreme republican party in Paris endeavors to influence the elections, which were taking place over France, in favor of the radicals by constant riots, the riot of 16 April, 1848 ; General Changarnier placed in command of the garrison and National Guard of Paris ; he defeats the insurgents.

Meeting of the Constituent Assembly (27 April, 1848) , the moderate character and antecedents of the majority of its members ; it declares that France is a Republic and prepares to draw up a republican constitution on conservative lines ; it maintains the Provisional Government in office , riot of 15 May in Paris, and attempt of the democratic party to overthrow the Constituent Assembly ; suppression of the riot and flight of Louis Blanc.

Critical position in Paris , the working classes of the Faubourg Saint Antoine prepare for insurrection ; the moderate republicans resolve to resist ; General Cavaignac appointed provisional War Minister he concentrates regular troops in Paris

Severe fighting in Paris (23–26 June) ; storming of the barricades by the troops ; Paris declared in a state of siege , supreme executive authority entrusted to Cavaignac , suppression of the radical party in Paris

The Constituent Assembly, now that peace was restored, proceeds to draw up a republican constitution ; the Constitution of 1848 places the supreme executive authority in the hands of a president of the republic, elected directly by the people, and the legislative authority in the hands of a single Chamber

Louis Napoleon, son of Louis Bonaparte king of Holland and Hortense de Beauharnais, and nephew of the first Napoleon, is elected President of the Republic (10 Dec., 1848) , he receives 5,562,834 votes, Cavaignac 1,469,166 votes, Ledru-Rollin 377,236 votes, Raspail 37,106, and Lamartine 21,000.

Character and previous career of Louis Napoleon ; difficulties of his position , he is distrusted by the Constituent Assembly, and both feared and hated by the extreme republicans

Foreign policy of the Prince President ; he sends a French army under Oudinot to Rome, which after a repulse (20 April) occupies Rome (3 July), overthrows the Roman Republic and reestablishes the authority of the Pope

Dissolution of the Constituent Assembly, and instalment of the Legislative Assembly (28 May, 1849), the position of parties in the new Assembly , the majority were moderates, in favor of parliamentary government after the English system, believers in limited monarchy, and very suspicious of the Prince President, whom they suspected of planning to restore the Empire , the minority called itself the Mountain, and, under the leadership of Ledru-Rollin, hoped to establish a democratic republic.

The deputies of the Mountain appeal to the people of Paris ; insurrection of 13 June, 1849 ; arrest of the deputies of the Mountain ; they are expelled from the Assembly , escape of Ledru-Rollin.

The majority of the Legislative Assembly becomes frankly reactionary, and endeavors to establish a bourgeois republic ; influence of Thiers, Berryer, Molé, Montalembert, and De Broglie, by the law of 31 May, 1850, the suffrage is restricted to three years' residents in a commune or canton, practically disenfranchising the working classes ; declaration of Thiers on this subject

The Legislative Assembly on adjourning left a permanent commission of deputies to watch the proceedings of the government ; disgust of the Prince President at this action ; he resolves to appeal to France ; his first provincial tour

The political position in 1851 , the incurable distrust reigning between the Prince President and the Assembly , constant struggle between the executive and legislative authority, and frequent changes of ministry

The Prince President, having made himself popular in France by provincial tours, declares himself in favor of universal suffrage and the sovereignty of the people , his explanation of the ideas of the Empire ; he demands that the Assembly should repeal the law of 31 May, 1850 (4 Nov., 1851)

The Coup d'État of 2 Dec , 1851 ; the Prince President declares the Legislative Assembly dissolved, universal suffrage reestablished, and Paris in a state of siege , the advisers of Louis Napoleon, and his agents , his half brother, the Duc de Morny, General de Saint Arnaud, Minister of

War, and M. de Maupas, Prefect of Police; arrest of the leading members of the Legislative Assembly; the troops shoot down opponents of the Coup d'État in Paris

The Prince President submits a new Constitution to a plébiscite of the people, establishing a strong executive, and institutions resembling those of the Consulate and the Empire; the Constitution accepted (21 Dec) by 7,481,231 votes out of 8,165,630 votes, and promulgated 14 Jan , 1852

The Prince President's provincial tour of 1852 ; his reception , enthusiasm in the army ; he declares at Bordeaux (9 Oct.) " L'Empire, c'est la paix" ; the Senate votes the re-establishment of the Empire (7 Nov), it is voted by a plébiscite (22 Nov), and the Prince President declares himself Napoleon III, Emperor of the French (1 Dec , 1852)

Authorities · On the history of the second French Republic, see *Garnier-Pagés*, Histoire de la Révolution de 1848, *Louis Blanc*, Histoire de la Révolution de 1848, *Lamartine*, Histoire de la Révolution de 1848, *Pierre*, Histoire de la République de 1848, with *Normanby*, A Year of Revolution, *Odilon Barrot*, Mémoires, *Falloux*, Mémoires d'un Royaliste, *Berryer*, Discours Parlementaires, *Thiers*, Discours Parlementaires, and *Véron*, Mémoires d'un Bourgeois, for the coup d'état of 1851, see *Maupas*, Mémoires sur le Second Empire, *Kinglake*, The invasion of the Crimea, *Victor Hugo*, Histoire d'un Crime, *Ténot*, Le Coup d'État, *Jerrold*, Life of Napoleon III, *Delord*, Histoire du Second Empire, and *Viel Castel*, Mémoires

---

LECTURE XIII.

THE REVOLUTION OF 1848 IN ITALY

The condition of Italy from the suppression of the insurrectionary movement of 1830 by Austria, to the outbreak of the revolutions of 1848 , the work of the Carbonari and of other secret societies , constant attempts made upon the lives of the Italian princes, and repeated outbreaks in different cities and country districts

Double tendency to be perceived in the popular movements in Italy ; with regard to government the middle classes desired representative constitutions and limited monarchy, while the secret societies advocated pure democracy , with regard to the unity of Italy, one section desired a federal government either monarchical or republican, while the other favored an Italy, one and indivisible, either monarchical or republican , these different tendencies prevented partisans of the national spirit and of political revolution from acting harmoiously together ; the most influential writer and thinker was Mazzini, but his advanced republican ideas made him obnoxious to moderate men.

Condition of the different Itatlan states at the outbreak of the revolutionary movement in 1848 ; the severe and arbitrary government of Naples and Sicily under Ferdinand II, afterwards called King Bomba , unpopularity of the Austrian government in Lombardy and Venetia ; Parma and Modena, ruled by the Empress Marie Louise and Duke Francis V, were entirely under Austrian influence , death of Marie Louise (18 Dec., 1847), and accession of Charles II, formerly Duke of Lucca , the government of Leopold II, Grand Duke of Tuscany ; he annexes Lucca (1845), and grants a constitution (1847) , Charles Albert, King of Sardinia, was desirous of setting himself at the head of the national Italian movement, but he was afraid of the republicans and the Carbonari ; he favored parliamentary government and granted a constitution to his kingdom in 1846

The worst governed provinces of Italy were those of the States of the Church, in which Pope Gregory XVI ruled in the most arbitrary manner with cardinals, priests and bishops as his only ministers and administrators , yet it was in the States of the Church that the first impulsion was given to the revolutionary movement of 1848 , death of Gregory XVI, (1 June, 1846)

Election of Pope Pius IX—Mastai-Ferretti—(16 June, 1846), his known liberal and national ideas , his reforms in internal administration , he reorganizes the tribunals, establishes munincipal government, permits the raising of civic guards, and allows a measure of liberty to the press , he proposes a Customs Union between the States of the Church, Tuscany and Sardinia , he calls an assembly for the organization of a new government ; Metternich protests against the reforming policy of Pius IX , but the people of Rome accuse him of not going far enough.

Outbreak of insurrection at Palermo (12 Jan , 1848) which spreads through the whole of Sicily.

Effect of the Revolution of February in Italy ; the people of Milan rise in insurrection and expel the Austrian garrison (11–15 Mch., 1848); formation of a provisional government which appoints Garibaldi commandant of its troops , similar movement in Venice (16–22 Mch); where Daniel Manin is elected Dictator , Francis V driven from Modena ; Charles II driven from Parma (9 Apr)

Charles Albert, King of Sardinia, summoned by all Northern Italy, sets himself at the head of the National movement ; he enters Milan (26 Mch); concentration of the Austrian troops under Radetzky , the Austrians defeated at Goito (8 Apr.); Leopold of Tuscany compelled by his people to send troops to assist Charles Albert , Ferdinand II, King of the Two Sicilies, forced to grant a constitution to Naples, and to send a fleet to assist Venice and an army under Pope to join Charles Albert , the papal troops, under Durando, join the Sardinians ; Charles Albert takes Peschiera ; desperate position of Radetzky, who asks for reinforcements

Desperate position of the Austrians in Italy ; terms offered to Charles Albert , he declines the intervention of England and France

Ferdinand II withdraws his constitution and dissolves the Neapolitan parliament (15 May); he vigorously pursues the war with the Sicilian insurgents, and calls back his fleet from Venice, and his army ; nevertheless, Pepe with 3,000 men throws himself into Venice, of which he takes military command

Pope Pius IX disavows the action of General Durando , he issues a Fundamental Statute for the goverment of his states, establishing lay government and ministerial responsibility (14 Mch.), Mamiani appointed Minister of the Interior (4 May)

Radetzky, joined by Nugent, defeats Charles Albert at Custozza (25 July) and occupies Milan (6 Aug) , armistice proclaimed between Sardinia and Austria (9 Aug) , gallant defence of Venice.

The Austrian victories encourage the other monarchs of Italy ; the Pope dismisses Mamiani (14 Sept.) ; appointment of Rossi, who desires to form an Italian Federation , assassination of Rossi (15 Nov.) , the Pope escapes to Gaeta (24 Nov) ; provisional government appointed in Rome under the triumvirate of Mazzini, Gioberti and Cernuschi (11 Dec) , meeting of the Roman Constituent Assembly , proclamation of the Roman Republic (9 Feb., 1849) , the triumvirs appoint Garibaldi commander-in-chief , Pius IX solemnly appeals to the Catholic rulers of Austria, France, Spain, and Naples for help (18 Feb 1849)

Progress of the revolution in Sicily , England recognizes the revolutionary government of Palermo (6 Sept , 1848) ; the Sicilians offer the throne to the second son of Charles Albert.

Progress of the revolution in Tuscany ; Montanelli appointed chief minister (26 Oct.) ; a liberal constitution granted ; flight of the Grand Duke Leopold II to Gaeta ; the Florentine Republic proclaimed under the triumvirate of Montanelli, Guerrazzi, and Mazzoni.

Difficult position of Charles Albert . he is forced to form a radical ministry under Rattazzi (15 Dec , 1848) ; he declares the armistice at an end and appeals to united Italy (12 Mch., 1849) ; Radetzky utterly defeats Charles Albert at Novara (23 Mch., 1849) ; Charles Albert abdicates in favor of his son, Victor Emmanuel ; favorable terms of peace granted to the Sardinians (6 Aug , 1849).

Triumphant progress of the Austrians , they restore Fran-

cis V to Modena and Charles III to Parma ; they overthrow
the Florentine Republic and re-establish the Grand Duke
Leopold II (28 July), who withdraws the constitution he
had granted ; capitulation of Venice to the Austrians (24
Aug)

Ferdinand II cruelly suppresses the Sicilian insurrection.

The Prince President of the French Republic, afraid of
allowing Austria too much predominance in Italy, sends a
French army under Oudinot to Rome , repulse of the French
(30 Apr); the siege of Rome ; the French capture Rome
(3 July) ; Garibaldi withdraws to the mountains where his
troops are cut up by the Austrians , Pius IX returns to
Rome (12 Apr , 1850) and re-establishes the Papal government under the charge of Cardinal Antonelli ; a French
garrison retained in Rome

Causes of the entire and disastrous failure of the Italian
revolutions in 1848 , Victor Emmanuel alone maintains parliamentary government in his dominions.

Authorities On the Italian insurrection, see *Cantu*, Della Indipendenza Italiana, *Ricciardi*, Histoire de la Révolution d'Italie, *Ulloa*,
Guerre de l'Indépendance Italienne, *Perrens*, Deux Ans de Révolution
en Italie, *Pepe*, Memoirs and Histoire des Révolutions et des Guerres
d'Italie en 1847, 1848, et 1849, *Balleydier*, Histoire de la Révolution de
Rome, *Bianchi*, Storia documentata della diplomazia Europea in
Italia, *Costa de Beauregard*, Les dernières années du Roi Charles Albert, *Rattazzi*, Ratazzi et son Temps, *Mazzini*, Works, *Martin*, Daniel Manin,*Montanelli*, Memoirs,*Cantu*, Storia ragionata e documentata
della rivoluzione Lombarda, *Cattaneo*, L'insurrection de Milan en
1848, *Garibaldi*, Memoirs, *Mario*, Garibaldi e i suoi tempi, *Sirao*,
Storia della revoluzioni d'Italia dal 1846 al 1866, and *Hubner*, Une
Année de ma Vie

LECTURE XIV.

THE REVOLUTION OF 1848 IN AUSTRIA.

Internal condition of the Austrian dominions during the
reign of the Emperor Ferdinand I ; the home policy of
Metternich ; he encourages the national spirit in the different

provinces of the Empire in order to play off one province against another, but he sternly represses all aspirations to self-government

The growth of national spirit was specially perceptible in Hungary and Bohemia, but it was also to be found in smaller districts, such as Transylvania, Croatia and Galicia ; condition of the German provinces ; the diverse nationalities of which the Empire was composed, prevented any tendency towards union, and encouraged schemes of federation or of entire independence

The national spirit in Hungary , the amount of local self-government allowed to the Magyars , the growth of Magyar literature and of attachment to the Magyar language , the national spirit in Hungary becomes, under the guidance of its men of letters, also democratic ; the Diet of 1833 abolishes serfdom , attitude of the Magyars to other nationalities within the limits of Hungary , influence of Szechenyi, Kossuth, Deak and Petöfi.

The national spirit in Bohemia , revival of the Czech language and literature , the Czechs desire to place themselves at the head of the Austrian Slavs ; in Bohemia as in Hungary the national spirit becomes also democratic, and demands are made not only for national but also for popular government , influence of Dobrouski, Kollar and Polacky.

The German spirit concentrated in Vienna, where democratic ideas, resembling those in vogue among the working classes in Paris and Berlin take deep root

Effect of the news of the Revolution of February in Austria ; insurrection of 13 March in Vienna , the Emperor Ferdinand dismisses Metternich from office ; the disgraced minister escapes to England ; Ficquelmont appointed minister , the Emperor promises a representative constitution

Effect of the fall of Metternich upon the Austrian provinces ; general demands for liberty and popular government , insurrections in Croatia, Bohemia and Galicia

The Hungarian Diet seizes the opportunity to demand the formation of a responsible Hungarian ministry with entire self-government, the Emperor yields (17 Mch.) and appoints Louis Batthyany prime minister, with Kossuth as Minister of the Interior; delight of the Magyars at this success, a Constituent Diet is summoned to draw up a constitution for Hungary

The Emperor further promises constitutions and self-government to the Slavonic Provinces (28 Mch —8 Apr) the Czechs summon a Pan-Slavonic assembly to meet at Prague on 31 May

Dissatisfaction of the people of Vienna at the prospect of the Austrian Empire being split into autonomous provinces, disgust of the working classes at the non-recognition of democratic principles; second popular insurrection in Vienna (15 May); dismissal of Ficquelmont, and convocation of a Constituent Assembly for the whole Austrian Empire to meet in Vienna, the Emperor Ferdinand escapes to Innsbruck, and throws himself upon the fidelity of the Tyrolese

Desperate position of the Austrian monarchy; seeming approach of disintegration, the strength of the opposition to Austria in Italy, Hungary and Bohemia, attitude of the Parliament of Frankfort to the Hapsburgs, desire expressed to keep Austria out of re-constituted Germany

From the diversity of aims of the different revolutions, the Austrian monarchy finds safety, the Emperor Ferdinand to please the Germans, resolves to act vigorously against the Slavs, Prince Windischgratz bombards Prague (12–14 June) and breaks up the Pan-Slavonic Congress, reduction of Bohemia to obedience

Despatch of an Austrian army under Nugent to re-enforce Radetzky in Italy, Jellachich, the newly appointed Ban of Croatia instructed to raise the Croatians against the Magyars

Progress of the revolution in Hungary; meeting of the Constituent Diet (5 July); the new Hungarian Constitution, influence of Kossuth, the Magyars issue oppressive decrees against the Slavs and Roumanians in Croatia, Slavonia, the Banat of Temesvar and Transylvania, insurrections in these districts against the Magyars, at the demand of the Diet the

Emperor disgraces Jellachich, the Emperor enters into negotiations with the Tsar Nicholas, who occupies the Danubian provinces

After the news of the victory of Custozza, the Emperor resolves to act more firmly against Hungary, Jellachich reinstated as Ban of Croatia (3 Sept), the Diet prepares to resist, the Palatine of Hungary, the Archduke Stephen, refuses to obey the Diet and escapes to Vienna ; murder of Lamberg at Pesth (27 Sept), the Emperor declares the Hungarian Constituent Diet dissolved, and orders Jellachich to invade Hungary, Kossuth appointed Dictator of Hungary.

Proceedings of the Constituent Assembly at Vienna ; dismay felt at the advance of the Hungarian army, third insurrection in Vienna (6 Oct.), the Emperor directs the members of the Constituent Assembly to leave Vienna and to assemble at Kremsier ; only the Slavs deputies obey, the German deputies remain in Vienna to form a provisional government, they negotiate with the German parliament at Frankfort, which recognizes them, and sends Robert Blum and two other deputies to their assistance, Windischgratz bombards Vienna (31 Aug) conquers the city, establishes martial law and shoots Robert Blum, wrath of the Parliament of Frankfort

Schwarzenberg appointed minister (21 Nov.), abdication of the Emperor Ferdinand in favor of his nephew Francis Joseph (2 Dec)

Vigorous policy of Schwarzenberg, Windischgratz and Jellachich occupy Pesth (5 Jan, 1849); Kossuth and the Diet withdraw, formation of Hungarian armies, placed under the command of Dombrovski, Bem, and Gorgei, the Hungarian armies re-occupy Pesth

Schwarzenberg dissolves the Diet of Kremsier (4 Mch), and promises a Unitary Constitution to the Austrian Empire, Kossuth and the Diet declare the independence of Hungary (14 Apr)

The Emperor Francis Joseph requests the assistance of the Tsar Nicholas; a Russian army under Paskevitch enters

Hungary (May), the armies under Paskevitch, Haynaw, Nugent and Jellachch defeat the Hungarians and drive them towards the Turkish frontier ; resignation of Kossuth, who escapes into Turkey (11 Aug.), capitulation of Gorgci (13 Aug.), surrender of Klapka at Komorn (2 Oct), end of the armed resistance of the Hungarians

The German policy of Schwarzenberg ; his attitude towards the Parliament of Frankfort , he prevents Frederick William IV of Prussia from accepting the Imperial throne offered to him by the Parliament , he claims the right of Austria to be treated as a constituent part of Germany

Authorities *Balleydier*, Histoire des Révolutions de l'Empire de l'Autriche, *Maurice*, The Revolutionary Movement of 1848–49 in Italy, Austria and Hungary, *Pillersdorf*, Rückblick auf die Politische Bewegung in Œsterreich in den Jahren 1848 und 1849, *Ficquelmont*, Aufklarungen uber die Zeit vom 20 Marz bis zum 4 Mai 1848, *Frobel*, Briefe uber die Wiener Oktober–Revolution mit Notizen uber die Letzten Tage Robert Blums. *Auerbach*, Tagebuch aus Wien, *Hubner*, Une Année de ma Vie, *Hetfer t* Geschichte Œsterreich vom Ausgange des Wiener Oktober-Aufstandes, *Berger*, Felix Fürst zu Schwarzenberg, *Windischgratz*, Einer Lebens-Skizze ; aus den Papieren eines Zeit-genossen der Sturmjal re 1848 und 1849, *Yranyi and Chassin*, Histoire Politique de la Révolution de Hongrie en 1847-49, *Bury*, Souvenirs et Récits des Campagnes d'Autriche, *Martin*, Guerre de Hongrie en 1848 et 1849, *Gorgei*, Mein Leben und Wirken in Ungarn, *Klapka*, Der Nationalkreig in Ungarn und Siebenbergen, of which there is an English translation, and *Kossuth*, Memoirs.

LECTURE XV.

THE REVOLUTION OF 1848 IN GERMANY

Effect of the Revolution of February in Germany ; general development of the desire for popular government in Western Germany , the states upon the Rhine and in the former kingdom of Westphalia were especially forward in this direction , there had been numerous riots in Rhenish Prussia, Hesse-Cassel and Brunswick ; as in Italy, the national spirit and the democratic movement were sometimes in harmony and sometimes opposed to each other , one section of advocates of German unity looked to Prussia to lead them ; the other, which was more democratic hoped for an independent and possibly republican German nation

Both the national and the democratic spirit were most evident in the smaller states and in Rhenish Prussia ; but they were also developed to some extent in the South German states of Bavaria, under King Louis I. of Wurtemberg, under King William I, and of Baden, under the Grand Duke Charles Leopold, while in Hanover, under Ernest I, they were especially developed

The share of the German Universities in promoting the national and liberal spirit ; the dismissal of Gervinus, Dahlmann, Ewald and the two Grimms, from their chairs at Gottingen, for protesting against the abolition of the Hanoverian constitution by Ernest I, in 1837.

The first effect of the Revolution of February was seen in risings in the great cities, similar to those which occurred in Paris and in Vienna , the most important of the risings were in Berlin and in Munich

The first insurrection in Berlin·(15-19 Mch) , Frederick William IV gives way before the popular feeling, sends his brother and heir, Prince William, who was suspected of opposition to popular wishes, away to England, convokes the States-General, and summons a Constituent Assembly to draw up a constitution for Prussia

Insurrection in Munich against King Louis I, who is accused of showing too much favor to his mistress, Lola Montes , he abdicates the throne (20 Mch) in favor of his son Maximilian Joseph II, who promises reforms

A group of German patriots and unionists meet at Heidelberg (5 Mch) and summon a Vor-Parlament, which assembles at Frankfort (31 Mch) , this Assembly convokes a Constituent Parliament, to be elected by universal suffrage by the whole of Germany, which should organize a federal German government under a monarch ; it was resolved that the decisions of this Constituent Parliament should be soveriegn, and not subjected to the control of the Federal Diet.

The Federal Diet, as established by the Congress of Vienna, withdraws its decrees of 1832–1834 controlling state representative governments and then ceases to oppose the new movement

In the face of the strength of the revolutionary movement, the German Princes permit the elections to the new Parliament

Meeting of the Parliament of Frankfort (18 May), it elects Heinrich von Gagern as its president ; it elects the Archduke John of Austria as Vicar of the Empire (28 June), he takes office (12 July), dissolves the Federal Diet, and appoints Schmerling his chief minister , the Parliament of Frankfort, with long debates, draws up a German Constitution ; the un-democratic nature of this Constitution causes republican risings in many of the cities of Germany and general uneasiness.

The position in Prussia ; Frederick William IV takes advantage of the condition of affairs in Denmark to stand forward as the defender of German interests

Death of Christian VIII of Denmark and accession of Frederick VII (20 Jan. 1848) ; insurrection in Denmark (18 Mch) , the king promises to summon the Consitituent Assembly by universal suffrage to draw up a Constitution which should unify Denmark and the Duchies of Schleswig and Holstein in spite of the latter being parts of the German Confederation , wrath in Germany at this news ; the Duke of Augustenburg sets himself at the head of the opposition in the two duchies , Prussia with the sanction of the Parliament of Frankfort, invades the duchies (6 Apr) and had almost conquered the whole of Denmark when the great powers intervened and insist on the signature of the armistice of Malmoe (26 Aug).

Frederick William IV of Prussia though he showed himself by his conduct in Denmark in favor of German interests, also showed himself the enemy of democracy ; at the request of the Parliament of Frankfort, he sent Prussian troops to that city to put down a republican insurrection (18 Sept) and then, also at their request, put down democratic risings throughout the Rhenish territories

Second insurrection in Berlin (Nov , 1848); the king dissolves the Prussian Constituent Assembly which had shown in the Junker party a strong minority opposed to democratic ideas, he declares Berlin in a state of siege, appoints Brandenberg and Manteuffel his ministers, and issues of his own authority a new constitution for Prussia giving a moderate amount of representative government (5 Dec., 1848)

Later history of the Parliament of Frankfort ; Gagern succeeds Schmerling as chief minister (Dec , 1848) ; completion of the new German Constitution with two chambers, the Volkhaus elected by universal suffrage, and the Staatenhaus chosen by the parliaments of the different states, recognizing no direct representation of the German princes, establishing parliamentary government, and only giving to the supreme executive authority a suspensive veto

The question of the admission of Austria with her non-German populations, as part of the new German Empire ; it is resolved that Austria shall be completely excluded (14 Jan , 1849), it is decided to offer the imperial crown to Frederick William IV of Prussia (28 Mar), he declines to accept unless invited by the princes of Germany, and eventually, under the influence of Schwarzenberg, refuses unconditionally

Indignation of Schwarzenberg at the Decree of 14 January , he withdraws the Austrian deputies from the Parliament of Frankfort

Last days of the Parliament of Frankfort , Gagern resigns office (8 May), and with his followers forms a secession parliament ; Prussia withdraws its deputies ; the Parliament, reduced to 105 members, is forced to leave Frankfort (30 May), it meets at Stuttgart and is eventually broken up by the King of Wurtemberg (19 June)

Frederick William IV of Prussia lends troops to the Kings of Saxony and Hanover to establish order in their dominions ; under the command of Prince William of Prussia order is also reestablished by Prussian soldiers in Baden and along the Rhine

Continuation of the Danish war , Frederick VII of Denmark grants a liberal constitution (5 June, 1849) , the Danes make a gallant struggle against the Prussians ; conclusion of peace (2 July, 1850), it is eventually arranged that the duchies of Schleswig and Holstein shall be garrisoned by a joint force of Austrians and Prussians, and that their fate shall be decided by a conference of the great powers

Result of the revolutionary movement of 1848 in Germany ; entire failure both of the democratic party and of the supporters of the parliamentary system , postponement of the unity of Germany.

Authorities . There are several reports of the proceedings of the Parliament of Frankfort, of which the most complete is *Wigard*, Stenographischen Bericht, 9 vols, , see also *Duncker*, Zur Geschichte der Deutschen Reichsversammlung in Frankfort, *Raumer*, Briefe aus Frankfurt und Paris, *Biedermann*, Erinnerungen aus der Paulskirche, *Ranke*, Politische Denkschriften aus den Jahren 1848-1851, in his Werke, vols XLIX-L, *Deym*, Graf Deym und die Oesterreichische Frage in der Paulskirche, *Becker*, Die Reaktion in Deutschland gegen die Revolution von 1848, *von Sybel*, Die Begrundung des Deutschen Reiches, vols. I, II, *von Moltke*, Geschichte des Krieges gegen Danemark, 1848-49, *Bunsen*, Memoirs, *Malet*, Journal, and *Bismarck*, Reden

---

LECTURE XVI.

EUROPE AFTER THE REVOLUTIONS OF 1848

The institutions of the Second Empire in France ; relations of the government to the Council of State, the Senate and the Legislative Body , while granting the widest extension of the franchise for electing the Legislative Body, the administration systematically interferes to promote the election of government candidates

Napoleon III and his ministers , the Bonapartists and some of the partisans of the Monarchy of July rallied to him, but he has to face the opposition of the Legitimists and the Republicans , he is unfortunate in the selection of ministers and has to make use of men of doubtful honesty in the work of administration , the influence of the Duc de Morny, Persigny, Rouher, and Maupas

Parliamentary opposition during the Second Empire ; Thiers ; exile or deportation of the leading Republicans

Internal policy of Napoleon III , he professes, owing to his selection by *plébiscite*, to represent the sovereignty of the people, and stands forth as the opponent of bourgeois or middle class politics , he exploits the wealth of France in extravagant buildings and public works , Haussmann rebuilds Paris , corruption of the administration ; Napoleon III attempts to blind the people by a successful and vigorous foreign policy.

Foreign policy of Napoleon III , though he declares the Empire to mean peace, he really desired war, in order to establish himself firmly at home and abroad , excellence of the army, trained in the Algerian wars , Napoleon's attachment to the idea of nationality , his views with regard to Italy

Attitude of the Great Powers towards the Second Empire : England, hoping for the assistance of France in the settlement of the Eastern Question, at once recognizes him as Emperor , the Tsar Nicholas recognizes him in an insulting fashion, and is followed by Austria and Prussia ; Napoleon's first foreign ministers , Drouyn de Lhuys and Walewski

Being unable to obtain the hand of a foreign princess, Napoleon III marries Eugénie de Montijo, Comtesse de Teba, (29 Jan , 1853)

Influence exercised by Prussia in Germany after her suppression of the revolutionary movement ; Frederick William IV hopes to exclude Austria and to be chosen Emperor by the princes of Germany , the League of the Three Kings—

Prussia, Saxony, and Hanover ; scheme of a Restricted Union , Prussia prepares a scheme for a united Germany under her leadership to be submitted to a revived German Parliament at Erfurt and to the German princes , only the petty princes accept the Prussian scheme.

Austria, having put down all rebellion and supported by Russia, resolves to intervene , the Archduke John resigns his authority as Vicar of the Empire to a committee of four, appointed half by Austria and half by Prussia (20 Dec , 1849)

Beust's scheme of a Middle Germany ; treaty of alliance made between Saxony, Bavaria, and Wurtemberg, (27 Feb , 1850).

The Parliament of Erfurt (29 Mar.–29 Apr 1850); it is only attended by Prussia and representatives of the petty princes , part played by Bismarck ; the Parliament refuses to accept the Prussian scheme , and so does the College of Princes, which met at Berlin (10 May)

Growing influence of Austria in German affairs under the ministry of Schwarzenberg , *ad interim* revival of the Diet of the Germanic Confederation or Bundestag, which undertakes the settlement of the disturbances in Schleswig-Holstein and Hesse-Cassel , opposition of Prussia , approach of war , the Prussian and the German federal troops supported by Austria face each other in Hesse-Cassel ; the Tsar Nicholas intervenes and threatens to attack whichever side begins war

Frederick William IV gives way ; Manteuffel appointed chief Prussian Minister , the Convention of Olmutz (29 Nov , 1850) , Prussia apologises, restoration of the Bundestag (15 May, 1851) , Bismarck appointed Prussian representative at Frankfort.

Negotiations for the renewal of the Zollverein , Austria endeavors to enter the Union ; opposition of Prussia , the Steuerverein declares its readiness to enter the Zollverein (7 Sept , 1851); reconstitution of the Zollverein on this basis with Austria excluded (10 Mar , 1853)

General reaction in Germany , most of the German princes

withdraw or modify the Constitutions they had granted in 1848, the Bundestag repudiates the Grundrechte decreed by the Parliament of Frankfort (23 Aug, 1851)

The reaction in Prussia; repressive administration of Manteuffel, Prince William commences to reorganize the army

The reaction in Austria, the Emperor Francis Joseph withdraws the Constitution of 4 March, 1849, (31 Dec, 1851), death of Schwarzenburg (5 April, 1852); appointment of Buol-Schauenstein as chief Austrian minister

Settlement of the Schleswig-Holstein question, Frederick VII of Denmark issues a unitary constitution for all his dominions, Prince Christian of Glucksburg recognized as heir to the throne of Denmark by the Conference of London (8 May, 1852)

The revolutionary movement of 1848 in Holland; the reign of William II (1840-49), he is succeeded by William III (17 Mar., 1849); the parliamentary Constitution is re-modeled in a more liberal sense; administration of Thorbecke

The revolutionary movement of 1848 in Belgium, excitement caused by the news of the revolution of February, Leopold I evades a republican movement by skilful policy, his ability as a parliamentary sovereign

The revolutionary movement of 1848 in England; the Chartists, results of the abolition of the Corn-laws

Authorities For the general history of this period see *Rothan* L'Europe et l'avénement du Second Empire, *Debidour*, Histoire diplomatique de l'Europe, and *Viel-Castel*, Memoirs, for the Second Empire, *Delord*, Histoire du Second Empire, *Jerrold*, Life of Napoleon III, *Harcourt*, Les quatre ministères de M Drouyu de Lhuys, *Maugny*, Souvenirs of the Second Empire, *Falloux*, Mémoirs d'un royaliste, and *Thiers*, Discours parlementaires, for Germany, see *Berger*, Felix, Furst von Schwarzenberg, *Bunsen*, Memoirs, *Beust*, Memoirs, *Lowe*, Life of Prince Bismarck, *Bismarck*, Gesammelte Werke and Politische Reden, *Hahn*, Furst Bismarck, *Kohl*, Furst Bismarck, and *Simon*. Histoire du Prince de Bismarck, and for English foreign policy *Martin*, Life of the Prince Consort, *Dalling* and *Ashley*, Life of Lord Palmerston, *Walpole*, Life of Lord John Russell, and *Malmesbury*, Memoirs of an ex-Minister

LECTURE XVII

THE CRIMEAN WAR

The history of the Eastern Question from the settlement of the crisis in 1841

England and France protest against the pressure placed upon the Turks by Russia and Austria to surrender Polish and Hungarian fugitives, an English fleet enters the Dardanelles (1849).

England's interest in the preservation of the independence of Turkey ; the Tsar Nicholas proposes to divide the territories of the " Sick Man " with England

The attitude of the Tsar Nicholas towards the Turks, consistency of his policy since the Treaties of Adrianople and Unkiar Skelessi , he occupies the Danubian Provinces in 1848, but at the request of the powers withdraws behind the Preuth (1851)

The Tsar Nicholas believes the time propitious for the final overthrow of the Turks , Francis Joseph of Austria is bound to him by gratitude for his assistance in 1849, and almost dependent on him , Frederick William IV of Prussia is his brother-in-law and desirous of obtaining his help to establish his power in Germany ; England cannot fight without allies and may be induced to share the spoil, while Napoleon III is distrusted by the European powers, and the strength of his position in France doubtful.

The condition of Turkey ; reforms attempted by the Sultan Abdul Medjid

Disputed questions likely to lead to war , the difficulty about Montenegro , the quarrel with France about the holy places in Palestine , Conversations of Nicholas with the English ambassador, Sir George Hamilton Seymour

Mission of Menshikov to Constantinople in 1853 , Nicholas demands to be recognized as official protector of the Greek Christians in the Turkish dominions ; the Russian ultimatums of 5 May and 31 May , Nicholas' Note to the

powers (11 June); the Russians occupy the Danubian
Provinces (July); the English and French fleets enter the
Dardanelles (Sept).

The Turks declare war against Russia (4 Oct); destruction of the Turkish fleet at Sinope (30 Nov); the English
and French fleets undertake the protection of Constantinople
(27 Dec).

England and France sign a treaty of alliance with Turkey
(13 Mar., 1854) and declare war against Russia ; alliance
signed between England and France (10 Apr).

The attitude of the German powers , tortuous policy of
Austria and Prussia.

Gallant defence of Silistria by the Turks (May, 1854) ,
the Russians evacuate the Danubian Provinces ; English and
French armies under Raglan and Saint-Arnaud land at
Varna

Austria occupies the Danubian Provinces ; the difficulty felt
by the Allies in effectively attacking Russia while Austria
refuses to declare war ; indignation of the Tsar Nicholas and
of the Allies at the conduct of Austria , Francis Joseph kept
in check by the attitude of Prussia and the German Confederation ; the Vienna Notes (8 Aug).

The campaign in the Crimea ; battles of the Alma
(20 Sept), Balaklava (25 Oct.), and Inkerman (5 Nov);
siege of Sevastopol , defence of the city by Todtleben ;
sufferings of the allied armies during the siege.

The English and French fleets in the Baltic under Sir
Charles Napier and Parseval-Deschênes ; capture of Bomar-
sund (16 Aug)

Continued vacillation of Austria

Death of the Tsar Nicholas (2 Mar , 1855); accession of
Alexander II

Campaign of 1855 before Sevastopol ; attack on the Redan
and the Mamelon (7 June) and failure to capture the
Malakov ; death of Lord Raglan (28 June); Victor
Emmanuel, King of Sardinia, joins the Allies (26 June), and
sends an army under LaMarmora to the Crimea ; battle of
the Chernaia (16 Aug) ; capture of the Malakov (8 Sept.).

Campaign of 1855 in the Baltic ; the English and French bombard Sveaborg and Helsingfors (7–11 Aug)

Campaign of 1855 in Armenia ; gallant defence of Kars ; its surrender (28 Nov).

The Tsar Alexander II negotiates for peace ; exhaustion of Russia

Congress of Paris for the settlement of terms of peace ; meeting of the Congress (25 Feb , 856) , plenipotentiaries present were . for France, Walewski and Bourqueney, for England Clarendon and Cowley, for Russia, Orlov and Brunnow, for Austria, Buol and Hubner, for Sardinia, Cavour and Vallamarina, and for Turkey, Ali Pacha and Djemil Effendi ; the Prussian representatives, Manteuffel and Hatzfeldt, not admitted till 18 March

By the Treaty of Paris (30 Mar) the independence and territorial integrity of Turkey was recognized, the Black Sea neutralized, and the Danube declared a free river , the Danubian Principalities of Moldavia and Wallachia were kept separate but given entire local self-government under their own princes, with national armies and free constitutions guaranteed by the powers, but under the suzerainty of Turkey , Servia receives the same advantages but a Turkish garrison is maintained in Belgrade and in three other cities

By the Declaration of Paris (16 Apr.) privateering is forbidden, neutral goods, even when carried in the ships of belligerents, are protected, and blockades are recognized only when effective.

Before the Congress broke up Cavour brought forward the condition of Italy, and the proceedings of Ferdinand II, King of the Two Sicilies, against his subjects were condemned

The most conspicuous results of the Congress of Paris were the isolation of Austria and the favorable attitude of the powers towards Sardinia

Authorities *Kinglake*, The Invasion of the Crimea, its Origin and account of its Progress to the death of Lord Raglan, *Hamley*, The Story of the campaign of Sebastopol, *Russell*, The British Expedition to the Crimea, *Sandwith*, Narrative of the siege of Kars, *Forçade*, Histoire des causes de la guerre d'Orient, *Rousset*, Histoire de la guerre de Crimée, *Rothan*, La Prusse et son Roi pendant la guerre de Crimée, and *Geffcken*, Zur Geschichte des Orientalischen Krieges

---

LECTURE XVIII.

THE UNITY OF ITALY.

Condition of Italy after the revolutionary movement of 1848, cruel government of Ferdinand II, King of the Two Sicilies, reactionary government of Pope Pius IX, the Grand Duke Leopold II of Tuscany, Duke Francis V of Modena, and Duke Charles III of Parma ; assassination of Charles III of Parma (26 Mch., 1834), and accession of Robert I ; arbitrary military government of the Austrians in Lombardy and Venetia

The only constitutional, parliamentary and moderate government in Italy was that of Sardinia, character of Victor Emmanuel I, Cavour becomes chief minister of Sardinia, his sagacious policy, Victor Emmanuel and Cavour hope to accomplish the unity of Italy under the constitutional government of the House of Savoy

Progress of the revolutionary movement in Italy ; it is mainly republican and democratic, and looks to the formation of an Italian Republic ; opposite points of view of Cavour and Mazzini, the former wishes to accomplish the unity of Italy by policy, with the countenance and assistance of Europe, the latter by means of popular insurrection, Mazzini's attempt to raise an insurrection in Genoa (June, 1857).

The Austrians continue to occupy Parma, Modena and the Legations, while the French occupy Rome since 1849

Political effect obtained by Cavour in joining the Anglo-

French alliance against Russia in 1855, and in sending an army to the Crimea , he thus obtains the right to be present at the Congress of Paris, and to lay the claims of Italy before the great powers

Interest taken in England and in France in the cause of Italian unity ; indignation at the cruelties of King Bomba , conspiracies formed, and money obtained ; the work of the secret societies and spread of democratic and unitary principles

Napoleon III takes into consideration the possibility of assisting the Italian cause; his sympathy with the idea of nationality , his scheme for the creation of an Italian confederation of the Italian Princes under the leadership of the Pope and the King of Sardinia , attempt of Orsini on the life of Napoleon (14 Jan , 1858)

The condition of affairs in Europe in 1858 favors the policy of Napoleon III and Cavour ; in Prussia Prince William had been declared regent owing to the insanity of Frederick William IV (Oct , 1857); the new regent hates Austria and is ready to be on friendly terms with France , the Tsar Alexander II is also friendly with France ; which seconds his ideas with regard to the Danubian principalities , Charles Cousa elected Prince of Moldavia (7 Jan , 1859), and of Wallachia (5 Feb); Milosch Obrenovitch overthrows Alexander Karageorgevitch, and becomes Prince of Servia (12 Jan., 1859), England, though less friendly with France than during the Crimean War. is too much occupied with the suppression of Sepoy Mutiny in India to wish to interfere in the affairs of Europe , Austria, the power most opposed to Italian reform and unity, is therefore isolated

Napoleon III and Cavour agree at Plombières (20 July, 1858), that Sardinia shall cede Savoy and Nice to France in return for assistance against Austria in Italy.

The relations between Sardinia and Austria ; Austria declares war (26 Apr , 1859); Napoleon III declares his intention of aiding Sardinia.

The campaign of 1859 in Italy ; the French defeat the

Austrians at Montebello (20 May) and at Magenta (4 June);
Napoleon III and Victor Emmanuel enter Milan (8 June);
Napoleon appeals to the Italians to unite for the freedom of
their country

General insurrection in Italy , the Grand Duke Leopold is
driven from Florence (April); Duke Robert I from Parma
(May); and Duke Francis V from Modena (June); Francis
II succeeds as King of the Two Sicilies (22 May), and is
prevented from aiding the Austrians by insurrections ; the
Austrians withdraw from the Legations , provisional governments formed at Florence, Modena and Bologna ; Cavour
resigns in order to be more free to persuade the Italian insurgents to unite with Sardinia (13 July).

The French defeat the Austrians at Solferino (24 June),
Napoleon III startled at the spread of the revolutionary
movement in Italy, and afraid of the establishment of a
strongly unified monarchy, instead of an Italian Federation
makes an armistice with Austria (8 July)

By the treaty of Villafranca (12 July), Austria makes
peace with France and cedes Lombardy, but not Venetia to
Napoleon III, eventually (24 Mch , 1860,) Napoleon III
cedes Lombardy to Victor Emmanuel in exchange for Savoy
and Nice.

Causes of the treaty of Villafranca ; both Austria and
France are afraid of the Prince Regent of Prussia who mo-
bilizes the Prussian army

Progress, of the movement for amalgamation with Sardinia in Italy , Tuscany, the Legations, Romagna, and the
Duchies of Parma and Modena vote for union with Sardinia
(Aug. Sept), Buoncampagni's government of Tuscany ,
the central Italian provinces elect the Prince of Carignan as
regent (7 Nov.), Garibaldi resigns the command of their
army

Napoleon III appeals for a conference of the great powers
to settle the affairs of Italy ; England formally opposes ;
Palmerston, who had become prime minister in June, declares for non-intervention and that the central Italian states

had a right to decide on their own government, and demands that the French should evacuate Rome

Victor Emmanuel accepts the union of Tuscany and the Legations with the kingdom of Sardinia (22 Mch , 1860)

Garibaldi lands in Sicily with a body of followers (5 Apr , 1860), his movement is entirely independent , he dislikes Cavour, and is an adherent of republicanism rather than of the House of Savoy ; Garibaldi conquers all Sicily by the end of June , Francis II, King of the Two Sicilies re-issues the constitution which his father had granted in 1848, and afterwards had withdrawn (30 June), Garibaldi crosses to the mainland, conquers Calabria and occupies Naples (7 Sept); Francis II escapes to Gaeta , Mazzini joins Garibaldi, and projects the establishment of an Italian Republic

Action of Victor Emmanuel and Cavour at this juncture , they represent themselves as forced by circumstances to intervene in the affairs of southern Italy , they are encouraged by England , wrath of the Pope, who excommunicates Victor Emmanuel ; Cialdini, with a Sardinian army, defeats the Papal troops at Castelfiardo (18 Sept), occupies Ancona and the Marches, avoids the Patrimony of St Peter and enters Neapolitan territory.

The Parliament of Turin, consisting of deputies from all northern Italy authorize Victor Emmanuel to unite the Marches, Naples and Sicily with the Sardinian dominions (2 Oct); Victor Emmanuel proceeds to Naples , patriotic conduct of Garibaldi ; the Marches, Naples and Sicily vote for union with northern Italy (21 Oct , 1860).

Surrender of Gaeta (13 Feb., 1861).

Meeting of the first Italian Parliament at Turin (18 Feb), Victor Emmanuel declared King of Italy

Italy thus formed into a United Kingdom within eighteen months of the outbreak of war, the only districts not ruled by the House of Savoy being Venetia, occupied by the Austrians, and Rome, with the Patrimony of St. Peter, garrisoned by French troops

Causes of this startling success , the ability of Cavour ,

formation of Italy into a limited monarchy under the House of Savoy.

Death of Cavour (6 June, 1861)

Authorities *Cantu*, Della Indipendenza Italiana, *Ideville*, Journal d'un Diplomat en Italie 1859-1862, *Mazade*, Le Comte de Cavour, *Bianchi*, Storia documentata della diplomazia Europea in Italia, *Rattazzi*, Rattazzi et son temps, *Zeller*, Pie IX et Victor Emmanuel, *Garibaldi*, Memoirs, *Mazzini*, Works, *Godkin*, Life of Victor Emmanuel, *Butler*, Correspondence of Cavour with Madame de Circourt, *Cavour*, Discorsi parlamentari, and Lettere, *D'Azeglio*, Souvenirs, *Bianchi*, La politique du Comte Camille de Cavour, *Mario*, Garibaldi e i suoi Tempi, and *Bazancourt*, Histoire de la guerre d'Italie

LECTURE XIX

.

THE OVERTHROW OF AUSTRIA

Position of the great powers towards each other after the formation of the kingdom of Italy.

The restless policy of Napoleon III , continuance of the alliance with England but on less cordial terms ; the joint expedition to China (1860) ; French interference in Syria (1860) , the French expedition to Mexico (1862) , election of the Archduke Maximilian as Emperor of Mexico (1864) ; disastrous result of the French interference in Mexico (1866)

Development of the Eastern Question , friendship between Napoleon III and Alexander II ; union of the provinces of Moldavia and Wallachia into the Principality of Roumania (1861) , death of Sultan Abdul Medjid and accession of Abdul Aziz (25 June, 1861) , overthrow of Prince Charles Couza (1865) , election of Prince Charles of Hohenzollern as Prince of Roumania (25 Mar., 1866)

Revolution in Greece , overthrow of King Otho (Oct , 1862) ; election of Prince George of Denmark as King of the Hellenes (30 Mar., 1863) ; England cedes the Ionian Islands to the kingdom of Greece

The position in Italy ; the ministries of Ricasoli and Rattazzi, longing of the Italians for Rome and Venice, negotiations with France for the withdrawal of the French garrison from Rome , Garibaldi makes an attempt on Rome ; he is defeated at Aspromonte (29 Aug , 1862) ; ministry of La Marmora (1864) , he negotiates with Prussia

The policy of Tsar Alexander II ; he emancipates the Russian serfs (5 Mar., 1861) ; outbreak of insurrection in Russian Poland (15 Jan , 1863) ; England, Austria, and France make a joint representation in favor of the Poles (17 Jan , 1863) , indignation of the Tsar , Prussia offers to assist Russia in suppressing the insurrection , gratitude of Alexander

The internal policy of Austria ; the ministry of Rechberg ; the Emperor Francis Joseph promulgates a unitary constitution (20 Oct , 1860) ; the Hungarians and Venetians refuse to send deputies to the new parliament.

Growing strength of Prussia ; accession of William I (2 Jan , 1861), his character and previous career ; his military instincts , reorganization of the Prussian army by von Roon and of the general staff by von Moltke , King William's belief in the unity of Germany and in the mission of Prussia to dominate Germany

Position of parties in the Prussian Landtag ; Bismarck appointed chief minister (24 Sept , 1862); he is unable to obtain a parliamentary majority, but raises taxes and governs without it , character of Bismarck's policy ; he works for the isolation of Austria and the destruction of her influence in Germany as the first step towards German unity

The weakness of the Bundestag, or Federal Diet , the schemes of the middle states, headed by Saxony, Hanover, Bavaria, for independence of both Austria and Prussia.

The Schleswig-Holstein question , its position at the death of Frederick VII of Denmark (15 Nov , 1863); the Duke of Augustenburg puts forward his claim to the duchies , at the request of the Bundestag, Hanover and Saxony occupy Holstein and Lauenburg (21 Dec , 1863), and Prussia and

Austria occupy Schleswig (1 Feb, 1864); resistance of the Danes, battles of Duppel; England makes useless representations, Christian IX of Denmark forced to yield, by the treaty of 1 August, confirmed 30 October, 1864, he surrenders the duchies to Prussia and Austria

The Bundestag, led by Bavaria and Saxony, demands that the duchies should be given up to the Duke of Augustenburg; Bismarck scornfully refuses, by the Convention of Gastein (14 Aug, 1865) Prussia and Austria agree to a condominium in the duchies, Austria occupies Holstein, while Prussia occupies Schleswig and purchases Lauenburg

Bismarck prepares for war with Austria, the friendliness of Russia towards the Prussian schemes; Bismarck's negotiations with Napoleon III to whom he offers Belgium and Luxemburg in return for neutrality

Bismarck signs an offensive and defensive treaty with Italy (8 Apr., 1866), and promises to attack Austria within three months

Bismarck refuses to submit the question of the duchies to the Bundestag (9 Apr., 1866), and attacks Austria's administration of Holstein as favoring the pretentions of the Duke of Augustenburg.

Outbreak of the Seven Weeks' War, a Prussian army under Manteuffel attacks the Austrians in Holstein (8 June)

Bismarck proposes to the Bundestag that a German parliament shall be elected by universal suffrage, that Austria shall be excluded from Germany, and that the forces of Germany shall be divided into two armies, of which the northern shall be commanded by the King of Prussia and the southern, by the King of Bavaria

Bismarck declares the Pact of Federation broken (14 June), Prussian troops occupy Saxony, Hanover, and Hesse-Cassel, Manteuffel prevents the South German states from lending effective aid to Austria

The Campaign of 1866 in Italy; the Italian army invades Venetia and is defeated by the Archduke Albert at Custozza (24 June), the Italian fleet defeated by Tegetthoff at Lissa

(20 July); preliminaries of peace signed between Austria and Italy (10 Aug), and definitive peace (3 Oct), by which Austria cedes Venetia to Italy.

The Campaign of 1866 in Bohemia ; von Moltke's strategical combinations ; junction of the armies of the Crown Prince of Prussia and Prince Frederick Charles , the Austrians under Benedek utterly defeated at Sadowa, or Königgratz (3 July); armistice signed 22 July, followed by the Preliminaries of Nikolsberg (26 July), and the Treaty of Prague (23 Aug)

By this treaty Austria loses no territory except Venetia, but she agrees to the dissolution of the Germanic Confederation, and promises to make no opposition to a new constitution of Germany in which she shall have no part

Prussia's chief advantages from the war were not gained from Austria but by the annexation of the following states , Hanover, Hesse-Cassel, Hesse-Homburg, Nassau, the city of Frankfort, and Schleswig-Holstein, which gave her an uncontested superiority in Germany , she makes favorable treaties of peace with Saxony , Bavaria, Wurtemberg, and Hesse-Darmstadt

When the great blow had been struck and it was too late for him to interfere effectively, Napoleon III, by his ambassador Benedetti, asks for Rhenish Bavaria and Rhenish Hesse, as his reward for non-interference , William I and Bismarck refuse and by making known the request rouse German feeling against France

Results of the Seven Weeks' War on the position of European politics

Authorities *Debidour*, Histoire diplomatique de l'Europe, 1814-78, *Lefèvre*, Histoire de l'intervention française au Mexique, *Masseras*, Un Essai d'Empire au Mexique, *Gaulot*, L'Empire de Maximilien, *Zeller*, Pie IX et Victor Emmanuel, *Garibaldi*, Memoirs. *Martin*, Pologne et Muscovie, *Batsch*, La Question polonaise dans la Russie occidentale, *Araminski*, Histoire de la Révolution polonaise, *Leroy-Beaulieu*, Un Homme d'état russe, Nicholas Milutine, *Von Sybel*, Die Begrundung des Deutschen Reiches durch Wilhelm I, Denkwurdigkeiten aus dem Leben des Grafen von Roon *von Moltke*, Gesammelte

Schriften und Denkwurdigkeiten, *Muller*, Graf Moltke, *Hahn*, Furst
Bismarck, *Kohl*, Furst Bismarck, *Busch*, Our Chancellor, *Lowe*, Life of
Bismarck, *Simon*, Histoire du prince de Bismarck, *Bismarck*, Gesam-
melte Werke, Briefe, Politische Briefe, and Politischen Reden, *Beust*,
Memoirs, *Vitzthum*, St Petersburg and London, 1852-64, and London,
Gastein und Sadowa, *Loftus*, Diplomatic Reminiscences, *Hansen*, À
travers la diplomatie, 1864-67, *Renouf*, Les coulisses de la diplomatie,
Rothan La politique française en 1866, *Benedetti*, Ma mission en
Prusse, *Klaczko*, Les préliminaires de Sadowa, and Two Chancellors,
Bismarck and Gortchakoff, *Viel-Castel*, Memoirs, *Gramont*, (pseud
Memor), L'Allemagne nouvelle, *La Marmora*, Un peu plus de lumière
sur les évènements militaires et politiques de l'année 1866, *Bonghi*,
L'alhanza prussiana e l'acquisto del Veneto, *Harcourt*, Les quatre
ministères de M de Drouyn de Lhuys, *Hahn*, Zwei Jahre preussisch-
deutsche Politik, 1866-67, *Treitschke*, Zehn Jahre Deutscher Kampfe
1865-74, *Hozier*, The Seven Weeks' War, *Lecomte*, Guerre de la Prusse
et de l'Italie contre l'Autriche et la Conféderation germanique, *Borb-
stadt*, Preussens Feldzuge gegen Oesterreich, *Rustow*, Der Krieg von
1866 in Deutschland und Italien, *Fontane*, Der deutsche Krieg von
1866, and the official accounts of the War of 1866 by the German
and Austrian general staffs

LECTURE XX

THE RE-CONSTITUTION OF GERMANY AND AUSTRIA

After the signature of the Treaty of Prague, Prussia propounded a new organization for Northern Germany , the
victories of her armies and the great preponderance she had
obtained over the other states by the annexation of Hanover,
etc., caused Bismarck's plan to be promptly accepted by the
Northern States (8 Feb , 1867).

Germany, north of the Main, was formed into the North
German Confederation, which consisted of the two kingdoms of Prussia and Saxony, the four grand duchies of
Mecklenburg-Schwerin, Mecklenburg-Strelitz, Saxe-Weimar, and Oldenburg, five duchies, seven principalities, and
the three free cities of Hamburg, Bremen, and Lubeck.

The federal power extending over foreign affairs, the army, coinage, and all matters not strictly provincial, was entrusted to the King of Prussia as President of the Confederation, whose executive minister was the chancellor appointed by himself, the King of Prussia was also commander-in-chief of the army and navy, Bismarck appointed chancellor.

The federal legislative authority was to be administered by the Federal Parliament or Reichstag, elected by universal suffrage in proportion to population

Between the President and the Reichstag was established the Federal Council or Bundesrath, consisting of forty-three members appointed by the governments of the different states, Prussia nominating seventeen.

This constitution was accepted by the Constituent Reichstag (17 April, 1867), which voted taxes for the maintenance of the army for four years

Von Roon applies the military organization of Prussia to the whole of the North German Confederation

The South German states, Bavaria, Wurtemberg, Baden, and Hesse-Darmstadt, maintained their independence, but the Zollverein, or Customs-Union, was renewed between them and the North German Confederation, its affairs being regulated by a Zollparlament.

The condition of the Austrian empire after the Treaty of Prague, failure of the constitution granted in 1861, owing to the abstention of Hungarian deputies; the struggle between the federalists, including the different Slavonic provinces, and the dualists, headed by Hungary, the Emperor Francis Joseph resolves on a dual constitution, Beust appointed Austrian chancellor.

The Constitution of 8 February, 1867; the empire split into two parts, Austria and Hungary, each having separate parliaments, ministries, budgets, and complete internal autonomy, imperial foreign policy, finance, and military administration carried on by an imperial ministry responsible to a Reichstag, consisting of delegations from the Austrian and Hungarian parliaments

Delight of the Magyars at the Dual Constitution, which was mainly the work of Deak , their attitude towards subject populations and compromise with Croatia

Wrath of the Slavonic populations at the Dual Constitution , the Slavs of the north, headed by the Czechs, being thus separated from the Slovaks, Slavonians, Croatians, and Servians in the south

Russia encourages the Pan-Slavist idea , and the Slavs of Austria look to Russia for help.

The condition of Russia , liberal policy of the Tsar Alexander and his ministers, except with regard to Poland

Russia's advance in Central Asia , conquest of Samarcand (1866), and Bokhara (1868)

Condition of the Eastern Question ; growth of Roumanian claims for independence under Prince Charles , the Turks withdraw their garrisons from Belgrade and the other Servian fortresses (18 April, 1867) , assassination of Michael Obrenovich (10 June, 1868), and accession of Milan as Prince of Servia , insurrection in Crete (1866–68)

Italian affairs after the Treaty of Prague ; the Italians demand from France the evacuation of Rome, which has a French garrison ; the garrison withdrawn (Dec., 1866); Garibaldi attacks Rome (25 Oct , 1867); a French army under De Failly arrives in Rome to defend the Pope (30 Oct); defeat of Garibaldi at Mentana (3 Nov.)

Negotiations of Napoleon III with Bismarck , his schemes on Belgium ; his schemes on Luxemburg, which was ruled by the King of the Netherlands as a German state, but had not joined the North German Confederation , equivocal position of Luxemburg which is garrisoned by Prussia , William III of the Netherlands ready to sell Luxemburg to France, but unwilling to do so without the consent of Prussia

Napoleon III appeals to Europe on the question of Luxemburg ; a conference of the great powers by the Treaty of London (11 May, 1867) direct that the province shall be evacuated by Prussia, that the fortress shall be dismantled, and that its neutrality shall be guaranteed by Europe

Growing weakness and unpopularity of the Second Empire in France ; effect of the final failure of the Mexican expedition (1867); strength of the parliamentary opposition under Thiers, Napoleon III resolves to rule more in harmony with popular feeling, he grants a measure of liberty to the press (May, 1868), and the right of public meeting (June, 1868), and eventually establishes real parliamentary government (8 Sept, 1869).

Napoleon's concessions taken as a confession of weakness, general hatred and contempt expressed for the Empire in France ; the republican party grows in strength and threatens revolution, Gambetta, elected deputy for Paris in 1869, comes into prominence ; influence of the " International," a democratic society of workingmen directed by Mazzini, Kossuth, and Ledru-Rollin.

Napoleon regards a successful war as the only means practicable for restoring the authority of the Empire, he is falsely told that the army is efficient ; he resolves on war with Prussia because Bismarck had foiled his designs on Luxemburg and he could promise the French people a restoration of the natural limits of France ; he endeavors to obtain allies, Austria is afraid to join him from fear of Russia and Italy declines because of the French occupation of Rome.

William I and Bismarck also desire war with France, they wish to incorporate the South German states and to complete German unity by a great national triumph.

Napoleon III forms a liberal ministry under Émile Ollivier (4 Jan, 1870), he appeals to a plébiscite and by 7,836,434 votes to 1,560,709 France declares herself satisfied with the Empire (8 May, 1870).

The pretext for war derived from the situation in Spain

Recent history of Spain, unpopularity of Queen Isabella II ; domination of the army and frequency of military pronunciamentos, the second Carlist war (1854–56)

Repeated changes of ministry and alternation of power between Espartero, Narvaez and O'Donnell, frequent wars, with Morocco (1859-60), with Peru (1864-66), with San Domingo (1864-65), state of insurrection in Cuba

After the deaths of Narvaez and O'Donnell, Isabella is abandoned, insurrection of September, 1868 ; Isabella escapes to France, formation of a provisional government under Serrano, Prim, and Topete.

Meeting of a constituent assembly at Madrid (Feb, 1869), it elects Serrano regent and declares in favor of constitutional monarchy, candidates for the throne of Spain, Don Carlos, the Duc de Montpensier, and Prince Ferdinand of Saxe-Coburg-Gotha ; Prim suggests the candidature of a prince of the house of Hohenzollern, King William I of Prussia gives permission for the candidature of his relative Prince Leopold of Hohenzollern (May, 1870)

Napoleon III resolves to make out of this candidature a *casus belli* with Prussia, Benedetti sent to Ems to demand an explanation of King William ; his interviews with the King (9-11 July), candidature of Prince Leopold for the throne of Spain withdrawn (12 July), Benedetti's instructions to demand yet more from the King of Prussia ; the King leaves Ems (13 July); Bismarck prepares for war, mobilization of the German armies

Excitement in Germany at the behavior of France ; the South German states prepare to assist the North German Confederation ; enthusiasm felt at the prospect of war with France

England endeavors to mediate but Napoleon is bent upon war, France declares war (17 July), European public opinion regards the war as wanton and sympathises with Prussia

Authorities *Von Sybel*, Die Begrundung des Deutschen Reiches durch Wilhelm I, *Maurenbrecher*, Grundung des Deutschen Reiches. *Oncken*, Das Zeitalter des Kaisers Wilhelm, *William I*, Politische Correspondenz, *Treitschke*, Zehn Jahre Deutscher Kampfe, and Deutsche Geschichte im 19ten Jahrhundert, *Binding*, Die Grundung des Norddeutschen Bundes, *Bulle*, Geschichte des zweiten Kaiserreiches und des Konigreiches Italien, *Delord*, Histoire du Second Empire, *Rothan*, La politique française en 1866, L'Affaire de Luxembourg, and La France et sa politique extérieure en 1867, *Thiers*, Discours parlementaires, *Gramont* (pseud *Memor*), La France et la Prusse avant la guerre, *Ollivier*, Mémoires, and Le 19 Janvier , papiers et correspondance de la famille impériale, *Beust*, Memoirs, *Benedetti*, Ma Mission en Prusse, *Hahn*, Der Krieg Deutschlands gegen Frankreich und die Grundung des Deutschen Kaiserreichs, *Sorel*, Histoire diplomatique de la guerre franco allemande, *Poujade*, La diplomatie du Second Empire et celle du quatre Septembre 1870, *Hubbard* Histoire contemporaine d Espagne, *Mazade*, Les révolutions de l'Espagne contemporaine, *Laveleye*, La Prusse et l'Autriche depuis Sadowa, *Loftus*, Diplomatic Reminiscences, and many of the books cited under Lecture XIX, including those on Bismarck

LECTURE XXI.

THE FRANCO-GERMAN WAR

Attitude of the powers of Europe at the outbreak of the Franco-German War ; England declares neutrality (19 July, 1870), and English public opinion is roused against France by the publication of Napoleon III's propositions to Bismarck for seizing Belgium , Russia declares neutrality (23 July), and threatens to attack Austria if that power should join France ; Austria therefore remains neutral ; Italy refuses to join France because of the French occupation of Rome ; Denmark alone prepares to aid Napoleon if the French armies won some immediate success ; formation of the League of Neutrals (Aug)

Enthusiasm for the war in Germany ; the Crown Prince of Prussia takes command of the contingents of the South German states.

Excitement in Paris , the Emperor Napoleon III leaves to take command of the army (28 July).

Rapid mobilization of the German army ; Moltke's plan of campaign , inferiority of the French military administration ; change in the French plan of campaign owing to the adhesion of the South German states to Prussia.

First campaign of 1870; the skirmish at Saarbrück (2 Aug); battle of Wissembourg (4 Aug), the Crown Prince of Paussia utterly defeats Mac Mahon at Worth, or Froschwiller, and Prince Frederick Charles defeats Frossard at Spicheren, or Forbach (6 Aug); Moltke, having thus broken the French line forms the siege of Strasbourg and advances against the main French army under Bazaine , Bazaine defeated at Borny (14 Aug), at Mars–La–Tour, or Vionville (16 Aug. , and at Gravelotte, or Saint–Privat (18 Aug), Bazaine's army shut up in Metz and besieged by Prince Frederick Charles

Excitement caused in Paris by the news of the French defeats , the Empress Eugénie, who had been appointed regent, dismisses Ollivier, and appoints a new ministry under Montauban, Comte de Palikao

The campaign of Sedan ; the Army of Châlons under Mac Mahon, and accompanied by the Emperor marches to relieve Metz ; it is utterly defeated by the main German army at Sedan (1 Sept); the French army capitulates (2 Sept), and the Emperor Napoleon III is sent a prisoner into Germany

Revolution of 4 September in Paris , the Imperial Government is overthrown , the deputies for Paris in the Legislative Body, with the exception of Thiers, form themselves into the Government of National Defence, with General Trochu, Commandant of Paris, as their president , this provisional government forms a ministry consisting of Jules Favre, Minister of Foreign Affairs, Gambetta, Minister of the Interior, General Le Flo, Admiral Fourichon, Crémieux, Ernest Picard, Jules Simon, Dorian, and Magnan , the other members of the National Defence were, Emmanuel Arago, Jules Ferry, Garnier–Pagés, Eugene Pelletan, Glas–Bizoin and Henri Rochefort

The first measures of the new French government ; its mistakes , it does not immediately summon a constituent assembly ; it persists in remaining in Paris , it sends Thiers to endeavor to obtain allies.

Thiers' journey , his reception in England, Russia, Austria and Italy , the French garrison withdrawn from Rome ,

the Italians take Rome, (20 Sept), and declare it the capital of the Kingdom of Italy

Continued success of the German armies in France , the
siege of Paris formed (19 Sept.), surrender of Toul (23
Sept.), and of Strasbourg (28 Sept), the Germans advance
south and take Orleans (11 Oct), Bismarck's negotiations
with Bazaine , his attitude towards the Government of National Defence , surrender of Bazaine and of Metz (27 Oct)

Gambetta leaves Paris and organizes a branch of the government at Tours , his extraordinary energy and success in
calling France to arms , he advocates war *à outrance* ; he
organizes the Army of the Loire , French success at Coulmiers
(9 Nov.), the Germans evacuate Orleans , the Army of the
Loire advances to the relief of Paris ; critical position of the
German besieging army , sortie of Trochu from Paris and
battle of Villiers–Champigny

Prince Frederick Charles breaks the Army of the Loire in
two, and reoccupies Orleans , the branch government retires
from Tours to Bordeaux (9 Dec), surrender of Verdun (8
Nov), Thionville (14 Nov), and Montmédy (14 Dec.), brilliant defence of Belfort

Effect of the German victories upon German popular
opinion , the South German States enter the North German
Confederation (15–25 Nov), the Reichstag offers the king
of Prussia the title of Emperor ; he declines to accept it
until it is offered to him by the German Princes , this is done
and William I of Prussia is proclaimed German Emperor at
Versailles (18 Jan , 1871).

Russia takes advantage of the war and of the existence of
a pacific ministry in England to declare the abrogation of
the terms of the Treaty of Paris of 1856 ; conference of the
powers upon this subject at London (17 Jan); the Treaty of
Paris modified so as to permit Russia to maintain a fleet in
the Black Sea (13 Mar), causes of France not being present
at the conference ; the policy of Bismarck with regard to the
Government of National Defence.

Final campaign of 1871 , the Germans commence the bombardment of Paris (5 Jan.); operations of the Army of the North under Faidherbe , battle of Pont de Noyelles (23 Dec , 1870); Faidherbe's success at Bapaume (3 Jan., 1871), surrender of Mezières (2 Jan.) ; and of Péronne (10 Jan.), Faidherbe utterly defeated by Von Góben at Saint Quentin (19 Jan); operations of the Second Army of the Loire under Chanzy ; he is defeated by Prince Frederick Charles at Le Mans (14–16 Jan). operations of the Army of the East under Bourbaki ; he is defeated at Héricourt (17 Jan.), and driven into Switzerland , last sortι from Paris under Ducrot; battle of Buzenval (19 Jan); Paris forced to surrender (28 Jan.).

The armistice of 28 Jan , 1871 ; its terms , its blunders ; conduct of Jules Favre ; tactical mistakes of the Government of National Defence ; Gambetta resigns his authority in the provinces , elections held for the meeting of a constituent assembly

Meeting of the Constituent Assembly at Bordeaux (12 Feb) , Thiers is elected chief of the executive power , he signs preliminaries of peace with Germany (22 Feb) ; the treaty accepted by the Assembly (3 March) ; by it France cedes Alsace and part of Lorraine, including Metz, to Germany, and promises to pay a war indemnity of five milliards of francs , a definitive treaty signed at Frankfort (10 May, 1871)

The Constituent Assembly declares the overthrow of the Empire and the proclamation of the third French Republic (1 March, 1871).

Formation of the Government of the Commune (18 March, 1871), its leaders and their doctrines ; Thiers concentrates an army against the Commune ; the government of the Commune resists and shoots the Archbishop of Paris and other hostages . the war with the Commune , MacMahon conquers the Commune and occupies Paris (21–28 May) ; burning of the Tuileries and of the Hôtel de Ville

The most important results of the Franco-German war were, the completion of the unity of Germany and the over-

throw of the second empire in France ; but the cession of
Alsace and Lorraine, more than the result of the war, raised
inextinguishable hatred between the two nations

Authorities *Sorel*, Histoire diplomatique de la guerre Franco-
Allemande, *Angeberg*, Recueils des Traités, conventions, etc , concernant la guerre Franco-Allemande, *Hahn*, Der Krieg Deutschlands
gegen Frankreich und die Grundung des Deutschen Kaiserreichs,
Meding, De Sadowa à Sedan, *Washburne*, Correspondence relating to
the Franco-German War, and Recollections of a Minister to France
(1869-77), *Daily News*, War Correspondence, *Forbes*, My experience
of the Franco-German war, *Russell*, My diary during the last great
war, *Rustow*, The war for the Rhine frontier in 1870, *Borbstädl*, The
Franco German War, *Hooper*, The Campaign of Sedan, *Labou-
chere*, Diary of the besieged resident in Paris, *Bingham*, Journal of
the Siege of Paris, *Bazaine*, L'Armée du Rhin, *Jarras*, Souvenirs,
Mazade, La guerre de France, and, Monsieur Thiers, *Trochu*, l'Empire et la défense de Paris, *Chanzy*, Mémoires, *Ducrot*, La défense de
Paris, *Rothan*, l'Allemagne et l'Italie, 1870-71, *Hippeau*, Histoire diplomatique de la troisième république Francaise, *Andlau*, Metz, *Jules
Favre*, Le gouvernement de la Défense nationale *Jules Simon*, Mémoires, Souvenirs du 4 septembre, and Le gouvernement de M. Thiers,
Glas-Bizoin, Dictature de cinq mois, *Valfrey*, Histoire de la diplo-
matie du gouvernement de la Défense national, *Maquest*, La France et
l'Europe pendant le siège de Paris, *Duret*, Histoire de quatre ans,
Busch, Our Chancellor, and Conversations of Prince Bismarck during
the Franco-German war, *Moltke*, Geschichte des Deutsch-Franzosischen
Krieges von 1870-71, *Hanneken*, Bazaine und die Kapitulation von
Metz, *Blume*, Operations of the German armies in France, *Von Sybel*,
Der Frieden von 1871, and *Lissagaray*, Histoire de la Commune

LECTURE XXII.

THE GERMAN EMPIRE.

Condition of Germany after the successful conclusion of
the Franco-Prussian War ; enthusiasm felt for a union
achieved on the field of battle ; important effect of the war
indemnity paid by France , creation of a national German

coinage ; the reconstitution of the North German Confederation as the German Empire , the Bundesrath increased by
six voices for Bavaria, four for Wurtemberg, two for Baden,
and two for Hesse-Darmstadt ; the Reichstag increased by
the additional representatives of the South German states,
chosen in the ratio of one deputy to each one hundred
thousand population

In spite of the triumph of national unity, particularism
makes itself felt in the Reichstag ; though the German
princes remain true to the Empire, the Polish, Schleswig,
and Hanoverian deputies form separate and irreconcilable
parties, while Alsace-Lorraine refuses to elect any deputies
at all.

The administration of Alsace-Lorraine as a *Reichsland*, or
territory of the Empire

Increased power given to the Catholic Church in German
by the absorption of the South German states into the Empire , Bismarck's dislike of Ultramontanism, which he regards as impairing the spirit of national unity , owing to the
strength of the Ultramontane party in the Reichstag, Bismarck attacks the Roman Catholic Church in Prussia only,
where the Protestants have a majority in the Landtag , the
Kulturkampf , the May Laws (1872), restraining the power
of the Catholic Church , expulsion of the Jesuits from
Prussia (June, 1872); attitude of Pope Pius IX ; the South
German states, and especially Bavaria, protest against Bismarck's anti-Catholic policy.

The reorganization of France , by the policy of Thiers
and the financial skill of Pouyer-Quertier, the war indemnity
is paid and France finally evacuated by the German army
(March, 1873).

The Constituent Assembly at Versailles , the position of
parties , the majority consists of monarchists and ultra-
montanes , deliberate tardiness shown in drawing up a new
constitution for France ; the presidency of Thiers renewed
until the constitution shall have been completed (Aug , 1871)

The majority of the Assembly, which favored monarchy,

divided into Legitimist, Orleanist, and Bonapartist parties, and therefore unable to agree upon a king or emperor; meanwhile the republican minority, led by Gambetta, makes way in France

The monarchical majority in the Assembly forces Thiers to resign (24 May, 1873), and elects MacMahon to the temporary presidency of the Republic, the administration of the Duc de Broglie; he prepares the way for the restoration ot monarchy by appointing anti-republican prefects and officials; fusion of the Legitimist and Orleanist parties; the Comte de Paris recognizes the Comte de Chambord as the legitimate king; regarding himself as next heir to the throne as the representative of hereditary, not of parliamentary, monarchy (Aug, 1873); the impracticable character of the Comte de Chambord; he refuses to abandon the white flag or to make any recognition of parliamentary institutions (27 Oct.), the Duc de Broglie and the parliamentary monarchists abandon the support of Comte de Chambord; election of MacMahon as President of the French Republic for seven years.

Completion of the French Constitution (25 Feb, 1875): its conservative nature, the Senate and the Chamber of Deputies; the presidency to be held for seven years and the president to be elected not by popular vote, but by the joint ballot of the two chambers; the working of parliamentary government in France; frequent changes of ministry, the result of the existence of parliamentary groups instead of well-defined parties

Condition of Spain; election of Amadeus, second son of Victor Emanuel to be King of Spain, assasination of Marshal Prim (30 Dec., 1870), Amadeus commences his reign (2 Jan,, 1871), Don Carlos, grandson of the first Don Carlos, raises a rebellion in the northern provinces (1872); the Carlist War not discouraged in the southern provinces of France, owing to the monarchical character of the Constituent Assembly and its desire to please the Comte de Chambord, difficult position of Amadeus; he resigns the throne of Spain.

Proclamation of a Spanish Republic , Emilio Castelar elected President , General Pavia dissolves the Cortes by armed force (3 Jan., 1874) ; Serrano assumes the presidency ; insurrection at Cartagena.

Pronunciamento of Martinez Campos (30 Dec , 1874) , overthrow of Serrano , Alfonso XII, only son of Queen Isabella, recognized as King of Spain , suppression of the Carlist rebellion.

The foreign policy of Bismarck , he aims to prevent France from obtaining any allies in Europe , he remains on friendly terms with Russia, whose Tsar, Alexander II, was the nephew and friend of the Emperor William, but suspects the Russian Chancellor, Gorchákov ; being unwilling to trust entirely to Russia, he looks for other allies ; England under Gladstone (1868-74) refuses to interfere in continental politics , he therefore enters into close relations with Austria.

The position of Austria ; discontent of the Slavs with the Dual Constitution , they look to Russia for assistance , therefore, in spite of the memory of Sadowa, the Emperor Francis Joseph is ready to enter into alliance with the Emperor William ; dismissal of Beust, the enemy of Prussia, and appointment of Andrassy as Austrian Chancellor (14 Nov , 1871).

Formation of the Dreikaiserbund, or Alliance of the Three Emperors, of Germany, Russia, and Austria (Sept., 1872) ; comparison between the Dreikaiserbund and the Holy Alliance , its aims (1) to maintain the *status quo* in Europe, (2) to act in harmony on the Eastern Question, (3) to oppose the progress of revolutionary, socialist, and nihilist movements

Triumphant position of Bismarck , he becomes the Dictator of Europe as Metternich formerly had been , characteristics of his diplomacy.

Authorities *Muller*, Kaiser Wilhelm, *Hahn*, Wilhelm, der erste Kaiser des neuen Deutschen Reichs, *Simon*, L'Empéreur Guillaume et son règne, *Forbes*, William of Germany, *Heigel*, König Ludwig II, von Bayern, *Lowe*, Life of Bismarck, *Busch*, Our Chancellor, *Hahn*,

Furst Bismarck, *Kohl*, Furst Bismarck, *Muller*, Reichskanzler Furst Bismarck, *Simon*, Histoire du prince de Bismarck, *Klaczko*, The Two Chancellors, *Mohl*, Das Deutsche Staatsrecht, *Whitman*, Germany, *Hahn*, Geschichte des Kulturkampfes in Preussen, *Schulte*, Geschichte des Kulturkampfes in Preussen, *Pressensé*, La politique réligieuse de la Prusse, *Véron*, Histoire de l'Allemagne depuis Sadowa, *Jules Simon*, Le Gouvernement de M Thiers, *Mazade*, Monsieur Thiers, *Hippeau*, Histoire diplomatique de la troisième république, *Chaudordy*, La France et la suite de la guerre de 1870-71, *Gambetta*, Discours, *Beust*, Memoirs, *Houghton*, Origin of the Restoration of the Bourbons in Spain, *Valras* Don Carlos VII et l'Espagne Carliste, and *Gallenga*, Iberian Reminiscences

---

LECTURE XXIII

RUSSIA'S ATTEMPT TO SOLVE THE EASTERN QUESTION.

Condition of the Turkish Empire during the latter years of the Sultan Abdul Aziz, growing weakness of the civil and financial administration, the pledges given after the Crimean war for the more tolerant government of the Christians broken, relying on the protection of the Western powers, all reforms are refused

Attitude of the Sultan towards Egypt, increased importance of that country to England after the completion of the Suez Canal (1869), in 1867 the Khedive of Egypt is given authority to govern without reference to Constantinople, and to negotiate with foreign powers, in 1872 succession by primogeniture in the family of Mehemet Ali is established.

Continued interest taken by Russia in the Eastern Question, the Tsar Alexander II, having freed himself from the humiliating restrictions of the Treaty of Paris in 1871, desires to intervene on behalf of the Christian subjects of Turkey ; by pursuing vigorously the classic policy of Russia he hopes to counteract the growth of Nihilism.

The progress of Russia in Central Asia, conquest of Khiva (1871) and Khokand (1876), Russia's intrigues in Afkanistan, her gradual approach to the frontiers of India.

Growth of the Panslavic idea in Russia; influence of Katkov

Character and policy of Gorchákov.

Attitude of Europe towards the Eastern Question; England, where Disraeli succeeded Gladstone (1874), is apprehensive of Russia's advance on India and Constantinople; purchase of the Khedive's Suez Canal shares; Austria's jealousy of Russia's interference of South Eastern Europe, and dislike of the Panslavic propaganda, France is too much occupied with internal disputes to interfere; Bismarck declares the Eastern Question '' not worth the bones of a Pomeranian grenadier ''

Outbreak of insurrection among the Christians of Bosnia and Herzegovina (July, 1875), encouraged by Servia and Montenegro; the great powers present a joint note to the Sultan (30 Jan., 1876), demanding reforms and religious liberty for the people of Bosnia and Herzegovina.

Russia forbids the Turks to attack Servia or Montenegro, the Dreikaiserbund threatens the Turks with punishment if reforms are not granted (11 May, 1876), England refuses to act with the other powers

Excitement among the Muhammadan population of Turkey, policy of Midhat Pasha; palace revolution (30 May, 1876), overthrow and subsequent murder of Abdul Aziz; Murad V proclaimed Sultan

Prince Milan of Servia declares war against the Turks (30 June, 1876); the Servian army is organized and commanded by Russian officers under Chernaiev, Prince Nicholas of Montenegro declares war against the Turks (2 July), Bosnia and Herzegovina annex themselves to Servia and Montenegro

Excitement in Turkey, defeat of the Servians; the Bulgarian massacres; the great powers intervene in the name of humanity.

Deposition of Murad V, and accession of Abdul Hamid II (31 Aug.), the Turks promise reform, and the creation of a Turkish parliament; illusory nature of this step; Ignatiev presents an ultimatum to the Sultan demanding the effective protection of the Christians in Turkey

Conference of the great powers at Constantinople (Dec 1876), the Turks refuse the demands made of them ; overthrow of Midhat Pasha (5 Jan , 1877)

Both Russia and Turkey prepare for war ; military enthusiasm in both countries , peace signed between Servia and Turkey (1 Mch., 1877).

Russia declares war against the Turks (24 Apr., 1877)

The campaign of 1877 , Loris Melikov advances into Armenia and the main Russian army under the Tzar crosses the Danube and invades Bulgaria ; successes of the Turks , Loris Melikov retreats, and the main Russian army is checked by Osman Pasha at Plevna , reinforcement of the Russian armies , Loris Melikov takes Kars (Nov), and Todtleben storms Plevna (10 Dec , 1877) , the Russians advance on Constantinople ; an English fleet enters the Dardanelles ; Convention of Adrianople (30 Jan., 1878) ; conclusion of an armistice ; the English fleet anchors before Constantinople

Treaty of San Stefano (3 Mch , 1878) between Russia and Turkey ; the Turks agree to a great increase of Roumania, Servia, and Montenegro, and to the creation of a principality of Bulgaria ; Russia receives Kars and Batoum and the retrocession of Bessarabia from Roumania , by this treaty the power of the Turks in Europe was destroyed

General alarm in Europe , Austria protests against the increase of the authority of Russia ; England, where Salisbury succeeds Derby as Foreign Minister (2 Apr., 1878), demands that the Treaty of San Stefano shall be submitted to a Congress of the Powers ; England makes a secret convention with the Turks (4 June) by which she receives Cyprus and the charge of defending the dominions of Turkey in Asia ; Bismarck declares himself '' an honest broker.''

The Congress of Berlin (13 June–13 July, 1878), the representatives present were, for Germany, Bismarck, Werther and Hohenlohe, for Austria, Andrassy, Karolyi and Haymerlé, for Russia, Gorchakov, Schuvalov and Oubril, for England Beaconsfield, Salisbury, and Odo Russell, for France, Waddington, Saint-Vallier and Desprez, for Italy, Corti and De Launay, and for Turkey, Caratheodori Pasha, Sadullah Bey and Mehmet Ali Pasha

By the Congress of Berlin, the Treaty of San Stefano was profoundly modified ; Russia retained the accessions of territory she had received ; Servia and Roumania were made independent kingdoms and received small additions of territory ; Austria received Bosnia and Herzegovina, a small principality of Bulgaria was created, and a semi-independent administration established for Eastern Roumelia, Greece received a small extension of frontier

Disgust of Alexander II and Gorchakov at the proceedings of the Congress of Berlin, but Russia was too weak to undertake actual opposition ; particular resentment felt by Alexander and Gorchakov towards Bismarck, whom they declared wanting in gratitude for the services Russia had rendered to Germany in 1866 and 1870 ; practical dissolution of the Dreikaiserbund, or Alliance of the Three Emperors.

Authorities Most of the books cited under Lecture XXII deal also with the period of the Russo-Turkish war, but see also *Gallenga*, Two Years of the Eastern Question, *Holland*, The European Concert on the Eastern Question, *Vambery*, Central Asia and the Anglo-Russian Frontier Question, and The Coming Struggle for India, *Hellwald*, The Russians in Central Asia, *Rawlinson*, England and Russia in the East, *Popowski*, Rival Powers in Central Asia, *H'yrouboff*, La Question d'Orient et le Traité de Berlin, *Le Faure*, Histoire de la guerre d'Orient, 1877-78, *Farcy*, La guerre sur le Danube, 1877-78, *Green*, The Russo-Turkish War, *Baker*, The War in Bulgaria, *Williams*, The Armenian Campaign, *Daily News*, War Correspondence, 1877-78, *Gay*, Plevna, the Sultan and the Porte, and *Brunswick*, Le Traité de Berlin

LECTURE XXIV.

THE TRIPLE ALLIANCE.

Germany having to fear the resentment of Russia, Bismarck draws closer to Austria, and signs an offensive and defensive alliance with the Emperor Francis Joseph (15 Oct.. 1879) , this alliance is joined in 1882 by Italy, and becomes the Triple Alliance, which agreed to check the desire of France to recover Alsace and Lorraine and the ambitions of Russia in the East

Internal policy of Bismarck , after the death of Pope Pius IX and the election of Pope Leo XIII, Bismarck softens the application of the May Laws and enters into negotiations with the Papacy ; end of the Kulturkampf (1881)

Bismarck and Socialism , his legislation against the Socialists ; after the murder of the Tsar Alexander II (1881) by the Nihilists, he forms once more friendly relations with Russia , the attitude of the new Tsar, Alexander III , Gorchakov succeeded by De Giers (1882).

Until the end of the administration of Bismarck the Triple Alliance is on more or less friendly terms with Russia and dominates Europe and keeps the peace

The situation in France ; the Duc de Broglie forms a government (16 May, 1877), and makes another effort for the re-establishment of the monarchy ; he is overthrown (14 Oct.), and from that time the government of France becomes frankly republican , resignation of MacMahon (30 Jan , 1879) , Jules Grévy elected President of the French Republic , influence of Gambetta ; commencement of a struggle with the Catholic Church not unlike Bismarck's Kulturkampf (1879–81) ; material prosperity of France, but increasing discredit of parliamentary government.

Position in Italy ; death of Victor Emmanuel (6 Jan., 1878) and of Pope Pius IX (7 Feb., 1878) ; accession of King Humbert and election of Pope Leo XIII , financial distress of Italy.

Rivalry of England and France in the Mediterranean ,

dual control established over the government of Egypt, which was practically bankrupt (1878) ; deposition of the Khedive Ismail (1879) ; France establishes a protectorate over Tunis (12 May, 1881) ; Arabi Pasha raises an insurrection against the Khedive Tewfik (1881) ; England intervenes, bombards Alexandria, overthrows Arabi Pasha in the battle of Tel-el-Kebir (13 Sept , 1882) and maintains a garrison in Egypt, England defends Egypt against the Mahdi , expedition up the Nile, and death of Gordon Pasha (1885) ; campaign in the Sudan (1886).

The condition of Russia , assassination of the Tsar Alexander II by the Nihilists (13 March, 1881) ; nature of the government of the Tsar Alexander III , progress of Russia in Central Asia , the Russians take Merv (1884) ; the affair of Penjdeh (30 March, 1885) ; war averted between England and Russia , the progress of Nihilism

The Eastern Question ; Alexander of Battenberg elected Prince of Bulgaria (1879) , union of Bulgaria and Eastern Roumelia (18 Sept , 1885) , war between Servia and Bulgaria , victory of the Bulgarians at Slivnitza (Nov , 1885) , anger of Russia ; Alexander of Battenberg deposed and removed from Bulgaria (6 Sept , 1886) ; election of Ferdinand of Saxe-Coburg as Prince of Bulgaria (Aug , 1887) ; King Milan of Servia abdicates (May, 1889) in favor of his son Alexander.

Death of the Emperor William I (9 March, 1888) , death of his successor, the Emperor Frederick (15 June, 1888) ; accession of the Emperor William II , his character and policy ; he maintains the Triple Alliance, and endeavors to remain on friendly terms with Russia.

Dismissal of Bismarck (1890) , retrospect of his twenty years' dictatorship over Europe.

Attempt to form a Franco-Russian alliance to counter balance the Triple Alliance

Authorities It is not possible to give an adequate list of authorities on the latest phase of Modern European History , reference may be made to several of the books already cited, and a general view can be found in *Dilke*, The Present Position of European Politics, published in 1887

APPENDICES.

Appendix 1

Names of Ministers—not necessarily Prime Ministers—but most important Ministers—in Italics

	House of Hapsburg, Holy Roman Emperors to 1805, aft 1805, Emperors of Austria	France	Great Britain	Spain	House of Hohenzollern, Kings of Prussia, and after 1851 also German Emp	Russia
1801	Francis II (since 1792) *Cobenzl*	Bonaparte, Cambacérès, and Lebrun, Consuls (since 1799)	George III (since 1760) *Addington*	Chas IV (since 1788) *Godoy*	Frederick William III (since 1797) *Haugwitz*	Alexander I. *Panine*
1802	. . . .		*Pitt* .		*Hardenberg* .	*Voronzov*
1804	. . . .	Napoleon, Emperor				
1805	. . . .		*Grenville* For, For S			
1806	*Stadion* .		*Fox,* For Sec *Portland*		*Haugwitz* (Feb) *Hardenberg* (Nov)	
1807			*Canning,* For S		*Stein*	
1808	*Metternich* .	.	*Perceval*	Joseph Bonaparte		
1809			*Wellesley,* For. S			
1810	. . .		*Liverpool*		*Hardenberg*	*Rumianzov*
1812	. . .		*Castlereagh,* F S			
1814	. . .	Louis XVIII, King of France. *Richelieu*		Ferdinand VII		
1815	. . .					
1816	. . .	*Decazes Richelieu Villèle*	George IV			*Nesselrode.*
1818	. . .					
1820	. . .					
1821	. . .					

	Austria	France	Britain	Spain	Prussia	Russia
			Canning, For. S		*Bernstorff*	
1822						
1824		Charles X, King of France				Nicholas I
1825			*Canning*, Prime M			
1827			*Goderich.*			
1828		*Martignac*	*Wellington*			
1829		*Polignac*				
1830		Louis Philippe, King of the French.	William IV			
		Laffite	*Grey*			
1831		*Casimir Perier*				
1832		*Soult.*				
1833				Isabella II		
				(Christina, Regent)		
1834			*Melbourne.*			
			Peel			
			Melbourne			
1835	Ferdinand I	*Broglie*				
1836		*Thiers*				
1837		*Molé*	Victoria			
1840		*Guizot.*		(Espartero, Reg)	Frederick Wm. IV.	
					Eichhorn	
1841			*Peel*			
1843				*Narvaez*		
				Pacheco		
1846			*Russell*	*Narvaez*		
1847						
1848	Francis Joseph I	Louis Napoleon, Pres			*Brandenburg.*	
	Schwarzenberg					
1850				*Murillo*	*Manteuffel.*	
1851						
185?		Napoleon III, Emp	*Derby*, (Feb)			
		Drouyn de Lhuys	*Aberdeen*, (Dec)			
1853	*Buol-Schauenstein*					
1854				*Espartero*		

Appendix I.—Continued.

House of Hapsburg; Holy Roman Emperors to 1805, aft 1805, Emperors of Austria.	France.	Great Britain.	Spain.	House of Hohenzollern; Kings of Prussia, and after 1851 also German Emp	Russia
1855 .	*Walewski*	*Palmerston*			Alexander II *Gorchikov.*
1856 .		*Derby*	*Narvaez* *O'Donnell*	(William, Regent) *Hohenzollern*	
1858		*Palmerston*			
1859 . *Rechberg*,	*Thouvenel.*				
1860 .					
1861	*Drouyn de Lhuys*			William I *Bismarck*	
1862 *Mensdorff*					
1863 . *Belcredi*		*Russell*	*Narvaez*		
1865 .	*Moustier* .	*Derby*	*O'Donnell* *Narvaez*		
1866					
1867 *Beust*		*Disraeli.* *Gladstone*	Provisional Gov't.— Serrano, Prim and Topete		
1868					
1869 .	*La Valette*		(Serrano, Regent) Amadeus I		
1870 .	Ollivier, (Jan) Government of Nat Defence, (Sept.)				
1871 . *Andrassy.*	Thiers, President MacMahon, Pres't	*Disraeli*	Castelar, President Serrano, President Alfonso XII		
1873					
1874					

	Austria	France	England	Spain	Germany	Russia
1879	Haymerlé.	Grévy, President				Alexander III *De Giers*
1880			*Gladstone*			
1881	*Kálnoky*					
1882						
1885			*Salisbury,* *Gladstone*			
1886			*Salisbury*	Alfonso XIII (Christina, Regent)		
1887		Carnot, President				
1888					Frederick III William II *Caprivi*	
1890			*Gladstone*			
1892			*Rosebery*			
1894		Casimir Perier, President			*Hohenlohe*	
1895		Faure, President.				Nicholas II *Lobánov.*

Appendix II.

Sweden	Denmark	Turkey	Portugal	The Protestant Netherlands: Holland	The Catholic Netherlands: Belgium
Gustavus IV (since 1792)	Christian VII (since 1766) (Pr. Fr'd'ck, Reg.)	Selim III (since 1789)	Maria I (since 1777) (Pr. John, Regent)	Batavian Republic (since 1795)	Annexed to France (since 1792)
	Frederick VI	Mustapha IV Mahmud II		Louis Bonaparte	
				Annexed to France	
				William I, King of the Netherlands	
Chas. XIV (Bernadotte)			John VI		
			Pedro IV. Maria II Miguel		
			Maria II	William I	Leopold I
	Christian VIII.	Abdul Medjid.			
	Frederick VII			William II	
Oscar I.					

Charles XV

Oscar II.

Christian IX

Abdul Aziz

Murad V
Abdul Hamid II

Pedro V
Luis I

Carlos

Wilhaun III

Wilhelmina

Leopold II

Appendix III.

The Popes	House of Savoy. Kings of Sardinia; aft 1861, Kings of Italy	The Two Sicilies	Tuscany	Parma	Modena.
Pius VII (Chiaramonti) (since 1800)	Chas Emmanuel II (since 1796)—Ruler of Sardinia only; Piedmont annexed to France. Victor Emmanuel I	Ferdinand IV (since 1759) after 1815, Ferdinand I		Louis of Parma, King of Etruria (1801) Annexed to France (1801)	Part of the Cisalpine Republic (1801)
			Charles Louis, King of Etruria		Part of the Kingdom of Italy.
		Naples *Sicily* Joseph Ferdinand Bonaparte IV Joachim Murat	Annexed to France.		
	Recovered Piedmont, and added Genoa Charles Felix	Recovered Piedmont, Ferdinand I.	Ferdinand III, Grand Duke, restored	Emp Marie Louise	Francis IV
Leo XII (Della Genga)		Francis I	Leopold II.		
. Pius VIII (Castiglioni)		Ferdinand II			
Gregory XVI (Capellari)	Charles Albert				

1846
1847 Pius IX (Mastai-Ferretti)

1849
1854 Victor Emmanuel II
1859

1861
1878 Leo XIII (Pecci)

Francis II .

Ferdinand IV.

Charles II (formerly King of Etruria.)
Charles III.
Robert I

Francis V

Victor Emmanuel I, King of Italy
Humbert

Appendix IV.

...rs, after 1805 ...s of Bavaria	Electors, after 1806 Kings, of Saxony	Electors, after 1814 Kings, of Hanover	Dukes, after 1803 Electors, after 1806 Kings, of Wurtemberg	Margraves, after 1803 Electors, after 1809 Grand Dukes, of Baden	Landgraves, after 1803 Electors, after 1814 Grand Dukes, of Hesse-Cassel	Landgraves, after 1806 Grand Dukes, of Hesse-Darmstadt.
Maximilian Jo-seph II (since 1799) aft. 1805 King Maximilian Jos I	FrederickAugustus I (since 1763)	George III (King of Great Britain) (since 1760)	Frederick II (since 1797) after 1806 King Frederick I	Charles Frederick (since 1746)	William IX (since 1785) after 1814 William I	Louis X (since 1790) after 1806 Louis I
		Mergedin Kingd'm of Westphalia	Mergedin Kingd'm of Westphalia		Mergedin Kingd'm of Westphalia	
		Geo III, restored	William I	Charles Louis, Frederick.	William I, restored	
		Geo IV, King of Great Britain		Louis I	William II	Louis II
	Anthony	William IV, King of Great Britain		Charles Leopold Frederick	(Frederick Wm, Regent)	
Louis I.	Frederick Augustus II					

1837
1847
1848 Maximilian Jo-
        seph II

1851
1852

1854 · John
1856
1864 Louis II.
1866 · Albert.
1873
1877
1886 Otho (Leopold,
        Regent)

1891
1892

Ernest I

George V

Annexed to Prussia

William II

Charles I

Louis II (Frederick,
        Regent)

Frederick I

Frederick Wm I   Louis III

Annexed to Prussia   . Louis IV

Louis V

CORNELL UNIVERSITY.

- -- ---

SYLLABUS

OF A

COURSE OF EIGHTEEN LECTURES

ON THE

HISTORY OF THE FRENCH REVOLUTION

FROM THE MEETING OF THE STATES-GENERAL TO
THE DECLARATION OF THE REPUBLIC
(1789-92)

BY

H. MORSE STEPHENS.

—

ITHACA
ANDRUS & CHURCH.

THE FRENCH REVOLUTION.

LECTURE I

FRANCE ON THE EVE OF THE REVOLUTION: ADMINIS-TRATIVE AND ECONOMIC CONDITION

The administration of France in the 18th century identical with that established by Richelieu, Mazarin and Louis XIV in the 17th century and based on the idea of the absolute power of the king.

The central administration   *i* The king   *ii* The ministers. *iii*. The bureaucracy

The provincial administration . *i*. the pays d'élection and the pays d'état   the attempt to stimulate provincial government : the Provincial Assemblies · *ii*. The intendants and their work   *iii*. The towns and villages.

The financial administration · *i* The expedients of finance ministers : *ii*. The farmers-general : *iii* The chief taxes : the taille, the gabelle, and the douanes.

The judicial administration : *i* The Parlements · *ii*. The lawyers,—avocats, procureurs and notaries : *iii*. The law administered : the droit coutumier and the droit écrit.

The military and naval administration.

The methods employed to maintain the administration the police : arbitrary authority   lettres de cachet.

The economic condition of France in the 18th century due to the system adopted in the 17th century

The state (i) of agriculture   tenure of agricultural property · influence of copyhold tenures   traces of feudalism · absence of serfdom   the corvée   the effect of the administration · effect of the theories of the physiocrats · (ii) of industry · effect of Colbert's legislation   the guilds   the commercial treaty with England : (iii) of commerce : the West India trade : commercial monopolies : smuggling.

The existence of "privilege" due to the historical growth of the administrative system in the 17th century : its evil effect ; its influence on the economic condition of France.

By the end of the 18th century France had outgrown the conditions of the 17th century : the administrative and economic reasons for welcoming a change.

It was because the French bourgeois, farmers, peasants and workmen were better off and better educated than in the rest of Europe that they welcomed the Revolution.

Authorities : *De Tocqueville*, L'Ancien Régime et la Révolution ; *Taine*, Les origines de la France contemporaine : l'ancien régime ; *Doniol*, La Révolution française et la feodalité ; *Rocquain*, L'esprit révolutionnaire avant la Révolution ; *Vicomte de Broc*, La France sous l'ancien régime : *Pizard*, La France en 1789 : *Boiteau*, État de la France en 1789 ; *D'Argenson*, Considérations sur le gouvernement ancien et présent de la France : *Senac de Meilhan*, Du gouvernement, des mœurs et des conditions en France avant la Révolution ; *Mathieu*, L'ancien régime dans la province de Lorraine et de Barrois ; *Krug-Basse*, L'Alsace avant 1789 ; *D'Hugues*, Essai sur l'administration de Turgot dans la généralité de Limoges ; *Clerc*, Histoire des États-Généraux et des libertés publiques en Franche Comté : *Lavergne*, Les Assemblées sous Louis XVI ; *Lucay*, Les Assemblées provinciales sous Louis XVI ; *Necker* De l'administration des finances de la France : *Stourm*, Les finances de l'Ancien Régime et de la Révolution : *Vührer*, Histoire de la dette publique en France ; *Dareste*, La justice administrative en France ; *Flammermont*, La réforme judiciare du chancelier Maupeou ; *Boscheron des Portes*, Histoire du Parlement de Bordeaux : *Dubédat*, Histoire du Parlement de Toulouse ; *Bos*, Les avocats aux conseils du roi ; *Arthur Young*, Travels in France ; *Levasseur*, La France industrielle en 1789 ; *Calonne*, La vie agricole sous l'ancien régime en Picardie et en Artois, and *Babeau*, *La Province sous l'ancien régime, La Ville sous l'ancien régime, Le Village sous l'ancien régime, La vie rurale dans l'ancienne France, *Les Artisans et les Domestiques d'autrefois, and *Les Bourgeois d'autrefois

[Books marked with a * are *not* in the University Library.]

LECTURE II

FRANCE ON THE EVE OF THE REVOLUTION POLITICAL AND SOCIAL CONDITION

The political condition of France in the 18th century and its most important factors   *i* The king · his actual authority dependent on his personality controlled by the court, the bureaucracy, political tradition, and public opinion.   *ii* The court . its political power . its representation of public and class opinion . influence of royal favourites   *iii* The bureaucracy · authority of the ministers and administrators . their relations with the king, the court, and public opinion.   *iv* Political tradition its tendencies and its power   *v* Public opinion the power of the press, of social action, of current ideas

The existence of provincialism in France in the 18th century despite the centralization of the administration

The political power of Paris and other cities

The social condition of France in the 18th century.   *i* The noblesse . A The court noblesse attitude towards the crown. B The petite noblesse   C The noblesse de la robe   D The noblesse de finance et de commerce   *ii* The clergy : A The dignitaries the Gallican and Ultramontane ideas . attitude towards the crown   B The parish curés C The monks and friars   D The Protestants   *iii*. The bourgeois   *iv*. The peasants and farmers   *v* The ouvriers or working classes.   *vi* The poor.

Education in France in the 18th century   *i* Primary education : the village schools ·   *ii* Secondary education · the Oratorians .   *iii* Higher education · the universities and colleges

The intellectual forces which influenced French thought in the 18th century   *i* Diderot and the Encyclopædists ·

ii Montesquieu and the political philosophers   *iii* Voltaire and the anti-clericals :   *iv* Rousseau and the sentimental Deists.

Political and social preparation for the ideas of the Revolution

Authorities : Consult the list added to Lecture I, and add **Jobez*, La France sous Louis XVI , *Sorel*, L'Europe et la Révolution française , Vol. i, Les mœurs and les traditions , **Renée*, Louis XVI et sa cour, the Mémoires of *Besenval*, **Allonville*, **Augeard* and *Madame Campan*, *Loménie*, Beaumarchais et son temps, *D'Haussonville*, Le Salon de Madame Necker, **Allain*, L'instruction primaire en France avant la Révolution, *Duruy*, L'instruction publique et la Révolution, *John Morley*, Diderot, Rousseau and Voltaire, **Vian*, Histoire de Montesquieu and *Sorel*, Montesquieu.

[Books marked with a * are *not* in the University Library]

LECTURE ·III.

THE PRELIMINARIES OF THE REVOLUTION

Accession of Louis XVI to the throne of France (10 May, 1774) · his character   the influence of Marie Antoinette the attitude of the Court . the Comte de Maurepas (1774–81).

The foreign policy of Louis XVI · the War of American Independence · Vergennes (1774–87) . France checkmated on the Dutch question (1786–87)

The internal policy of Louis XVI · financial questions being of paramount importance : the finance ministers shape the internal policy of the King.

The administration of Turgot (1774–76) : his previous career · his physiocratic views . his attempt to introduce economy . he frees the corn trade in France   " encore un mémoire " . effect of his reforms

The administration of Clugny (1776–77)

The first administration of Necker (1777–81) : his character : a banker rather than a statesman : he publishes a balance sheet of France : the " Compte rendu " : the Provincial Assemblies.

The administrations of Joly de Fleury (1781–83) and D'Ormesson (1783).

The administration of Calonne (1783–87) : the affair of the Necklace : the deficit : the Assembly of the Notables (1787).

The administration of Loménie de Brienne (1787–88) : the struggle with the Parlements.

The events in Dauphiné (1788) : Mounier : the assemblies of Vizille and Romans.

The States-General definitely summoned for 1 May, 1789.

The second administration of Necker (1788–89).

Authorities : *Chérest*, La chute de l'ancien régime ; *Droz*, Histoire du règne de Louis XVI ; *Arneth*, Correspondance secrète entre Marie Thérèse et le Comte de Mercy-Argenteau ; *La Rocheterie*, Histoire de Marie Antoinette ; *Campardon*, Marie Antoinette et le procès du Collier ; *Neymarck*, Turgot, et ses doctrines : *Foncin*, Essai sur le ministère de Turgot ; *Tissot*, Études sur Turgot ; *Léonce de Lavergne*, Les Assemblées provinciales sous Louis XVI ; *Lanzac de Laborie*, Jean Jacques Mounier.

[Books marked with a * are *not* in the University Library.]

LECTURE IV.

THE ELECTIONS TO THE STATES-GENERAL.

The effect of the movement in Dauphiné on the situation.

The States-General of past days : impossibility of reproducing it : historical investigations : the two problems of double representation for the Tiers État and of vote par ordre or vote par tête.

The second meeting of the Notables (Nov., 1787).

Necker's decision : the "Résultat du Conseil" and "Rapport au Roi" (27 Dec., 1787) : the system of election decreed : 1000 deputies to be chosen in 250 deputations of four members each by the royal bailliages and sénéchaussées.

The outburst of pamphlets : Sieyès publishes *Qu'est-ce que le Tiers Etat ?*

Tenacity of local opinion : troubles in Brittany and Franche-Comté : the influence of Dauphiné and of Mounier.

The "Règlement du Roi," (24 Jan., 1789) : it lays down the procedure of the elections : the cahiers.

The primary elections.

The electoral assemblies : the question of suppléants : supplementary règlements.

The elections of the nobility : the old and the new noblesse : differences of opinion as to the meaning of the Règlement : the liberal nobility.

The elections of the clergy : the revolt of the curés.

The elections of the Tiers État : the rural elections : the city elections : the tendency of the elections : election of Mirabeau.

The elections in Paris.

Influence of the electoral period on the constituition of the States-General of 1789.

Authorities: *Morse Stephens*, History of the French Revolution, Vol. i, chapter 1 ; *Chassin*, Le génie de la Révolution, Vol. i. Les cahiers des curés ; Les élections et les cahiers de Paris en 1789, 4 vols.; **Labot*, Convocation des États-généraux et législation électorale de 1789 ; the Mémoires of *Bailly*, **Beugnot* and *Malouet* : for the cahiers *Mavidal et Laurent*, Archives Parlementaires, vols. ii–vii.

LECTURE V.

THE MEETING OF THE STATES-GENERAL : THE OATH OF THE TENNIS COURT.

The meeting of the States-General : the sermon of the Bishop of Nancy (4 May) : the opening session (5 May) : the speech of Necker.

The struggle between the orders on the question of vote par tête : masterly inactivity of the Tiers État : the conferences.

The Tiers État resolve to organize (June 12) : debates on their name and character : Mirabeau comes to the front : the deputies declare themselves the National Assembly (June 15).

The Oath of the Tennis Court (20 June).

The National Assembly joined by the majority of the Order of the Clergy (22 June).

The Séance Royale (23 June) : Mirabeau takes the lead.

The National Assembly joined by the minority of the Order of the Noblesse (25 June) and by the remainder (27 June).

Troops concentrated in the neighborhood of Paris.

Mirabeau proposes an address to the King for the withdrawal of the troops (8 July).

Dismissal of Necker (12 July).

Authorities : *Mavidal et Laurent, Archives Parlementaires*, vol. viii ; *Dugour*, Collection de pièces intéressantes, vols. i, ix, x ; *Buchez et Roux*, Histoire parlementaire de la Révolution française, vols. i, ii ; *Loménie*, Les Mirabeau, vol. iii ; *Mirabeau, Œuvres*, vol. vii ; certain speeches of Mirabeau selected in *Morse Stephens'* Orators of the French Revolution, vol. i.

LECTURE VI.

THE TAKING OF THE BASTILLE.

The interest with which the Parisians followed the proceedings of the National Assembly.

The disorderly elements in Paris : the sack of Réveillon's factory (28 April).

The garrison of Paris : the Gardes Françaises : the mutiny among them (30 June).

The excitement caused in Paris by the concentration of the troops.

The reception of the news of Necker's dismissal : the events of July 12 in Paris : riots and pillaging of shops : the troops disinclined to act.

The Electors of Paris meet (13 July) and organize the National Guard.

The events of 14 July : the taking of the Bastille : attitude of the Assembly.

The king recalls Necker and forms a liberal ministry.

The king's visit to Paris (17 July): Bailly appointed Mayor of Paris, and Lafayette Commandant of the National Guard : adoption of the tricolour.

The murder of Foullon and Berthier (21 July).

The first emigration.

Effect of the taking of the Bastille in France and in Europe, on Paris, the King and the Assembly.

The Duke of Orleans : his position and his party.

Authorities : *Pitra*, La Journée de 14 Juillet, edited with a valuable preface discussing all the authorities by *Aulard* ; *Dusaulx*, De l'insurrection parisienne et de la prise de la Bastille ; *Bord*, La prise de la Bastille, and *Lecocq*, La prise de la Bastille et ses anniversaires.

LECTURE VII

- - —

THE REVOLUTION IN THE PROVINCES

The waiting attitude of the Provinces . vague expectations of immediate relief and benefits

Effect of the news of Necker's dismissal, and of the taking of the Bastille, in the Provinces

Outbreak of jacquerie in the rural districts . the "guerre aux châteaux" universality of the jacquerie, proof that it was not directed by any single man or association the idea of the peasants in attacking the châteaux and destroying the muniments

Outbreak of riots in the cities and towns . their causes pillage of baker's shops sympathy shown by the soldiers

Breakdown of the administrative machinery, and general refusal to pay taxes

The "great fear" and its results

Formation of National Guards all over France, and establishment of a sort of local government

The National Guards of the towns put down the jacquerie in the rural districts result of the antagonism thus created between town and country

Startling effect of Salomon's report on the state of France on the National Assembly the night of 4 August general abandonment of "privilege" : inadequacy of this abandonment to restore good government failure of the Assembly to grasp the situation

The establishment of National Guards and of self-government in Paris after the taking of the Bastille, and in the provinces after the "great fear", the natural result of the breakdown of the administrative machinery

Authorities : *Seilhac*, Scènes et portraits de la Révolution en Bas-Limousin , *Boivin-Champeaux*, La Révolution dans l'Eure , *Le Duc*, Histoire de la Révolution dans l'Ain, vols 1, 11 *Sommier*, Histoire de la Révolution dans le Jura · *Desmasures*, Histoire de la Révolution dans le département de l'Aisne *Duval*, Archives révolutionnaires du département de la Creuse *Véron-Réville*, Histoire de la Révolution

dans le département du Haut-Rhin +*Lallié*, Le district de Mache-
coul *Pothier, Roanne pendant la Révolution . *Balleydier, Histoire
du peuple de Lyon pendant la Révolution, vol 1 *Lecesne*, Arras sous
la Révolution, vol 1 *Ramon*, La Révolution à Péronne *Babeau*,
Troyes pendant la Révolution, vol i : *Seinguerlet*, Strasbourg pendant
la Révolution, and *Gosselin, Journal des principaux épisodes de
l'époque révolutionnaire à Rouen

[Books marked with a * are *not* in the University Library]

LECTURE VIII.

THE INSURRECTION OF 5 AND 6 OCTOBER

The proceedings of the National Assembly after the capture of the Bastille had induced the King to recall Necker
want of practical statesmanship among the deputies

Absence of the spirit of party, and its effect . importance
of oratory . waste of time caused by the inexperience of the
deputies

The Declaration of the Rights of Man

The two first questions raised for the future constitution
of France · (1) the question of the royal veto Mirabeau
supports the absolute veto the suspensive veto eventually
carried (2) the question of one or two chambers . rejection of the scheme of two chambers · resignation of the ad-
mirers of the English constitution led by Mounier, Clermont-
Tonnerre, and Lally-Tollendal

Necker's helplessness as Minister of Finance he proposes
a loan, and an income tax of twenty-five per cent : approach
of national bankruptcy Mirabeau's great speech patriotic
gifts

Public opinion in Paris importance of political journalism Loustalot, Camille Desmoulins and Marat · suspicions
entertained of the sincerity of the King poverty and starva-
tion in Paris

The second attempt of the Court to stop the Revolution and dissolve the National Assembly by force · concentration of troops on Versailles attempt made by the Court to secure the fidelity of the soldiers · the banquet in the Orangerie (1 October)

Importance of the crisis

The women of Paris, led by Maillard, march on Versailles, (5 Oct) · the King prevented from withdrawing further from Paris behaviour of the women in front of the palace and in the National Assembly : arrival of Lafayette with the National Guard of Paris (10 P M) · Lafayette goes to bed the mob breaks into the palace (5 A M , 6 Oct) · Lafayette induces the King and Queen to come to Paris . their journey, and establishment at the Tuileries.

Effect of the transference of the King to Paris on the history of the Revolution · he becomes practically a prisoner the project of the Revolution being checked by force averted . the second emigration.

Authorities : For the history of the Assembly see the books cited under Lecture V with the Mémoires of *Ferrieres* , for the events of 5 and 6 October see the authorities cited in *Morse Stephens*, History of the French Revolution, vol 1, p 220

LECTURE IX

EUROPE AND THE REVOLUTION

Startling effect of the news of the capture of the Bastille (14 July), and of the transference of the King to Paris (6 Oct) upon the monarchs and peoples of Europe.

General admiration expressed in England enthusiasm of the English Radicals sympathy expressed by the educated classes. ·

Effect caused in the countries bordering on France . in-

surrections among the peasants upon the Rhine and in Savoy
cruel suppression of these insurrections

The monarchs of Europe approve or disapprove of the
Revolution according to their desire to see France strong or
weak   they all believe the movement to be temporary, but
fear the extension of '' French principles ''

Catharine II of Russia, and her expectation that the excitement in Western Europe would leave her free to deal
with Poland

Charles IV of Spain, and his fear that the Pacte de Famille
between France and Spain would be endangered.

Gustavus III of Sweden, and his royalist attitude

The Dutch republicans, recently overthrown by England
and Prussia, look to France for help

Effect of the position in France upon the insurgent dominions of the Emperor Joseph II.

The Belgian revolution of Oct 1789 . the Austrians driven
out of Belgium , formation of the Belgian Republic (10 Jan ,
1790) : parties in Belgium   they look for help to France

Death of the Emperor Joseph II (20 Feb., 1790)   contrast between the reforms effected by a benevolent despot
and a people acting together

Importance of the early stages of the French Revolution
in the history of Europe.

Authorities : *Morse Stephens*, History of Europe, 1789-1815, chapter 11

LECTURE X

THE FIRST YEAR'S WORK OF THE CONSTITUENT ASSEMBLY

The Assembly follows the King to Paris, and is established
in the Riding School close by the Tuileries · effect of the
change

Growing importance of journalism in forming public opinion in Paris, and in acquainting the Provinces with the course of events.

Rise of political clubs the Jacobins and the Cordeliers

Preponderant weight exercised over the Assembly by Paris · Bailly and Lafayette their efforts to govern Paris.

Proceedings of the Constituent Assembly. it sets to work to draw up a constitution for France want of method and order contrast between its destructive and constructive work

The Assembly's fear of strengthening the executive Mirabeau's scheme of selecting a ministry from the Assembly rejected (7 Nov) disastrous effect of maintaining a weakened executive

The Assembly's financial policy confiscation of the estates of the Church : first issue of assignats economic effect of the Assembly's financial policy. further issue of assignats (Aug, 1790) retirement of Necker

The Assembly's policy toward the Church · the civil constitution of the clergy · schism created

The foreign policy of the Assembly its neglect of international obligations threatening position caused by affairs at Avignon and the rights of the Princes of the Empire in Alsace : the dispute about Nootka Sound · debate on the right of declaring war and peace Mirabeau's policy as reporter of the Diplomatic Committee

The Federation of 14 July, 1790

The Assembly's attitude toward the army and navy insubordination and disorganization Bouillé puts down a military mutiny at Nancy (31 August, 1790)

Gradual pacification of France as the new local institutions come into operation

Authorities : *Mavidal et Laurent*, Archives Parlementaires, vols ix–xviii *Bailly*, Mémoires *Bacourt*, Correspondance entre Mirabeau et La March *Sciout* Histoire de la constitution civile du clergé, vols 1, 11 , *Bouillé*, Mémoires. *Duruy*, L'Armée royales en 1789 and *Maire*, Histoire de l'affaire de Nancy

[Books marked with an * are *not* in the University Library]

LECTURE XI

THE POLICY OF MIRABEAU.

Mirabeau alone perceives the real danger of the situation . his desire to avert foreign war, to ward off bankruptcy, and to strengthen the executive

Mirabeau enters into communication with the Court the nature of the arrangement made : in return for the payment of his debts Mirabeau becomes the secret adviser of the King, but his advice is never followed

The character of Mirabeau's Notes for the Court the fund of political wisdom contained in them

Mirabeau's enemies and the way in which they thwarted his schemes vanity and weakness of Lafayette

Mirabeau clings to the monarchy as the only institution around which a strong executive can be formed, but he desires a limited monarchy subject to the controlling voice of the representatives of the nation

Mirabeau's endeavors to establish a strong executive · foiled in his first scheme he tries to form a party of order in the Assembly.

Mirabeau's sense of the importance of good government he hates anarchy as much as despotism.

Mirabeau's attitude on the financial situation · his fear of national bankruptcy

Mirabeau's views on foreign affairs . he foresees the danger of foreign war, but is not afraid of civil war : in this his ideas run counter to those of the King

Mirabeau's great plan , he wishes the Court to escape from Paris but not to move toward the frontier or to rely on foreign help he desires the King to accept the new constitution but to superadd to it a strong executive authority · he understands the importance of public opinion and endeavors to form a sentiment in favor of order

Mirabeau's assistants : how his speeches were written

Mirabeau's private life and its effect upon his political position

Mirabeau's character.

Mirabeau's latter days . his struggle with the triumvirate of Dupart, Lameth and Barnave he is accused of treachery The death of Mirabeau (2 April, 1791).

Authorities : *Loménie,* Les Mirabeau, vols iii–v : *Mézières,* Vie de Mirabeau. *Bacourt,* Correspondance entre Mirabeau et La Marck . *Plan,* Un collaborateur de Mirabeau * *Duquesnoy,* Journal sur l'Assemblée Constituante.

[Books marked with a * are *not* in the University Library.]

<hr />

LECTURE XII.

THE FLIGHT TO VARENNES

Effect of Mirabeau's death on the political situation the Court, the Assembly and the people are left without any experienced guide

The King and Queen, despite Mirabeau's advice, resolve to appeal for foreign help

The Emperor Leopold II : his exceptional political ability he restores tranquility in the Austrian dominions and reconquers Belgium · he becomes the leading monarch in Europe · Marie Antoinette appeals to him for active help

Exasperation of the French people at the knowledge of the intrigues going on between the French Court and the Emperor, an exasperation increased by the mystery surrounding them : anger caused by the menaces of the émigrés . growth of a feeling that Europe wished to prevent France from working out her political freedom

The increasing distrust of the Court, and general belief in the insincerity of the King and Queen.

This belief justified by the flight to Varennes, which finally destroyed all sympathy between the King and the mass of the people.

The plan of the escape from the Tuileries · its weak points :

flight to the frontier attempted: the King leaves behind a declaration annulling his assent to previous reforms . the royal family is stopped at Varennes (21 June, 1791) and brought back to Paris . dramatic character of the episode · tragic effect of the flight to Varennes

The Emperor Leopold issues the Manifesto of Padua (6 July, 1791) and is supported by most European powers   together with the King of Prussia he issues the Declaration of Pilnitz (27 Aug , 1791) . anger of the French people at the threats of Europe

Effect of the flight on the Assembly   the majority fears it has gone too far, and revises the constitution · the Cordeliers Club prepares a petition for the dethronement of the King , the bourgeois become apprehensive   Bailly and Lafayette determine to act · the massacre of the Champ de Mars (17 July)

Louis XVI accepts the new constitution (21 Sept., 1791) and the Constituent Assembly dissolves

Authorities : The Mémoires sur l'affaire de Varennes   *Bimbenet,* La Fuite de Louis XVI à Varennes . *Aucelon,* La vérité sur la fuite et l'arrestation de Louis XVI à Varennes   *Gabriel,* Louis XVI, le Marquis de Bouillé et Varennes   *Fournel,* L'événement de Varennes , *Klinckowstrom,* Le Comte de Fersen et la cour de France, vol i   and *Browning,* The flight to Varennes, exposing the inaccuracies of Carlyle's account

[Books marked with a * are *not* in the University Library]

LECTURE XIII.

THE CONSTITUTION OF 1791

The characteristics of the new French Constitution   (1) the abolition of privilege and of all relics of feudalism   (2) the mania for election   (3) the weakening of the executive authority

The effect of the abolition of feudalism on land tenure, on local government, and on the position of the nobility

Division of France into departments, districts and cantons · consequent abolition of provincial spirit this redistribution, the most lasting part of the work of the Constituent Assembly.

The new system of local government . the councils and directories of the departments and districts · the functions of the procureur-syndic and the procureur-général-syndic the new municipalities : rage for creating local offices to be filled by election.

The new legislature method of its election its powers

The new judicial system abolition of the parlements and former courts of justice : the system of election applied to all grades of judges . introduction of the jury system

Restriction of the franchise : unpopularity of this restriction, which threw all power into the hands of the middle classes

The position of the executive under the new constitution the weakening of the King's power functions assigned to the ministers, who are given responsibility without power this is the worst part of the Constitution of 1791.

Effect of the attempt to apply the system of election to the Church

Constitution of 1791 satisfied neither the Royalists nor the Democrats : it was a bourgeois compromise which satisfied only the middle classes nevertheless, it was not given a fair trial, owing to the interference of Europe in the affairs of France · its great credit is to have remodelled France into departments, and to have extirpated the feudal system

LECTURE XIV.

THE LEGISLATIVE ASSEMBLY

The meeting of the Legislative Assembly (22 Sept , 1791) : its distinctive character   absence of experienced men owing to the resolution passed by the Constituent Assembly on the motion of Robespierre that none of its members could be elected to the Legislative

The most important leaders in the new Assembly · (1) the Constitutionalists . (2) the Girondins

The nature of the Girondin party ; the brilliance of its orators, Vergniaud, Guadet, and Gensonné : its political director, Brissot.

The influence of the Jacobin Club upon the Legislative Assembly · importance of the debates in the Jacobin Club . Robespierre temporarily excluded from active political life becomes important there   the position of Danton, the former leader of the Cordelier Club . Marat and his journal, the *Ami du Peuple*

By the Constitution of 1791 the Legislative Assembly is prevented from touching constitutional questions · it therefore devotes itself to current politics

The two questions mainly discussed during the first months of the session of the Legislative Assembly had reference to the treatment of the priests and bishops who had refused to take the oath to the Civil Constitution of the Clergy, and to the émigrés   the action taken on these two questions

Indignation caused in the Assembly and in France by the position taken up by the Emperor Leopold and by the King of Prussia, and the general belief that the King and Queen were traitors and in sympathy with the foreign powers

The policy of Narbonne · his endeavor to prove the patriotism of the King by placing three armies in readiness on the frontier

The question of war becomes of paramount importance . the Girondins support the idea of war   Marat and the extreme party oppose it.

Profound mistrust felt of the honesty of the King and Queen : Pétion elected Mayor of Paris

Authorities: *Rabusson-Lamothe,* Lettres sur l'Assemblée Législative *Guadet,* Les Girondins *Sorel,* L'Europe et la Révolution française, vol ii Mémoires of *Bertrand de Moleville, *Beugnot,* and *Madame Roland*

[Books marked with a * are *not* in the University Library]

LECTURE XV

THE OUTBREAK OF WAR

The pacific character of the Emperor Leopold ; his desire to aid his sister Marie Antoinette not strong enough to induce him to wish for war he is forced by the Diet of the Empire to protest against the violation of the rights of the Empire in Alsace . he defends the conduct of the princes on the Rhine in sheltering French émigrés

Catharine of Russia hopes that in a war between the German powers and France she will be left unhindered to carry out her projects against Poland

The Emperor and the King of Prussia sign an offensive and a defensive alliance.

The policy of the Legislative Assembly in forcing the Emperor to declare himself the Emperor's despatch read in reply on 1 March, 1792 death on the same day of the Emperor Leopold

Growing excitement in France at the approach of war · formation of the Girondin ministry : the internal policy of Roland . the foreign policy of Dumouriez

Change caused in the position on the Continent by the death of the Emperor Leopold followed by that of Gustavus III of Sweden : the King of Prussia becomes the leader of the alliance against France

War declared by France against Austria (20 Apr., 1792).

Marie Antoinette communicates with the new Emperor, Francis II.

Conviction in France that the powers of Germany at the request of the Court intended to undo the work of the Revolution : exasperation against the King and Queen.

The disorganization of the French army leaves France badly prepared for war : the schemes of Dumouriez to procure allies are foiled : France is looked upon as an easy prey by the German powers.

Attitude of England and of Spain.

With the outbreak of war the history of the Franch Revolution enters on a new phase : France fights desperately to maintain her rights to settle the form of her government : the monarchs of Europe fail to understand the meaning of national opposition.

Authorities : *Sorel*, L'Europe et la Révolution française, vol. ii *Bourgoing*, Histoire diplomatique de l'Europe pendant la Révolution française, vols. i, ii : *Masson*, Le département des affaires étrangères pendant la Révolution : *Sorel*, Un général diplomate au temps de la Révolution in the " Revue des Deux Mondes " for 1884 : *Browning*, Despatches of Earl Gower : * *Ernouf*, Le duc de Bassano : *Von Sybel*, Geschichte der Revolutionszeit, vol. i : *Ranke*, Ursprung und Beginn der Revolutionskriege : *Arneth*, Marie Antoinette, Joseph II und Leopold II : *Vivenot*, Quellen zur Geschichte der deutscher Kaiserpolitik Œsterreichs während der französischen Revolutionskriege, 5 vols.: *Beer*, Joseph II, Leopold II und Kaunitz : and *Hüffer*, Diplomatische Verhandlungen aus der zeit der französischen Revolution, 3 vols.

[Books marked with a * are *not* in the University Library.]

LECTURE XVI.

THE INVASION OF THE TUILERIES.

The first disasters of the war : murder of Dillon.

Austria and Prussia determine to act together : their plan for the joint invasion of France.

Projects for the formation of a camp near Paris and for the deportation of priests who had refused to take the oath to the Civil Constitution of the Clergy

The king dismisses the Girondin ministers (12 June) and vetoes the decrees of the Assembly on these two questions

The hopeless position of the Court

The attitude of Paris, and of the mayor, Pétion.

The events of 20 June the monster petition presented to the Assembly the petitioners break into the Tuileries · the gravity of the situation · the mob is persuaded to retire without doing any damage

The famous fifty days between 20 June and 10 Aug , 1792 . deliberate preparations made for the overthrow of the monarchy the leaders of the movement the Secret Directory of the Insurrection the part played by Danton.

The bourgeois of the Provinces sympathize with the king Lafayette leaves his army and comes to Paris · the King and Queen refuse to trust Lafayette

The identification of the Court with the foreign enemies . Vergniaud's speech of 3 July the progress of the invaders the country declared in danger (11 July)

The Duke of Brunswick as general commanding the invading Prussian army issues a threatening manifesto against Paris and the Revolution effect of this manifesto . the enrollment of volunteers

Attempt made to establish an alliance between the Court and the Girondins.

General expectation of an insurrection which should overthrow the monarchy

Arrival of the battalion of the Marseillais in Paris, singing the Marseillaise (30 July)

Authorities *Mortimer-Ternaux*, Histoire de la Terreur, vol 1 *Roederer*, Chronique de cinquante jours 20 juin–10 août 1792 Vergniaud's speech in *Morse Stephens* Orators of the Revolution, vol 1 *Pollio et Marcel*, Le bataillon du 10 août

LECTURE XVII

THE CAPTURE OF THE TUILERIES

Final arrangements made for the attack on the Tuileries · the expectant attitude of the people of Paris and the Provinces   the policy of the Legislative Assembly · various schemes proposed for the safety and escape of the King and Queen

Causes of the breakdown of the administrative machinery when put to the test of foreign war the weakness of the executive makes itself felt   Danton and others perceive that a strong administration cannot be established as long as the monarchy is maintained in its false position

The insurrection of 10 August   the plan of battle   the Tuileries attacked   the royal family and ministers place themselves under the protection of the Assembly : the Swiss Guards defend the Tuileries   capture of the palace

The Legislative Assembly declares Louis XVI suspended from office   it is resolved that a National Convention shall be summoned to draw up a new constitution for France

The former Girondin ministers, Roland, Clavière, and Servan, reappointed, and three new ministers, Danton, Monge, and Lebrun elected.

Danton becomes the real chief of the executive council or ministry, and devotes all his energies to organizing the national defence against the Prussians and the Austrians   he is aided by Vergniaud as reporter of the Committee of Twenty-one

Deputies sent through the provinces and to the armies to announce the capture of the Tuileries, the suspension of the King, and the summons of a National Convention

The insurrectionary commune or municipality of Paris takes a prominent part · former members of the secret directory of insurrection join the Commune and are reinforced by the leading republican statesmen including Robespierre,

Marat, and Billaud-Varenne · the Commune causes domiciliary visits in Paris to be made, and fills the prisons with persons suspected of opposition to the Revolution the Commune sends emissaries into the provinces recommending that its example should be followed.

Effect of the news of the capture of the Tuileries in the armies and in the provinces : desertion of Lafayette (20 Aug.)

Authorities : *Mortimer-Ternaux*, Histoire de la Terreur, vol in · *Vatel*, Vergniaud · *Robinet*, Danton

LECTURE XVIII.

THE MASSACRES IN THE PRISONS

Rapid advance of the invaders . the Austrians lay siege to Lille and the émigrés to Thionville : the Prussians take Longwy (27 Aug) and Verdun (2 Sept.) the way to Paris left open

Panic caused in Paris by the successful advance of the invaders : Danton and Vergniaud endeavor to provide for the defence of Paris and France · volunteers refuse to march while the prisons are full of suspected enemies of the Revolution

The massacres in the prisons (Sept. 2–6) . probably eleven hundred persons killed · the part played by Maillard : the massacres in the prisons of Paris imitated in the provinces

Responsibility for the massacres in the prisons how far was the Commune of Paris, the Legislative Assembly, the Executive Council and the people of Paris responsible . apathy of the mass of the Parisians : the refusal of the National Guard to interfere

Effect of the massacres in the prisons on the political situation : they were an act of defiance to the foreign invaders

they terrified out of existence attempts at reaction . they influenced the eléctions to the convention   they sealed the fate
of the monarchy

Dumouriez withdraws into the Argonne, and repulses the
Prussians at Valmy (20 Sept) . retreat of the Prussians
Paris saved from the danger of a siege

The National Convention meets at Paris and declares that
France is a Republic (21 Sept).

End of the first period of the French Revolution.

Authorities . *Chuquet*, La Campagne de l'Argonne . *Mortimer-
Ternaux*, Histoire de la Terreur, vol iii · **Granier de Cassagnac*,
Histoire des massacres de Septembre   Mémoires sur les journées de
Septembre, in *Berville et Barrière*, Collection des mémoires

CORNELL UNIVERSITY.

SYLLABUS

OF

LECTURES XIX===L

ON

THE FRENCH REVOLUTION,

BY

H. MORSE STEPHENS.

ITHACA :
ANDRUS & CHURCH.

TABLE OF CONTENTS

THE FRENCH REVOLUTION.

LECTURE XIX

THE FIRST DAYS OF THE REPUBLIC

Parties in the Convention , absence of party feeling in the modern sense , reasons for the refusal of French politicians to form political parties ; no bonds of party loyalty , the majority of the Convention prided itself on its independence and impartiality

The Girondins ; the two principal sections , (1) the Girondins of the Legislative Assembly—Vergniaud, Guadet, Gensonné, influenced by Brissot, sometimes called the *Brissotins* , (2) the young men who met in Madame Roland's *salon*— Louvet, Barbaroux, Valazé, influenced by Buzot, sometimes called the *Buzotins* ; both sections to some extent aided by certain former members of the Constituent Assemby, such as Lanjuinais and Durand-Maillane.

The Mountain , the two principal sections : (1) the radical leaders of the Legislative Assembly—Merlin of Thionville, Chabot, Basire , (2) former members of the insurrectionary commune of Paris—Billaud-Varenne, Collot d'Herbois ; apart from them and in no way party leaders were Robespierre, Danton, and Marat

The Center, Marsh, or Plain , "the Frogs of the Marsh ;" great ability of many of the men of the Center ; their sincere patriotism , their endeavor to maintain an open mind between the two extremes ; Barère the typical character of the Marsh in the early days of the Convention

Declaration of war between the Girondins and the Mountain ; Louvet's attack on Robespierre (29 Oct , 1792) , Robespierre's reply (5 Nov.) , the Girondins declare the Mountain guilty of the massacres of September in the prisons and stigmatize them as men of blood ; the deputies of the Mountain accuse the Girondins of enmity towards Paris and assert that they desire to raise the provinces against her with a view of forming a federal and divided republic ; the attitude of Danton ; the unpopularity of Marat in the Convention

The Convention and the government , weakness of the Executive Council or ministry after the resignation of Danton ; the influence of Roland, the Minister of the Interior , he assists the Girondins

The Convention and the provinces , disorganization of the local governments of the departments, districts and cities.

The Convention and the armies ; the first Deputies on Mission to the armies.

Rejection of the proposal to give the President of the Convention executive power and special rank ; Pétion, the former Mayor of Paris, elected first President of the Convention

Authorities : The condition of parties sketched in this lecture is founded on *Morse Stephens*, History of the French Revolution, vol ii, chap. v , but see also *Michelet*, Histoire de la Révolution française, vol. v, *von Sybel*, History of the French Revolution, vol ii, *Mortimer-Ternaux*, Histoire de la Terreur, vol iii, and *Aulard*, Les Orateurs de la Législative et de la Convention   Among PRIMARY AUTHORITIES consult the account of the first debates in the Convention in the *Moniteur*, with the text of Louvet's accusation against Robespierre and Robespierre's reply in *Morse Stephens*, Orators of the French Revolution, vol. i, pp. 458–474, vol ii, pp 332–357.

LECTURE XX.

THE REVOLUTIONARY PROPAGANDA

The foreign policy of the Convention ; the schemes of Lebrun-Tondu, the Minister for Foreign Affairs ; the attitude of Danton , the center of French diplomacy not in Paris but in the camp of the victorious general, Dumouriez.

The policy of Dumouriez ; his desire to break up the alliance between Austria and Prussia ; his negotiations with the Prussians, he permits the Prussians to retreat after Valmy without pressing them hard

After the retreat of the Prussians, Dumouriez concentrates all his force against the Austrians ; he regards Austria as the hereditary enemy of France, recurring to the policy of Richelieu and Mazarin, the heroic defence of Lille ; Dumouriez raises the siege of Lille (7 Oct)

Dumouriez invades the Catholic Netherlands or Belgium (28 Oct , 1792) ; he defeats the Austrians at Jemappes (6 Nov.) , he occupies Brussels and Antwerp, conquers the whole of Belgium, and fixes his headquarters at Liége

The campaign on the Rhine ; Custine invades Germany and takes Spires (23 Sept), Worms (24 Sept), and Mayence (20 Oct) , the proceedings of Custine upon the Rhine.

The campaign in the South ; Montesquiou takes Chambéry (25 Sept) and occupies the whole of Savoy ; Anselme takes Nice (29 Sept)

Effect of the news of these victories upon the Convention ; the members go wild with patriotic enthusiasm ; they believe that their conquests were due, not to the weakness of their opponents or to the favor with which their armies were received, but to the fact that France had adopted the republican form of government

Declaration of the Revolutionary Propaganda ; by the Decree of 18 November it is declared that the French Republic was waging war on behalf of all peoples against all kings, that it would aid other nations to gain their liberty, and did not intend to make any annexations , Decree of 15 December.

Effect of the Revolutionary Propaganda upon Europe , the war changes its character ; foreign rulers feel that it is necessary to crush the French Republic at any cost , peoples of Europe were not ready for the enfranchisement promised them by France ; the war becomes one of ideas.

Contrast between the theories and practice of the Convention ; the annexation declared of Savoy and Nice, (9 Nov) and of Belgium (13 Dec)

Divergence between the policy of Dumouriez and the patriotic exaltation of the Convention , mission of Danton to the camp of Dumouriez

Attitude of Dumouriez and the Convention towards England , the mission of Chauvelin and Talleyrand to London ; position of Pitt and Grenville ; Dumouriez wishes to conquer Holland in order to intimidate England , the Convention declares the Scheldt open to commerce (28 Nov) and orders Dumouriez to invade Holland (30 Nov), effect of these measures on English public opinion

Authorities: The only satisfactory analysis of the foreign policy of the Convention during this period is contained in *Sorel*, L'Europe et la Révolution française, vol iii M Sorel in this volume gives complete references to the PRIMARY AUTHORITIES For the campaigns of Dumouriez and Custine, the best SECONDARY AUTHORITIES are *Chuquet*, Jemappes et la conquête de la Belgique, and L'Expédition de Custine, and *Rambaud*, Les français sur le Rhin, and for the gallant defence of Lille *Foucart et Finot*, La défense nationale dans le Nord, and *Derode*, Le siège de Lille en 1792.

·

LECTURE XXI.

- — — —

THE KING'S TRIAL

Questions of internal government , abolition of the Revolutionary Tribunal of 17 August on the motion of Lanjuinais (13 Nov) , dissolution of the insurrectionary commune and installment of a duly elected municipality for Paris (2 Dec) with Chaumette as procureur and Hébert as one of his substitutes ; Saint Just becomes prominent by proposing a law to fix the price of food (20 Nov) , Decree of 18 December punishing with death anyone who exported food out of the country, and Decree of 16 December punishing with death anyone proposing the destruction of the Republic

The question of the King's trial , debate on the question

whether Louis XVI should be tried as a traitor to the nation, the younger Girondins advocate an elaborate trial, the views of Robespierre, a trial resolved upon and a committee appointed to draw up charges against the King (3 Dec)

Louis XVI appears before the Convention (11 Dec), and presents his defence by means of counsel (26 Dec.)

Division of parties upon the question, some of the Girondins follow Lanjuinais and Vergniaud, in demanding that the case should be referred to the primary assemblies and not dealt with by the Convention

This motion was lost and it was resolved (14 Jan, 1793) that the following questions should be put to the Convention (1) was Louis guilty of conspiracy against the nation; (2) shall the judgment be subject to the sanction of the people; and (3) what shall be the penalty

On the first question 683 members out of 739 voted that Louis was guilty, on the second question, 424 members to 284 voted against the appeal to the people, on the third question 361 members voted for death, 26, for death, the execution to be postponed, and 334, for detention until a general peace and then banishment.

The divisions in the Girondin party on these questions, they become more marked on the question of postponing the execution of the King, which is rejected by 380 to 310.

Execution of Louis XVI (21 Jan 1793)

Effect of the execution of the King on Europe; France declares war against England and Holland (1 Feb) and Spain declares war against France (7 Mar); indignation felt against France in the courts of Europe; attitude of Catherine II of Russia, Portugal, Tuscany, the Two Sicilies, and the Holy Roman Empire declare war against France.

Effect of the execution of Louis upon parties in the Convention, Danton's appeal for harmonious action in the face of the war with Europe

Authorities: The best account of the trial of the king is given in *Mortimer-Ternaux*, Histoire de la Terreur, vol iv, but a more dramatic narrative is that of *Michelet*, Histoire de la Révolution française, vol v. The *Marquis de Beaucourt* has collected the official documents and other material in his Captivité et derniers moments de Louis XVI. Among PRIMARY AUTHORITIES may be noted the various speeches and opinions delivered in the Convention during the king's trial. The list of these contained in the President White Library can be found in the catalogue of books on the French Revolution, pp 95–104. The most important of these speeches are those of Robespierre on 3 Dec, 1792, and of Vergniaud on 31 Dec., reprinted in *Morse Stephens*, Orators of the French Revolution, vol ii, pp 357–366, and vol i, 326–345, and that of Barère on 4 Jan, 1793

LECTURE XXII.

THE STRUGGLE BETWEEN THE GIRONDINS AND THE MOUNTAIN

Increased bitterness of the extreme parties after the execution of the King, resignation of Roland, the Girondin Minister of the Interior, and of Pache, the Jacobin Minister of War, who are succeeded by Garat and Bournonville ; Pache elected mayor of Paris

Danton endeavors to secure the more efficient conduct of the war, formation of the Committee of General Defence (3 Jan., 1793), the Convention through this Committee endeavors to direct the Executive Council and undertake the charge of the general administration, the decrees of 1 and 15 February, the first ordering the issue of 800,000,000 livres in assignats, the second, a levy of 300,000 men, Deputies on Mission sent to superintend the new levy

The effect of news from the frontiers upon the situation in Paris.

Miranda driven from before Maestricht (4 Mar.) by the Austrians, Mayence besieged by the Prussians, and Custine driven out of Germany.

Danton's second mission to Dumouriez, riots in Paris (9 Mar); resignation of Bournonville (10 Mar.), Danton's

appeals for union , establishment of the Revolutionary Tribunal to punish with death all crimes against the nation
(10 March).

Outbreak of insurrection in La Vendée as a result of the
levy of 300,000 men ; Dumouriez defeated at Neerwinden
(18 Mar) and driven from Belgium by the Austrians and
the English , formation of the second Committee of General
Defence

Desertion of Dumouriez (5 Apr); its effect upon the Convention , formation of the First Committee of Public Safety ;
its members, power, and functions , Danton's effort to create
a strong executive in this Committee ; enactment of the Law
of the Maximum (3 May).

Impossibility for the Girondins and the Mountain to act
together , the Girondin leaders attack both Danton and
Robespierre ; Robespierre's reply (10 Ap..), Camille Desmoulins publishes his *Histoire des Brissotins*

The dangerous situation of France does not check the
strife between the two parties

Authorities : For this period see *Mortimer-Ternaux*, Histoire de
la Terreur, vol v, and *Morse Stephens*, History of the French Revolution, vol ii, chap vii. Among PRIMARY AUTHORITIES should be
noted the documents printed in *Buchez et Roux*, Histoire parlementaire de la Révolution française, and the debates in the Convention,
of which the most important speeches are reprinted with notes in
Morse Stephens, Orators of the French Revolution. On the desertion of Dumouriez see *Sorel*, L'Europe et la Révolution française,
vol iii, *Chuquet*, La trahison de Dumouriez, and the Memoirs of Dumouriez himself. In this place it may be well to note some of the
chief books upon the Girondins individually and as a party. *Lamartine*, Histoire des Girondins, is a mere rhapsody without any historical
value, and reference should be made rather to *Guadet*, Les Girondins,
Autard, Les Orateurs de la Législative et de la Convention, vol i,
Bué, La légende des Girondins, *Vatel*, Vergniaud, *Dauban*, Mémoires
inédits de Pétion et Mémoires de Buzot et de Barbaroux, *Madame
Roland*, Mémoires, ed Dauban, and *Bailleul*, Examen critique de
l'ouvrage posthume de Madame De Stael

LECTURE XXIII.

THE OVERTHROW OF THE GIRONDINS.

The internal divisions in the Girondin party prevent it from acting effectively against the Mountain ; nature and causes of the difference of opinion existing among the Girondin leaders.

The Convention, on the demand of the Girondins, by 220 votes to 92 orders that Marat be sent for trial before the Revolutionary Tribunal , tactical mistake of this measure , thirty-five out of the forty-eight sections of Paris, led by Pache and Hébert, demand the expulsion of twenty-two of the leading Girondins from the Convention as disturbers of the public peace (15 Apr.) , acquittal of Marat (22 Apr), significance of his trial

Some of the Girondins perceiving that Paris is opposed to them wish to appeal to the provinces , Paris prepares to support the Commune and the Mountain against the Girondins and the Federalists , Guadet proposes that the Convention should leave Paris (30 Apr.) and that it should meet at Bourges (18 May)

The influence of the Girondins over the Convention shown by the election of Isnard as President (15 May) , election of the Committee of Twelve, consisting of Girondins and depputies of the Center to report upon the safety of the Convention (20 May)

Open preparations made in Paris for a *coup d'état* to overthrow the Girondins , the power of the Commune , the weakness of the Girondins.

Arrest of Hébert by the Committee of Twelve (24 May) , the Commune petitions against the arrest (26 May) ; Isnard threatens Paris (27 May) ; Garat, Minister of the Interior, declares the idea of danger to the Convention imaginary, and the Committee of Twelve is dissolved , the Committee is reestablished (28 May).

The *coup d'état* of 31 May ; formation of an insurrection-

ary commune ; Hanriot appointed Commandant of the National Guard ; the people of Paris surround the Convention ,
Barère secures the dissolution of the Committee of Twelve
and the grant of extended powers to the Committee of Public Safety.

The *coup d'état* of 2 June , under pressure of the Commune and of the people of Paris thirty-one leading Girondins are ordered under arrest.

Significance of the overthrow of the Girondins ; the triumph of the Mountain

Authorities : The most recent and most complete work on the
overthrow of the Girondins is *Wallon*, La révolution de 31 Mai et le
fédéralisme en 1793, ou la France vaincue par la commune de Paris
The animus of this work is obvious from its title, but can be counter-
acted by a study of the primary authorities quoted by M. Wallon
himself The daily reports of the spies employed by the Department
of the Interior during the month of May, 1793, printed in *Schmidt*,
Tableaux de la Révolution française, vol 1, are of the greatest value
and interest

LECTURE XXIV

THE CRISIS OF THE SUMMER OF 1793.

Critical position of France and of the Convention during
the summer months of 1793.

Disasters upon the frontiers ; the English and Austrians
take Condé (10 July), and Valenciennes (28 July) ; the
Duke of York and the Prince of Coburg quarrel ; the English lay siege to Dunkirk and the Austrians to Le Quesnoy ;
the Prussians take Mayence (28 July) , the Austrians and
Imperialists invade Alsace ; the Spaniards invade Roussillon
in the Eastern Pyrenees and cross the Bidassoa in the Western Pyrenees

The insurrection in La Vendée ; the Vendéans take Saumur (10 June), fail in an attack on Nantes (29 June), and take Châtillon (5 July)

The insurrection of the great cities (June, 1793), Bordeaux refuses to receive deputies sent on mission, Marseilles and Toulon arrest deputies on mission and declare against the Convention, in Lyons the movement is more pronounced and on 17 July Chalier, the mayor, is guillotined, several cities make arrangements to send deputies and national guards to Bourges

The rising in Normandy; the escape of most of the arrested Girondin deputies from Paris, they assemble at Caen and raise an army, most of the departments of Normandy and Brittany incline to support them; Saint-Just's report on the proscribed Girondins (9 July)

Murder of Marat by Charlotte Corday (13 July), discovery of the Petition of the Seventy-three, a petition against the exclusion of the Girondins signed by members of the Convention, which had hitherto been kept secret

Measures taken by the Convention under the direction of the Mountain to meet these dangers, promulgation of the Constitution of 1793; a force from Paris sent against the Norman insurgents, who are defeated at Pacy-sur-l'Eure (13 July); flight of the Girondin deputies from Caen, pacification of Normandy by Robert Lindet, the fugitive Girondin deputies declared outlaws (28 July); their wanderings and melancholy fate

Submission of Bordeaux (2 Aug.), troops sent against Marseilles, Toulon, and Lyons; gallant defence of Dunkirk

Dissolution of First Committee of Public Safety (10 July), its example and its work

Authorities: For the disasters upon the frontiers, see *Sorel*, L'Europe et la Révolution française, vol III, *Chuquet*, Mayence [1792-93], and Valenciennes, *Fervel*, Les campagnes de la révolution française dans les Pyrénées Orientales, and *Foucart*, La défense nationale dans le Nord de 1792 à 1802. For the insurrection in La Vendée, see *Chassin*, La préparation de la guerre de Vendée, the Mémoires sur la Vendée in *Berville et Barrière*, Collection des mémoires, *Savary*, Guerres des Vendéens et des Chouans, *Turreau*, Mémoires, *Proust*, Archives de

l'Ouest, and Mémoires sur la Vendée, éd. Lescure. For the resistance
of the cities, see *Wallon*, cited under lecture XXIII, *O'Reilly*, Histoire
de Bordeaux, part ii, *Vivié*, La Terreur à Bordeaux, *Laborde*, Histoire
de la Révolution à Marseille, *Balleydier*, Histoire du peuple de Lyon
pendant la Révolution, *Morin*, Histoire de Lyon depuis la Révolution,
and the Mémoires of the *Abbé Guillon*. For the rising in Normandy
see *Vaultier*, Souvenirs de l'insurrection Normande, and *Boivin-
Champeaux*, Histoire de la Révolution dans le département de l'Eure.
For the murder of Marat see *Chevremont*, Marat, *Bougeart*, Marat,
Passy, La Mort de Marat, and *Chéron de Villiers*, Charlotte de Corday
d'Armant. For the wanderings of the proscribed Girondins, see *Meil-
lan*, Mémoires, *Louvet*, Mémoires, and *Vatel*, Charlotte Corday et les
Girondins. For the First Committee of Public Safety and its work,
see *Aulard*, Recueil des actes du comité de salut public, and
Cambon's report on the state of the Republic, reprinted in *Morse
Stephens*, Orators of the French Revolution, vol. i, pp. 507-541.

LECTURE XXV.

THE GREAT COMMITTEE OF PUBLIC SAFETY.

The Great Committee of Public Safety ; the nine members
originally elected (10 July) : Barère, Couthon, Gasparin,
(to 27 July), Herault de Séchelles, Robert Lindet, Prieur of
the Marne, Jean Bon Saint-André, Saint-Just, and Thuriot
(to 20 Sept.) ; Robespierre succeeds Gasparin (27 July) ;
Carnot and Prieur of the Côte d'Or added (14 Aug.) ; Billaud-Varenne and Collot d'Herbois added (6 Sept.) ; retirement of Thuriot (20 Sept.)

Characters of the men composing the Great Committee of
Public Safety ; solidarity of the committee ; division of labor among its members ; the importance of Barère ; position
of Robespierre.

The Great Committee gradually organizes the Reign of
Terror, of which the chief weapons had been forged in the
Convention before the fall of the Girondins.

Attitude of Danton towards the Committee , he proposes
that the ministers shall act as its subordinates, and that it
shall thus become the recognized executive power.

The ideas of the Terror foreshadowed in Barère's first report (1 Aug) ; importance of this report

The festival of 10 August on the anniversary of the capture of the Tuileries ; characteristic features of the festivals
of the Revolution.

The despotism of the Great Committee and the stringency
of its methods of government, the Reign of Terror, made
necessary by the defeats of the French armies on the frontiers,
and by the pressure of internal dissensions and civil war

Authorities : This lecture is based upon *Morse Stephens,* History
of the French Revolution, vol 11, chap 1x   Barère's report is printed
in *Morse Stephens,* Orators of the French Revolution, vol 11, pp 10-38

LECTURE XXVI.

THE REIGN OF TERROR

The measures of 5 September, 1793 ; the representations
of the Commune of Paris and of Chaumettte ; the Revolutionary Tribunal divided into sections so as to try more cases ,
formation of the *sans-culotte* army of 18,000 men , reorganization of the revolutionary committees of the sections and the
granting of salaries to them , Terror declared ʻʻ the order of
the day ''

The Committee of General Security, elected on 11 September, dissolved to make way for a Committee more in harmony with the Great Committee of Public Safety (14 Sept)

Adoption of the Law of the Suspects (17 Sept.) drafted
by Merlin of Douai

Amar's report of 3 October, by which 21 Girondin deputies

were again declared outlaws, 43 were then ordered to be tried by the Revolutionary Tribunal, and 65 were placed under arrest for injuring the Protest of the Seventy-three.

The legal bases of the Terror; Saint-Just's decree of 10 October, declaring the Constitution of 1793 suspended and Billaud-Varenne's decree of 14 Frimaire (14 Dec.), containing the scheme of revolutionary government

The system of the Terror, the Committee of Public Safety recognized as controlling the executive authority, assisted by the Committee of General Security in charge of all matters of police, by the deputies on mission entrusted with the government of the provinces, and by the deputies on mission with the armies carrying out the orders of the Committee

The methods of the Terror for reducing all mal-contents to absolute obedience and frightening away any attempt at opposition or reaction, by means of the Law of the Suspects and the Law of the Maximum pretexts were given for filling the prisons, the revolutionary committees under superintendence of the Committee of General Security, and aided by the practice of denunciation and the institution of *cartes de sûreté* filled the prisons, the Revolutionary Tribunal and the guillotine kept the prisons from overflowing

Procedure of the Revolutionary Tribunal, life in the prisons of Paris

The Terror in the provinces; the unlimited powers of the deputies on mission; some of these proconsuls maintained the peace by an appearance of ferocity, some by sending prisoners to Paris, and some by making use of revolutionary tribunals and military commissions for themselves.

The atrocities of Carrier at Nantes, and of Joseph Le Bon at Arras, the punishment of Bordeaux, Marseilles, and Lyons for their opposition to the Convention; Tallien, Barras, and Fouché.

The Terror with the armies; Saint Just and Le Bas at Strasbourg, restoration of discipline by strong measures

Reorganization of the military system, the work of the Military Committee; Dubois-Crancé

Robespierre's decree of 8 Brumaire (29 Oct.) increasing the activity of the Revolutionary Tribunal; fifty executions in October, fifty-eight in November, and sixty-nine in December, among which may be noted those of Marie Antoinette (16 Oct.), twenty-one Girondin leaders (31 Oct.), the Duke of Orleans (4 Nov.), Madame Roland (8 Nov.), and Madame Dubarry (8 Dec.)

Authorities: For the government of the Terrors in Paris, and in the provinces, see *Morse Stephens*, History of the French Revolution, vol. ii, chapters x and xi. For the Revolutionary Tribunal the authorities are *Wallon*, Histoire du Tribunal Révolutionnaire de Paris, avec le journal de ses actes, and *Campardon*, Le Tribunal Révolutionnaire de Paris; for the prisons of Paris *Dauban*, Les Prisons de Paris sous la Révolution d'après les relations des contemporains; for the government of the deputies on mission *Wallon*, Les représentants du peuple en mission, corrected by the correspondence of the deputies themselves with the Committee of Public Safety contained in *Aulard*, Recueil des actes du Comité de Salut Public; for the Terror in the provinces *Lallié*, Les Noyades de Nantes and Les Fusillades de Nantes, *Paris*, Histoire de Joseph Le Bon, *Lecesne*, Arras sous la Révolution, *Vivié*, La Terreur à Bordeaux, *Raveral*, Lyon sous la Revolution, *Salomon de la Chapelle*, Lyon et ses environs sous la Terreur, and *Seinguerlet*, Strasbourg pendant la Révolution, and for the reorganization of the army, *Iung*, Dubois-Crancé.

LECTURE XXVII.

FIRST RESULTS OF THE TERROR.

Justification of the Reign of Terror found in the vigorous prosecution of the foreign war and the suppression of internecine strife.

The thirteen armies of the Republic; their organization; the restoration of discipline; the selection of efficient officers; the improvement of equipment; the arrangements made for feeding and clothing the soldiers ; France becomes one vast arsenal.

The work of Carnot ; his strategy ; his direction of the armies of the Republic ; aided in his work by Prieur of the Côte d'Or, by the Military Committee of the Convention, and by the Topographical Bureau.

The first successes of the reorganized armies on the frontiers ; the English, Dutch, and Hanoverians forced to raise the siege of Dunkirk, defeated at Hondschoten (6 Sept.), and driven into Belgium ; the Austrians forced to raise the siege of Maubeuge, defeated at Wattignies (15 Oct), and driven across the frontier ; Hoche defeats the Austrians and Prussians at the Geisberg (25 Sept) ; Pichegru relieves Landau and drives the Austrians and Imperialists across the Rhine ; Dugommier retakes Toulon (18 Dec.), which had been surrendered to the English and Spaniards on 4 August.

Successes of the Committee of Public Safety against insurgents in France ; submission of Marseilles (23 Aug.) ; bombardment of Lyons ; its capture (9 Oct.) ; progress of the war in La Vendée ; services rendered by the former garrison of Mayence ; great defeat of the Vendéan army at Cholet (17 Oct.) ; the Vendéans continue a desultory warfare ; the "destruction" of La Vendée.

The attempt to create a republican navy ; the efforts of Jean Bon Saint-André.

The foreign policy of the Great Committee ; advantages derived from the neutrality of Switzerland ; Robespierre's report on the manifestoes of the allied kings against the Republic, 15 Frimaire (5 Dec.)

Owing to these successes France submits to the despotism of the Great Committee and its system of government, the Reign of Terror.

Authorities : The latest monograph upon the military organization of the Terror is *D'Hauterive*, L'Armée sous la Révolution, and *Jung*, Dubois-Crancé still remains indispensable. For Carnot the chief authorities are his Mémoires and the Mémoires sur Carnot by his son. The French government has just commenced the publication of Carnot's correspondence under the able editorship of M. Charavay. For

the campaigns on the frontiers see *Chuquet*, Wissembourg ; Hoche et
la lutte pour l'Alsace ; and Houdschote et Wattignies, and *Jomini*,
Histoire critique et militaire des guerres de la Révolution, vol. i. For
the war in La Vendée and the great cities see the authorities cited
under Lecture XXIV. For the attempt to create a Republican navy
see *Guérin*, Histoire maritime de la France, vol. v, *Chevalier*, Histoire
de la marine française sous la première République, and *Nicolas*, Jean
Bon Saint-André. The foreign policy of the Great Committee is ana-
lysed and described by *Sorel*, L'Europe et la Révolution française,
vol. iii, iv.

LECTURE XXVIII.

THE WINTER OF 1793-94.

The attitude of the Convention towards the Great Committee of Public Safety and the Reign of Terror ; the position of Danton that while supporting the Committee in all
executive measures, the Convention preserved its legislative
rights.

The work done in other Committees of the Convention by
the members of the Center during the Reign of Terror ; men
like Sieyès and Merlin of Douai confined themselves to this
work in order not to hamper the Committees of Government
by their criticisms.

The work done in the Legislative Committee ; Cambacérès
lays the bases of the civil code and Merlin of Douai, of the
penal code.

The work of the Committee of Public Instruction ; Gré-
goire and Sieyès ; its schemes for national education ; its
reform of weights and measures and introduction of the
metric system ; the Republican Calendar.

Symptoms of opposition to the Terror ; wrath of the pro-
pagandists at the abandonment of the idea of the revolutionary propaganda ; Cloots and other exiled foreigners intrigue
against the Committee of Public Safety.

The leaders of the Commune of Paris disliked the despotism of the Committee and favor the establishment of Municipal independence, the character of Chaumette; his municipal reforms; the character of Hébert; the *Père Duchesne.*

The Cordéliers Club becomes the headquarters of these two sections and is joined by many of the men who accomplished the *coup d'état* of 2 June

The episode of the Worship of Reason; it is fostered by the Cordéliers; a Goddess of Reason received in the Convention (10 Nov), Gobel, Bishop of Paris, and other ecclesiastics resign the priesthood; the character of the Worship of Reason in Paris, its extension to the provinces; the Worship of Reason to some extent a manifestation of a spirit of patriotism.

Danton attacks the Worship of Reason as disgraceful, and Robespierre secures the expulsion of its promoters from the Jacobin Club, they prepare for resistance and form the party known as the Hébertists.

The independents in the Convention; the Great Committee afraid of the influence of Danton, in spite of the support he gives them, he is accused of want of sympathy with the Terror; the party of the " indulgents ; " Camille Desmoulins becomes the spokesman of those who believed the Terror was being carried too far; publication of the *Vieux Cordélier*

Position of Robespierre in the Committee of Public Safety, in the Jacobin Club, and in the Convention; he is regarded in France and in Europe as the master of the Committee; his seeming power and real weakness; he is permitted to pose as the exponent of the system of the Terror, his two reports, of 5 Nivôse (25 Dec) on the principles of revolutionary government and of 17 Pluviôse (5 Feb.) on the principles of political morality which should govern the administration of the Republic.

Authorities : For the work done in the committees of the Convention no SECONDARY AUTHORITY can be mentioned and recourse must be had to the reports published by them during the Terror. For the party of the Hébertists and their schemes see *Avenel*, Anacharsis Cloots; for the Worship of Reason, *Aulard*, Le culte de la Raison et le culte de l'Être Suprême; for Danton and his party, *Robinet*, Danton, and Mémoires sur la vie privée de Danton *Bougeart*, Danton, *Clarelle*, Camille et Lucile Desmoulins, and above all the works of Camille Desmoulins, particularly his *Vieux Cordélier*; for Robespierre, *Hamel*, Histoire de Robespierre, and Robespierre's reports.

LECTURE XXIX.

OVERTHROW OF THE DANTONISTS AND HÉBERTISTS.

The position in the Great Committee of Public Safety; the distinction becomes more marked between the views of Robespierre and his friends and those of the working members of the Committee; both sections agree in the necessity of dealing promptly with the parties of the Cordeliers or Hébertists and the Indulgents or Dantonists.

Fabre-d'Églantine, a friend of Danton, attacks the Hébertists; and secures the arrest of Vincent and Ronsin on 27 Frimaire (17 Dec.); Fabre is himself arrested (24 Nivôse— 13 Jan. 1794) as an accomplice in a stock-jobbing machination of Chabot; Danton proposes that the Committee should find means for rendering justice to the victims of arbitrary arrest (4 Pluviôse—24 Jan.); release of Vincent and Ronsin (14 Pluviôse—2 Feb.)

The Convention decrees the abolition of negro slavery (16 Pluviôse—4 Feb.); the position in the French colony of San Domingo; effect of the Revolution there.

The Great Committee resolves to strike at the Hébertists and the Dantonists; Saint-Just's report against the Hébertists (23 Ventôse—13 Mar.); arrest of the Hébertist leaders the following day; their trial; execution of nineteen of them (Germinal—24 Mar.), including Hébert, Cloots, Momoro, Vincent, and Ronsin.

Chaumette subsequently executed (24 Germinal—13 Apr.); the control of the Commune passes to the leaders of the Jacobin Club, which, since the *épuration*, consisted chiefly of Robespierre's followers ; Lescot-Fleuriot appointed Mayor of Paris and Payan, National Agent

Arrest of the Dantonist leaders (10 Germinal—30 Mar), Saint-Just's report against them the following day , effect of this event upon the Convention and upon Paris ; Robespierre prevents Danton's being heard at the bar of the Convention , the trial of the Dantonists , execution of Danton and thirteen others, including Fabre-d'Églantine, Camille Desmoulins, Hérault de Séchelles, Chabot, and Basire (16 Germinal—5 Apr.)

Effect of these blows the reorganization of the Commune of Paris and the establishment of the Reign of Terror in the Convention itself

Authorities: Upon the overthrow of the Hébertists see Saint-Just's report of 23 Ventôse and *Schmidt*, Tableaux de la Révolution française, vol 11, pp 141-203 , upon the overthrow of the Dantonists, *Robinet*, Le procés des Dantonistes and Saint-Just's report of 11 Germinal, reprinted in *Morse Stephens*, Orators of the French Revolution, vol 11, pp 506-539.

LECTURE XXX.

THE TERROR AT ITS HEIGHT

Passive condition of France under the government of the Committee of Public safety ; Paris being controlled by the Commune, and the provinces by the deputies on mission.

Entire acquiescence of the Convention in the supremacy of the Committee after the fall of the Dantonists ; immediate consent given to the monthly reelection of the members of the Committee and to all executive measures proposed , academic character of debates in the Convention , smallness of the attendance

Contrast between the views of Robespierre and those of the majority of the Committee , only Couthon and Saint-Just sympathize with Robespierre's views ; while deemed the master of the Committee his influence was really small, because he managed no department ; Robespierre's attempt to create a department of police, which brought him into collision with the Committee of General Security , Couthon's failure to oust Barère as reporter of the Committee.

Robespierre's position in France , he is considered the author of the Reign of Terror yet the deputies on mission do not correspond with him

Robespierre's position in Paris ; enthusiasm felt for him and his ideas in the Jacobin Club

Robespierre's position in the Convention ; hatred and fear felt for him

Robespierre's views ; he desires to use the power of the Committee to establish a Reign of Virtue, based on the ideals of Rousseau ; Utopian character of his dreams

Robespirre's religious views , belief in the necessity and value of religion ; his Puritanism , his desire to make France virtuous by force of terror

Robespierre regards the Reign of Terror as a means to an end, the establishment of a Reign of Virtue ; his colleagues in the Committee regard it as a temporary expedient for the concentration of the force of France against her enemies

Robespierre's great speech of 18 Floréal (7 May, 1794), establishing the worship of the Supreme Being and recognizing the immortality of the soul , celebration of the Festival of the Supreme Being in Paris (20 Prairial—8 June) , the culmination of Robespierre's apparent ascendancy

Law of 22 Prairial, moved by Couthon ; expediting the procedure of the Revolutionary Tribunal and depriving prisoners of counsel.

The height of the Terror in Paris ; executions average 196 per week between 22 Prairial and 9 Thermidor

The height of the Terror in the provinces; the diversity of methods employed by deputies on mission.

Authorities: *Hamel,* Histoire de Robespierre, *Aulard,* Le culte de la Raison et le culte de l'Être Suprème, and of primary importance, Robespierre's speech of 18 Floréal, reprinted in *Morse Stephens,* Orators of the French Revolution, vol. ii, pp 390-418

LECTURE XXXI.

REVOLUTION OF 9 THERMIDOR

Condition and position of the armies of the Republic in the spring of 1794, want of enthusiasm in the opposing armies, the King of Prussia quarrels with England and thinks more of the Polish question than the conquest of France; the Emperor Francis II, under the influence of Thugut, also turns his attention to Poland; withdrawal of Prussian and Austrian troops from the Rhine and Belgium.

England, influenced by the *émigrés* remains hostile; negotiations between France and the United States; Jean Bon Saint-André's endeavors to build up a Republican fleet; a fleet sent from Brest to protect a convoy from America, battle of the First of June; Lord Howe defeats the French fleet, legend of the *Vengeur*

Successes of the French armies on the northeastern frontier; formation of the army of the Sambre-et-Meuse; victory of Fleurus (8 Messidor–26 June), conquest of Belgium completed by the capture of Antwerp (5 Thermidor–23 July); the English retire to Holland, and the Austrians, southwards; the Prussians defeated at Kaiserslautern (24-27 Messidor– 12-15 July), similar successes against the Sardinians and the Spaniards.

These victories proved the efficacy of the measures of the Terror, but made its continuance unnecessary

The position of Robespierre; he perceives that his colleagues in the Committee wish to make him the scapegoat for the atrocities of the Terror; growing difference of opinion between him and his colleagues, he prepares to attack the Committee of General Security, in which he has but one friend, and the Financial Committee; his unpopularity in the Convention, especially among the surviving friends of Danton; resentment felt at the conspicuous part taken by him in the Festival of the Supreme Being (20 Prairial–8 June); he is made ridiculous by the report of Vadier on the case of Catherine Théot (29 Prairial)

Robespierre retires from the Committee and the Convention to prepare a speech which should induce the Convention to proscribe his opponents

Robespierre reads his speech to the Convention and to the Jacobin Club (8 Thermidor–26 July), its reception

The Revolution of 9 Thermidor, Robespierre, Couthon, Saint-Just, Le Bas, and Augustin Robespierre ordered under arrest by the Convention; they are rescued by the Commune of Paris, they are outlawed by the Convention, the Hôtel de Ville is occupied, and their attempt at insurrection foiled

Execution of Robespierre and his friends (10 Thermidor).

Significance of the Revolution of Thermidor, end of the Reign of Terror

Authorities Upon the campaigns on the frontiers see *Jomini*, Histoire critique et militaire des guerre de la Révolution, vol ii, corrected with regard to the Army of the Moselle by *Moreaux*, Le Général René Moreaux, and supplemented by Barère's reports some of which are reprinted in *Morse Stephens*, Orators of the French Revolution, vol. ii, pp 69-138 On the Revolution of 9 Thermidor, Mémoires sur les Journées révolutionaires, in *Barrière-Lescure*, Bibliothèque des Mémoires, *D'Héricault*, La Révolution de Thermidor, *Hamel*, Histoire de Robespierre, and Histoire de Saint-Just, with Robespierre's last speech in the Convention and Barère's reports printed in *Morse Stephens*, Orators of the French Revolution, vol ii, pp 421-467, and pp 138-157.

LECTURE XXXII

THE RULE OF THE THERMIDORIANS.

Although the Revolution of 9 Thermidor terminated the Reign of Terror, it did not lead to an alteration of the system of government by the committees, the government of the committees remained arbitrary but ceased to be sanguinary.

Berlier's report (26 Thermidor); to prevent the permanent ascendancy of any group of men, while providing for stability of policy, it was resolved that the Committees of Public Safety and General Security should be renewed by a quarter every month, and that the retiring members should not be eligible for reelection until a month had passed, Committee of General Security increased to sixteen

The government of the Thermidorians (July 1794 to March 1795); this party consisted of those members of the Committees who had not been directly concerned in the internal administration of the Terror, and of the members of the Mountain who had taken part in overthrowing Robespierre, the leading Thermidorians were Carnot, Prieur of the Marne, Merlin of Douai, and Treilhard.

The foreign policy of the Thermidorians; they continue the war with vigor, but abandon the ideas of the Revolutionary propaganda and prepare the way for peace, Merlin's report of 14 Frimaire (4 Dec., 1794); the theory of the natural boundaries of France

The internal policy of the Thermidorians, the outcry against the Terrorists; the worship of Marat; the rising to importance of the *jeunesse dorée* led by Fréron; Carrier sent before the Revolutionary Tribunal (21 Brumaire–11 Nov.) and executed

Hoche suppresses the guerrilla warfare of the Chouans in Brittany and the smouldering insurrection in La Vendée pacification of La Jaunaye (15 Feb, 1795).

Continued successes of the armies on the frontiers; Pichegru invades Holland, occupies Amsterdam, and captures the Dutch fleet in the Texel with his cavalry, by January 1795, the whole of Holland is in the hands of the French, formation of the Batavian Republic.

Other successes of the French armies ; Jourdan defeats the Austrians at Aldenhoven (2 Oct) and occupies Aix-la-Chapelle, Cologne, and Coblentz ; Moreaux occupies the Palatinate and Tréves ; Dugommier and Moncey invade Spain ; the Sardinians defeated at Loano (24 Nov.)

These further victories preclude any desire to restore the Terror and increase the outcry against the Terrorists

Action of the Thermidorians ; closing of the Jacobin Club (8 Brumaire–18 Nov), recall of the survivors of the Seventy-three Girondin Sympathisers (18 Frimaire–8 Dec), repeal of the Law of the Maximum (4 Nivôse–24 Dec)

The position during the winter of 1794–95

Authorities No authoritative work exists upon the government of the Thermidorians and hardly any documents of importance have been published on this period The best sources of information are the reports, among which may be noted Berlier's report of 26 Thermi-dor, Robert Lindet's of 20 September, Romme's report on the crimes of Carrier, 21 Brumaire, and Merlin's report of 14 Frimaire The for-eign policy of the Thermidorians has been sketched by a masterly hand and due justice first done to it by *Sorel*, in his l'Europe et la Révolution française, vol iv, and the situation in Paris can be studied in *Schmidt*, Tableaux de la Révolution française, vol ii

----

LECTURE XXXIII

THE INSURRECTIONS OF GERMINAL AND PRAIRIAL

Increased outcry in Paris and in the provinces for the pun-ishment of the Terrorists,—who are stigmatized as the '' tail of Robespierre'' , effect of the report of Courtois on Robes-pierre's papers (16 Nivôse—5 Jan , 1795).

The Thermidorians who had been supporters or agents of the Terror begin to be ousted from the committees of government by deputies of the Plain and sympathisers with the Girondins

Rioting in Paris; overthrow of the worship of Marat; fighting between the *jeunesse dorée* or *jeunesse Fréronienne* and the survivors of the old Jacobin party.

Saladin's report on the conduct of the members of the Great Committee of Public Safety, condemning Billaud-Varenne, Collot d'Herbois, Barère, and Vadier (12 Ventôse— 2 Mar., 1795)

Recall to their seats in the Convention of the surviving Girondins, including Lanjuinais and Louvet (18 Ventôse)

Exasperation of the survivors of the Mountain at this measure; working upon the misery among the poorer classes of Paris, caused by the severity of the winter, they foment a rising

Insurrection of 12 Germinal (1 Apr., 1795), the mob of the faubourgs St. Antoine and St Marceau break into the Convention, shouting for "bread and the Constitution of 1793"

Results of the insurrection of 12 Germinal; Billaud, Collot, Barère, and Vadier are ordered to be deported to French Guiana without trial; a commission appointed to inquire into the conduct of the deputies on mission during the Terror; the Committee of Public Safety increased from 12 to 16 members (14 Germinal); power passes into the hands of the returned Girondins and the members of the Plain

Insurrection of 1 Prairial (20 May, 1795); the Convention invaded by the mob, who are encouraged by the survivors of the Mountain, murder of Féraud; gallant conduct of Boissy-d'Anglas; expulsion of the mob; disarmament of the faubourgs of St. Antoine and St. Marceau; end of mob influence in Paris

Condemnation, suicide, or execution of *les derniers Montagnards*.

Report of Durand-Maillane condemning the acts of the

deputies on mission during the Terror (13 Prairial—1 June), followed by numerous arrests.

Authorities · Upon the insurrections of Germinal and Prairial see *Schmidt*, Tableaux de la Révolution française, vol 11 and his Paris pendant la Révolution, *Claretie*, Les derniers Montagnards, *Marc de Vissac*, Romme le Montagnard, and *Louvet's* funeral oration on Féraud, reprinted in *Morse Stephens*, Orators of the French Revolution, vol i, pp 475-500

LECTURE XXXIV

CONSTITUTION OF THE YEAR III

After the insurrection of 1 Prairial the control of the Committees of Government passes into the hands of the returned Girondins and of the Deputies of the Plain , in foreign policy they follow the lines laid down by the Thermidorians and retain the greatest Thermidorian statesmen in office, who make the treaties of Basle , in internal policy they encourage the spirit of reaction and vengeance.

Not only the Terrorist members of the Convention who had taken active part in the government of the Terror, but also some of the leading Thermidorians are committed to prison after Durand–Maillane's report , the Convention declines, however, to send them for trial

The reaction in the provinces , the Deputies on Mission sent out in the summer of 1795 permit and sometimes encourage the persecution of local Terrorists , atrocities committed by the Companies of Jéhu in the South of France , Hoche maintains peace in Brittany and La Vendée, and defeats a force of émigrés at Quiberon (21 July).

The victories of the French armies, and still more the Treaties of Basle, cause a general outcry in France for the abolition of arbitrary government and the promulgation of a new constitution.

A committee of seven appointed (14 Germinal–3 Apr ,
1795), including Sieyès, Cambacérès, and Merlin of Douai,
to draw up the bases of a new constitution , the details
worked out by a committee of eleven, including Boissy–
d'Anglas and Daunou

The Constitution of the Year III , its principal point the
attempted separation of the legislative from the executive
authorities

The executive authority entrusted to five Directors elected
by the legislature, of whom one was to retire yearly and to
be ineligible for reelection ; the Directors were to live together in the Luxembourg Palace, and the will of the majority was to be taken as the will of the whole ; they were to
appoint the ministers, who were not to be members of the
legislature, and were to have complete control of the administration , treaties were to be submitted to the legislature for
ratification , the Directors controlled the expenditures but
could not impose taxes , they could not veto legislation

The legislative authority entrusted to two chambers, the
Council of Ancients, consisting of two hundred and fifty
members above forty-five years of age, and the Council of
Five Hundred ; one-third of each Council was to retire
yearly and elections were held in two degrees, with a property qualification for both electors and deputies ; the Council
of Five Hundred alone could impose taxes ; the Council of
Ancients was the court of appeal in diplomatic questions ,
in legislation the consent of the majority in each chamber
was necessary ; for the election of Directors the two Councils acted jointly.

In local administration the elected councils-general of the
departments and districts were maintained, but the elected
procureurs-syndics and *procureurs-généraux-syndics* were replaced by national agents nominated by the central government

The judicial system established in 1791 was maintained.

Rejoicing of the *bourgeois* and reactionaries in France at
the Constitution of the Year III ; the royalists begin to intrigue for the restoration of monarchy.

The Convention in order to counteract this movement, determines to elect the first Directors from among the regicides and decrees that two-thirds of the new legislature shall be elected by the departments from its own number (13 Fructidor–30 Aug.).

Indignation of the royalists and the *bourgeois* at this action of the Convention.

Authorities : For the internal history of France during this period, see the ordinary secondary histories, which are, however, very incomplete owing to ignorance of the authorities; for the condition of Paris see *Schmidt*, works cited under Lecture XXXIII ; for the reaction in the provinces, the various provincial histories, *Wallon*, Les représentants en mission, and *Daudet*, La réaction royaliste au Midi en 1795 ; for the character of the government, *Fain*, Manuscrit de l'An III ; and for the Constitution of the Year III, the text of the Constitution, the debates in the Convention and the reports of the constitutional committees.

LECTURE XXXV.

THE TREATIES OF BASLE.

The results of Merlin's report of 14 Frimaire (4 Dec., 1794) ; the Thermidorians resolve to show Europe that the French Republic has entirely abandoned the revolutionary propaganda and will not annex territory beyond the "natural limits" of France ; the Rhine, the Alps, and the Pyrenees.

The doctrine of the natural limits ; by recurring to it the Thermidorian statesmen assert themselves to be the successors of Richelieu, Mazarin, and Louis XIV ; the attainment of these limits held out as the reward of France for her sacrifices and victories.

The Thermidorians offer proof of their sincerity by not annexing Holland after its conquest by Pichegru ; Sieyès and Reubell organize the Batavian Republic.

Friendship shown by the neutral powers after the cessation of the Reign of Terror, notably by the U. S. of America, represented by James Monroe, and Denmark, communications opened with Prussia through Grouvelle, the French minister at Copenhagen

The first treaty of peace made by France with Tuscany (9 Feb., 1795).

The returned Girondins and members of the Plain, who filled the Committees of Government after the Thermidorians, followed their predecessors in foreign policy, under the leadership of Sieyès, Reubell, Treilhard, Cambacérès, Merlin of Douai, and Boissy-d'Anglas.

Attitude of the belligerent powers towards the Republic. Prussia desires to withdraw from the war because her attention is concentrated on Poland and England declines to pay subsidies unless she can control the Prussian armies, Spain desires peace because two French armies, having entered Spain threaten Madrid, the princes of the Empire dislike to continue the war, because their territories are being overrun by French armies, Austria and Sardinia, subsidized by England, are ready to continue the war, England becomes the most persistent enemy of the Republic.

Causes of England's pronounced hostility, reliance of Pitt and Grenville on the assurances of the *émigrés*, fears of the governing classes provoked by Burke, the national conscience aroused by the orgies of the Worship of Reason, general desire for revenge on France for her conduct during the war for American Independence, England captures all the colonies of France in Asia, Africa, and the West Indies except San Domingo, where the negroes are in insurrection.

Importance of the neutrality of Switzerland at this juncture, Berne, where Wickham, the English minister resided, the headquarters of the *émigrés*, and Basle, where Barthélemy, the French minister, resided the headquarters of sympathizers with France

Negotiations at Basle, Hardenberg, the Prussian minister signs with Barthélemy a treaty of peace between Prussia and France (5 Apr.), the open and secret clauses of this treaty,

Prussia promises the left bank of the Rhine to France and France grants neutrality to northern Germany

Treaty of peace and alliance made with the Batavian Republic (27 May)

Treaty of peace signed between Spain and France at Basle (22 July) ; its significance

Treaty with the Landgrave of Hesse-Cassel (29 Aug)

England and the *émigrés* , a force of *émigrés*, landed from English ships at Quiberon, annihilated by Hoche (21 July, 1795).

The campaign of 1795 on the Rhine ; treacherous communications entered into between Pichegru and the royalist exiles , effect of Pichegru's misconduct on military operations ; Jourdan forced to retire from Germany and Kléber forced to raise the siege of Mayence

By the Treaties of Basle, France reenters the comity of European nations , proposal to exchange Madame Royale for certain deputies of the Convention held prisoners in Austria ; death of Louis XVII (20 Prairial—8 June,.1795).

Authorities *Sorel*, L'Europe et la Révolution française, La paix de Bâle (Revue Historique, vols v–vii), *Fain*, Manuscrit de l'an trois, *von Sybel*, History of the French Revolution, vol iv, *Vivenot*, Herzog Albrecht von Sachsen-Teschen als Reichsfeldmarschall, vol. ii, *Combes*, Mémoire sur la correspondance officielle de Merlin de Thionville relativement aux Négociations·de Bâle, and of primary importance the Papiers de Barthélemy, ed. *Kaulek*

LECTURE XXXVI

THE INSURRECTION OF 13 VENDÉMIAIRE

The feeling in France with regard to the Constitution of the Year III , general approval of the Constitution, mingled with opposition to the law declaring that two-thirds of the first legislature must be elected from the Convention, elements of this opposition; a desire to punish the Terrorists still further, the wish of the Bourgeois to obtain at once the influence secured to them under the new Constitution, the royalist intrigues, and a general desire for reaction

The knowledge of the strength of the opposition unites the Convention in the face of common danger

The Constitution of the Year III solemnly submitted to the popular vote, and on 1 Vendémiaire (23 Sept, 1795) proclaimed the Constitution of France

The opposition in Paris determines to make a display of force which should compel the Convention the Decree of the Two-thirds, the movement organized by royalist intriguers, the *jeunesse dorée*, and the bourgeois sections

The Convention appoints Barras to provide for its defence, and Barras employs as his assistant Napoleon Bonaparte, who had been removed from active service the previous year

The National Guard of the bourgeois sections of Paris, accompanied by many volunteers, advanced to attack the Tuileries (13 Vendémiaire–5 Oct), they are repulsed by the artillery commanded by Bonaparte, complete victory of the Convention, character of the insurrection of 13 Vendémiaire compared with the other insurrections in Paris during the Revolution.

Armed opposition to the Decree of the Two-thirds in Paris alone; the rest of France acquiesces.

The Convention elects the first Directors, who are all regicides.

The Convention dissolves itself (4 Brumaire–26 Oct), after declaring a general amnesty to all prisoners for political offences

Authorities: *Larévellhère-Lépeaux*, Mémoires, *Réal*, Essai sur les journées des 13 et 14 vendémiaire, *Fain*, Manuscrit de l'an trois, *Danican*, Les brigands démasqués, and *Iung*, Histoire de Bonaparte

LECTURE XXXVII.

THE FIRST DIRECTORS.

The first Directors elected under the Constitution of the the Year III ; Larévellière-Lépeaux, Barras, Reubell, Carnot, and Letourneur ; character, previous career, and inclinations of the first Directors.

Reubell devotes himself to foreign affairs ; his experience and aptitude for this department.

Carnot and Letourneur, both formerly officers of the engineers, direct the military operations.

Larévellière-Lépeaux becomes the chief advocate of Theophilanthropy and devotes himself to its extension.

Barras does the least work but dominates the others and keeps them in harmony.

The first ministry of the Directory appointed 5 November ; Merlin of Douai, Minister of Justice, Charles Delacroix, of Foreign Affairs, Faypoult, of Finance, Benezech, of the Interior, Aubert-Dubayet, of War, and Truguet, of the Marine.

The first Councils ; importance of Sieyès, who refused to be a Director and preferred to sit in the Council of Five Hundred, in which sat also Cambacérès, Treilhard, Merlin of Thionville, Tallien, Boissy-d'Anglas, Daunou, Isnard, Louvet, and Prieur of the Côte d'Or, while Lanjuinais and Durand-Maillane sat in the Council of Ancients.

Difficulties presented in the attempt to carry out the arrangements of the Constitution of the Year III.

Authorities : There exists no modern or adequate history of the Directory and documents are lacking for the proper appreciation of the period. The most useful books, though old-fashioned and without references, are *Barante*, Histoire du Directoire, and *Thiers*, Histoire de la Révolution française. Reference should also be made to *Larévellière-Lépeaux*, Mémoires, *Barras*, Mémoires, *Carnot-Feullens*, Histoire du Directoire constitutionnel, and *Despaze*, Les cinq hommes.

LECTURE XXXVIII.

THE INTERNAL POLICY OF THE FIRST DIRECTORS

The first Directors in undertaking the government of France had to deal on the one hand with the royalists and other remnants of the party defeated on 13 Vendémiaire, and on the other hand, with the advanced democrats who looked back with regret on the ideas of the Reign of Terror.

Of these two factions the former was politically the stronger ; in the elections of the free third to the legislature it had obtained many important successes, in the election of Barbé-Marbois and other politicians who had taken no part in previous political assemblies and who detested the recollection of the Convention ; but the fact that the Convention had decreed that no new Director or new third of the legislature should be elected till 1797, prevented this party from getting a majority in the Councils.

The greater part of this party consisted of unavowed royalists, who wished to restore either the old monarchy or the constitutional monarchy established by the Constitution of 1791 ; the party was supported in great measure by funds obtained from England through Wickham and its headquarters was the Club de Clichy in Paris, from which it took its name as the Clichians ; its general was Pichegru, whose transactions with the *émigrés* were well known but not yet openly revealed.

To meet the danger caused by the intrigues of the Clichians and the conspiracies of the radicals, the Directors formed a Ministry of Police (Jan., 1796) which was organized by Merlin of Douai, who was succeeded by Cochon de Lapparent in April, 1796.

Babeuf forms a plot for the restoration of the Constitution of 1793, but his machinations became known to the police and he was arrested, with sixty-four of his accomplices (10 May, 1796) ; the ideas of Babeuf, his long trial before the High Court of Vendôme, Babeuf executed (27 May, 1797) after an attempt at suicide.

Second radical plot to seize the camp of Grenelle formed by Huguet, formerly a Constitutional Bishop, and a member of the Convention, distinction between the ideas of these conspirators and those led by Babeuf, failure of the attempt (10 Sept., 1796), Huguet and other ringleaders tried by a military commission and shot (6 Oct)

Condition of France in 1796; continued troubles in the south between the Terrorists and the reactionaries, the mission of Fréron, debates on this subject in the Councils; France declared by the Directors in a state of perfect internal peace (15 July, 1796); prevalence of brigandage; distinction between insurrection for political purposes and brigandage.

Effect of the victories of the armies in Italy on the position of the Directors; the financial situation improved by the money sent by Bonaparte; pride of France in the victories of the Republic, acquiescence of the people in the government of the Directory in spite of evidences of corruption, because it gave France victory abroad and internal peace.

Significance of the growing importance of the Department of Police, the army becomes more professional than national.

Authorities : Reference may be made for the condition of Paris to the reports of the police spies, in *Schmidt*, Tableaux de la Révolution française, and Paris pendant la Révolution ; and for Babeuf, to *Advielle*, Histoire de Babeuf

LECTURE XXXIX.

THE FOREIGN POLICY OF THE FIRST DIRECTORS

The foreign policy of the Directory left chiefly in the hands of Reubell, the Director, and Charles Delacroix, the Minister of Foreign Affairs; the personal enmity between

Sieyès and Reubell threatens to cause a breach between the Directors and the Councils in regard to foreign affairs

Anxiety felt in France for a general peace, Reubell and Delacroix, however, wish to continue the war with England, Austria, and Sardinia, they adopted the principles of the Thermidorians and would only make peace upon the basis of receiving the "natural limits" of France.

Reubell desires Prussia to make an offensive and defensive alliance with the French Republic, Frederick William II, though he had made peace, shrank from making an alliance with the Republic; such an alliance involved the cession of the left bank of the Rhine and Prussia did not wish to stand forth as sanctioning the division of the Empire

For these reasons the project of an alliance with Prussia failed, because Prussia had already obtained all she could by being allowed, owing to the "line of demarcation," to appear as the saviour of Northern Germany

Alteration caused in the position of Prussia by the results of the campaign of 1796, increased friendliness with France, secret supplement to the Treaty of Basle signed (5 Aug).

Reubell's negotiations with Spain, by the Treaty of San Ildefonso (19 Aug., 1796), Spain makes an offensive and defensive alliance with France and afterwards declares war against England, this alliance forced the English to abandon Corsica and placed a Spanish fleet at the disposal of the French Republic, defeat of the Spanish fleet at Cape St. Vincent by Sir John Jervis (14 Feb., 1797)

Relations between Austria and France, exchange of Madame Royale effected (20 Dec, 1796), the Directors resolve to pursue the war vigorously against the Austrians both in Italy and Germany, result of the victories of 1796 upon the position of Austria

The first Directors and England; the people of both countries desire peace, but the governments wish the prosecution of the war, disappointment of the Directors that the conquest of Holland has done so little to damage England, effect upon England of Bonaparte's victories in Italy and of the

Treaty of San Ildefonso ; Lord Malmesbury sent to Paris to
discuss the terms of peace (Nov , 1796) ; failure of the negotiations , Hoche prepares a scheme for attacking England
by way of Ireland , the expedition to Bantry Bay under
Hoche frustrated by bad weather

Modifications in the foreign policy of the first Directors
caused by Bonaparte's victories in Italy and the successes,
followed by reverses, of the campaign in Germany

Authorities . A short sketch of the foreign policy of the Directory
will be found in *Morse Stephens*, European History (1789-1815)   Ref
erence may be made to the inadequate secondary histories cited under
Lecture XXXVII, supplemented by the despatches of the Prussian
Minister in Paris, published in Preussen und Frankreich von 1795 bis
1807 , Diplomatischen Correspondenzen, ed *Paul Bailleu*, vol 1

———————

LECTURE XL.

THE CAMPAIGNS OF 1796 IN ITALY AND GERMANY.

The first Directors resolve on an active offensive campaign
in Italy with, as its aim, the invasion of Italy and the de-
tachment of the King of Sardinia from the Austrian alliance,
and treat the war in Germany as of secondary importance

The condition and military situation of the Army of Italy;
Schérer pushes forward and by the victory of Loano (24
Nov., 1795), opens communications with the Republic of
Genoa, which is well affected to France

Napoleon Bonaparte takes command of the Army of Italy
(27 Mar , 1796), causes of his appointment , his previous
career

Campaign of 1796 in Italy ; first stage , Bonaparte turns
the Maritime Alps and separates the Sardinian from the
Austrian army , he defeats the Sardinians under Colli at
Montenotte (12 Apr.), Millesimo (13 Apr.), Dego (15 Apr.),

Ceva (16 Apr), and Mondovi (22 Apr.), Victor Amadeus III of Sardinia, fearing for the safety of Turin, signs the Armistice of Cherasco (28 Apr.)

Treaty of peace signed between Sardinia and France (15 May), by which Victor Amadeus ceded Savoy and Nice to the French Republic

Campaign of 1796 in Italy, second stage, Bonaparte crosses the Po and (10 May) forces the passage of the Adda at the bridge of Lodi; the Austrians evacuate Lombardy, Bonaparte occupies Milan and besieges Mantua; the Dukes of Modena and Parma forced to submit and to contribute both money and works of art, Bonaparte occupies Bologna and Ferrara, Pope Pius VI signs the Armistice of Foligno (24 June).

Campaign of 1796 in Italy; third stage; an Austrian army under Wurmser invades Italy for the relief of Mantua, and is defeated at Castiglione (5 Aug.); in the following month Wurmser throws himself into Mantua

Campaign of 1796 in Italy, fourth stage, an Austrian army under Alvinzi invades Italy by the valley of the Brenta for the relief of Mantua, the French repulsed at Caldiero (12 Nov.); Bonaparte wins the battle of Arcola (16 Nov)

Campaign of 1796 in Italy; fifth stage; the Austrians make a last effort to relieve Mantua by way of Lake Garda; Bonaparte defeats Alvinzi at Rivoli (14 Jan., 1797); surrender of Mantua (2 Feb.)

Bonaparte's attitude towards the Italian people; his attitude towards the Pope, Pius VI signs the Treaty of Tolentino with the French Republic (19 Feb)

Campaign of 1796 in Germany; the Army of the Sambre-et-Meuse, under Jourdan, and the Army of the Rhin-et-Moselle, under Moreau, invade southern Germany; they are outmanœuvered by the Archduke Charles, who repulses Jourdan; Marceau killed in the battle of Altenkirchen (20 Sept); Moreau meanwhile advances; the Margrave of Baden, the Duke of Wurtemburg, and the Elector of Bavaria enter into negotiations with Moreau; the Treaty of Pfaffenhofen (7 Sept); the Archduke Charles turns upon Moreau, who accomplishes his famous retreat

Effect of the campaigns of 1796 on Europe, on France, and on the position of the Directors.

After these campaigns the armies of France become still further professional rather than national ; pronounced rivalry between the officers and soldiers of the armies which fought in Germany and those which fought in Italy.

Authorities Of Bonaparte's campaigns in Italy the most graphic account is contained in *Thiers*, Histoire de la Révolution française , these chapters have been edited with English notes in *Bowen*, The Campaign of Arcola All histories of Napoleon contain a description of his Italian campaigns For military details see the Correspondance of Napoleon, *Jomini*, Histoire critique et militaire de la Révolution, and *Pommereul*, Campagnes du Général Bonaparte en Italie For the campaign in Germany for a brief account, *Rambaud*, Les français sur le Rhin, *Pajol*, Vie de Kleber, *Thoumas*, Vie de Marceau, and for military details, *Jomini*

LECTURE XLI

THE POLITICAL SITUATION IN 1797

The victories of the Republican armies and the success of the foreign policy of the first Directors do not compensate for the ruinous result of continued war upon the prosperity of France

The disordered condition of the finances, the inflation of the paper currency, and the corruption of officials and contractors increase the general desire for peace , the blockade of France maintained by the English navy ruins French commerce and impoverishes the nation

The general desire for peace and the belief that the first Directors were wedded to a war policy caused the new third of the Councils, elected in 1797, to belong almost entirely to the Clichian party ; the most conspicuous new member was Pichegru, in spite of the suspicion of treason that rested upon him.

Barthélemy, negotiator of the Treaties of Basle, chosen a Director in the place of Letourneur (May, 1797).

The policy of the Clichians, a majority of them favor constitutional monarchy and would have been ready to advocate the return of the Bourbons if the *émigré* princes would have permitted a limitation of the old monarchical authority ; other sections were in favor of the eldest son of the late Duke of Orleans, or of princes belonging to foreign royal houses , some were declared absolutists

The Clichians support a peace policy ; negotiations entered into with Lord Malmesbury as representative of England at Lille (July, 1797) ; failure of these negotiations , the Councils blame the Directors and Ministers for this failure

The Directors at first incline to yield to the Councils , general change in the ministry, the most important new ministers being Talleyrand, of Foreign Affairs, François de Neufchâteau, of the Interior, and Schérer, of War

Importance of Talleyrand , his previous career ; his relations with Barras

Disgust of the chief generals of the Republic, of Hoche, who had succeeded to the command of the Army of the Sambre-et-Meuse, and of Bonaparte at the speeches and the pacific intentions of the Clichians

A struggle imminent and indeed necessary between the Councils and the Directory ; the impracticable nature of the Constitution of the Year III , failure of the attempt to divorce the executive and legislative functions of government

Authorities   See books cited under Lecture XXXVII

LECTURE XLII.

FRANCE AND EUROPE IN 1797.

Bonaparte invades the Tyrol (16 Mar, 1797) and advances on Vienna, he defeats the Archduke Charles and signs preliminaries of peace with Austria at Leoben (17 Apr.)

At the same time Hoche and Moreau invade Germany, and are only checked in their march by the news of the signature of these preliminaries.

By the preliminaries or Convention of Leoben, Austria agrees to recognise the Rhine as the frontier of France, which involved the cession of Belgium, and to receive Venice in exchange for the Austrian possessions in Lombardy, the question of peace with the Empire referred to a congress to be held at Rastadt; Bonaparte entrusted with negotiating a definitive peace with Austria

Bonaparte's policy in Italy; he forms the Cisalpine Republic out of Lombardy, the Legations, and the other States of Northern Italy (9 July), the Constitution of the New Republic based on the Constitution of the Year III

Bonaparte overthrows the ancient aristocratic government of Genoa and forms the Ligurian Republic (15 June)

Bonaparte occupies Venice, which he holds in readiness to surrender to Austria, but he annexes the Ionian Islands

The Directors approve of the policy of Bonaparte in setting up Republics in Italy as part of the policy inherited from the Thermidorians

The position and attitude of the Batavian Republic, after the conclusion of the Convention of Leoben, Hoche is placed in command of the united armies, of the Sambre-et-Meuse and of the Rhin-et-Moselle, and is directed to prepare an invasion of England or Ireland with the aid of the Dutch fleet in the Texel.

Perilous position of England in 1797, owing to mutinies in the navy and Irish discontent; the Directors owing to their quarrels with the Legislature miss the best opportunity of striking at England.

Hoche and Bonaparte, informed of the political situation by Talleyrand and others, press the Directors to overthrow the opposition in the Councils, Hoche sends them money, Bonaparte, a general

Effect of the *coup d'état* of 18 Fructidor upon foreign policy ; Austria, which had been delaying the signature of a final treaty, signs the Treaty of Campo Formio (17 Oct.) , the terms of this treaty follow those of the Convention of Leoben

The death of Hoche (18 Sept , 1797) prevents the accomplishment of his attempt on England ; nevertheless, the Dutch fleet sails out of the Texel, but is defeated by Admiral Duncan in the battle of Camperdown (11 Oct)

The situation at the end of 1797 , the triumph of the Directors and of a vigorous foreign policy , Bonaparte acknowledged the chief general of the Republic ; England the sole remaining enemy in arms against France

Authorities   See works cited under Lectures XXXVII, XXXIX and XL   For the Italian Republics see *Gaffarel*, Bonaparte et les Républiques italiennes ; for the Batavian Republic see La République Batave ou la Révolution française en Hollande, and for Hoche *Rousselin de Stint-Albin*, Vie de Hoche   A short sketch is given in *Morse Stephens*, European History [1789-1815]

———————

LECTURE XLIII

THE COUP D'ÉTAT OF 18 FRUCTIDOR

The situation in France in 1797 proved the impossibility of successfully separating the legislative and executive powers of government in France.

Ever since the elections of 1797 the difference of opinion between the majority of the Directors and the majority of the Councils had been a serious danger in both internal and foreign policy

The armies disliked the Clichians because of their desire for peace , republicans feared their designs against republican government ; and the French people generally sided with the Directors against the legislature, because the Councils represented but a small class of the population, owing to the restricted franchise.

The leadership in the Councils passed from the hands of former members of the Convention, like Sieyès, to the leaders of the Clichians, Barbé-Marbois and Pichegru, whose only ally in the Directory was Barthélemy, the newly elected Director , weakness of character of Barthélemy

Since the change of ministry in June, 1797, the majority of the original Directors, urged by Bonaparte and Hoche, the generals, and by Talleyrand, Merlin of Douai, and François de Neufchâteau, the ministers, had been ready to take strong measures against the Clichians , but Carnot, fearing the overthrow of the Constitution, opposed their views

Eventually Barras, Larévellière-Lépeaux, and Reubell determined to act, and took into their counsels one of Bonaparte's generals, Augereau, who had been sent from Italy for that purpose and placed in command of the military division of Paris

On 18 Fructidor (4 Sept , 1797) the regular troops under Augereau surrounded the Tuileries and fifty-five Clichian leaders were arrested by the police , they were at once deported to Sinnamari, French Guiana, without trial ; Barthélemy was deported also, but Carnot was permitted to escape from the Luxembourg and leave France , some of the most distinguished of the exiles, including Pichegru and Barthélemy, soon escaped and made their way to England

Merlin of Douai and François de Neufchâteau were elected Directors in the place of Barthélemy and Carnot, but the places in the Councils left vacant by the deportations were not filled up

The government, which under the influence of the Clichians had been hesitating, became more arbitrary and more republican , forty-two journals were suppressed ; the strict laws against the *émigrés*, which were being disregarded, were enforced , and republican clubs were again allowed

The results of the *coup d'état* were, at home stronger government and the repression of representative institutions, and abroad, greater determination in carrying out a warlike policy ; Austria at once signed the Treaty of Campo Formio, and the Dutch fleet set sail from the Texel to be defeated at Camperdown

Significance of the *coup d'état* of 18 Fructidor ; it was not a national or popular revolution, but a *coup d'état* made necessary by the impracticable nature of the Constitution of the Year III , it is distinguished from other important "days" of the Revolution by the fact that not a single drop of blood was shed, though many citizens were arbitrarily exiled

Authorities Upon the *coup d'état* of 18 Fructidor in addition to the general authorities upon the history of the Directory already cited, see Mémoires sur les Journées révolutionaires, in *Barrière et Lescure*, Bibliothéque de Mémoires, *Ramel*, Journal, being a narrative by one of those deported, *Barbé-Marbois*, Journal d'un déporté, and *Victor Pierre*, La Terreur sous le Directoire, and Le dix-huit fructidor

---

LECTURE XLIV.

THE POLICY OF BONAPARTE

Position and popularity of Napoleon Bonaparte after the Treaty of Campo Formio ; he arrives in Paris (5 Dec , 1797), since the death of Hoche he was without dispute the greatest general of France ; his reception in Paris ; attitude of the Directors towards Bonaparte.

The Directors resolve to carry on a vigorous war against England, the only remaining enemy of France ; Bonaparte, after being appointed to the command of the Army of the Interior, points out the difficulty of invading England while the English fleet commands the Channel ; he therefore suggests an expedition to Egypt, which should lead to the expulsion of the English from India

Bonaparte, in spite of his popularity, fears to attack the government of the Directory, strengthened as it had been, by the revolution of 18 Fructidor, and therefore desires to leave France ; the Directors wish to be rid of the popular general ; the expedition to Egypt is therefore undertaken

Bonaparte leaves France (9 May, 1798), he occupies Malta (9-12 June), he reaches Egypt (1 July) and occupies Alexandria (4 July), he defeats the Mamelukes in the Battle of the Pyramids (21 July) and occupies Cairo (24 July)

The English fleet under Nelson destroys the French fleet in Aboukir Bay, in the Battle of the Nile (1 Aug), Bonaparte and his army are thus entirely cut off from communication with France , the English fleet commands the Mediterranean, occupies Minorca, and besieges Malta

After Bonaparte's departure the Directors recur to the ideas of Hoche of attacking England through Ireland ; failure of the expedition of Humbert (Aug , 1798), slight assistance rendered to the French by the insurrection in Ireland of 1798

Bitterness of the war between France and England ; the extent of the naval war the effect of the blockade of the French ports by England , destruction of the naval power of France ; French privateers ravage English commerce, but French fleets are unable to cope with English fleets

The French and English in the West Indies ; the attempt of Victor Hugues to raise the Caribs and the negroes against the English ; reconquest of the French West India Islands by Abercromby , occupation of the Spanish colony of Trinidad and the Dutch colony of Demerara

The policy of Bonaparte essentially anti-English , his organization of Egypt , the Turks, disgusted at the invasion of Egypt, form an alliance with England.

Authorities In addition to the histories of the Directory and books on Napoleon already cited, see for the expedition to Egypt,

Gall, Bonaparte en Égypte, and *Boulay de la Meurthe*, La Directoire et l'expédition d'Égypte , for the French navy during this period, see *Guérin*, Histoire Maritime de la France, vol vi, *Chevalier*, Histoire de la marine française sous la prémière République, *Jurien de la Gravière*, Guerres maritimes sous la République et sous l'Empire, and *Rouvier*, Histoire des Marins français sous la République

LECTURE XLV.

THE FOREIGN POLICY OF THE FRUCTIDORIAN DIRECTORY

The Directors placed in complete power by the Revolution of 18 Fructidor, pursue a vigorous foreign policy and, imitating the policy of the Thermidorians and of Bonaparte, resolve instead of annexing neighboring countries, to set up republican governments in them

The Directors intervene in Switzerland , a revolution breaks out there ; peasants and people declare French principles and appeal for help to the French Republic , General Brune invades Switzerland to assist the popular movement and defeats the troops of the government of the Cantons . declaration of the Helvetian Republic, one and indivisible , with a constitution modelled after that of the Year III , reforms accomplished in Switzerland , abolition of relics of feudalism , arbitrary conduct of the French commissioner, Rapinat ; the Swiss people resent the continued presence of French troops and break out into constant petty insurrections.

The policy of the Directory in Italy , murder of General Duphot at Rome (27 Dec., 1797) , Berthier, who commanded the French troops in the Cisalpine Republic in succession to Bonaparte, occupies Rome ; Pope Pius VI escapes from Rome and is eventually taken prisoner to France, where he dies at Valence (29 Aug., 1799) , formation of the Roman Republic, depending for support on the French army in Rome

Attitude of Ferdinand IV, King of the two Sicilies, towards the French Republic; influence of his wife, Marie Caroline, during Bonaparte's campaign in Italy, he makes peace with France (12 Nov, 1796), assistance rendered by Ferdinand to Nelson, after the battle of the Nile, believing Bonaparte safely shut up in Egypt, Ferdinand resolves to attack the French, without formal declaration of war the Neapolitan army under the Austrian general, Mack, drives the French from Rome (29 Nov, 1798), Championnet, who had succeeded Berthier, expels Mack (15 Dec) and occupies Naples (Jan., 1799), flight of Ferdinand and Marie-Caroline, establishment of Parthenopean Republic.

Further aggressions of the French in Italy; Joubert occupies Piedmont (Nov., 1798), and Charles Emmanuel IV escapes to Sardinia, in spite of the wishes of the Grand Duke Ferdinand to remain at peace with France, the French occupy Florence (25 Mar, 1799)

The Directors make no appeal to the national spirit in Italy and no effort to establish a united Italian Republic

The Directors and Austria, the Emperor Francis II and his people believe their defeats by the French due to the genius of Bonaparte, their relief at the news of Bonaparte's departure to Egypt and delight at the result of the Battle of the Nile, Pitt and Grenville discover that Austria is not satisfied with the Treaty of Campo Formio and is ready to enter into another coalition against France, the position of Bernadotte, the French ambassador at Vienna; riot of 15 April, 1798, questions at issue between France and Austria

The Directors and Prussia; accession of Frederick William III (Nov., 1797); the Directors resolve to make another effort to obtain an alliance with Prussia, mission of Sieyès to Berlin (May, 1798); its failure; Frederick William III resolves to maintain strict neutrality.

The Directors and Russia; the Emperor Paul departs from the position of Catherine, whom he had succeeded in 1796, and meditates war with France, he takes into his service the *émigré* army under Condé and gives asylum to Louis XVIII, he is indignant at Bonaparte's expedition to Egypt, as indicating the intention of France to interfere in the East, he accepts the title of Grand Master of the Knights of St. John of Malta and occupies the Ionian Islands.

The Directors and the Congress of Rastadt, after the departure of Bonaparte for Egypt, the negotiations drag, since Austria determines to try another war with France in the absence of Bonaparte, attitude of the French envoys, Treilhard, Bonnier, and Roberjot, who insist upon the cession of the left bank of the Rhine to France and support the secularization of the ecclesiastical states of Germany

Position of the Directors in Europe in 1798; apprehensions caused by their conduct in Switzerland and Italy, formation of the second coalition against France

Authorities In addition to the general authorities already cited, see *Gaffarel*, Bonaparte et les républiques italiennes, *Vivenot*, Zur Geschichte des Rastadter Kongresses, *Bailleu*, Preussen und Frankreich von 1795 bis 1807, vol 1, and, for Bernadotte's mission to Vienna, *Masson*, Les Diplomates de la Révolution

--- --- ---

LECTURE XLVI.

INTERNAL POLICY OF THE FRUCTIDORIAN DIRECTORS

The Directory, as the supreme executive authority after the *coup d'état* of 18 Fructidor, entered upon a course of arbitrary government, submissive behavior of the Councils

The financial policy of the Directors, owing to the inflation of the paper currency, and the fall in the value of assignats, the Directors resolve, on the advice of Ramel, Minister of Finance, to issue no more assignats, they issued instead *mandats territoriaux*, distinction between the two forms of paper money, the Directors declare partial bankruptcy, maintaining only one-third of the national debt on the *Grand Livre*, and paying the other two-thirds in *mandats territoriaux*.

Distress caused in France by these financial measures ; corruption rife among officials , waste and peculation of the funds sent to Paris from conquered countries

Treilhard elected Director (May, 1798) in the place of François de Neufchâteau , he is succeeded as envoy at Rastadt by Jean Debry , Sieyès again refuses to be a Director, preferring to go as ambassador to Berlin

François de Neufchâteau becomes Minister of the Interior, and Bruix, Minister of the Marine

The elections to the Councils in 1798 resulted in the return of advanced republicans, for the Clichians and reactionaries dared not appear at the polls ; the Fructidorian Directors, disapproving of strong political sentiment in either direction, quashed the greater part of these elections and sent their own nominees to the Councils instead.

The Directors and the army , feeling the approach of a fresh European war, the Directors resolved to increase the army , experienced officers existed but there was a lack of soldiers ; it was no longer possible to call for volunteers or to summon the nation to arms, since the country was no longer in danger ; therefore on the demand of the Directors, the Councils passed the first Law of Conscription (5 Sept., 1798) , under this law all Frenchmen between 20 and 25 were declared subject to military service , they were divided into five classes, and the executive could call out one or more classes with the consent of the legislature

Condition of France in 1798 , brilliancy of social life in Paris , Madame Tallien, Madame Récamier, and Madame Bonaparte ; encouragement of literature, science, and art ; this brilliancy and prosperity confined to Paris, while the provinces suffered from the ruin of commerce and the prevalence of brigandage

Authorities See the general authorities with the addition of *Goncourt*, Histoire de la société française pendant le Directoire

LECTURE XLVII

THE CAMPAIGNS OF 1798

Bonaparte's campaign in Syria ; having conquered lower Egypt, Bonaparte leaves Desaix in command and advances into Syria to meet the advancing Turks (Feb , 1799); he conquers the whole of Palestine with the exception of Acre, which is gallantly defended with the help of English sailors under Sidney Smith , Bonaparte defeats the Turks at Mount Tabor (16 Apr.) and, raising the siege of Acre, retires to Egypt (20 May)

The position in Egypt ; Desaix had gone up the Nile ; the Mamelukes had reoccupied Cairo and the English had landed a Turkish army at Aboukir ; Bonaparte defeats the Mamelukes and the Turks , on the reception of news from France, Bonaparte leaves Egypt (22 Aug) turning over the command to Kléber.

Outbreak of war with the second coalition, of which the principal members were Austria, Russia, and England ; the Austrians attack the French in Italy and Germany, before a formal declaration of war ; the Archduke Charles defeats Jourdan at Stockach (25 Mar) and Kray defeats Schérer at Magnano (5 Apr.); the Congress of Rastadt breaks up and on leaving the city, two of the French envoys, Bonnier and Roberjot, are murdered by Austrian hussars and the third, Jean Debry, severely wounded

Effect of the massacre at Rastadt on the French people , general indignation, which rallies the country round the Directors

Campaign of 1799 in Italy ; the Russians under Suvórov, with the Austrians under Kray, drive the French army under Moreau, across Italy, occupying Milan and Turin, and besieging the remnant of the French army in Genoa ; the army in southern Italy under Macdonald defeated in the battle of the Trebbia (17–19 June); the French abandon all Italy except Genoa ; Joubert defeated by Suvórov at Novi (15 Aug), and Championnet by Melas at Genola (4 Nov.)

Campaign of 1799 in Switzerland , the Archduke Charles advances to the Rhine, leaving Korsákov with the army, with the Russian army to drive the French out of Switzerland ; splendid defensive campaign of Masséna , he defeats the Russians at Zurich (26 Sept); the Archduke Charles fears to cross the Rhine, while Masséna remains master of Switzerland ; Suvórov crosses the Alps to the assistance of Korsákov, but his army is practically destroyed by the severity of the weather

Campaign of 1799 in Holland ; an English army under the Duke of York and a Russian army under Hermann land at the Helder (27 Aug.), the remnant of the Dutch fleet in the Texel having been taken by Abercromby and Mitchell ; gallant defence made by French troops under Brune and the troops of the Batavian Republic under Janssens ; the battles of Bergen (2–16 Sept.); the Duke of York signs the Convention of Alkmaar (18 Oct), by which the English and Russians agree to evacuate Holland.

Effect of the campaigns of 1799 on Europe ; the Tsar Paul resolves to abandon the coalition , causes of his disagreement with Austria and England.

Effect of the campaigns of 1799 on France , in spite of the victories of Masséna and Brune, the French, owing to their expulsion from Italy, regard the war as disastrous, and condemn the government of the Directors ; general desire expressed for the return of Bonaparte from Egypt.

Authorities For Bonaparte's campaign in Syria, see works cited under Lecture XLIV , for the murders at Rastadt, see *Vivenot*, Zur Geschichte des Rastadter Kongresses, *Helfert*, Der Rastatter Gesandtenmord, and the Piéces officielles concernant l'assassinat commis sur les ministres français à Rastadt , for campaign in Italy, *Jomini*, with *Macdonald*, Mémoires , for campaign in Switzerland, *Jomini* , for campaign in Holland, *Bunbury*. Some passages in the great war with France , and for all the campaigns, *Mathieu Dumas*, Précis des événements militaires sur la campagne de 1799

LECTURE XLVIII.

THE COUP D'ETAT OF 30 PRAIRIAL

The elections of 1799 returned to the Councils a body of new deputies who were neither Clichians nor radicals, and who represented the general desire of France to be rid of the Directory, which had been discredited by its corruptness and had lost the vigor of the days of Fructidor.

Sieyès, who had returned from Berlin with the conviction that strong government was necessary and that the Constitution of the Year III was a failure, set himself at the head of the majority of the legislature, prepared with a new scheme for regulating the relations between the executive and legislative powers

To destroy the Directory, Sieyès permitted himself to be elected a Director (16 May) in the place of his enemy Reubell, who had to retire by lot.

Sieyès became President of the Directory in his turn and with the majority of the Councils effected the *coup d'état* of 30 Prairial (18 June).

This revolution was the direct reverse of that of 18 Fructidor; the legislature illegally and unconstitutionally interfered with the Directors, just as in Fructidor the Directors had interfered with the legislature.

The majority of the Councils with the support of Sieyès declared Treilhard and Merlin of Douai to have been illegally chosen Directors, and therefore deposed them, and also forced Larévellière-Lépeaux to resign, their places were filled by Gohier, Roger Ducos, and General Moulin, three friends of Sieyès and men of no influence, Barras acquiesces in the *coup d'état* and is permitted to remain in office.

The Directors at once appointed a fresh ministry consisting mainly of former members of the Convention, including Robert Lindet, Minister of Finance, Fouché, of Police, Cambacérès, of Justice, Reinhard, of Foreign Affairs, and Bernadotte, speedily succeeded by Dubois-Crancé, of War.

France acquiesced in the *coup d'état* of 30 Prairial because people were disgusted with the Directors, and full of consternation at the expulsion of the French armies from Italy, perilous situation of France

Authorities On this *coup d'état* see the Memoirs of *Larévellière-Lépeaux*, *Barras*, and *Gohier*

LECTURE XLIX

THE REVOLUTION OF 18 BRUMAIRE

Growing discredit of the government of the Directory; the defeat and death of Joubert at Novi (15 Aug) destroyed the last hope of the Directors; increase of brigandage and outbreak of local disturbances

Both the people and the army regard Bonaparte as the one man capable of restoring internal order and defeating the foreign enemies.

Representatives of the different political parties in Paris all hope to win the assistance of Bonaparte; Sieyès looked upon him as likely and able to establish the new Constitution he had devised; Talleyrand, who had been turned out of the Ministry of Foreign Affairs by the *coup d'état* of 30 Prairial. and Fouché, who at that time became Minister of Police, both regarded him as the coming man

Information, containing the hopes of the different informants, of the *coup d'état* of 30 Prairial reached Bonaparte in Egypt and caused him to take his departure.

After a long and dangerous voyage, owing to the English cruisers in the Mediterranean, lands at Fréjus (9 Oct , 1799), and reaches Paris (16 Oct) , he is received with rapturous delight in France and with apprehension, mingled with a hope of getting his assistance, by all parties in Paris

Bonaparte consults Talleyrand, Sieyès, Fouché and others, but resolves to take his own course; the Directors give him an official reception, the Council of Five Hundred elects Lucien Bonaparte its President, and the whole legislature gives him a banquet (6 Nov.)

Bonaparte resolves on a military revolution, relying on the assistance of General Lefebvre, the commander of the military division of Paris

On 18 Brumaire, Year VIII (9 Nov., 1799), the Councils were summoned to meet at Saint-Cloud, where the palace was surrounded by troops, Sieyès and Roger Ducos, who were in the plot, at once declared their resignations, Barras was induced to agree ; Gohier and Moulin were made prisoners in the Luxembourg by Moreau

On 19 Brumaire after a stormy scene, the Council of Five Hundred was dissolved by Bonaparte's soldiers ; in the evening a few deputies, at the instigation of Bonaparte and Sieyès, decreed the suppression of the Directory and the establishment of a provisional government, consisting of three Consuls, Bonaparte, Sieyès, and Roger Ducos ; commissions were appointed to aid the Consuls in revising the Constitution and drawing up new laws for the Republic

Comparison between the *Coup d'état* of 18 Fructidor and the Revolution of 18 Brumaire, both were bloodless and military, but while the former established the power of five directors, the latter established the power of one man, the idol of the army and the greatest general and statesman of the Republic.

End of the French Revolution, after more than ten years of struggle, the Revolution had ended in placing the fortunes of France in the hands of an adventurer who was far more powerful than Louis XVI had ever been, since the Reign of Terror and the Directory had concentrated and centralized the administration of France, and the wars of the Republic had created a professional army entirely devoted to its chief.

Authorities The histories and memoirs referred to under the Lectures on the Directory give much space to the Revolution of Brumaire, all histories and lives of Napoleon, especially *Lanfrey*, Histoire de Napoleon, describe it at length, but additional reference may be made to *Lucien Bonaparte*, Mémoires

LECTURE L

THE GREAT DAYS OF THE REVOLUTION

The following list of events and their dates will aid in fixing the remembrance of the course of the French Revolution ·

1789

Meeting of the States-General, 5 May.
Oath of the Tennis Court, 20 June
Taking of the Bastille, 14 July.
Abolition of Privileges, 4 August
The King brought to Paris, 6 October.

1790.

The First Federation, 14 July
Suppression of military mutiny at Nancy, 31 August.

1791.

Death of Mirabeau, 2 April.
Flight to Varennes, 21 June
Massacre of the Champ de Mars, 17 July
Declaration of Pilnitz, 21 August
Meeting of Legislative Assembly, 22 September.

1792

War declared against Austria, 20 April
The mob invades the Tuileries, 20 June.
Storming of the Tuileries and suspension of the King, 10 August
Massacres in the Prisons, 2–6 September
Battle of Valmy, 20 September
Meeting of Convention and Declaration of the French Republic, 21 September.

1793

Execution of Louis XVI, 21 January.
First Committee of Public Safety, 7 April
Overthrow of the Girondins, 31 May–2 June
Great Committee of Public Safety, 10 July
Terror declared the order of the day, 6 September.

1794.

Execution of the Hébertists, 24 March.
Execution of the Dantonists, 5 April.
Battle of Fleurus, 26 June.
Revolution of 9 Thermidor, 27 July

1795.

Insurrection of 12 Germinal, 1 April
Insurrection of 1 Prairial, 20 May.
Treaties of Basle · Prussia, 5 April ; Spain, 22 July.
Insurrection of 13 Vendémiaire, 5 October
Dissolution of the Convention, 26 October.

1797.

Coup d'état of 18 Fructidor, 4 September
Treaty of Campo Formio, 17 October

1799.

Murder of the French envoys at Rastadt, 27 April
Coup d'état of 30 Prairial, 18 June.
Revolution of 18 Brumaire, 9 November.

CPSIA information can be obtained
at www.ICGtesting.com
Printed in the USA
LVHW101618090919
630422LV00018B/828/P